# Lecture Notes in Artificial Intelligence    11308

Subseries of Lecture Notes in Computer Science

More information about this series at http://www.springer.com/series/1244

Adrian Groza · Rajendra Prasath (Eds.)

# Mining Intelligence and Knowledge Exploration

6th International Conference, MIKE 2018
Cluj-Napoca, Romania, December 20–22, 2018
Proceedings

Springer

*Editors*
Adrian Groza (ID)
Technical University of Cluj-Napoca
Cluj-Napoca, Romania

Rajendra Prasath (ID)
Indian Institute of Information Technology
Sri City, India

ISSN 0302-9743          ISSN 1611-3349   (electronic)
Lecture Notes in Artificial Intelligence
ISBN 978-3-030-05917-0      ISBN 978-3-030-05918-7   (eBook)
https://doi.org/10.1007/978-3-030-05918-7

Library of Congress Control Number: 2018964609

LNCS Sublibrary: SL7 – Artificial Intelligence

This Springer imprint is published by the registered company Springer Nature Switzerland AG
The registered company address is: Gewerbestrasse 11, 6330 Cham, Switzerland

# Preface

This volume contains the papers presented at MIKE 2018: the 6th International Conference on Mining Intelligence and Knowledge Exploration held during December 20–22, 2018, at the Technical University of Cluj-Napoca, Cluj-Napoca, Romania (http://www.mike.org.in/2018/). We received 93 qualified submissions from 29 countries and each qualified submission was reviewed by a minimum of three Program Committee members using the criteria of relevance, originality, technical quality, and presentation. A rigorous review process with the help of the distinguished Program Committee led to the acceptance of 33 of these submissions for presentation at the conference. Hence, the overall acceptance rate for this edition of MIKE is 35.48%.

The International Conference on Mining Intelligence and Knowledge Exploration (MIKE) is an initiative focusing on research and applications on various topics of human intelligence mining and knowledge discovery. Human intelligence has evolved steadily over several generations, and today human expertise excels in multiple domains and in knowledge-acquiring artifacts. The primary goal was to focus on the frontiers of human intelligence mining toward building a body of knowledge in this key domain. The focus was also to present state-of-the-art scientific results, to disseminate modern technologies, and to promote collaborative research in mining intelligence and knowledge exploration. At MIKE 2018, a specific focus was placed on the "learning to explore smart and intelligent systems."

MIKE 2018 identified ten tracks topic wise, each led by two to three track coordinators to contribute and also to handle submissions falling in their areas of interest. The involment from each of them along with the supervision of the Program Chairs ensured the selection of quality papers for the conference. Each track coordinator took responsibility to fulfil the tasks assigned to them since the first call for papers was circulated. This is reflected in the quality of every paper appearing in these proceedings.

The accepted papers were chosen on the basis of research excellence, which provides a body of literature for researchers involved in exploring, developing, and validating learning algorithms and knowledge-discovery techniques. Accepted papers were grouped into various subtopics including evolutionary computation, knowledge exploration in IoT, artificial intelligence, machine learning, image processing, pattern recognition, speech processing, information retrieval, natural language processing, social network analysis, security, fuzzy rough sets, and other areas. Researchers presented their work and had an excellent opportunity to interact with eminent professors and scholars in their area of research. All participants benefitted from discussions that facilitated the emergence of new ideas and approaches.

We were pleased to have the following notable scholars serving as advisory members for MIKE 2018: Prof. Ramon Lopaz de Mantaras, Artificial Intelligence Research Institute, Spain; Prof. Mandar Mitra, Indian Statistical Institute, Kolkata, India; Prof. Agnar Aamodt, Prof. Pinar Ozturk, Prof. Bjorn Gamback and Dr. Kazi Shah Nawaz Ripo, Norwegian University of Science and Technology, Trondheim,

Norway; Prof. Sudeshna Sarkar and Prof. Niloy Ganguly, Indian Institute of Technology, Kharagpur, India; Prof. G. Kannabiran, Indian Institute of Information Technology, Sri City, India; Prof. Philip O'Reilly, University College Cork, Ireland; Prof. Nirmalie Wiratunga, Robert Gordan University, UK; Prof. Paolo Rosso, Universitat Politecnica de Valencia, Spain; Prof. Chaman L. Sabharwal, Missouri University of Science and Technology, USA; Prof. Tapio Saramaki, Tampere University of Technology, Finland; Prof. Vasudeva Verma, Indian Institute of Technology, Hyderabad, India; Prof. Grigori Sidorov, NLTP Laboratory CIC–IPN, Mexico; Prof. Genoveva Vargas-Solar, CNRS, France; Prof. Ildar Batyrshin, National Polytechnic Institute, Mexico; and Dr. Krishnaiyya Jallu, Bharat Heavy Electronics Limited, Hyderabad, India.

We sincerely express our gratitude to Prof. Bayya Yegnanarayana, INSA Senior Scientist, International Institute of Information Technology, Hyderabad, India, and Prof. Chaman Lal Sabharwal, Missouri University of Science and Technology, Rolla, USA, for their continuous support of MIKE 2018. Their guidance, suggestions, and constant support were invaluable in planning various activities of MIKE 2018.

Several eminent scholars, including Prof. Sankar Kumar Pal, Distinguished Scientist and Former Director, Indian Statistical Institute, Kolkata, Prof. Sung-Bae Cho, Yonsei University, South Korea, Prof. Alexander Gelbukh, Instituto Politecnico Nacional, Mexico, and Prof. N. Subba Reddy, Gyeongsang National University, Jinju, South Korea, also extended their kind support in guiding us to organize the MIKE conference even better than the previous edition.

Prof. Radu Grosu, The Vienna University of Technology, Vienna, Austria, Prof. Sudip Misra, Indian Institute of Technology, Kharagpur, West Bengal, India, and Prof. Vasile Rus, Institute for Intelligent Systems, The University of Memphis, USA, delivered invited talks on "Biophysical Recurrent Neural Networks," "IoT," and "Conversational Intelligent Tutoring Systems," respectively.

A large number of eminent professors, well-known scholars, industry leaders, and young researchers participated in making MIKE 2018 a great success. We recognize and appreciate the hard work put in by each author of the articles published in these proceedings. We also express our sincere thanks to the Technical University of Cluj-Napoca, Romania, for hosting MIKE 2018.

We thank the Technical Program Committee members and all reviewers for their timely and thorough participation in the reviewing process. We thank Prof. Rodica Potolea, Technical University of Cluj-Napoca (TUCN), Romania, for her support in organizing MIKE 2018 in TUCN this year. We appreciate the time and effort put in by the members of the local organizing team at TUCN, Romania, and IIIT Sri City, India. We are very grateful to all our sponsors for their generous support of MIKE 2018.

Finally, we acknowledge the support of EasyChair in the submission, review, and proceedings creation processes.

We are very pleased to express our sincere thanks to Springer staff members, especially Alfred Hofmann, Anna Kramer, and the editorial staff, for their support in publishing the proceedings of MIKE 2018.

December 2018                                             Adrian Groza
                                                       Rajendra Prasath

# Organization

## Program Committee

| | |
|---|---|
| Goutham Reddy Alavalapati | Kyungpook National University, South Korea |
| Lasker Ershad Ali | Peking University, Republic of China |
| Gloria Inés Alvarez | Pontificia Universidad Javeriana Cali, Colombia |
| Zeyar Aung | Khalifa University of Science and Technology, Masdar Institute, United Arab Emirates |
| Costin Badica | University of Craiova, Romania |
| Tanmay Basu | Ramakrishna Mission Vivekananda Educational and Research Institute, India |
| Victoria Bobicev | Technical University of Moldova, Moldova |
| Isis Bonet | EIA University, Colombia |
| Remus Brad | Lucian Blaga University of Sibiu, Romania |
| Michael Breza | Imperial College London, UK |
| Matteo Ceriotti | University of Duisburg-Essen, Germany |
| Basabi Chakraborty | Iwate prefectural University, Japan |
| Snehashish Chakraverty | National Institute of Technology Rourkela, India |
| Emil St. Chifu | Technical University of Cluj-Napoca, Romania |
| Camelia Chira | Babes-Bolyai University, Romania |
| Sung-Bae Cho | Yonsei University, South Korea |
| Florin Craciun | Babes-Bolyai University, Romania |
| Horia Cucu | University Politehnica of Bucharest, Romania |
| Radu Danescu | Technical University of Cluj-Napoca, Romania |
| Liviu P. Dinu | University of Bucharest, Romania |
| Irina Dragoste | Technical University Dresden, Germany |
| Shiv Ram Dubey | Indian Institute of Information Technology, Sri City, India |
| Madalina Erascu | West University of Timisoara, Romania |
| Cristina Feier | University of Bremen, Germany |
| Debasis Ganguly | IBM Ireland Research Lab, Ireland |
| Alexander Gelbukh | Instituto Politécnico Nacional, Mexico |
| Ashish Ghosh | Indian Statistical Institute, Kolkata, India |
| Sujata Ghosh | Indian Statistical Institute, Chennai, India |
| Mircea Giurgiu | Technical University of Cluj-Napoca, Romania |
| Sergio Alejandro Gomez | Universidad Nacional del Sur, Argentina |
| Adrian Groza | Technical University of Cluj-Napoca, Romania |
| Anca Hangan | Technical University of Cluj-Napoca, Romania |
| Marko Hölbl | University of Maribor, Slovenia |
| Bogdan Iancu | Technical University of Cluj-Napoca, Romania |
| Oana Iova | National Institute of Applied Sciences, France |

| | |
|---|---|
| Saurav Sahay | Georgia Institute of Technology, USA |
| Gheorghe Sebestyen | Technical University of Cluj-Napoca, Romania |
| Manish Shrivastava | International Institute of Information Technology, Hyderabad, India |
| Jamuna Kanta Sing | Jadavpur University, India |
| Arif Ahmed Sk | Haldia Institute of Technology, India |
| Radu Razvan Slavescu | Technical University of Cluj-Napoca, Romania |
| Cristina Slavescu Kinga | Iuliu Hatieganu University of Medicine and Pharmacy, Romania |
| Tripti Swarnkar | Indian Institute of Technology, Kharagpur, India |
| Kathirvalavakumar Thangairulappan | Virudhunagar Hindu Nadars' Senthikumara Nadar College, India |
| Veerakumar Thangaraj | National Institute of Technology Goa, India |
| Birjodh Tiwana | LinkedIn Inc., USA |
| Levente Torok | Analytical Minds, Hungary |
| Denis Trcek | University of Ljubljana, Slovenia |
| Turki Turki | King Abdulaziz University, Saudi Arabia |
| Odelu Vanga | Birla Institute of Technology and Science Pilani, Hyderabad Campus, India |
| Jose R. Villar | University of Oviedo, Spain |
| Venkatesh Vinayakarao | Indian Institute of Information Technology, Sri City, India |
| Anil Kumar Vuppala | International Institute of Information Technology, Hyderabad, India |
| Sergiu Zaporojan | Technical University of Moldova, Moldova |

## Additional Reviewers

Abburi, Harika
Alluri, Knrk Raju
Cignarella, Alessandra Teresa
De la Peña, Gretel Liz
Ghanem, Bilal

Kopeć, Mateusz
Smywiński-Pohl, Aleksander
T. Kathirvalavakumar
T. Kumaran
Vikström, Antti

# Contents

# FCA-Based Ontology Learning from Unstructured Textual Data

Simin Jabbari[1,2(✉)] and Kilian Stoffel[1]

[1] University of Neuchâtel, Neuchâtel, Switzerland
{simin.jabbari,kilian.stoffel}@unine.ch
[2] Diagnostics Data Science Lab, F. Hoffmann-La Roche Ltd., Basel, Switzerland

**Abstract.** Ontologies have been frequently used for representing domain knowledge. They have lots of applications in semantic knowledge extraction. However, learning ontologies especially from unstructured data is a difficult yet an interesting challenge. In this paper, we introduce a pipeline for learning ontology from a text corpus in a semi-automated fashion using Natural Language Processing (NLP) and Formal Concept Analysis (FCA). We apply our proposed method on a small given corpus that consists of some news documents in IT and pharmaceutical domain. We then discuss the potential applications of the proposed model and ideas on how to improve it even further.

**Keywords:** Ontology engineering · Semantic knowledge extraction
Formal concept analysis · Natural language processing · Concept lattice

## 1 Introduction

Advancing knowledge in a domain in which one is not familiar with is an interesting yet a difficult challenge. Ontologies have been used as promising tools for knowledge representation by giving structure to unstructured data (such as text) [8,11,13]. One idea for giving structure to texts is to define a set of concepts and identify relationship between them. In this paper, we focus on how to build an ontology from a text corpus (a bunch of documents that are available in a domain of interest) using Natural Language Processing (NLP) [1,6] and Formal Concept Analysis (FCA) [9,10]. NLP and FCA have been recognized as powerful tools for such purposes [2,5,7,14,16–18,20]. The built ontology can be later used for reasoning and semantic knowledge extraction. We mainly focus on the ontology learning and we discuss how one can use such ontology for reasoning and extracting semantic knowledge.

As mentioned earlier, the proposed pipeline for such automatic ontology learning is based on applying a sequence of NLP operators to text corpus for text processing, and then a sequence of FCA operators to build taxonomies and concept hierarchies. The latter is then followed by a set of further operators to define relationship between concepts and bringing knowledge expertise to refine the ontology we are trying to learn. In the following, we first describe

© Springer Nature Switzerland AG 2018
A. Groza and R. Prasath (Eds.): MIKE 2018, LNAI 11308, pp. 1–10, 2018.
https://doi.org/10.1007/978-3-030-05918-7_1

the sequence of NLP and FCA operators being used for our proposed ontology learning method. We then apply our method to a text corpus which consists of documents regarding news about companies in IT and pharmaceutical industries. We further discuss about the potential applications of ontology for indexing and knowledge extraction.

## 2    Methode

In this section, we focus on describing the pipeline for learning ontology from unstructured textual data. Our proposed method consists of three major components (see Fig. 1). In the first component, a formal context is generated as an outcome of text processing and extracting triplets of the form *(subject, predicate, object)*. The second component then generates a set of formal concepts using FCA and builds a concept hierarchy as a taxonomy for our ontology. The third component is then used for converting concept lattice into ontology by defining ontological concepts (from formal concepts) and relationship between them (thanks to the triplets that have been extracted in the first component of the pipeline). The constructed ontology is then improved by incorporating domain knowledge and can be used for generating general form of relation between different ontological concepts from real instances. In the following, we will describe this topic with more detail.

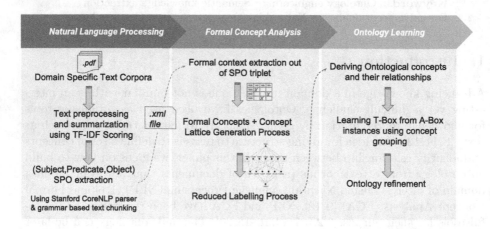

**Fig. 1.** The pipeline for learning ontology from text corpus consists of three main components. The first step is the preprocessing of the text corpus using NLP. Then a concept hierarchy is generated by FCA. Finally, the concept lattice is transformed into an ontology by defining ontological concepts and the relationship between them, i.e., generating TBox from ABox.

## 2.1 Extracting Meaningful Triplets from Text Corpus Using Natural Language Processing (NLP)

Natural Language Processing (NLP) consists of a set of processing techniques to be applied on textual data for the purpose of text mining. To derive ontology from textual data, the first step is to convert the documents from *.pdf* to *.txt* format, and store them in a text corpus. The next step is then preprocessing of the corpus by *parsing* (i.e., separation of sentences), *tokenization* (i.e., separating words of each sentence), and *POS-tagging* (i.e., labelling each word by its corresponding Part-Of-Speech tag such as noun or verb). We then use the POS-tagged tokens to define a *chunk grammar* to extract triplets of the form *(subject, predicate, object)*. Note that for the purpose of chunking, grammar is defined in such a way that it increases the chance of extracting proper subjects and objects from sentences, by ignoring auxiliary information about them. For instance for the sentence *"The small white cat went to the beautiful garden."*, the words *cat* and *garden* will be recognized as the proper subject and object, respectively, by ignoring the further info on the size, color, and beauty of them in the sentence. Moreover, all components of the triplet will be represented by their original form, after lemmatization. For instance the triplet *(cat, go, garden)* is extracted from sentence above, where the verb *went* has been replaced by its lemmatized form *go*.

Also note that in the above approach, a chunk is defined by the sequence of *<NP><VP><NP>*, where *NP* denotes a noun phrase (such as *the small white cat* or *the beautiful garden*) and *VP* denotes a verb phrase (such as *went*).

Once all triplets of the above form are extracted from text corpus, the next step is to build a formal context that describes each subject and object in syntactical sense (here, *cat* and *garden*) by the verb associated to (here *go*). The method that we use for describing subjects/objects by their corresponding verb is the following. For a given triplet *(cat, go, garden)*, both subject and object in the syntactical sense (i.e., *cat* and *garden*) will be considered as two objects in the formal context (as two rows of the binary table) to be described by the verb *go* in the present *(going)* and past participle form *(gone)* as formal context attributes, respectively. In other words, *cat* is an object that has capability of *going* as an attribute, and *garden* is an object that is characterized by attribute *gone* which indicates it can be considered as a place that something (like *cat*) can *go* into. To formalize such definition, we define formal context attributes by adding suffix *-ing* and *-ed* to the lemmatized version of each verb in the existing triplets (here, *go-ing* and *go-ed*, although *go-ed* is meaningless from syntactical point of view). To ensure that the above explanation is well understood, we provide another example. For the sentence *"the big pharmaceutical enterprise Roche has been producing breast cancer medicine Herceptin"*, the triplet *(roche, produce, herceptin)* is translated into two additional rows in existing formal context as (1) *roche* which has attribute *produce-ing* and (2) *herceptin* which has attribute *produce-ed*. Once the formal context is generated (see Fig. 2 as an example), we then use FCA to define formal concepts as described in the following section.

| | Hire–ing | Hire–ed | Produce–ing | Produce–ed | Study–ing | Study–ed | Sell–ing | Sell–ed | Collaborate–ing | Collaborate–ed |
|---|---|---|---|---|---|---|---|---|---|---|
| Roche | X | | X | | | | X | | X | X |
| Herceptine | | | | X | | X | | X | | |
| HealthKit | | | | X | | | | X | | |
| Apple | X | | X | | | | | X | | |
| John | | X | | | | | | | | |
| Genentech | X | | X | | X | | | | X | X |
| Novartise | X | | X | | X | | | X | | |
| Alex | | X | | | | | | | | |
| Clozapine | | | | X | | X | | X | | |

**Fig. 2.** A formal context created by triplets of the form (subject, predicate, object). All subjects and objects of the sentences (in syntactical sense) are considered as objects (i.e., rows) of the formal context. Attributes of the formal context is then determined by the predicates (i.e., verbs) of the sentences or triplets. For each verb, there are two attributes: in the present form (i.e., verb-ing) and the past participle form (i.e., verb-ed). Subjects of the sentences are connected to verb-ing, and object of the sentences are linked to verb-ed.

## 2.2 From Meaningful Triplets to Concept Hierarchies Using Formal Concept Analysis (FCA)

Formal Concept Analysis (FCA) [9,10] helps in defining taxonomy in a given domain of interest and is being used for automatically defining formal concepts as well as learning concept hierarchies from a formal context. The formal context is defined as a triplet $K := \langle G, M, I \rangle$, where $G$ denotes set of objects, $M$ denotes set of attributes and $I$ is a binary relation between $G$ and $M$. A formal context can be represented as a binary table (see Fig. 2), where each object (row) is characterized by a set of attributes (columns) based on inserted relations between them by the cross signs.

Assume $A \subset G$ and $B \subset M$ denote a subset of objects $G$ and attributes $M$, respectively. Then a pair $(A, B)$ is a formal concept if and only if $A^u = B$ and $B^d = A$. Here, $A^u$ denotes a set of those attributes that all objects in $A$ have in common. Similarly $B^d$ denotes a set of those objects that all attributes in $B$ have in common. $A$ and $B$ are known as extent and intent of that formal concept. We denote by $\{(A_1, B_1), (A_2, B_2), \cdots, (A_p, B_p)\}$ the set of all $p$ formal concepts embedded in a given formal context. To make story short, a formal concept is characterized by a subset of attributes that are common in a set of objects. Those formal concepts mimic the human interpretation of a real concept in the real world, yet represented in a mathematical form. Note that we may also refer to a formal concept $(A, B)$ only by its extent $A$ or intent $B$, or simply a name that is assigned to that pair.

The *concept lattice* is then used for describing hierarchies between the formal concepts, i.e., sub-concept and super-concept relationships between formal concepts. For instance *mammals* (as a formal concept) can be considered as a sub-concept of a bigger formal concept labeled as *animals*. That means each creature (i.e., object) that belongs to the set of *mammals* also belongs to the set of *animals* but not vice versa.

There are many different algorithms proposed in the literature for extracting formal concepts [10,12,15,19], as well as concept lattices [3,4,9] which are being used for transforming data into human understandable structures, knowledge representation [18] and data mining [20]. In this paper we use a tool called *CONEXP* for building formal concepts and concept lattice.

In previous section we explained how triplets *(subject, predicate, object)* extracted from a text corpus can create a formal context. Once the formal context is created, then we apply FCA in order to build the concept hierarchy. We then use a reduced labelling method to simplify representation of formal concepts in the lattice. Reduced labelling ensures that each object $g$ and attribute $m$ of the formal context is represented only once in the lattice. Mathematically speaking, for each object $g \in G$ in the formal context, there is a formal concept $(A, B)$ such that $\gamma(g) := (\{\{g\}^u\}^d, \{g\}^u) = (A, B)$. Similarly, for each attribute $m \in M$, there is also a formal concept $(C, D)$ such that $\mu(m) := (\{m\}^d, \{\{m\}^d\}^u) = (C, D)$. Here, $\gamma(.)$ and $\mu(.)$ denote *object concept* and *attribute concept* of $g$ and $m$, respectively. The formal concepts $(A, B)$ and $(C, D)$ are then replaced by their corresponding object concepts and attribute concepts. Note that it is possible to have a subset of objects $g_1, g_2, \cdots, g_n$ and attributes $m_1, m_2, \cdots, m_m$ that can be assigned to a given formal concept $(A, B)$. However, if $g_1$ is assigned to formal concept (A,B) , there is no formal concept $(C, D) \neq (A, B)$ such that $g_1$ can be assigned to, meaning that $g_1$ will be assigned to one and only one formal concept, i.e., one lattice node.

Figure 3 demonstrates the concept lattice that has been generated using FCA on the formal context that is depicted in Fig. 2, but after reduced labelling.

## 2.3    From Concept Lattice to Ontology Using Relations and Domain Knowledge

The first step towards learning ontology from a concept lattice is to define ontological concepts from formal concepts. The former can be interpreted as a label for the latter. For instance, verbs {*hiring, producing, earning*}, as the intent of a formal concept, are characteristics of an ontological concept *company*, and objects {*Roche, Novartis*} are just instances of that ontological concept. Similarly, the formal concept {*produced, sold, treating*} can be labeled as an ontological concept *medication*, where {*Herceptin, Perjeta*} are just instances of that concept. In order to build an ontology, we not only need ontological concepts, but also relationship between the concepts. This is not a difficult task because it can be done by connecting objects that are elements of the same triplets. For instance, objects *Roche* and *Herceptin* must be linked to each other because *(Roche, produce, Herceptin)* is an existing triplet already extracted from text corpus. The ontological relationships between *Roche* and *Herceptin* then can be defined as follows: "*Roche – Produces $\rightarrow$ Herceptin*" and "*Herceptin – ProducedBy $\rightarrow$ Roche*". Similarly all objects $O_1$ and $O_2$ for which there is a triplet $(O_1, verb, O_2)$ in the text corpus will be linked to each other.

Once the relationships between all objects are inserted into the lattice, the next step is to define TBox using instances of ABox already represented in the lattice. In other words, *(Roche, produce, Herceptin)* as well as other instances such as *(Novartis, produce, Clozapine)* are converted to the following object property in the ontology that links to classes: *(company, produce, medication)*.

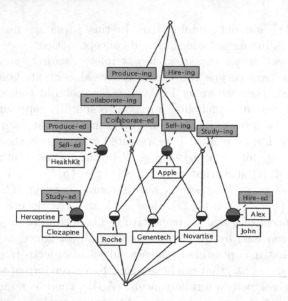

**Fig. 3.** The concept lattice that is generated after applying FCA to the formal context of Fig. 2. This figure depict the concept hierarchy after reduced labelling. By looking at this lattice, one can immediately recognize that objects such as *Roche, Novartis, Genentech,* and *Apple* belong to the same class (i.e., *companies*) which have in common properties such as *hiring* and *producing*, but maybe different in some aspects such as *collaborating* and *studying*. Similarly, Objects such as *Herceptin, Clozapine,* and *HealthKit* are all instances of a same class (i.e., *products*) that are common in attributes such as *being produced, studied,* and *sold (i.e., sell-ed). Alex* and *John* will also be recognized as a separate class (i.e., *persons*) that have a common characteristics as *being hired.* This example shows how such lattice can be of great help for learning about new terminologies. For instance, if someone knows *Herceptin* as a *product* (or medication) but has never heard about *Clozapine*, he can deduce that it should also be a *product* or *medication* and not a *company* or a *person!*

This is how a TBox can be eventually constructed using instances of ABox. Note that the domain knowledge and refinement of the concept lattice according to the comments from a subject matter expert can provide a great support for completing the ontology. In other words, the proposed method is just a starting point towards creation of an ontology from unstructured textual data and can further be adjusted according to a domain knowledge.

In this work, *Owlready2* is used for creating domain ontology with afore-mentioned classes, relationships and individuals. Figure 4 depicts the ontology presented in Protégé based on the concept lattice shown in Fig. 3.

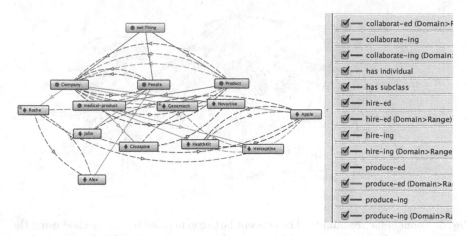

**Fig. 4.** The ontology represented in *Protégé* based on the concept lattice shown in Fig. 3. The ontological concepts such as company, people, product, medical-product, etc. are linked to each other via relationships that have been defined based on the verbs in the triplets. The ontology is then be adjusted by adding further info such as the fact that medical-product is a sub-class of product. The description of the arrows and how they link different concepts to each other are also represented.


## 3    Result

We applied our proposed model to a given dataset which consists of 22 .pdf files (2–6 pages each) containing information about news on companies and products in IT and pharmaceutical domain. After preparing the corpus and some preprocessing, we could identify 138 sentences from which we extracted triplets of the form *(subject, predicate, object)*. This gave us a formal context with 123 objects (rows) and 40 attributes (columns). Note that the subjects, objects, and verbs in the triplets might be repeated more than once. This is why at the end, we ended up with a smaller formal context. We also excluded some of the sentences that had no meaningful interpretation. Figure 5 depicts the concept lattice generated by our proposed method on the dataset we described above.

Although the graph looks complex, one can find interesting insights by looking at such lattice. The instances of the same category (such as *products, diseases, companies, people,* etc.) have been automatically appeared in more or less the same locations in the graph. This is because the instances of the same category share the same characteristics (i.e., attributes) as they appear quite frequently with the same kind of verbs. Moreover, grouping such instances facilitates learning TBox which is essential for learning final ontology. Completing this graph with additional edges that indicates the relationship between ontological concepts can be used for deriving implication rules, and semantic reasoning.

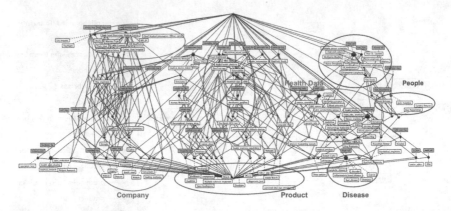

**Fig. 5.** Zoom in for readability. The concept lattice generated by our method using the documents on pharmaceutical and IT news. This corpus is made of 138 sentences from 22 pdf files (2–6 pages each). The corresponding formal context consists of 123 objects (rows) and 40 attributes (columns). The encircled nodes determine instances of similar concepts such as companies (pink), products (orange), people (red), etc., which shares the same attributes (gray boxes). Note that a node in the lower layers of lattice inherits characteristics of its parents from upper layers (i.e., those through which it reaches to the root node indicating the most general concept). (Color figure online)

## 4    Discussion

Nowadays, new data are being produced more than any time before, and so many new scientific and non-scientific disciplines have been proposed to the globe. It is often the case that someone wants to discover a new domain but he lacks a basic knowledge about that context. Building ontologies from unstructured data is a good starting point for deriving a set of taxonomies and concept hierarchies for a given unknown domain. Besides building the cornerstone of a knowledge model, our proposed model can be used to classify new words into one of existing ontological concepts (or a perhaps a new one) depending on the characteristics or attributes that the new words share with existing ones (i.e., previously learned words). Moreover, we can use this method for indexing documents to be used by smart search engines (where documents are tagged by not only their own keywords, but also by other words that are somehow linked to the content of the documents in a semantic way). Another application of the proposed method for learning ontology is to derive implication rules and semantic knowledge. The possibility to further adjust the built ontology and to incorporate subject matter expert knowledge to come up with a more accurate ontology is also appealing.

We would also like to mention some of the future works to be done for the purpose of improving our proposed method. The first topic is around NLP, and how to improve text preprocessing so that more meaningful triplets are extracted from the corpus. Dealing with huge number of documents is also another challenge. Using entity detection (e.g., which word is disease or medication) for building entity-specific ontologies (such as ontologies for diseases and medications, separately) and then connecting those ontologies via relational formal contexts (such as the one that links diseases to medications) also seems to be a right approach for learning more accurate and complete ontologies in a given domain of knowledge (such as medicine). As another example for future topic, we can also mention how to effectively update an ontology that has been created some time ago after receiving more documents in a given corpus. Adding more and more automation for handling big and complex graphs (as a consequence of a big corpus) is also a topic of interest for research.

## 5  Conclusion

We proposed a pipeline for generating ontology from a text corpus. This method is based on NLP and FCA, and gives structure to unstructured textual data. The application of the proposed method is to build a cornerstone for a knowledge model (especially when one has no clue about the context of available documents), which will be later used for semantic knowledge extraction and reasoning. The proposed method was described by a toy example (for simpler explanation) and was also tested on a real use case using a corpus of news documents (in .pdf format). The underlying method was able to identify concepts and instances that are similar in sharing the common attributes. The new proposed approach for learning ontology from a text corpus gives a promising approach for generating knowledge models in a more automated way than before, which helps a lot in acquiring knowledge about a previously unknown context.

## References

1. Allen, J.F.: Natural language processing. In: Encyclopedia of Cognitive Science (2006)
2. Bendaoud, R., Hacene, A.M.R., Toussaint, Y., Delecroix, B., Napoli, A.: Text-based ontology construction using relational concept analysis. In: International Workshop on Ontology Dynamics-IWOD 2007 (2007)
3. Bordat, J.P.: Calcul pratique du treillis de galois d'une correspondance. Mathématiques et Sciences humaines **96**, 31–47 (1986)
4. Carpineto, C., Romano, G.: GALOIS: an order-theoretic approach to conceptual clustering. In: Proceedings of ICML, vol. 293, pp. 33–40 (1993)
5. Castellanos, A., Cigarrán, J., García-Serrano, A.: Formal concept analysis for topic detection: a clustering quality experimental analysis. Inf. Syst. **66**, 24–42 (2017)
6. Chowdhury, G.G.: Natural language processing. Ann. Rev. Inf. Sci. Technol. **37**(1), 51–89 (2003)
7. Cimiano, P., Hotho, A., Staab, S.: Learning concept hierarchies from text corpora using formal concept analysis. J. Artif. Intell. Res. (JAIR) **24**, 305–339 (2005)
8. Dou, D., Wang, H., Liu, H.: Semantic data mining: a survey of ontology-based approaches. In: 2015 IEEE International Conference on Semantic Computing (ICSC), pp. 244–251. IEEE (2015)
9. Ganter, B.: Two Basic Algorithms in Concept Analysis. Springer, Heidelberg (2010)
10. Ganter, B., Wille, R.: Formal Concept Analysis: Mathematical Foundations. Springer, New York (2012)

11. Gómez-Pérez, A., Fernández-López, M., Corcho, O.: Ontological Engineering: with Examples from the Areas of Knowledge Management, e-Commerce and the Semantic Web. Springer, London (2006)
12. Krajca, P., Vychodil, V.: Distributed algorithm for computing formal concepts using map-reduce framework. In: Adams, N.M., Robardet, C., Siebes, A., Boulicaut, J.-F. (eds.) IDA 2009. LNCS, vol. 5772, pp. 333–344. Springer, Heidelberg (2009). https://doi.org/10.1007/978-3-642-03915-7_29
13. Maedche, A., Staab, S.: Ontology learning for the semantic web. IEEE Intell. Syst. 16(2), 72–79 (2001)
14. Moraes, S., de Lima, V.L.S.: Combining formal concept analysis and semantic information for building ontological structures from texts: an exploratory study. In: LREC, pp. 3653–3660 (2012)
15. Nourine, L., Raynaud, O.: A fast algorithm for building lattices. Inf. Process. Lett. 71(5), 199–204 (1999)
16. Velardi, P., Fabriani, P., Missikoff, M.: Using text processing techniques to automatically enrich a domain ontology. In: Proceedings of the international conference on Formal Ontology in Information Systems, vol. 2001, pp. 270–284. ACM (2001)
17. Velardi, P., Navigli, R., Cuchiarelli, A., Neri, R.: Evaluation of OntoLearn, a methodology for automatic learning of domain ontologies. Ontol. Learn. Text Methods Eval. Appl. 123(92), 92–107 (2005)
18. Wille, R.: Lattices in Data Analysis: How to Draw Them with a Computer. Springer, Heidelberg (1989)
19. Xu, B., de Fréin, R., Robson, E., Foghlú, M.Ó.: Distributed formal concept analysis algorithms based on an iterative MapReduce framework. In: Domenach, F., Ignatov, D.I., Poelmans, J. (eds.) ICFCA 2012. LNCS (LNAI), vol. 7278, pp. 292–308. Springer, Heidelberg (2012). https://doi.org/10.1007/978-3-642-29892-9_26
20. Zaki, M.J., Parthasarathy, S., Ogihara, M., Li, W., et al.: New algorithms for fast discovery of association rules. KDD 97, 283–286 (1997)

# Meaningful Clusterings of Recurrent Neural Network Activations for NLP

Mihai Pomarlan[✉] and John Bateman

University of Bremen, Bremen, Germany
{pomarlan,bateman}@uni-bremen.de

**Abstract.** Recurrent neural networks have found applications in NLP, but their operation is difficult to interpret. A state automaton that approximates the network would be more interpretable, but for this one needs a method to group network activation states by their behavior. In this paper we propose such a method, and compare it to an existing dimensionality reduction and clustering approach. Our method is better able to group together neural states of similar behavior.

**Keywords:** Recurrent neural networks
Natural language processing · Interpretability

## 1 Introduction

For several years, AI has been enjoying a "summer": a period of increased research enthusiasm, exciting new results, and raised expectations. Deep learning techniques are a chief cause of this, and they have proven able to tackle many challenging domains such as image recognition and captioning, machine translation, game playing, and others. However, while deep neural networks appear to perform better than rival approaches, they are also difficult to interpret.

Interpretability matters because a human user would like to hold the network to account for its decisions. To trust a decision, it should be possible to have it explained in an understandable way. It is also useful to "debug" the network during its training and development, to ensure it learns "the right thing". This can be easily seen for image classifiers. In [22], an artificially constructed example is presented of how, because of biases in the training data, a network learns the wrong features to classify by (in their example, the network sees a husky dog because the background is snow). Without having to mistrain the network, researchers have shown that while a deep reinforcement learning agent can master the game Breakout, it nevertheless gains no understanding of the game and does not have good performance on even small variations of it [13].

This work was partially funded by Deutsche Forschungsgemeinschaft (DFG) through the Collaborative Research Center 1320, EASE.

© Springer Nature Switzerland AG 2018
A. Groza and R. Prasath (Eds.): MIKE 2018, LNAI 11308, pp. 11–20, 2018.
https://doi.org/10.1007/978-3-030-05918-7_2

In this paper we are interested in applications of deep learning for natural language processing. There are tools to visualize and "debug" a network: LSTMVis [23] and RNNVis [20] offer visualizations of recurrent neural networks trained for NLP. Activation states (and the character or word sequences that produce them) are clustered using a distance metric. Often, clustering is preceded by some dimensionality reduction techniques such as tSNE [21]. Both the clustering and the dimensionality reduction typically employ the Euclidean distance metric. In this paper, we argue that this is not entirely appropriate and suggest, and experimentally compare, an alternative approach.

The idea behind clustering activation states is, if two activation states are close, they should "mean" the same thing and respond similarly to the same sequences of input tokens. Ideally, clustering would reveal "states" analogous to the states of an automaton: one could then extract what grammar the network has learned, and an interpretable representation of a program it approximates.

Note however that recurrent neural networks typically contain non-linearities, and thus it is not necessarily the case that activations close to each other (under the Euclidean distance metric) will in fact behave similarly.

Our approach is to sample the behavior of an activation state, by computing the most likely suffixes, as predicted by the network from the activation state. Two activation states are clustered only if they have the same most likely suffixes.

For our investigation, we use as an example an LSTM network trained for a semantic entailment task. We cluster activation levels of the trained network, first via a tSNE and DBSCAN [8] pipeline, then by the novel method presented here. We evaluate the methods in terms of how the clusters they discover actually group activation states that behave similarly when excited with the same suffixes. We show how the extracted clusters help understanding the network's mistakes.

## 2   Background

A **recurrent neural network** is an artificial neural network where some of the inputs to a neural layer come from the layer's previous activation state, thus implementing memory, and so is suitable for processing sequential data, e.g. text. Several variants of recurrent networks exist; the one we will be using in this paper is "long short-term memory" (**LSTM**) [11], which were developed to address a vanishing gradient problem of the original recurrent networks: error gradients often tended to zero or "exploded" during training. LSTM solves this by maintaining a "cell state" that interacts linearly with itself and non-linearly with the input; the output function is also non-linear in the cell-state.

Recurrent networks for NLP can be trained to work at word or character level, depending on what are the input tokens. A **character level network** would be fed characters one by one, usually in a "one-hot" encoding fashion. We use character level networks for this paper.

A **language model** is a procedure to estimate the probability distribution for the next input token, given a prefix of already seen tokens. Neural networks can be trained as language models by preparing pairs of form (prefix, next word/character) from some training text corpus.

The network **activation state** is the configuration of activation levels of all neurons in the network. A sequence of tokens fed to the a network uniquely determines its activation state. Because of this tight correspondence, we will often identify a network activation state with the prefix that caused it.

A language model can generate text, given a prefix, by continuing the prefix based on the probability distribution for the next token [14]. For example, for a prefix $p_k$ (of k tokens), the language model might select the token that appears most likely, conditional on this prefix. Let that token be $c$, then a new prefix would be $p_{k+1} = p_k + c$, and the procedure would repeat as much as needed.

Neural networks can be trained for several objectives at once. For example, they can be trained as language models, and to resolve semantic entailment, by weighing the training data for semantic entailment more heavily.

**Semantic entailment** is a type of natural language inference task which is about discovering the logical relation between sentences: entailment (one of the sentences is implied by the other), contradiction (the two sentences cannot both be true), or no relation. The Stanford Natural Language Inference corpus [3] provides several thousand pairs of premise/query, annotated with correct relations between them. The corpus was constructed to train and test neural architectures for natural language inference. We use part of this corpus for this paper.

## 3   Clustering by Most Likely Suffixes

In this section we present our method to cluster neural network activation states.

Network activation states take values from a continuous space, but clusters of activation states may be used to construct a discrete, automaton-like representation of a network, e.g. a finite state machine. Such automata will only approximate the network behavior, and will likely be very large (so further simplification or state selection mechanisms will be needed), but in principle they are a more interpretable representation of the network's operation. In particular, for NLP, an automaton representation closely corresponds to a grammar.

We want to obtain clusters of network states that are interpretable as the states of an automaton. Automata states are defined as equivalence classes of an "indistinguishability" relation: prefixes $p_1$, $p_2$ are equivalent if, for every suffix $s$, the automaton produces the same output for strings $p_1 + s$ and $p_2 + s$.

In the neural network case, every prefix corresponds to a network activation state. Two network activation states are indistinguishable if they respond the same to every string input to the network. Formally, let $U(h, s)$ be an update function for the new network activation state given the previous state $h$ and some input string $s$, and $O(h)$ be an output function parameterized on the current state. Two activation states $U(h_0, s_1)$ and $U(h_0, s_2)$ are indistinguishable if and only if for every input string $s$ we have $O(U(U(h_0, s_1), s)) = O(U(U(h_0, s_2), s))$.

It is impossible to test every possible suffix, so we approximately capture the network's behavior from an activation state by sampling only a few suffixes instead. Consider a neural network trained as a language model. As described in Sect. 2, language models can be used for generation. Then, we use the function

---

**Algorithm 1. mlSuffix(model, prefix, len)**

suffix ← ""
for k upto len do
  c ← argmax(predict(model, prefix))
  suffix ← suffix + c
  prefix ← prefix + c
  if c is terminating then
    break
  end if
end for
return suffix

---

---

**Algorithm 2. likelySuffixTree(model, prefix, len)**

suffixes ← {}
likeliest2 ← argkmax(predict(model, prefix), 2)
for c in likeliest2 do
  if c is terminating then
    suffixes ← suffixes ∪ {c}
  else
    nextlikeliest2 ← argkmax(predict(model, prefix + c), 2)
    for d in nextlikeliest2 do
      if d is terminating then
        suffixes gets suffixes ∪ { c + d }
      else
        suffixes ← suffixes ∪ { mlSuffix(model, prefix + c + d, len-2) }
      end if
    end for
  end if
end for
return suffixes

---

given in Algorithm 1 to compute a greedy approximation of the most likely suffix given a neural network *model* and an activation state of it caused by *prefix*. The function always continues the prefix with the most likely next token, until some suffix length *len* is reached or a terminating token is generated.

Two activation states of a language model are "the same" if they give the same probability distribution over suffixes. We test whether the two activation states deem the same few suffixes as most likely (cf. Algorithm 2). Given a language model and a prefix, it finds the two most likely tokens (as estimated by the model), and for each of those tokens, the two most likely tokens to follow it.

Algorithm 2 is the method we use to cluster network activation states, and which we compare with clustering methods using Euclidean distance in Sect. 4.

The method as described is only applicable to language models. For this paper, we apply it to a network with a mixed training objective (a main task, and a language model task). In the future, we will investigate the application of a technique from [1] to convert a general NLP neural network to a language model, by replacing the output layer of the network with a classifier trained to give a next token probability distribution from the network activation state.

## 4   Evaluation

### 4.1   Network Training

We use part of the SNLI corpus [3]: premise/query pairs of 70 characters or fewer, with no rare words, in natural English. An example training entry:

```
a dog runs:the dog is running home:#
```

The ":" separates premise, query, and result ("#": no relation; "|": contradiction; "<": entailment). Special characters do not appear in the premises/queries.

We use an LSTM with three recurrent layers, of 64 units each, and a Dense output layer with softmax activation. Training is done for a mixed objective: language model and semantic entailment. We generate training pairs of form (prefix, next character). Only prefixes that end in a separating character (" " and ":") are used. For the example sentence above, the training pairs include

```
("a dog ", "r")
("a dog runs:", "t")
("a dog runs:the dog is running home:", "#")
```

Pairs where the second element (the next character) is one of the result characters "#","|", "<" are given five times the weight of other training pairs, to more strongly train the network to respond to the semantic entailment task.

### 4.2   Clusters of Prefixes

Since a prefix uniquely defines a network activation state, we use cluster of prefixes and cluster of network activation states interchangeably.

We first look at clusters obtained by methods using Euclidean distance. Since a network activation state has a large dimensionality (384 in our case), and clustering methods aren't robust in such cases, we perform a dimensionality reduction step using tSNE, a well established method for activation state visualization.

We generate the activation states of the network trained in Sect. 4.1, corresponding to every prefix in the training text, and run a tSNE on the results to map them to a two-dimensional space. A part of this space is shown in Fig. 1. Notice that tSNE tends to project activation states into thin long "strips". For this reason, we select DBSCAN as our clustering technique, since it is more able to separate strips that are close together than the K-means approach used in [7].

We observe that prefix clusters tend to group prefixes from the same string together. For example, a part of one of the obtained clusters is in Listing 1.1.

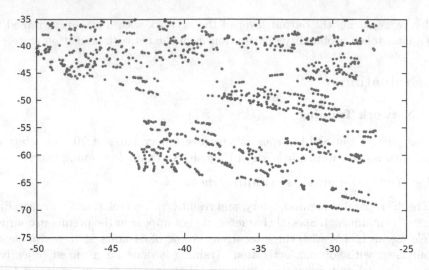

**Fig. 1.** A fragment of the tSNE projection of network activation states.

**Listing 1.1.** Part of a DBSCAN cluster

```
"a boy in a large pool:nobody "
"a boy in a large pool:nobody is "
"a boy in a large pool:nobody is in "
"a boy in a large pool:nobody is in a "
```

Such clusters are not appropriate as automaton states: the responses from a prefix should change as the prefix lengthens.

Therefore, we post-processed the DBSCAN clusters by removing a prefix from a cluster if it is a prefix of some other one in the same cluster. An example cluster obtained like this is given in Listing 1.2. This post-processing makes the DBSCAN clusters more appropriate to interpret as automaton states.

**Listing 1.2.** Post-processed DBSCAN cluster, keeping only distinct maximal strings

```
"a boy in a large pool:nobody is in a "
"a young boy in a pool:nobody is in the "
```

We then cluster the activation states using our method from Sect. 3. An example cluster is given in Listing 1.3. Our method produces more and smaller clusters than DBSCAN. The clusters also seem appropriate as automaton states; they show no tendency to group prefixes of the same string together.

**Listing 1.3.** Cluster obtained by most likely suffix grouping

```
"two young boys play together at a park:two young boys are "
"two young children playing in the grass:the children are "
"two young children playing on the street:two children are "
```

### 4.3    Cluster Quality

We formalize quantifying the quality of a cluster of network activation states
as an agreement assessment problem: given discrete sets of raters, items, and of
categorical ratings, measure the agreement between raters.

In our case, the raters are the network activation states in a cluster. Each
such activation state corresponds to a prefix from the training text. To get the
set of items, we select up to 30 suffixes that appear in the training text after the
prefixes in the cluster; the suffixes will not include the final, result character on
a training text line. So for the example line in Sect. 4.1, we could have a prefix
"a dog runs:", for which the suffix would be "the dog is running home:".

The categorical rating will be one of "#", "|", "<". Each prefix in the cluster
rates each of the up to 30 suffixes by asking the network what its response
is to the string prefix+suffix. To measure agreement, we use the Fleiss kappa
score. For each method we evaluate, we compute a weighted average score: each
cluster receives a kappa score, weighted by cluster size. Table 1 shows average
scores for our method based on most likely suffixes, and for tSNE+DBSCAN
with different eps values (eps is a DBSCAN parameter controlling the maximum
distance between two points such that they are considered part of the same
neighborhood). For DBSCAN, we only select clusters of at least 5 points.

**Table 1.** Weighted average Fleiss kappa scores for clusters

| Clustering method | Cluster# | Avg. Fleiss Kappa |
|---|---|---|
| DBSCAN (eps = 0.125) | 102 | 0.242343 |
| DBSCAN (eps = 0.25) | 676 | 0.459795 |
| DBSCAN (eps = 0.5) | 1857 | 0.620173 |
| DBSCAN (eps = 1.0) | 597 | 0.594576 |
| DBSCAN (eps = 2.0) | 26 | 0.308523 |
| Most likely suffixes | 1956 | 0.824841 |

### 4.4    Explaining Errors

We would like to have good clusters of activation states so as to produce an
automaton that approximates the network's behavior, and is more readily interpretable. We show here a brief example of why such an automaton is useful.

The network trained in Sect. 4.1 correctly answers 83% of the training queries,
and 74% of the test queries. An example input producing an error is

"a family smiling on the couch:people are on a couch:"

for which the correct answer is "<" (entailment), but the network answers "|" (contradiction). We look at clusters containing prefixes of this string and observe the following cluster obtained by our most likely suffix method:

```
"a group of people dancing together:people are "
"a crowd of people dancing together:people are "
"three people playing in the snow:people are "
"a family smiling on the couch:people are "
```

So the network seems to arrive at a state where it remembers the premise involves a group of people, and the query asks about a group of people also, but it may be confused about what the people in the premise are doing. To test whether this is the case, we compute the network responses to strings formed from these prefixes plus suffixes "dancing:", "dancing together:", "outdoors:", and "on the couch:". We find perfect agreement, with suffixes "outdoors", "dancing:", and "dancing together:" resulting in "<" (entailment), and "on the couch" resulting in "|" (contradiction). This confirms that the network in these cases reaches a state in which it "forgets" about the exact action in the premise.

Note that in the process of finding a plausible explanation for the network's mistake, we also generate more strings on which the network makes mistakes. Such analysis can be used to create a corpus of text that is still problematic for the network, so that it can be trained further and its performance improved.

## 5   Related Work

There are two approaches to interpreting NLP neural networks. The oldest, and the one most relevant to this paper, is to use recurrent networks for grammar inference. One method, presented in [10], is to partition the network's state space into discrete regions. A more recent method is shown in [7], where K-means clustering of activation state vectors is used to extract some simple regular grammars from recurrent networks. Partitioning into discrete bins doesn't scale to the sizes of contemporary networks however, and our work here suggests that k-means might also not behave well once the grammars become more complex.

The second approach uses statistical techniques. Visualization of word/sentence embeddings was used to discover patterns of negation and compositionality [17]. Some version of "salience", defined as the impact of a cell on the network's final decision, is the basis for other visualization techniques. Representation erasure has been used to analyze a network [18], by tracking how a network changes state or output when deleting word vector representation dimensions, input words, or hidden units. In [15], an error analysis for character-level language model LSTMs vs ngram models is presented, including neural activation levels while the network processes a sequence. Recent developments on visualization tools are summarized in [5,12]. LSTMVis [23] and RNNVis [20] are two such tools; they use Euclidean distance to group network activations.

Different network architectures and training regimes show different ability to capture grammatical features, which has been investigated in [19], with particular focus on noun-verb number agreement. A very interesting approach to quantify how well a representation (e.g. bag of words or LSTM) can capture grammatical features is described in [1]: can one train an accurate classifier for that feature, with the representation as input (rather than the original sentence)?

Positive samples are not enough to learn regular grammars, but stochastic samples can replace negative samples [2]. A polynomial time algorithm to learn a regular grammar from stochastic samples is given in [6]; it constructs a prefix tree automaton and merges states based on the language sample's statistical properties. Our activation clusters can be used by a Carrasco-like algorithm for grammar inference to merge states in a prefix tree.

Natural language inference has received a lot of attention, and it has been shown that recurrent networks can learn logical semantics (or at least learn enough to give that appearance) [4]. A large text corpus to train classifiers has been made available [3], and several neural network architectures have been empirically tested for performance at the semantic entailment task [9]. A combination of semantic entailment and generation is presented in [16], where the network's task is to generate a statement implied by a premise given as input.

## 6   Conclusions and Future Work

In this work we have presented a method to group recurrent neural network activation states in a meaningful way, in order to obtain a more interpretable representation of how the network operates. We compare our method to a Euclidean clustering approach, and use Fleiss kappa scores to quantify how appropriate the clusters are as states of an automaton approximating the network behavior.

The performance of the Euclidean clustering methods is better than we expected, if one applies some simple post-processing (only keep maximal strings in a cluster) to remove an artifact resulting from tSNE. Even so, our method based on groupings by most likely suffixes shows better average Fleiss kappa scores, and is better suited to extract an approximating automaton from a neural network.

In future work we will investigate learning a metric on the network activation states based on kappa scores, and look at extending the most likely suffix method to networks that are not language models, using a technique from [1].

## References

1. Adi, Y., Kermany, E., Belinkov, Y., Lavi, O., Goldberg, Y.: Fine-grained analysis of sentence embeddings using auxiliary prediction tasks. CoRR abs/1608.04207 (2016)
2. Angluin, D.: Identifying languages from stochastic examples. Technical report, YALEU/ DCS/RR-614, Yale University, Department of Computer Science, New Haven, CT (1988)
3. Bowman, S.R., Angeli, G., Potts, C., Manning, C.D.: A large annotated corpus for learning natural language inference. In: Proceedings of the 2015 Conference on Empirical Methods in Natural Language Processing (EMNLP) (2015)

4. Bowman, S.R., Potts, C., Manning, C.D.: Recursive neural networks for learning logical semantics. CoRR abs/1406.1827 (2014)
5. Choo, J., Liu, S.: Visual analytics for explainable deep learning. CoRR abs/1804.02527 (2018)
6. Carrasco, R.C., Oncina, J.: Learning deterministic regular grammars from stochastic samples in polynomial time. ITA **33**(1), 1–20 (1999)
7. Cohen, M., Caciularu, A., Rejwan, I., Berant, J.: Inducing regular grammars using recurrent neural networks. CoRR abs/1710.10453 (2017)
8. Ester, M., Kriegel, H.P., Sander, J., Xu, X.: A density-based algorithm for discovering clusters a density-based algorithm for discovering clusters in large spatial databases with noise. In: Proceedings of the Second International Conference on Knowledge Discovery and Data Mining. AAAI Press (1996)
9. Evans, R., Saxton, D., Amos, D., Kohli, P., Grefenstette, E.: Can neural networks understand logical entailment? In: Intntl Conf on Learning Representations (2018)
10. Giles, C.L., Miller, C.B., Chen, D., Sun, G.Z., Chen, H.H., Lee, Y.C.: Extracting and learning an unknown grammar with recurrent neural networks. In: Proceedings of the 4th International Conference on Neural Information Processing Systems, NIPS 1991. Morgan Kaufmann Publishers Inc., San Francisco (1991)
11. Hochreiter, S., Schmidhuber, J.: Long short-term memory. Neural Comput. **9**(8), 1735–1780 (1997)
12. Hohman, F., Kahng, M., Pienta, R., Chau, D.H.: Visual analytics in deep learning: An interrogative survey for the next frontiers. CoRR abs/1801.06889 (2018)
13. Kansky, K., et al.: Schema networks: zero-shot transfer with a generative causal model of intuitive physics. In: ICML (2017)
14. Karpathy, A.: The unreasonable effectiveness of recurrent neural networks. http://karpathy.github.io/2015/05/21/rnn-effectiveness/. Accessed 29 Jan 2018
15. Karpathy, A., Johnson, J., Fei-Fei, L.: Visualizing and understanding recurrent networks. CoRR abs/1506.02078 (2015)
16. Kolesnyk, V., Rocktäschel, T., Riedel, S.: Generating natural language inference chains. CoRR abs/1606.01404 (2016)
17. Li, J., Chen, X., Hovy, E., Jurafsky, D.: Visualizing and understanding neural models in NLP. In: Proceedings of NAACL-HLT, pp. 681–691 (2016)
18. Li, J., Monroe, W., Jurafsky, D.: Understanding neural networks through representation erasure. CoRR abs/1612.08220 (2016)
19. Linzen, T., Dupoux, E., Goldberg, Y.: Assessing the ability of LSTMs to learn syntax-sensitive dependencies. TACL **4**, 521–535 (2016)
20. Ming, Y., et al.: Understanding hidden memories of recurrent neural networks. CoRR abs/1710.10777 (2017)
21. van der Maaten, L., Hinton, G.: Visualizing data using t-SNE. J. Mach. Learn. Res. **9**, 2579–2605 (2008)
22. Ribeiro, M.T., Singh, S., Guestrin, C.: "Why should i trust you?": explaining the predictions of any classifier. In: Proceedings of the 22nd ACM SIGKDD International Conference on Knowledge Discovery and Data Mining. ACM, New York (2016)
23. Strobelt, H., Gehrmann, S., Huber, B., Pfister, H., Rush, A.M.: Visual analysis of hidden state dynamics in recurrent neural networks. CoRR abs/1606.07461 (2016)

# Automatic Extraction of Structured Information from Drug Descriptions

Radu Razvan Slavescu[1]([⊠]) [iD], Constantin Maşca[1] [iD],
and Kinga Cristina Slavescu[2] [iD]

[1] Department of Computer Science, Technical University of Cluj-Napoca,
Bariţiu 28, 400027 Cluj-Napoca, Romania
Radu.Razvan.Slavescu@cs.utcluj.ro, Constantin.Masca@student.utcluj.ro
[2] "Iuliu Hatieganu" University of Medicine and Pharmacy, Cluj-Napoca, Romania
Slavescu.Kinga@yahoo.com

**Abstract.** This paper describes a Conditional Random Field (CRF) based named entity extraction model that is used for identifying relevant information from drug prescriptions. The entities that the model is able to extract are: dosage, measuring unit, to whom the treatment is directed, frequency and the total duration of treatment. A corpus with 1800 sentences has been compiled and annotated by two experts from drug prescription texts. Using the set of features identified by us, the CRF model hits around 95% F1-measure values for unit, dosage and frequency detection.

**Keywords:** Conditional Random Field · Drug description
Named Entity Recognition

## 1 Introduction

Nowadays, prescribing drugs to patients becomes increasingly challenging, in part because of the amount of administration details like quantity, frequency, patient condition and treatment duration which must be memorized.

To address this, we developed a Named Entity Recognition (NER) model able to identify inside a text the position of the word sequences containing the chunks of information mentioned. It is based on Conditional Random Fields (CRF) and exploits context information in order to perform sequence labeling. Along with this, we extended the corpus introduced in [6] up to 1800 sentences and revisited the sentences in order to double check their labels. First, we crawled several drug prescription websites. Then, we manually extracted from the online texts those sentences which contained information of interest about the drugs. Sentences that contained at least one of the entities pursued were selected from the full description. For each word in these sentences, its Part-of-Speech (POS) tag was added to allow using it as a feature for various Machine Learning algorithms.

The key contributions of our work are as follows. First, the expanded annotated corpus could be used for further model creation and assessment. Second,

© Springer Nature Switzerland AG 2018
A. Groza and R. Prasath (Eds.): MIKE 2018, LNAI 11308, pp. 21–31, 2018.
https://doi.org/10.1007/978-3-030-05918-7_3

the paper proposes and assesses a CRF model based solution for extracting the aforementioned categories of information which are of interest for a medical practitioner. The overall performance assessment in terms of precision, recall and F1-measure prove the system's ability to identify the named entities is good.

The rest of the article is structured as follows. Section 2 summarizes the related work. Section 3 gives a brief overview of the Conditional Random Fields for Entity extraction. Section 4 describes the two datasets used for building and testing our model. The model features, parameters and implementation are then detailed in Sect. 5. Section 6 shows the obtained results. The last section concludes and describes the future developments we plan to pursue.

## 2   Related Work

Extracting sequences of interest from large, unstructured texts has been an open problem in Natural Language Processing (NLP) for decades. One initiative aiming to tackle this kind of problems in the medical texts field is lead by the i2b2 tranSMART Foundation[1]. Various annual competitions focused on medicine related NLP tasks have been organized. In the third workshop on NLP Challenges for Clinical Records [10], the focus was on the identification of medications, their dosages, modes (routes) of administration, frequencies, duration, and reasons for administration in discharge summaries.

The winning system of that competition used a combination of machine learners with several rule-based engines [4]. They used different features for the CRF model. Gazetteers and lexicons were used for multiple entity detection. Suffixes and prefixes of words were also taken as features. Several other features were obtained, such as POS tags, orthographic information and medical category of the words. For each named entity a different feature set was used in order to accommodate the data found in the texts. For example, for the frequency/duration, the system relied on a gazetteer and a pattern matching mechanism, while for the mode, it used a gazetteer generated from the train set. The final results of the system were good, averaging 0.9 over all entities besides reason and duration. The low performance on the two entities is probably due to the small frequency of the entities in the data set. Another reason is the ambiguous and diverse ways of expressing this kind of information. For extracting the reason part, the system relies heavily on pattern matching and does not generalize well.

The paper [9] describes a three steps pipeline for extracting drug administration details: named entity identification, filtering, and Relation Extraction using scope detection. The named entity identification is achieved via a rule-based approach. A standard CRF-based solution added to the rule-based one did not improve the performance. The authors explain this by the limited amount of training data. When additional training data, even if inaccurate, was added, applying CRF improved the performance.

---

[1] http://transmartfoundation.org.

The machine learning based solution proposed in [5] aims at extracting content (active ingredient, interaction effects, etc.) from the Summary of Product Characteristics, focusing mainly on drug-related interactions. The authors compare the performances of two different classifiers, one based on CRFs and one based on Support Vector Machines, on a corpus of 100 manually annotated drug interaction descriptions. The two models exhibit similar overall performance. The reported overall accuracy for each of them is around 91%.

Paper [8] addresses the problem of extracting medicine prescriptions from discharge summaries written as unstructured free texts. The solution relies on a machine learning approach consisting of two extraction steps: medication information extraction and relation extraction. Each of them is treated as a sequence labeling problem. This approach achieves a phrase-level F1-measure of 86.4%.

## 3 Conditional Random Fields for Entity Extraction

### 3.1 CRF Model

CRFs are sequence predicting probabilistic models [7], which exploit contextual information of input variables. Their output is the most likely sequence of labels for a given sequence of input variables. The general linear chain CRF is defined as follows. Let $X$ and $Y$ be random vectors representing the input and output variables respectively. Let $\theta = \{\theta_k\} \in \mathbb{R}^K$ be a parameter vector and $\mathcal{F} = \{f_k(y, y, x_t)\}_{k=1}^K$ be a set of real-valued feature functions. Then a linear-chain conditional random field is a distribution $p(y|x)$ that takes the form:

$$p(y|x) = \frac{1}{Z(x)} \prod_{t=1}^{T} \exp\left\{ \sum_{k=1}^{K} \theta_k f_k(y_t, y_{t-1}, \mathbf{x}_t) \right\},$$

where $Z(x)$ is an input-dependent normalization function

$$Z(\mathbf{x}) = \sum_{y} \prod_{t=1}^{T} \exp\left\{ \sum_{k=1}^{K} \theta_k f_k(y_t, y_{t-1}, \mathbf{x}_t) \right\}.$$

In our case, $X$ is the feature vector corresponding to the words in a sentence, while $Y$ corresponds to the labels we search for. Factors are functions of the form $\Psi_a(\mathbf{y}_a)$, $a \in \mathbb{N}$, such that each of them depends only on a subset $Y_a \subseteq Y$ of the variables. The parameter vector $\theta$ is learned from data using the maximum likelihood algorithm.

### 3.2 CRFs for Named Entity Recognition

The goal of NER is to classify text segments into predefined classes (i.e., entities). For example, let us consider the sentence "Take 200 mg. of medicine X, twice daily, with food". Here, the task of NER may be to figure out the sequence of words in the sentence which gives the frequency with which the drug is administrated, i.e., "twice daily". Such entities should be identified correctly even if they appear infrequently in the training set. Section 4 lists the whole set of entities we aimed to identify.

To achieve this one idea would be to rely not on a the word alone, but also on its neighbors and their respective features. Besides the neighboring words, some other features might help, and among them, suffixes, prefixes, capitalization or position in the sentence. Another feature which pays off for the task is the word POS tag, like noun (NN), verb (VBZ), adverb (RB) etc. A POS is a category of words sharing similar grammatical properties and roles.

Various methods for NER have been proposed, and among them, hand-crafted rules, grammar-based techniques or statistics based methods. We opted for CRFs because they can handle sequences that vary in length and are more flexible when the training set is modified. Unlike the probabilistic models, the rule-based systems need new rules to be added manually when some unforeseen cases appear in the training set.

Before applying the CRF based training, texts are split into sentences, which are further tokenized into individual words. Then, the CRF model is built. The set of features selected for model generation heavily impacts the system performance. Part-of-speech tags are used in most models. Word-based features such as suffixes, lengths, whether it contains a number or not, etc. are usually present as well, given that they are easy to extract. The full set of features we used for our work is given in Sect. 5.

## 4　Corpus Description

### 4.1　Our Corpus

As previously stated, our corpus consists of 1800 sentences which describe the way a specific, known drug should be administrated. It expands the corpus presented in [6] with about 600 new sentences and revisits the previous labeling to fix some inconsistencies, using a similar methodology. The sentences were extracted manually from texts containing official drug descriptions scraped from public web sources. After separating each sentence of interest from the whole text, it was labeled in an semi-automatic, iterative manner. In the first iteration, 500 sentences were manually labeled by two experts working independently. This resulted in a Cohen correlation coefficient value of 0.63. After a first reconciliation step, the labels were manually corrected and the resulting corpus was used in order to train a first model. This model was further used to annotate a new set of sentences, which were then manually checked for erroneous/missing labels. After that, the new sentences were added to the corpus, a new model was generated and used for labeling. After 3 iterations, a final check over the obtained corpus was manually performed.

The entities we intend to extract, considered of interest for medical practitioners, and their respective labels are:

1. quantity (DOS) e.g., 10, 5.2, two, three to four etc.
2. measuring unit (UNIT) e.g., mg, tablespoons etc.
3. to whom the treatment is directed (WHO) e.g., children under 5 years of age, adults etc.
4. frequency (FREQ) e.g., twice daily, once a month etc.
5. total duration of treatment (DUR) e.g., two weeks, three months etc.

An example of labeled sentence is presented in Table 1. It corresponds to the sentence *The recommended dose is 600 mg twice daily with food.* The labeling was done in the Begin-Inside-Outside (BIO) style, hence the B-FREQ and I-FREQ labels attached to the *twice daily* part of the sentence, which contains the frequency of the drug administration.

**Table 1.** Example of a labeled sentence

| The | DT | O |
|---|---|---|
| recommended | VBN | O |
| dose | NN | O |
| is | VBZ | O |
| 600 | CD | B-DOS |
| mg | NN | B-UNIT |
| twice | JJ | B-FREQ |
| daily | RB | I-FREQ |
| with | IN | O |
| food | NN | O |
| . | . | O |

Some statistics about the data in our corpus, i.e., the number of words with a particular label and their distribution are presented in Table 2.

**Table 2.** Data set statistics

| Entity | Occurrences | Frequency (%) |
|---|---|---|
| DOS | 1953 | 5.14 |
| UNIT | 1803 | 4.75 |
| DUR | 1595 | 4.20 |
| FREQ | 415 | 1.09 |
| WHO | 3048 | 8.03 |
| O | 29146 | 76.78 |

## 4.2   i2b2 Dataset

In order to test our approach on some other datasets, we prepared a second one starting from the dataset used in the i2b2 challenge [10]. The i2b2 dataset was generated from the actual description of the dosage administration procedure. The de-identified clinical records used in this research were provided by the i2b2 National Center for Biomedical Computing. i2b2 data is constructed from discharge records which include the description of the medication regimen a patient has gone through while being hospitalized. Therefore, the language is more diverse and with more expressive diversity. Unlike our corpus, which is more narrative and continuous, i2b2 contains much information that is written with no context and because of this sentences are not always properly constructed. The original challenge was to extract the following:

1. medication name and its offset (marker "m")
2. dosage and its offset (marker "do")
3. mode/route of administration and its offset (marker "mo")
4. frequency and its offset (marker "f")
5. duration and its offset (marker "du")
6. reason and its offset (marker "r")
7. event (marker "e")
8. temporal marker (marker "t")
9. certainty (marker "c")
10. found in list/narrative of the text (marker "ln")

We focused on the same types of information as in the self-prepared dataset.

## 5   Proposed Model Parameters

The vector of features pertaining to a word can dramatically impact the model performance. After several tests, we selected the following set of features:

1. the word's POS tag
2. prefix of the POS tag (first 2 letters)
3. whether or not the word is written in lower case
4. the last 2 and 3 letters of the word
5. whether or not the word is entirely uppercase
6. whether or not the word is a title
7. whether or not the word contains digits

When generating a word's feature vector, we used a 3-word wide context for a word. The value for the window width was obtained by trial-and-error after more tests performed.

Regarding the POS tag set, the Natural Language Toolkit we employed provided 36 different tags. However, some of them were connected to some others, such as the adjective (JJ) and the superlative adjective (JJS). Since we noticed the related POS's behave in a similar manner (e.g., in the JJ/JJS case), we collapsed them into just one value. Quite often, the drug's name is written either in uppercase or has the first letter uppercased. Two different CRF input features are used to gather this information. At the same time, information on the presence of digits has a separate feature reserved. We decided though to have a feature describing whether the word comprises digits only, since the POS tags already contains this information. This also covers both the case when a word comprises only digits and when it is written in letters, like "four".

Before generating the model, a pre-processing phase was triggered. It consisted in splitting the raw text into sentences, then tokenizing each sentence into words and performing POS tagging over them, using the NLTK API [1]. The rest of the labels are generated and attached to each word via an in-house code.

The training via gradient descent search was done using the Limited Memory Broyden Fletcher Goldfarb Shanno (L-BFGS) algorithm. The implementation was based on a Python wrapper of the CRFsuite library [2]. For regularization, we chose the randomized search, based on sampling the hyperparameter distribution 50 times, using 3-fold cross validation. As performance measures, we used precision, recall and F1-measure.

## 6 Results

The system's performance on the training set is given in Table 3, where on can see the values for precision, recall and F1-measure obtained by the 10-fold cross

**Table 3.** Precision P, recall R and F1-score on a train set using 10-fold

| Label | Precision | Recall | F1-score |
|---|---|---|---|
| B-DOS | 0.973 | 0.968 | 0.969 |
| O-DOS | 0.833 | 0.780 | 0.804 |
| B-DUR | 0.854 | 0.689 | 0.765 |
| I-DUR | 1.000 | 0.970 | 0.985 |
| O-DUR | 0.965 | 0.944 | 0.954 |
| B-FREQ | 0.979 | 0.969 | 0.973 |
| I-FREQ | 0.957 | 0.985 | 0.970 |
| O-FREQ | 0.983 | 0.971 | 0.977 |
| B-UNIT | 0.980 | 0.979 | 0.980 |
| I-UNIT | 1.000 | 0.774 | 0.873 |
| O-UNIT | 0.961 | 0.851 | 0.902 |
| B-WHO | 0.938 | 0.935 | 0.937 |
| I-WHO | 0.938 | 0.892 | 0.913 |
| O-WHO | 0.884 | 0.869 | 0.877 |
| Avg/Total | 0.957 | 0.946 | 0.952 |

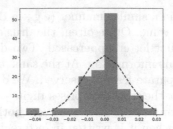

**Fig. 1.** Error distribution for total F1-measure

validation. The error distribution for this test is given in Fig. 1 and follows the normal distribution pretty well.

The next aspect we investigated was the impact of the train set dimension over the overall performance. To this end, we conducted a 9-round experiment. In each round, we prepared train sets of 500, 700, 900, 1100 and 1300 sentences out of a total of 1400 sentences; these sets were then used them for training. The components of the 500-sentences train set were selected randomly in each round, then 200 more sentences, selected randomly, were successively added, to get the 700, 900, 1100 and 1300-sentence sets. A model was then generated using the

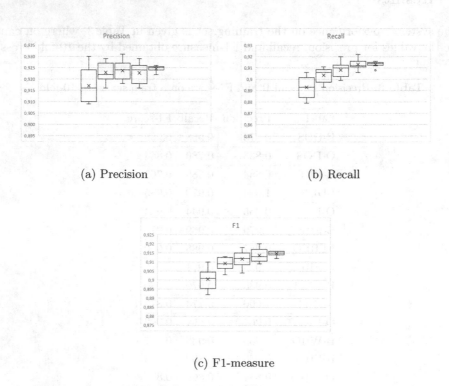

(a) Precision                                  (b) Recall

(c) F1-measure

**Fig. 2.** Performance of models trained on sets of 500, 700, 900, 1100, 1300 sentences

**Table 4.** Precision P, recall R and F1-score on the test set

|  | P | R | F1 |
|---|---|---|---|
| WHO | 0.780 | 0.948 | 0.856 |
| UNIT | 0.969 | 0.944 | 0.957 |
| DOS | 0.980 | 0.956 | 0.968 |
| FREQ | 0.967 | 0.928 | 0.947 |
| DUR | 0.600 | 0.800 | 0.686 |
| Avg/Total | 0.935 | 0.938 | 0.935 |

current train set and evaluated over a separate 400-sentence dataset. The results
are summarized in Fig. 2.

Table 4 shows the results obtained on the test set containing 400 sentences
by a model trained using 1400 sentences. The results are computed per entity in
a micro-averaged manner.

The results obtained on the i2b2 dataset are presented in Table 5. This time,
the model has been trained and tested on the data provided by i2b2. The set
of entities we aimed are the same as above, so we focused only on a subset of
the targets required by the i2b2 competition. For comparison, we present the
performance of our system (left) and the results obtained by the best system in
the competition [3] for the corresponding tasks (right).

The results are comparable, however the i2b2 winner performs slightly better
on all tasks. We believe this is because of the style the text is written in the
two cases. For our corpus, the style is somehow more formal, with sentences
following a (more or less) standard structure, while the i2b2 is compiled from
discharge texts written in different ways by different human agents, with no
special attention to standard formulations.

**Table 5.** Results on i2b2 dataset: our system (left) v. i2b2 challenge winner (right)

| Task | Precision | Recall | F1 | Precision | Recall | F1 |
|---|---|---|---|---|---|---|
| Frequency | 0.923 | 0.872 | 0.896 | 0.962 | 0.932 | 0.947 |
| Medication name | 0.935 | 0.893 | 0.914 | 0.913 | 0.914 | 0.914 |
| Reason | 0.669 | 0.272 | 0.386 | 0.697 | 0.461 | 0.555 |
| Dosage | 0.947 | 0.918 | 0.932 | 0.963 | 0.934 | 0.949 |
| Mode of administration | 0.968 | 0.941 | 0.954 | 0.959 | 0.946 | 0.952 |
| Duration | 0.748 | 0.566 | 0.640 | 0.806 | 0.519 | 0.631 |
| Avg/Total | 0.914 | 0.847 | 0.874 | 0.928 | 0.888 | 0.908 |

# 7    Conclusions and Future Work

We developed a solution for extracting information of interest about drug administration from medicine description written in natural language. The obtained results prove that a CRF based model can offer a solution to the task at hand and leads to promising results, especially in case of standard description of drugs. The typical use would consist in quickly obtaining the information of interest by highlighting the relevant word sequence inside large texts.

We have compiled and labeled a corpus of 1800 sentences. This represents a 50% increase compared to the previous version, as well as fixing some ambiguous labels. Using the same methodology, we plan to enrich it with texts written in slightly different styles, to increase the generalization capabilities of the model.

One direction we envisage is to explore in more detail the structure of the sentences in the corpus. We will try to group sentences based on the order in which groups of entities appeared inside them. Hopefully this will reveal how many ways of phrasing the details of a prescription there actually are. The approach described in [11] for Semantic Role Labeling could help in this respect. This may open the possibility for additional information extraction, such as relationships between the extracted entities.

**Acknowledgments.** The work for this paper has been supported in part by the Computer Science Department of the Technical University of Cluj-Napoca, Romania.

# References

1. Bird, S., Klein, E., Loper, E.: Natural Language Processing with Python. O'Reilly Media, Inc., Sebastopol (2009)
2. Okazaki, N.: CRFsuite: a fast implementation of Conditional Random Fields (CRFs) (2007)
3. Patrick, J., Li, M.: A cascade approach to extracting medication events. In: Proceedings of the Australasian Language Technology Association Workshop 2009, pp. 99–103 (2009)
4. Patrick, J., Li, M.: High accuracy information extraction of medication information from clinical notes: 2009 i2b2 medication extraction challenge. J. Am. Med. Inf. Assoc. **17**(5), 524–527 (2010)
5. Rubrichi, S., Quaglini, S.: Summary of product characteristics content extraction for a safe drugs usage. J. Biomed. Inform. **45**(2), 231–239 (2012)
6. Slavescu, R.R., Masca, C., Slavescu, K.C.: Sequence labeling for extracting relevant pieces of information from raw text medicine descriptions. In: Proceedings of the International Conference on Advancements of Medicine and Health Care through Technology, October 2018, Cluj-Napoca, Romania (2018, In press)
7. Sutton, C., McCallum, A.: An introduction to conditional random fields. Found. Trends Mach. Learn. **4**(4), 267–373 (2012)
8. Tao, C., Filannino, M., Uzuner, Ö.: Prescription extraction using CRFs and word embeddings. J. Biomed. Inform. **72**, 60–66 (2017)
9. Tikk, D., Solt, I.: Improving textual medication extraction using combined conditional random fields and rule-based systems. J. Am. Med. Inform. Assoc. **17**(5), 540–544 (2010)

10. Uzuner, Ö., Solti, I., Cadag, E.: Extracting medication information from clinical text. J. Am. Med. Inform. Assoc. **17**(5), 514–518 (2010)
11. Zhang, Y., Jiang, M., Wang, J., Xu, H.: Semantic role labeling of clinical text: comparing syntactic parsers and features. In: AMIA 2016, American Medical Informatics Association Annual Symposium, Chicago, IL, USA (2016)

# From Open Information Extraction to Semantic Web: A Context Rule-Based Strategy

Julio Hernandez[1]([✉]), Ivan Lopez-Arevalo[1], Jose L. Martinez-Rodriguez[1], and Edwyn Aldana-Bobadilla[2]

[1] Cinvestav Tamaulipas, Ciudad Victoria, Mexico
{nhernandez,ilopez,lmartinez}@tamps.cinvestav.mx
[2] Conacyt-Cinvestav, Mexico City, Mexico
ealdana@tamps.cinvestav.mx

**Abstract.** The Web represents a valuable data source of information that is presented mainly as unstructured text. The extraction of structured and valuable information from sources such as the Web is an important challenge for the Semantic Web and Information Extraction areas, where elements representing real-world objects (aka named entities) and their relations need to be extracted from text and formally represented through RDF triples. Thus, extracting such information from the Web is manually unfeasible due to its large scale and heterogeneity of domains. In this sense, Open Information Extraction (OIE) is an independent domain task based on patterns to extract any kind of relation between named entities. Hence, one step further is to transform such relations into RDF triples. This paper proposes a method to represent relations obtained by an OIE approach into RDF triples. The method is based on the extraction of named entities, their relation, and contextual information from an input sentence and a set of defined rules that lead to map the extracted elements with resources from a Knowledge Base of the Semantic Web. The evaluation demonstrates promising results regarding the extraction and representation of information.

**Keywords:** Open Information Extraction · Semantic Web
Named entity recognition · Named entity linking

## 1 Introduction

The automatic analysis of text to extract valuable information is a fundamental task to transform a set of characters into machine-readable data. The field of Information Extraction (IE) analyzes the content of text to identify information like named entities (NE[1]) and the relationships between them [13]. However, the

---

[1] A named entity, mainly, refers to names of people, companies, and geographical places. However, the types of NEs varies according to the domain.

© Springer Nature Switzerland AG 2018
A. Groza and R. Prasath (Eds.): MIKE 2018, LNAI 11308, pp. 32–41, 2018.
https://doi.org/10.1007/978-3-030-05918-7_4

output of IE systems is provided as structured data constituted by text elements. As a consequence, this kind of output cannot be automatically analyzed by a computer. In this sense, the Semantic Web (SW) field tries to make computer understandable the content of unstructured data provided by the Web [4]. The SW describes and relates entities through a structure called RDF *triple*, which is constituted a *subject*, *predicate*, and *object*, each one represented by a unique URI. Both, IE and SW, describe information as binary relations; However, the latter can be processable by computers meanwhile the former only by humans.

According to Jurafsky and Martin [11], IE involves the identification of instances of a particular class in a natural language text and the extraction of relations between them. IE approaches are built based on a set of predefined target relations. This kind of approaches can not be directly applied to open domains like the Web. In this sense, the work of Banko *et al.* [8] introduced the notion of Open Information Extraction (OIE). OIE is based on free domain rules to extract relations patterns from any domain. The OIE output structure is the same as the SW. However, while a relation in SW is constituted by URI elements, an OIE relation is constituted by strings.

In this work, we proposed a lightweight domain-independent approach following a self-supervised method to annotate and relate entities based on their context[2] interaction. For this purpose, we define a *relation context* as the interaction between two or more NEs in a sentence, i.e., it is considered their indexes, their classes, and their dependencies according to the syntactic and semantic analysis. To achieve the above goal, we proposed a set of domain-independent rules to map OIE relations to SW triples.

The next section presents the works related to the mapping process between IE and SW. In Sect. 3 it is explained the proposed methodology to map OIE triples to SW triples based on the context interaction and rules. In Sect. 4 are presented the experiments and results applying the proposed methodology. Finally, the conclusions of the work are presented in Sect. 5.

## 2   Related Work

With the growth of the SW, the works based on free domain strategies to map relations from text to SW structures have gained importance [14]. In this sense, works such as LODifier [2], Pikes [5], and FRED [10] define a set of rules to related two NEs following a semantic analysis technique, e.g., Semantic Role Labeling (SRL) or Discourse Representation Structures (DRS). In a different way, our proposal takes into account the interaction between two entities considering their context relation based on the OIE paradigm.

There have been a few studies about the effectiveness to map OIE tools' output to SW. Zouaq *et al.* [14] studied different OIE tools and, according to their results, the authors concluded that OIE systems are not directly applicable to SW due to their unstructured nature and the lack of information to exactly

---

[2] In this work, the term *context* refers to the words between two NEs in a sentence.

determine which members of the triple are part of the tuple (text triple). In the proposed work we evaluate the mapping process from OIE tools output to RDF triples based on domain-independent rules, considering the context of NEs.

Another free-domain paradigm to extract relations is based on distant supervision, which exploits large KBs, e.g., Yago or Freebase, to automatically label entities in text using machine learning algorithms. A set of features are extracted from labeled entities to train a classifier. According to Augenstein et al. [1], this kind of approaches depends on the quality of the input corpus to define a good set of features to describe, uniquely, a relation between two entities. Our approach differs from distant supervision methods because our work did not perform any classification task since our main objective is to find a relation between two NEs considering their local context. Hence, in the proposed work, OIE relations are mapped to SW triples based on domain-independent rules, which take into account the context interaction between NEs. This method is described in the next section.

## 3   Proposed Method

The proposed method extracts relations from plain text sentences based on syntactic and semantic analysis. Both analyses are combined through a set of defined rules and queries to discover open relations taking into account their relation context.

The semantic analysis is based on the discovery of frames to relate two NEs. According to Baker [3] a frame is a generalization over groups of words which describes similar states of affairs, sets of roles, and syntactic patterns, e.g., the **Possibility** frame generalize the words: *can, could, might,* and *may,* which express conditionality.

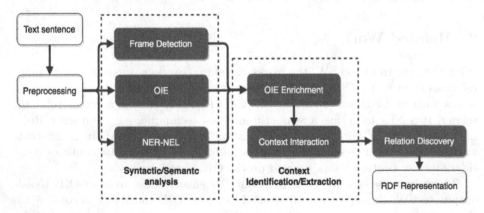

**Fig. 1.** Overview of the proposed method to extract relations based on domain-independent rules considering the context interaction between two NEs.

As Fig. 1 shows, the proposed method combines the output of syntactic (*OIE* and *NER-NEL*) and semantic tools (*Frame Detection*) to identify the context of a sentence. The output of these tools is merged by a middleware module (*OIE Enrichment*). Then, a rule-based module (*Context Interaction*) identifies the NEs whose context related them and a query-based module (*Relation Discovery*) identifies their corresponding predicate in a KB of the SW. Finally, an RDF representation (*RDF Representation*) is generated. The modules and their function are described as follows:

- **Preprocessing:** identifies text features such as tokens, part-of-speech tags, token indexes, etc.
- **Syntactic/Semantic Analysis:** the preprocessed sentence is parsed to identify NEs, frames, and binary relations.
  - *NER-NEL:* identifies words or phrases which evoke a NE, tagging them with their corresponding class, e.g., *New York City* as *Location.* Finally, NEs are linked to their corresponding resources from a KB of the SW.
  - *Frame Detection:* analyzes the content of the sentence to detect frames.
  - *OIE:* extracts binary relations from text[3]. Generally, the result of this task is a triple of subject, verb, and complement. The verb corresponds to the relation between the subject and the complement.
- **Context Identification/Extraction:** the *OIE* output is enriched with NEs and frames extracted from the *NER-NEL* and *Frame Detection* modules.
  - *OIE enrichment:* enriches the OIE module's output tagging the NEs, identified by the *NER-NEL* module, in the subject and complement content. Additionally, the verb element content is tagged with the identified frames.
  - *Context Interaction:* determines if the subject and complement of the *OIE* output are candidates to create an RDF triple according to a set of predefined domain-independent rules (see later).
- **Relation Discovery:** looks for the predicate between two NEs through a SPARQL query over a KB of the SW.
- **RDF representation:** generates the output as RDF triples.

The *Context Interaction* module is based on domain-independent rules to define the possible relation between two NEs from the *OIE* output module. A relation between two NEs exists iff one of the following rules occurs:

- **Rule 1 (NER-NEL + OIE):** the subject and complement of an OIE triple contain NEs.
- **Rule 2 (Frame + OIE):** the OIE triple contains a frame in their verb element and their subject and complement contain NEs.

The above rules define the contextual scenarios to identify the subject and object of an RDF triple. After determining the context interaction, the next step

---

[3] In this work we focus on binary relations, but, the OIE output could also be represented as n-ary relations.

consists on defining the RDF triple's predicate. This step follows a query-based method. In this sense, the following rules are defined to discover the predicate between the identified NEs:

- **Direct Relation Rule:** this rule is divided into two cases: (i) a predicate between two identified NEs it's defined by a KB of the SW, e.g., the query[4] *dbr:The_Beatles ?p dbr:Liverpool* returns *dbo:hometown*, and (ii) two identified NEs are related by a frame, e.g., *?s rdfs:label "Leadership"*, where *?s* is a *pmofn:Frame* type. The second case queries the frame name in the Premon[5] KB, setting the returned URI as the predicate.
- **Indirect Relation Rule:** only one NE of the relation is linked to a resource in a KB of the SW. However, the class of the remaining NE is known in advance. The query for this rule relates a class member (e.g., *Person*, *Location*, etc.) with an specific resource (e.g., a person's name). For example, the query to find a relation between a person class and the resource *dbr:The_Beatles* is as follows: *?s ?p dbr:The_Beatles*, where *?s* is of type *dbo:Person*. From the resulting list of predicates (returned by the *?p* variable), a majority voting scheme is followed to select the triple's predicate.
- **Default Relation Rule:** the generic relation *ContextRelated* is set.

The first and second rules are based on a query-based search to extract the corresponding predicate from a KB of the SW. If both rules fail, the last rule is applied. This rule denotes the existence of a relation, even when the context information gives minor evidence about the specific relation. In particular, the second rule occurs when a NE could not be linked to a KB and thus, the NER system assigns a class to the NE.

## 4 Experiments

This section describes the experiments and results for evaluating the proposed method.

### 4.1 Dataset and Metrics

The dataset used for the experiments corresponds to a set of 200 English sentences extracted from DBpedia. The extraction process was performed through a SPARQL query to retrieve the abstracts (*dbo:abstract*) of a set of resources from a specific class. The class *Person* was selected for the experiments because it contains concrete information about people and helps to create a familiar scenario in the evaluation process. However, this class can be interchangeable by any other, e.g., *Location*, *Organization*, etc. On the other hand, We decided to extract 200 sentences inspired by other OIE works [7,9].

---

[4] We use URI prefixes (namespaces) in accordance with the service hosted at http://prefix.cc.

[5] https://premon.fbk.eu/.

From the set of retrieved abstracts, only the first sentence is kept for the experiments since this sentence does not contain any coreference, i.e. pronouns (he, she, it), whose resolution is out of the scope of this work.

For the evaluation, we obtained the precision of a set of relations extracted from the set of sentences. The evaluation considers a set of relations extracted from a sentence; then a user evaluates them as correct or incorrect. A relation is considered as correct if it is coherent with the sentence. On the other hand, a relation is not correct if the context of the sentence is not related with the assigned relation.

## 4.2 Implementation

The RE process is supported by different tools which, by themselves, tries to give a meaning to the input text, e.g., tagging tokens with their corresponding POS-tag, identifying NEs, etc. In this sense, the Stanford CoreNLP[6] [12] is used in the *Preprocessing* (tokenize, assign part-of-speech tags), *NER-NEL* (identified NEs), and *OIE* (extract relations) modules. The DBpedia Spotlight[7] system was used, in combination with Stanford CoreNLP, to detect and link entities from text to the DBpedia KB in the *NER-NEL* module. In the *Frame Detection* module, SEMAFOR[8] [6] is used as the Semantic Role Labeling tool to detect frames in text, this is based on probabilistic parsing to find words that evoke FrameNet[9] frames. The aforementioned tools can be changed by any other approach for the same task, giving flexibility to the proposed methodology. The remaining modules (*OIE Enrichment, Context Interaction*, etc.) identify, extract, and annotate the RDF triples from the text sentence.

## 4.3 Evaluation

The evaluation process tries to asseses how well was assigned a relation between two identified NEs. To achieve this, we follow a methodology based on human judgment like some OIE approaches [7,9]. The evaluation process was made by five persons, which determine the correctness of the relation according to the following considerations: (i) the subject appears before the object in the text, (ii) the relation is equal, or is similar in meaning with the text between the subject and object, (iii) if the relation is derived from frame rules, the frame's description has to be close in meaning with the context of the OIE triple, and (iv) if the relation is labeled as *ContextRelated*, the text between the subject and object has to related them.

A particular consideration is made for *ContextualRelated* relation; it represents a non-specific relation. A *ContextRelated* relation establishes the existence of a relation between two NEs according to their context information.

---

[6] https://stanfordnlp.github.io/CoreNLP/index.html.
[7] https://www.dbpedia-spotlight.org/.
[8] http://www.cs.cmu.edu/~ark/SEMAFOR/.
[9] https://framenet.icsi.berkeley.edu/fndrupal/.

However, the extraction process has no elements to define a specific relation from a KB of the SW. For example:

**Sentence:** Robert Leon Phillips, known as Bob Phillips (born June 23, 1951), is an American television journalist best known for his long-running program Texas Country Reporter.
**RDF Triple:** (dbr:journalist, exp:ContextRelated, dbr:Texas)

where the prefix *dbr* denotes a DBpedia resource[10] and *exp* denotes a generic URI. The triple extracted from the example is evaluated as incorrect because the *dbr:Texas* refers to a *location* and not to a *TV show* as the sentence suggests. Additionally, the text between NEs lacks of meaning to determine the relationship between *dbr:journalist* and *dbr:Texas*.

### 4.4   Results

This section presents the results of the extraction of relations between NEs and the number of such relations classified as correct or incorrect. Also presents the individual results for each proposed rule. The Table 1 shows the global results of the experiments, the row *others* groups the remaining relations whose total number of examples is less than 5, denoted by the number inside the parenthesis[11]. According to the Table 1, the *occupation* relation got the largest number of correct evaluations, meanwhile, the *ContextRelated* relation got the second place. The last result demonstrates a high context dependency between entities, i.e. they are related under a specific context. Additionally, only 35% of the extracted relations have at least five examples (correct/incorrect), as a consequence of the open scenario, in which the experiment was evaluated. The best results were obtained when the proposed rules are taken into account. Finally, Fig. 2 illustrates the best ten relations evaluated as correct, following the proposed rules (*Frame + ORE* and *NER-NEL + OIE*).

Table 2 illustrates the results of the experiments taking into account only those relations extracted with the *Frame + OIE* rule. According to the results, the relations extracted based on frame detection is over half of the entire results. However, the precision is under 50%, that is to say, the frame rules extracted more relations but at least half of them were incorrect. From the relation extracted, the most common relation was *being_born* with the greatest number of correct and incorrect evaluations. Finally, Fig. 3 illustrates the comparison between the extracted relations following this rule.

The results for the rule based on *NER-NEL + OIE* are shown in Table 3. The number of relations extracted following this rule are less than those extracted with the *Frame + OIE* rule. However, the results are better than frame results. The *ContextRelated* is the second relation with the largest number of correct and the first for incorrectly evaluated relations. The Fig. 4 illustrates the comparison between the extracted relations following this rule.

---

[10] http://dbpedia.org/resource/.
[11] This explanation is used for the next tables.

**Table 1.** Relations extracted following the proposed rules.

| Relation name | Correct | Incorrect |
|---|---|---|
| Occupation | 291 | 28 |
| ContextRelated | 228 | 65 |
| Nationality | 112 | 16 |
| Being_born | 26 | 39 |
| Employing | 15 | 9 |
| Being_employed | 6 | 4 |
| Being_named | 5 | 14 |
| Employer | 5 | 1 |
| Profession | 5 | 0 |
| Assistance | 4 | 6 |
| Leadership | 4 | 8 |
| Others (26) | 44 | 22 |
| **TOTAL** | **745** | **212** |
| **Precision** | **77.85%** | |

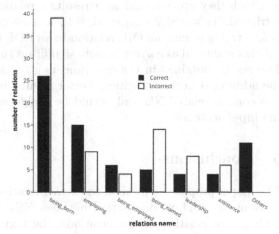

**Fig. 2.** A comparison between the extracted relations following the proposed rules.

**Table 2.** Relations extracted following the Frame + ORE rule.

| Frame name | Correct | Incorrect |
|---|---|---|
| Being_born | 26 | 39 |
| Employing | 15 | 9 |
| Being_employed | 6 | 4 |
| Being_named | 5 | 14 |
| Assistance | 4 | 6 |
| Leadership | 4 | 8 |
| Becoming_member | 2 | 5 |
| Participation | 2 | 3 |
| Others (20) | 27 | 7 |
| **TOTAL** | **91** | **95** |
| **Precision** | **48.92%** | |

**Fig. 3.** A comparison between the extracted relations following the Frame + ORE rule.

## 4.5  Discussion

The experiment's results demonstrate the feasibility to map OIE relations to RDF triples following the proposed approach. These results were obtained applying two rules based on syntactic and semantic analysis over the OIE output. As part of the applied rules, the *ContextRelated* relation was proposed to denote a generic relation between two NEs. The number of labeled examples with this relation are one of the best, only below of the *occupation* relation. In the *ContextRelated* relation the involved NEs are highly dependent on the context

**Table 3.** Relations extracted following the NER-NEL + OIE rule.

| Relation name | Correct | Incorrect |
|---|---|---|
| Occupation | 291 | 28 |
| ContextRelated | 228 | 65 |
| Nationality | 112 | 16 |
| Employer | 5 | 1 |
| Profession | 5 | 0 |
| StateOfOrigin | 4 | 1 |
| Others (6) | 9 | 6 |
| **TOTAL** | **654** | **117** |
| **Precision** | **84.82%** | |

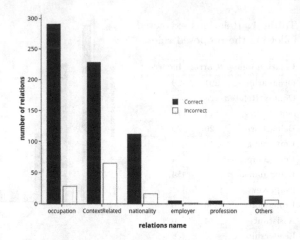

**Fig. 4.** A comparison between the extracted relations following the NER-NEL + OIE rule.

in which they appear, and as a result, a relation from DBpedia could not be retrieved. As stated Zouaq et al. [14], it is necessary to apply additional steps before trying to map an OIE relation to an RDF triple. However, *ContextRelated* entities evaluated as correct is more significant than those evaluated as incorrect. The results obtained in the experiments give us the opportunity to think that the additional work can achieve better results. In this sense, a relation between two context-related NEs only could be evaluated as valid under the context of the input sentence.

## 5   Conclusions

This paper proposed a method to extract relations from OIE tuples, taking into account the context interaction between NEs. Two rules considering aspects such as the position of the mentions, the text between them, and the frame description to determine a relation between two NEs were defined. Additionally, was proposed a generic relation (*ContextRelated*) to depicts a relation highly dependent on their context, i.e. this kind of relations does not appear in a generic KB like DBpedia.

The results demonstrated the feasibility to map the OIE output to RDF triples applying some rules based on syntactic and semantic analysis. According to the experiment's results, the frame rules get the largest number of different relations. However, over half of them were evaluated as incorrect. On the other hand, the NER-NEL rule gets promising results. In the particular case of the *ContextRelated* relation, the context interaction between two NEs was mapped as an RDF predicate, letting establish a connection between them. Additionally, the entities related as *ContextRelated* demonstrated a high dependency with the sentence's context.

# References

1. Augenstein, I., Maynard, D., Ciravegna, F.: Relation extraction from the web using distant supervision. In: Janowicz, K., Schlobach, S., Lambrix, P., Hyvönen, E. (eds.) EKAW 2014. LNCS (LNAI), vol. 8876, pp. 26–41. Springer, Cham (2014). https://doi.org/10.1007/978-3-319-13704-9_3
2. Augenstein, I., Padó, S., Rudolph, S.: LODifier: generating linked data from unstructured text. In: Simperl, E., Cimiano, P., Polleres, A., Corcho, O., Presutti, V. (eds.) ESWC 2012. LNCS, vol. 7295, pp. 210–224. Springer, Heidelberg (2012). https://doi.org/10.1007/978-3-642-30284-8_21
3. Baker, C.: FrameNet: a knowledge base for natural language processing. In: Proceedings of Frame Semantics in NLP: A Workshop in Honor of Chuck Fillmore (1929–2014), pp. 1–5. Association for Computational Linguistics (2014)
4. Berners-Lee, T., Hendler, J., Lassila, O.: The semantic web. Sci. Am. **284**(5), 34–43 (2001)
5. Corcoglioniti, F., Rospocher, M., Palmero Aprosio, A.: Frame-based ontology population with pikes. IEEE Trans. Knowl. Data Eng. **28**(12), 3261–3275 (2016)
6. Das, D., Schneider, N., Chen, D., Smith, N.A.: Probabilistic frame-semantic parsing. In: Human Language Technologies: The 2010 Annual Conference of the North American Chapter of the Association for Computational Linguistics, HLT 2010, pp. 948–956. Association for Computational Linguistics, Stroudsburg (2010)
7. Del Corro, L., Gemulla, R.: ClausIE: clause-based open information extraction. In: Proceedings of the 22nd International Conference on World Wide Web, WWW 2013, pp. 355–366. ACM, New York (2013)
8. Etzioni, O., Banko, M., Soderland, S., Weld, D.S.: Open information extraction from the web. Commun. ACM **51**(12), 68–74 (2008)
9. Fader, A., Soderland, S., Etzioni, O.: Identifying relations for open information extraction. In: Proceedings of the Conference on EMNLP, pp. 1535–1545. Association for Computational Linguistics, Stroudsburg (2011)
10. Gangemi, A., Presutti, V., Recupero, D.R., Nuzzolese, A.G., Draicchio, F., Mongiovà, M.: Semantic web machine reading with FRED. Semant. Web **8**(6), 873–893 (2017)
11. Jurafsky, D., Martin, J.H.: Speech and Language Processing: An Introduction to Natural Language Processing, Computational Linguistics, and Speech Recognition, 2nd edn. Prentice Hall Series in Artificial Intelligence. Prentice Hall, Pearson Education International (2009)
12. Manning, C.D., Surdeanu, M., Bauer, J., Finkel, J., Bethard, S.J., McClosky, D.: The Stanford CoreNLP natural language processing toolkit. In: ACL System Demonstrations, pp. 55–60 (2014)
13. Piskorski, J., Yangarber, R.: Information extraction: past, present and future. In: Poibeau, T., Saggion, H., Piskorski, J., Yangarber, R. (eds.) Multi-source, Multilingual Information Extraction and Summarization Theory and Applications of Natural Language Processing, pp. 23–49. Springer, Heidelberg (2013). https://doi.org/10.1007/978-3-642-28569-1_2
14. Zouaq, A., Gagnon, M., Jean-Louis, L.: An assessment of open relation extraction systems for the semantic web. Inf. Syst. **71**, 228–239 (2017)

# Reference Metadata Extraction from Korean Research Papers

Jae-Wook Seol, Won-Jun Choi, Hee-Seok Jeong, Hye-Kyong Hwang,
and Hwa-Mook Yoon$^{(\boxtimes)}$

Korea Institute of Science and Technology Information, Seoul, Korea
{wodnr754, cwj, hsjeong, hkhwang, hmyoon}@kisti.re.kr

**Abstract.** A large amount of research papers are published in various fields and the ability to accurately extract metadata from a list of references is becoming increasingly important. Moreover, metadata extraction is crucial for measuring the influence of a particular study or researcher. However, it is difficult to automatically extract data from most lists of references because they consist of unstructured strings with bibliographies structured in various formats depending on the proceedings. Thus, this paper presents an effective and accurate method for extracting metadata, such as author name, title, publication year, volume, issue, page numbers, and journal name from heterogeneous references using the conditional random fields model. To conduct an experiment measuring the effectiveness of the proposed model, 1,415 references from 93 different academic papers published in Korea were used and a high accuracy of 97.10% was obtained.

**Keywords:** Reference extraction · Metadata extraction
Conditional random fields

## 1 Introduction

A list of reference papers can help researchers find preexisting studies related to a specific topic. In addition, the impact factor (IF) of a paper or its field weighted citation impact (FWCI) are useful for recognizing authoritative and influential research in various fields. Extracting metadata from lists of references is crucial to this process. Metadata, such as author names and titles, are required for online library application programs, including article search, citation analysis, and topic modeling.

A list of references consists of unstructured strings. Each academic journal structures its bibliography using a different format and an extraction program is required to extract relevant bibliographical data from these strings. A large number of studies have been previously performed regarding metadata extraction from reference lists using supervised and unsupervised learning models. In particular, the conditional random field (CRF) [9] supervised learning model has exhibited high performance compared to other machine learning methods [11]. Thus, we propose an effective and accurate method of extracting metadata, including author name, publication year, title, proceeding, volume, issue, and page numbers, from heterogeneous references using the CRF model.

A. Groza and R. Prasath (Eds.): MIKE 2018, LNAI 11308, pp. 42–52, 2018.
https://doi.org/10.1007/978-3-030-05918-7_5

The metadata extracted using this proposed method can be used in a variety of applications. It can be used to create databases where metadata from academic articles are automatically constructed and integrated into scholarly search engines. The Korea Institute of Science and Technology Information (KISTI) is a government research institute that compiles the metadata of academic papers written in Korea. By applying the proposed model, the institute will be able to automate the manual process and increase its efficiency. In addition, based on the extracted bibliographical data, a researcher's influence can be measured and other researchers can be provided with materials related to the researcher of interest.

To verify the validity of the proposed model, 1,415 references cited in 93 academic papers released in Korea were used.

In the following sections, this paper introduces related studies (Sect. 2), describes the extraction model for the reference bibliographies using CRF (Sect. 3), discusses experimental results (Sect. 4), and concludes (Sect. 5).

## 2 Related Work

A large number of studies have been conducted regarding the extraction of metadata from lists of references. The methodologies used for these studies can be largely divided into unsupervised learning [1, 6–8], such as the knowledge-based method, and supervised learning [2–5], including the hidden Markov model (HMM). Table 1 lists previous studies regarding reference metadata extraction. Cortez et al. [6] and Guo et al. [7] extracted reference metadata using a pattern-based method. Pattern-based methods are effective and easy to implement but have difficulty recognizing new patterns. Hetzner et al. [2] and Ojokoh et al. [3] utilized HMM, while Gao et al. [4] and Tkaczyk et al. [5] used CRF to automatically extract metadata. Most studies that used supervised learning utilized HMM or CRF. HMM and CRF are statistical models that predict a series of labels in terms of the sequential and structured samples through their neighboring samples.

In particular, the CRF model has many applications, such as in DNA searches in the field of bioinformatics and object recognition and image segmentation in the field of computer vision. Additionally, it has exhibited high performance in partial parsing and named entity recognition [10] in natural language processing. In this study, CRF was used to extract author name, publication year, title, proceeding, volume, issue, and page numbers from heterogeneous reference sources.

Previous studies have mainly focused on English and Chinese academic papers and e-books used as references. In contrast, this research extracts metadata from 93 academic papers written in Korean across various fields, including science, technology, biology, and mechanics.

**Table 1.** Comparison of existing methodologies for reference metadata extraction.

| Method | | Data set | | Result |
|---|---|---|---|---|
| Unsupervised learning | INFOMAP and the Alignment Reference Citation Agent [1] | Source | PubMed digital library | 97.87% (Accuracy) |
| | | Test set | 500 | |
| | | Training set | – | |
| | | Category | 7 | |
| | Knowledge-based approach [6] | Source | ACM digital library | 96.04% (F1, Computer Science domain) |
| | | Test set | 300 | |
| | | Training set | – | |
| | | Category | 10 | |
| | Rule-based approach [7] | Source | IEEE & ACM digital libraries | 89.06% (Accuracy) |
| | | Test set | 2,157 | |
| | | Training set | – | |
| | | Category | 9 | |
| | Regular expression-based approach [8] | Source | ACM digital library | 89.02% (F1, Journal articles) |
| | | Test set | 385 | |
| | | Training set | – | |
| | | Category | 5 | |
| Supervised learning | Hidden Markov Model [2] | Source | Cora dataset | 74.7% (F1) |
| | | Test set | 142 | |
| | | Training set | 350 | |
| | | Category | 14 | |
| | Hidden Markov Model [3] | Source | Cora dataset | 89.66% (F1) |
| | | Test set | 500 | |
| | | Training set | | |
| | | Category | 13 | |
| | CRF [4] | Source | Chinese digital libraries | 95.2% (Accuracy) |
| | | Test set | 6,479 | |
| | | Training set | 1,368 | |
| | | Category | 14 | |
| | CRF [5] | Source | CiteSeer & Cora-ref | 89.84% (F1) |
| | | Test set | 5-fold cross-validation (3,438) | |
| | | Training set | | |
| | | Category | 5 | |

# 3  Reference Metadata Extraction

In this section, we propose a reference metadata extraction method based on supervised learning. Figure 1 shows an overall system flow diagram of the proposed model. When reference data are entered, variously-structured reference strings are normalized and bibliographical information is subsequently extracted using the CRF classifier based on the features generated by the feature vector generator. Finally, the extracted bibliographical data are stored in the metadata database through post-processing.

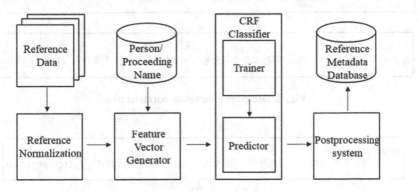

**Fig. 1.** System architecture.

## 3.1  Data Preprocessing

Metadata was extracted from 1,415 references cited in 93 academic articles published in the fields of science, technology, humanities, biology, and mechanics. A set of correct answers were constructed by tagging the author, publication year, title, proceeding, volume, issue, and page number information.

Bibliographical data were normalized in various patterns through metadata normalization. The CRF classifier was used to determine the class of the metadata word units (distinguished by spaces). Therefore, metadata undistinguished by spaces must be distinguished accordingly. Normalization was applied based on punctuation marks and particular words that appear with the metadata. Figure 2 illustrates the metadata normalization process. "김갑성.임승호.이상미", the co-authors in the original text, should be divided into three separate authors as follows: "김갑성", "임승호", and "이상미". Moreover, "24(1)," should be divided into the volume number "24" and issue number "1" through a space between the numbers. The spaces between "pp." and "135-155", and "Vol." and "12" were eliminated because "pp." and "Vol." are clue words, which indicate that the subsequent numbers are page and volume numbers, respectively. Thus, "pp." and "Vol." were configured as clue word features by the CRF model in the following feature generation step.

The normalized references were tokenized on a space-basis and each token assigned a B-I-O tag. B (begin) refers to the beginning of a field, I (inside) to its middle, and O is assigned if a token does not belong to a field we wish to extract.

Figure 3 illustrates an example of the assignments of B-I-O tags to each token. Author name, publication year, title, proceeding, volume, issue, and page numbers - the reference metadata we wish to extract - are expressed as *author, py, title, proc, volume, issue,* and *page*, respectively. To these, the prefix "b_" is added if the token is a beginning element of a field, and "i_" is prefixed for middle elements.

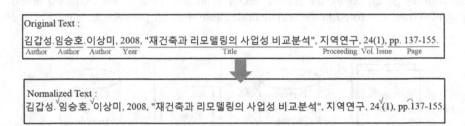

**Fig. 2.** Reference metadata normalization.

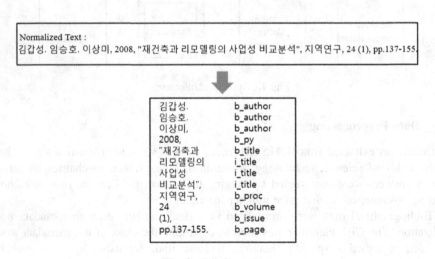

**Fig. 3.** B-I-O tagging.

## 3.2    Reference Metadata Extraction Based on Conditional Random Fields

This paper uses the CRF [12] machine learning model to extract reference metadata. CRF is a statistical model that can be used to predict a series of labels in sequential and structured samples through their neighboring samples. When features and tokens - strings included in the references normalized in Sect. 3.1 and distinguished through spaces - are input into the CRF classifier, a predicted label corresponding to each token is produced.

To increase the performance of the extraction, we applied the following features to the CRF: punctuation, number, capital letter, word length, person/proceeding dictionaries, and clue word.

- Punctuation feature: The punctuation feature refers to punctuations that appear in the tokens. Table 2 lists the types of punctuations used as a feature and examples of their use.

**Table 2.** Punctuation features.

| Punctuation | Field | Examples |
|---|---|---|
| , | All metadata fields | 정원규, 이성혐, *[Author]* |
| . | All metadata fields | 국민의 알 권리에 대한 고찰. *[Title]* |
| ; | Year | 2013; *[Year]* |
| : | Title, volume, issue | 27(4): *[Volume][Issue]* |
| - | Title, proceeding, page | pp.1947-1960. *[Page]* |
| () | Year, title, proceeding, volume, issue | (2001) *[Year]* |
| [] | Title, proceeding | 항공안전 관리시스템[SMS] 소개 *[Title]* |
| "" | Title, proceeding | "N-스크린 서비스의 발전 동향" *[Title]* |

- Number feature: Number feature indicates whether numbers are included in a token. Volume, issue, year, and page are tokens that include numbers.
- Capital letter feature: Capital letter feature indicates whether the first word in a token begins with a capital letter, in which case, it is likely the beginning of a field.
- Word length feature: Word length feature refers to the number of characters that constitute a token. The tokens year and Korean author, mostly consist of four and three characters, respectively. Hence, word lengths can act as clues for extracting these tokens.
- Person/proceeding dictionary feature: Person/proceeding dictionary feature refers to dictionaries that contain 2,133,854 Korean names and 4,245 proceeding names, respectively.
- Clue word feature: Clue word feature refers to words surrounding a field that help distinguish a particular field. Table 3 lists the types of clue words and corresponding examples.

**Table 3.** Clue word featrues

| Field | Clue word | Examples |
|---|---|---|
| Year | "년" | "2009년" |
| Volume | "권", "집", "Vol.", "V." | "32권", "Vol. 32" |
| Issue | "호", "No.", "N." | "5호", "No.5" |
| Page | "pp.", "p.", "p.p." | "pp.271-299", "p. 1-4" |
| Proceeding | "Journal of", | "Journal of Korea Tappi" |

Features that correspond to each token in labeled reference data are generated in the training process and converted into feature vectors. Subsequently, a classifier model is constructed with the feature vectors based on CRF. Likewise, in the testing process, features are generated on each token in the reference data and converted into feature vectors. Subsequently, the constructed classifier model extracts labels from the converted data. Figure 4 illustrates the CRF procedure for reference metadata extraction.

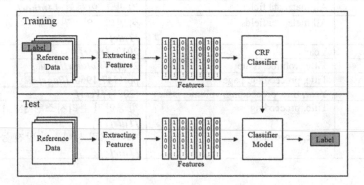

**Fig. 4.** CRF procedure for reference metadata extraction.

Figure 5 shows an example of a feature vector generated from reference data. The labeled data are used as training data to build a training model.

```
김갑성.          0 0 0 1 0 0 0 1 0 b_author
임승호.          0 0 0 1 0 0 0 1 0 b_author
이상미,          0 0 0 1 0 0 0 1 0 b_author
2008,           1 0 1 0 0 0 0 1 0 b_py
"재건축과        0 0 0 0 0 0 0 1 0 b_title
리모델링의       0 0 0 0 0 0 0 0 0 i_title
사업성          0 0 0 0 0 0 0 0 0 i_title
비교분석",       0 0 0 0 0 0 0 1 0 i_title
지역연구,        0 0 0 0 0 0 0 1 1 b_proc
24              1 0 0 0 0 0 0 0 0 b_volume
(1),            1 0 0 0 0 0 0 1 0 b_issue
pp.137-155.     1 0 0 0 0 0 1 1 0 b_page
```

**Fig. 5.** Example of CRF feature generation for use in a training model.

# 4   Experiments

## 4.1   Experimental Set-up

To validate the proposed reference metadata extraction method, we conducted experiments on a data set containing 1,415 references cited in 93 Korean academic papers in the fields of science, technology, humanities, biology, and mechanics. Table 4 lists the number of fields included in the 1,415 references.

**Table 4.** Data set.

| Field | The number of fields |
|---|---|
| Author | 3,225 |
| Title | 1,407 |
| Proceeding | 1,399 |
| Page | 1,132 |
| Volume | 1,299 |
| Issue | 1,170 |
| Publication year | 1,392 |

We evaluated the systems using Accuracy (Eq. (1)). These metrics rely on true positives (TP), true negatives (TN), false positives (FP), and false negatives (FN), which are defined as appropriate in order to provide exact and inexact evaluations of the tasks.

$$Accuracy = \frac{TP + TN}{TP + TN + FP + FN} \tag{1}$$

### 4.2 Experimental Results and Analysis

We used 5-fold cross validation, dividing the data set at random into 5 approximately equal-size parts. The training set and the test set consist of 283 references and 1,132 references, respectively. The performance was also measured by strict and lenient matching. Strict matching measures the number of correct predictions made on all tokens in a field, while lenient matching measures the number of correct predictions on a token-basis. Table 5 shows the results of the reference metadata extraction.

**Table 5.** Reference metadata extraction results.

| Fold | Accuracy | |
|---|---|---|
| | Lenient matching (Token) | Strict matching (Field) |
| 1-fold | 97.99% | 96.75% |
| 2-fold | 97.93% | 96.37% |
| 3-fold | 98.01% | 96.74% |
| 4-fold | 98.90% | 98.47% |
| 5-fold | 98.43% | 97.16% |
| Average | 98.25% | 97.10% |

Strict matching result of the reference metadata extraction yielded an average of 97.1% correct answers. The overall results were lower than that obtained with lenient matching because an incorrect answer on even a single word in a field resulted in an incorrect answer for the entire corresponding field. However, strict matching results are more relevant to this study, as the aim of this system is to correctly extract the fields that compose a list of references.

Table 6 and Fig. 6 illustrate the extraction results for each field. The extraction results for publication year were the most accurate at 99%, as the items corresponding to this field typically had simple patterns, such as "2002.", "(2008)", and "1998년". However, the accuracy of the results for the title were low compared to other fields because the number of words in the field was the largest, resulting in a high probability of error in defining its range.

**Table 6.** Extraction results for each field.

| Field | Accuracy | |
|---|---|---|
| | Lenient matching (Token) | Strict matching (Field) |
| Author | 98.61% | 98.61% |
| Title | 99.01% | 94.38% |
| Proceeding | 95.42% | 96.43% |
| Page | 98.41% | 98.41% |
| Volume | 96.78% | 96.78% |
| Issue | 95.25% | 95.25% |
| Publication year | 99.64% | 99.64% |

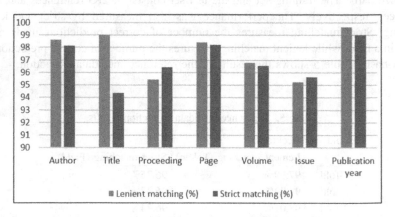

**Fig. 6.** Graph of the extraction results for each field.

Difficulties were encountered during metadata extraction from citations in news articles and reports. This is because even though the metadata was similar to those found in academic papers, such as author name, title, and publication year, the ordering and outlining patterns of the metadata differed significant and confounded the proposed model. These aspects of the model must be improved through future training on a variety of different data and patterns from various sources.

Table 7 shows the performance of CRF features to extract metadata. When dictionary feature were added, performance of extraction was improved the most. The author dictionary contains most of the Korean person names. Performance was improved from 69.58% to 97.36% when the feature were applied. Punctuation feature also improved performance. The feature act as a delimiter that divides each metadata. Thus, the feature is an important feature for extracting metadata from references.

**Table 7.** Extraction results for each feature.

| Feature | Accuracy | |
|---------|----------|---|
| | Lenient matching (Token) | Strict matching (Field) |
| Number + Capital letter | 88.66% | 80.73% |
| + Word length | 89.97% | 82.77% |
| + Dictionary | 96.41% | 94.16% |
| + Punctuation | 98.24% | 97.08% |
| + Clue word | 98.25% | 97.10% |

## 5 Conclusion

A large number of research papers on a variety of topics have been published on the web. Thus, the ability to accurately extract metadata from a list of references is of increasing importance. This study proposed a novel method for effectively and accurately extracting bibliographical data, such as author name, title, publication year, volume, issue, and journal name, from heterogeneous references using CRF. The CRF model was chosen because the fields in a list of references are often listed sequentially and have specific patterns. CRF is a statistical model for predicting a series of labels for the sequential and structured samples by considering their neighboring samples. To extract bibliographical data from a reference list, its structure was first normalized using its variously patterned field relations. Moreover, to increase the performance of the CRF classifier, a number of features were used, including punctuation, number, capital letter, word length, person/proceeding dictionaries, and clue words. Finally, to measure the effectiveness of the proposed model, 1,415 heterogeneous references cited in academic papers published in Korea were analyzed with a high accuracy of 97.10%.

Future studies will focus on developing a model that can extract bibliographical data from English and Korean references. They will attempt to extract metadata from a variety of reference sources, including news articles, reports, patents, and online content. Moreover, comparative experiments will be conducted by building a number of different deep-learning models, such as those based on RNN, to measure the performance of the reference metadata extraction model described herein.

**Acknowledgements.** This research was supported by Korea Institute of Science and Technology Information (KISTI).

# References

1. Day, M.Y., et al.: A knowledge-based approach to citation extraction. In: IRI-2005 IEEE International Conference on Information Reuse and Integration, Conference, pp. 50–55 (2005)
2. Hetzner, E.: A simple method for citation metadata extraction using Hidden Markov models. In: Proceedings of the 8th ACM/IEEE-CS Joint Conference on Digital Libraries, pp. 280–284. ACM (2008)
3. Ojokoh, B., Zhang, M., Tang, J.: A trigram Hidden MARKOV model for metadata extraction from heterogeneous references. Inf. Sci. **181**(9), 1538–1551 (2011)
4. Gao, L., Tang, Z., Lin, X.: CEBBIP: a parser of bibliographic information in chinese electronic books. In: Proceedings of the 9th ACM/IEEE-CS Joint Conference on Digital Libraries, pp. 73–76. ACM (2009)
5. Tkaczyk, D., Szostek, P., Dendek, P.J., Fedoryszak, M., Bolikowski, L.: Cermine–automatic extraction of metadata and references from scientific literature. In: 2014 11th IAPR International Workshop on Document Analysis Systems (DAS), pp. 217–221. IEEE (2014)
6. Cortez, E., da Silva, A.S., Gonçalves, M.A., Mesquita, F., de Moura, E.S.: FLUX-CIM: flexible unsupervised extraction of citation metadata. In: Proceedings of the 7th ACM/IEEE-CS Joint Conference on Digital Libraries, pp. 215–224. ACM (2007)
7. Guo, Z., Jin, H.: Reference metadata extraction from scientific papers. In: 2011 12th International Conference on Parallel and Distributed Computing, Applications and Technologies (PDCAT), pp. 45–49. IEEE (2011)
8. Tang, X., Zeng, Q., Cui, T., Wu, Z.: Regular expression-based reference metadata extraction from the web. In: 2010 IEEE 2nd Symposium on Web Society (SWS), pp. 346–350. IEEE (2010)
9. Lafferty, J., McCallum, A., Pereira, F.C.: Conditional random fields: probabilistic models for segmenting and labeling sequence data (2001)
10. Sun, W., Rumshisky, A., Uzuner, O.: Evaluating temporal relations in clinical text: 2012 i2b2 challenge. J. Am. Med. Inform. Assoc. **20**(5), 806–813 (2013)
11. Yu, J., Fan, X.: Metadata extraction from Chinese research papers based on conditional random fields. In: FSKD, pp. 497–501. IEEE (2007)
12. CRF++. https://taku910.github.io/crfpp/

# On the Impact of Semantic Roles on Text Comprehension for Question Answering

Anca Marginean$^{(\boxtimes)}$ and Gabriela Pricop

Technical University of Cluj-Napoca, Cluj-Napoca, Romania
anca.marginean@cs.utcluj.ro, gabriela.pricop@student.utcluj.ro

**Abstract.** New challenges for question answering are introduced by texts whose understanding require inference and commonsense knowledge. Task 11 - Machine comprehension using Commonsense Knowledge - from SemEval 2018 proposes a corpus of such texts, questions and answers. Since the predicates identified by Semantic Role Labeling aim to capture the semantic of a sentence, they seem appropriate to the task of text comprehension. We propose a Context-Novelty based model for identification of the correct answer for a question. This model relies on the SRL predicates of the text, question and answers and (i) it targets identification of the parts from the text which are relevant to the current question and (ii) it measures how well the answer matches that parts. The performance of the model was evaluated directly by counting the number of correctly answered questions and by its integration to a classical machine learning process.

**Keywords:** Semantic roles · ConceptNet · Commonsense reasoning

## 1 Introduction

Text comprehension is a common ability for humans, but still in its incipient phase for machines. Natural language processing addresses, with more or less success, many components involved in text comprehension, as main entities recognition, extraction of the relations between them, identification of events and their ordering in time, opinions. The task of text comprehension becomes more complex when knowledge outside the text is required, as it is the case of commonsense knowledge.

The representation of the text given by Semantic Role Labeling (SRL) identifies "who" did "what", "when", "to whom" and "in which manner". It relies on thematic roles like *AGENT*, *PATIENT* which are defined in FrameNet [1], or verb-specific roles *ARG*0, *ARG*1, *MNR* defined in PropBank [7]. The recent development of deep learning techniques as Long Short Term Memory or attention mechanism improved the quality of SRL systems. He et al. [3] reports $83.1F1$ on a CoNLL 2012, Roth et al. [9] reports $87.9F1$ on CoNLL 2009. Therefore, even though they do not work perfectly, they become a powerful tool in the extraction of text's semantics.

© Springer Nature Switzerland AG 2018
A. Groza and R. Prasath (Eds.): MIKE 2018, LNAI 11308, pp. 53–63, 2018.
https://doi.org/10.1007/978-3-030-05918-7_6

Taking a different perspective, ontology lexicalization takes also steps towards text comprehension, by targeting a text representation which supports inference. The idea is to define the way to express entities and relations from ontologies in natural language [10]. Once ontology lexicalization solved, text would be interpreted as a set of concepts and relations. Another effort towards inference on natural language is the natural logic, which is a system of logical inference which operates over natural language [4]. SRL, ontology lexicalization, and natural logic have a common objective in giving a proper representation of the text semantics.

The task 11 of SEMEval-2018 [6], Machine comprehension using commonsense knowledge, is a question answering task. The novelty of the task compared to other question answering challenges is the fact that it includes many questions which require commonsense knowledge for finding the correct answer. The texts are describing everyday activities and their understanding could involve extra commonsense information. Nonetheless, the current results indicate that the proposed corpus can be addressed with limited or even no commonsense knowledge. Most of the participating systems (10 out of 11) [5,6,11] used neural network-based approach, mostly LSTM and attention mechanism. There were 3 LSTM-based systems which obtained accuracy between 0.81 and 0.84, while the rest of the systems reported values between in $[0.61, 0.75]$.

From our knowledge, none of the participants used SRL. This paper proposes a way of analyzing text for identification of relevant parts for a question. The objective is similar to the one of the attentive reader model [2], but without the use of neural network. The aim is to answer the question: can meaning representation with semantic roles improve text comprehension even in the absence of deep learning applied for text comprehension?

Section 2 briefly enumerates the quantitative similarity measures used in the initial experiment. They are based on the counts of the common words, common predicates, or aggregated similarity of predicates. Section 3 introduces the proposed analysis of text, questions and answers. The core of this analysis are the SRL predicates and the context of an answer given by the question. Results and final remarks are presented in Sect. 4 and Conclusions.

## 2    Quantitative Similarity-Based Features for Comparing Text with Questions and Answers

Semantic role labeling returns for each sentence a set of predicates. We used pathLSTM [9] with PropBank. Each predicate $p$ contains a sense $sense(p)$ from PropBank and a set of arguments (roles). Each argument $arg_i(p)$ has a type $(A0, A1,..AM\text{-}TMP)$ and a span of words $w \in arg_i(p)$. It is possible a word to belong to more arguments of the same predicate, but also to arguments of other predicates. The words $w$ of an argument can at their turn be predicates. A basic example of SRL result can be observed in Fig. 1.

```
They used a picnic cloth.        They used a table.

 used(use.01)                     used (use.01)
    A0: They                         A0: They
    A1: a picnic cloth               A1: a table

What did they use?
```

Fig. 1. SRL annotated sentence

Several features were derived from each tuple ⟨text $t$, question $q$, correct answer $CA$, wrong answer $WA$⟩:

- number of common words between text and question, text and answers, and question and answers
- number of common predicates for ⟨$t, q$⟩, ⟨$t, CA$⟩, ⟨$t, WA$⟩, ⟨$q, CA$⟩, ⟨$q, WA$⟩, where a predicate is common for ⟨$e_1, e_2$⟩ if it has the same sense in both $e_i$
- similarity of predicates, where similarity of two predicates is computed as an aggregation of three similarities: between senses, between types of roles and between spans of roles [8].

Together with these, differences between values obtained for the correct and the wrong answer are included as features for a learning process. Random Forest or Decision Tree build models with accuracy values around 0.67. This revealed that there is a lot of information which is missed by these quantitative features, even though the intuition that common words indicate the correct answer is true. Therefore we developed a context aware model for weighting words' contribution.

## 3   Semantic Score Based on Context Dependent Similarity

### 3.1   Context Identification

In order for a phrase to be an answer, it does not need to be similar to the whole text, but to a certain part of the text which is relevant to the current question. We define the context of a question $q$ in the queried text $t$ to be a set of weights situated at different levels in $t$'s elements: predicate level, pair predicate argument, predicate sense level. Elements with higher weight are considered more relevant for the question's answer.

**Argument Similarity.** For two arguments $arg_1$ and $arg_2$ we define a similarity $S$ based on argument's type and common words. This can be replaced with word vectors similarity. In the following equations, we denote the words in the span of an argument $arg$ as $w \in arg$, while the type of the argument $arg^t$.

$$S(arg_1, arg_2) = \begin{cases} \alpha * |\{w | w \in arg_1 \wedge w \in arg_2 \wedge \\ \quad POS(w) \notin \{DT, CC, IN, PRP, TO, WDT\}|, & arg_1^t = arg_2^t \\ 0, & \text{otherwise} \end{cases}$$

(1)

$S(arg_1, arg_2)$ considers common words filtered by part of speech. A special case not included in formula 1 is the case of the pronouns $I$ and $we$ which are not filtered out in case the second argument belongs to an answer and it includes references to the person describing the action, as *author* or *narrator*. $\alpha > 1$ influences the importance of a common word.

$$S^{cohesion}(arg_1, arg_2) = S(arg_1, arg_2) * 10^{(S(arg_1, arg_2) - 1)}$$

(2)

Since our scores have additive nature, we need to differentiate between the following two situations: fewer arguments which share more words, respectively many arguments which share one word. A common measure for texts similarity which deals with this problem is the longest common sequence of words, used also in [5]. We do not use sequences of words, but we measure a degree of cohesion of common words, where the unit is the span of the arguments. In order to prefer common words in the same semantic component of the phrase, we increased the impact of the arguments sharing $n > 1$ words by $10^n$.

**Context of the Question.** The context of the question aims to emulate the attention model which proved appropriate for many NL tasks addressed with deep learning. The context gives higher weights to predicates or branches which seem to be involved in answer identification.

We started from the simplest case, where the question contains only one predicate $p_q$ and there is a predicate $p_t$ in the text such that (i) $sense(p_t) = sense(p_q)$, and (ii) there is at least a pair of arguments $arg_i(p_t)$, $arg_j(p_q)$ which have some meaningful words in common. Then, generally, the answer is the other argument of the predicate $p_t$. For example, in Fig. 2, $A0$ is common, the predicate sense is the same, and the answer is the other argument ($A1$).

We propose a weighting schema for predicates and their argument. In order to decide the weight of each (i) argument, (ii) pair ⟨argument, predicate⟩, respectively (iii) predicate of the text, we compare all these with all the arguments

```
I choose a stamp with heart design.
    choose (choose.01)
    A0:I
    A1: a heart design
What did I choose?
    choose (choose.01)
    A0: I
    A1: What
```

**Fig. 2.** Only one predicate in the question with common predicate in the text

and predicates from the question. In the current version, we do not consider the hierarchical nature of the SRL predicates.

$$S_{children}(p_t, p_q) = \sum_{arg_i \in Args_{p_t}} \sum_{arg_k \in Args_{p_q}} S(arg_i, arg_k) \tag{3}$$

$$S_w(p_t, p_q) = wordSim(sense(p_t), sense(p_q))$$

$$ContextScore(p_t) = \sum_{p_q \in Pred(q)} [PredError + S_w(p_t, p_q)^2] * S_{children}(p_t, p_q)$$

$$\tag{4}$$

$S_{children}$ computes a similarity between two predicates given only by the similarities of the arguments (roles). The similarity of senses $S_w$ is computed as cosine similarity of word vectors. Two embeddings were used: GoogleNews and ConceptNet. In case the cosine similarity is smaller than a threshold, the words are considered completely different. The best results were obtained with $thr = 0.7$.

$$wordSim(w_1, w_2) = \begin{cases} WV(w_1) * WV(w_2), & WV(w_1) * WV(w_2) > thr \\ 0, otherwise \end{cases} \tag{5}$$

$ContextScore(p_t)$ gives a weight to a predicate in text. All the question predicates are considered and the similarities of roles are weighted by the similarity of the predicates' senses $S_w$. By choosing $S_w^2$ instead of $S_w$ our model increases the impact of the predicates with the same sense compared to the ones with similar sense ($S_W \in [-1, 1]$). If $PredError = 0$, similarities of arguments are completely dependent on the similarity of predicate senses.

Each argument of a predicate $p_t$ of a text is compared to all the arguments of all the predicates $p_q$ in the question. Our context model assigns a context score to each argument of a predicate. Its context score relies on all similar arguments weighted by the word similarity of the predicates senses.

$$ContextScore(p_t, arg_i) = \sum_{p_q \in Pred(q)} \sum_{arg_k \in Args(p_q)} S_w(p_t, p_q) * S(arg_i, arg_k) \tag{6}$$

Let's apply the proposed context model on the text in Fig. 3 which is taken from the train set.

For the question in Fig. 4, the predicates with $ContextScore \neq 0$ include $write : 2$, $decide : 40$, $send : 240(A1 : 200)$, $send : 12(A1 : 10)$, $miss : 40$. Except for $send$, the ContextScores for arguments are all 0, since the senses of the predicates are completely different. It is possible to have the same predicate identified in more sentences. Current version do not computes a ContextScore for a sentence, but existing tests indicate that this could help, together with coreference. Even though $send$ obtained a high ContextScore 240, in the absence of coreference, the relation to $Shelly$ is not accessible from this predicate. Instead, it is accessible from $miss$ predicate, which also has a high Context Score.

```
I miss my best friend Shelly and so I decided to send her a
    letter telling her all about my trip to my sister's house
    in Alaska, and to also tell her that I hoped she was
    well. I finished writing my letter and as I went to find
    a stamp and an envelope I needed to send it, I had found
    that I did not have any. I went to a store that sells
    cards and envelopes, and chose a box of pretty purple-
    colored envelopes to mail my letter in. After that I
    went to the post office to purchase some stamps that are
    like small stickers, and chose a heart design that I
    liked. ...
```

**Fig. 3.** A text from training set

```
Who was the letter sent to?
sent (send.01)
        A1: the letter sent to
        A2: to
CA: their friend Shelly          friend (friend.01)
                                 A1: Their
                                 A0: Their friend
WA: the president                -
```

**Fig. 4.** Example of question

## 3.2   Context and Novelty-Dependent Analysis of the Answer

Once the context of a question is computed, the answers can be evaluated. The main assumption is that an answer should be related to the elements with high values for ContextScores, but it also must bring something new compared to the question.

**Novelty Condition.** In order to prefer new information to the information contained in the question, when comparing the answers' arguments with the text, the following condition is added to the conditions in the Eq. 1 of $S(arg_1, arg_2)$:

$$NoveltyCond_1 = ((w \notin Question \land \neg OrQuestion) \lor OrQuestion) \land w \notin OtherAnswer \tag{7}$$

According to this conditions, two types of answers' words are avoided: (i) words common with the question, in case this is not an OR question, (ii) words common to the other answer. For example, for the question *When did the cat ate?* we have two answers *A1: The cat ate in the morning, A2: in the evening.* The first answer includes a complete sentence, while the other one only a chunk of words. The entity doing the action is the *cat* in both answers, even though it is not present in the second answer. Since in the end we compare the scores of the two answer, the words common with the question (here *cat*) should not contribute to the additive score of the answer.

**Context-Dependent Analysis.** Both answers are compared to the text and a context dependent similarity score $V$ is computed (Eq. 8). The contribution of the arguments of predicate $p_t$ to the value of the answer is weighted by the value of ContextScore of $p_t$ in $S_{children}$. In case $\epsilon = 0$, if the predicate is considered irrelevant by the context model, the arguments will not be able to contribute to the value of the answer ($S_{children}$ will be 0). This is recommended behavior in case the Context model is very precise, otherwise, $\epsilon$ is better to be small, but different than 0.

$$S_{children}(p_t, p_a) = (\epsilon + ContextScore(p_t)) * \sum_{arg_i \in Args_{p_t}} \sum_{arg_k \in Args_{p_a}} S(arg_i, arg_k)$$

$$V_p(p_t, p_a) = [PredError + S_w(p_t, p_a)^2] * (S_{children}(p_t, p_a) + \alpha * S_w(p_t, p_a))$$

$$V(a) = \sum_{p_t \in Pred(t)} \sum_{p_a \in Arg_a} V_p(p_t, p_a)$$

$$(8)$$

$V_p(p_t, p_a)$ measures the value brought by the predicate $p_a$ to the answer according to its similarity to $p_t$. Predicates $p_t$ and $p_a$ with the same senses or at least similar ones should increase the value of the answer, no matter the arguments are similar or not. Therefore, the second factor in $V_p$ includes also the similarity between the senses of the predicates. The first factor of $V_p$ weights the contribution of $p_a$ with respect to the similarity of the predicate senses. $V(a)$ is the value of an answer in the context determined by its question.

For example, for the question *Why did they write the letter?* and the answers *They missed their friend, They asked the friend to come there*, the Context Model identifies *miss* as a predicate with *ContextScore* > 0. Due to the Novelty Condition, the word *friend* is not considered when evaluating the answers. Therefore, $S_{children} = 0$. But, since the similarity of the senses is added to $S_{children}$, the value of the first answer will be higher than the value for the second.

The formula $V(a)$ from Eq. 8 fails in case the answer contains no predicates: e.g. question *When do they expect the letter to arrive to its destination?* with the answers CA: *one week* and WA: *one day*. Therefore, in case $V(a) = 0$, we compare words from the answers to words in the arguments of all the predicates in text. $\beta$ is the number of words from $a$ for which similarity with words in an argument of a text predicate is higher than the threshold.

$$V_w(a) = PredError * \sum_{p_t \in Pred(t)} \sum_{arg_i \in p_t} 10^\beta \left( \sum_{w_t \in arg_i} \sum_{w_a \in a} \right.$$

$$\{\alpha * wordSim(w_t, w_a) * ContextScore(p_t) | POS(w_t) \notin \{DT, CC, IN,$$

$$\left. PRP, TO, WDT\} \wedge NoveltyCondition \wedge wordSim(w_t, w_a) > threshold\}\right)$$

$$(9)$$

Even though $V$ and $V_w$ are computed differently, we want to keep them comparable in case the answers are evaluated one with $V$ and the other with $V_w$. This is the reason for introduction of PredError in $V_w$ even though we do not compare predicates. In our tests, $PredError = 0.2$.

The final value $V_f(a)$ of an answer is $V$ if $V \neq 0$, otherwise is $V_w$. For a question with two answers, we defined $ValueDifference(a_1, a_2) = V_f(a_1) - V_f(a_2)$. A perfect model would ensure that whenever $ValueDifference(a_1, a_2) > 0$, $a_1$ is the correct answer. When the difference is 0, the model does not have enough information to select an answer: either both answers are evaluated to 0, either they have equal values.

## 4   Results

In order to evaluate our context model and its components, we counted first the number of questions with $ValueDifference(CA, WA) > 0$ (meaning that the correct answer $CA$ is correctly identified based only on this value). Higher this number, better the model in identifying the correct answer. Table 1 depicts the results of this experiment. We vary the word embeddings (E1 and E2), the use of cohesion (E3), and of the novelty condition (E4), respectively the threshold for similarity (E5). The total number of questions considered for this experiment is 1188 and they are taken from the development set of Task 11 SemEval 2018. In all our tests, the $Yes/No$ questions are eliminated. A question is a $Yes/No$ question if at least one of the answers contains just $yes$ or $no$.

Comparing E1 and E2, one can observe that the number of correctly answered questions ($\# > 0$) increases by using ConceptNet compared to GoogleNews with 20, while the number of wrongly answered questions ($\# < 0$) increases with 12. We considered E2 better than E1, therefore ConceptNet is used in the rest of the experiments E3, E4, and E5. Comparing E2, E3 and E4 we can conclude that (i) the impact of cohesion is not significant and (ii) the absence of cohesion or of the novelty-condition increases the number of situations where the model can not choose an answer ($\# = 0$ increases from 274 to 275, respectively 286). Apparently, the system with smaller threshold (E5) behaves better then E2 since the $\#$ of correctly answered questions increases to 656 from 628 for E2, while the $\#$ of questions with no selected answer decreases to 192 from 274 for E2. Yet, the price is a significant increase in $\#$ of wrongly answered questions to 340. The last row includes a ratio between $\#$ of correctly answered questions and $\#$ of all answered questions ($ValueDifference \neq 0$).

Another observation of this first experiment is that whenever $ValueDifference \neq 0$, the correct answer is indicated with an acceptable accuracy around 0.68. The main limitation of the model is indicated by still the large $\#$ of questions where $ValueDifference = 0$. For the most of these questions, both answers are evaluated to $V_f = 0$. One reason for this is the absence of coreference in our model. Due to this, the values of the context scores are not correctly propagated for the text. Another reason is the fact that $When$ questions are difficult to answer due to the time ordering which is completely ignored by the Context-Novelty model.

The second experiment aimed to measure how much influence has the ContextNovelty model on a learning process. The results are included in Table 2. We considered two basic learning algorithm: decision trees J48 and Random Forests. Either 10-fold cross validation on train corpus (L0, L1, L2), or the pair train-test corpus were used. The train corpus has 8153 questions, out of which 6165 can be answered without common sense knowledge. The considered features are the ones presented in Sect. 2 together with the differences between $V_f$ and $V_w$. Exception is $L0$, where no feature from ContextNovelty model was included. The version used for ContextNovelty model is E2 (see Table 1) which includes ConceptNet and full options.

**Table 1.** Ability of different versions of the *ContextNovelty* model to identify the correct answer with *ValueDifference*

| #questions | E1: GoogleNews full | E2: ConceptNet* full | E3: ConceptNet no cohesion | E4: ConceptNet no novelty | E5: ConceptNet full threshold = 0.6 |
|---|---|---|---|---|---|
| $\# > 0$ | 608 | 628 | 624 | 617 | 656 |
| $\# = 0$ | 306 | 274 | 275 | 286 | 192 |
| $\# < 0$ | 274 | 286 | 289 | 285 | 340 |
| $\frac{\#>0}{\#Answered}$ | 0.69 | 0.687 | 0.683 | 0.684 | 0.65 |

**Table 2.** Accuracy of learning with quantitative features and *ContextNovelty* model

| Exp | Data | J48 | Random Forest |
|---|---|---|---|
| L0 | Train corpus (8153) (10-fold CV) *without ContextNovelty model* | 0.668 | 0.70 |
| L1 | Train corpus (8153) (10-fold cross validation) | 0.753 | 0.781 |
| L2 | Train corpus without commonsense (6165) (10-fold cross validation) | 0.772 | 0.799 |
| L3 | Train (8153)/test corpus (2393) | 0.746 | **0.782** |
| L4 | Train(6165)/test corpus (1845) without commonsense | 0.773 | **0.794** |

Comparison of the experiments L0 and L1 revealed that the accuracy increased with almost 0.1 simply by introducing *ValueDifference* as a feature. Elimination of questions which need commonsense knowledge determined an increases in accuracy from 0.74 (L03) to 0.77 (L04) for J48. The most important conclusion of the experiment is related to the value of 0.782 obtained in experiment L3. This value is lower than the values obtained by the first three systems participating to the competition [0.81, 0.84]. But, (i) it is higher than the value 0.72 reported for the baseline [6], which is based on Attentive Reader,

(ii) it is obtained by a very simple classical learning process, without any search for hyper-parameters, (iii) it uses a context model which do not yet exploits coreference or hierarchical information for the SRL predicates. Therefore, the values of 0.78 (L03) and 0.79 (L04) supports the conclusion that for text comprehension, methods using SRL predicates are promising alternatives to deep learning methods.

## 5    Conclusions

We tackle the problem of text comprehension for question answering with a solution based on SRL predicates and an evaluation of the answers given the context identified in text. The context scores computed by our model express the degree of relevance of the text's semantic constituents to the question. The obtained results, with/without learning, support the conclusion that SRL predicates have great potential in giving a representation of the text on which formal models like inference can be applied. Further work is needed on better set and use of the context scores and coreference integration. VerbNet is considered for the future as a good candidate to mix natural logic with SRL predicates.

## References

1. Baker, C.F., Sato, H.: The FrameNet data and software. In: The Companion Volume to the Proceedings of 41st Annual Meeting of the Association for Computational Linguistics (2003)
2. Chen, D., Bolton, J., Manning, C.D.: A thorough examination of the CNN/daily mail reading comprehension task. In: Proceedings of the 54th Annual Meeting of the Association for Computational Linguistics (Volume 1: Long Papers), pp. 2358–2367. Association for Computational Linguistics (2016)
3. He, L., Lee, K., Lewis, M., Zettlemoyer, L.S.: Deep semantic role labeling: what works and what's next. In: ACL (2017)
4. MacCartney, B., Manning, C.D.: Natural logic for textual inference. In: Proceedings of the ACL-PASCAL Workshop on Textual Entailment and Paraphrasing, RTE 2007, pp. 193–200 (2007)
5. Merkhofer, E., Henderson, J., Bloom, D., Strickhart, L., Zarrella, G.: MITRE at SemEval-2018 Task 11: commonsense reasoning without commonsense knowledge. In: Proceedings of the 12th International Workshop on Semantic Evaluation, pp. 1078–1082. Association for Computational Linguistics (2018)
6. Ostermann, S., Roth, M., Modi, A., Thater, S., Pinkal, M.: SemEval-2018 Task 11: machine comprehension using commonsense knowledge. In: Proceedings of the 12th International Workshop on Semantic Evaluation, pp. 747–757. Association for Computational Linguistics (2018)
7. Palmer, M., Gildea, D., Kingsbury, P.: The proposition bank: an annotated corpus of semantic roles. Comput. Linguist. **31**(1), 71–106 (2005)
8. Rettinger, A., Schumilin, A., Thoma, S., Ell, B.: Learning a cross-lingual semantic representation of relations expressed in text. In: Gandon, F., Sabou, M., Sack, H., d'Amato, C., Cudré-Mauroux, P., Zimmermann, A. (eds.) ESWC 2015. LNCS, vol. 9088, pp. 337–352. Springer, Cham (2015). https://doi.org/10.1007/978-3-319-18818-8_21

9. Roth, M., Lapata, M.: Neural semantic role labeling with dependency path embeddings. In: Proceedings of the 54th Annual Meeting of the Association for Computational Linguistics (Volume 1: Long Papers), pp. 1192–1202. Association for Computational Linguistics (2016)
10. Walter, S., Unger, C., Cimiano, P.: M-ATOLL: a framework for the lexicalization of ontologies in multiple languages. In: Mika, P., et al. (eds.) ISWC 2014, Part I. LNCS, vol. 8796, pp. 472–486. Springer, Cham (2014). https://doi.org/10.1007/978-3-319-11964-9_30
11. Wang, L., Sun, M., Zhao, W., Shen, K., Liu, J.: Yuanfudao at SemEval-2018 Task 11: three-way attention and relational knowledge for commonsense machine comprehension. In: Proceedings of the 12th International Workshop on Semantic Evaluation, pp. 758–762. Association for Computational Linguistics (2018)

# Solving the Traveling Tournament Problem with Predefined Venues by Parallel Constraint Programming

Ke Liu$^{(\boxtimes)}$ ⓘ, Sven Löffler, and Petra Hofstedt

Department of Mathematics and Computer Science,
Brandenburg University of Technology Cottbus-Senftenberg,
Konrad-Wachsmann-Allee 5, 03044 Cottbus, Germany
{liuke,sven.loeffler,hofstedt}@b-tu.de

**Abstract.** The Traveling Tournament Problem with Predefined Venues (TTPPV) is a practical problem arising from sports scheduling. We describe two different modeling approaches for this problem, each of which is suitable for different sizes of instance. The experimental results show that our modeling approaches lead to improved performance compared to previous techniques in terms of the number of feasible solutions and the optimal value. Furthermore, we present how to execute the models in parallel through data-level parallelism. The parallel versions do not only gain speedup but also attain significant improvement on optimal value since more subtrees are searched independently.

**Keywords:** Sports scheduling · Constraint programming
Parallel constraint solving · TTPPV

## 1 Introduction

The Traveling Tournament Problem with Predefined Venues (TTPPV), i.e. 068 problem in CSPLib [1], was originally presented in [2] and seeks a compact single round-robin schedule for a sports tournament that minimizes the total distance traveled by all teams participating in the tournament. The Traveling Tournament Problem (TTP) and TTPPV have been studied in the constraint programming and integer programming communities [3], where TTPPV is a special case of TTP by adding the predefined venues for each particular game. The predefined venues denote that the home-away assignment of each game is known beforehand. Specifically, i.e. team A plays against team B at team A's home or B's home is already determined before the scheduling. The problem of scheduling TTP usually consists of two sub-problems, the construction of the timetable, which schedules that each team plays against other teams in which round, and the home-away pattern (HAP) table that determines home and away games for each team in each round. Hence, a complete scheduling of TTP and TTPV is composed of the timetable and the HAP. Moreover, since home-away

© Springer Nature Switzerland AG 2018
A. Groza and R. Prasath (Eds.): MIKE 2018, LNAI 11308, pp. 64–79, 2018.
https://doi.org/10.1007/978-3-030-05918-7_7

assignment rules out some HAPs that are incompatible with predefined venues, the overall search space of TTPPV is much smaller than TTP for the same number of teams.

**Table 1.** A feasible solution for the TTPPV problem for 8 teams within a HAP table of the solution starting at the second column, where a symbol ∗ indicates an away game for the team at the beginning of each row, otherwise home game.

| | | | | | | | |
|---|---|---|---|---|---|---|---|
| 1 | 7 | ∗6 | ∗5 | 4 | 3 | ∗2 | ∗8 |
| 2 | ∗4 | 3 | ∗8 | ∗6 | 5 | 1 | ∗7 |
| 3 | ∗5 | ∗2 | 6 | 8 | ∗1 | ∗7 | 4 |
| 4 | 2 | 5 | ∗7 | ∗1 | 8 | 6 | ∗3 |
| 5 | 3 | ∗4 | 1 | 7 | ∗2 | ∗8 | 6 |
| 6 | 8 | 1 | ∗3 | 2 | 7 | ∗4 | ∗5 |
| 7 | ∗1 | ∗8 | 4 | ∗5 | ∗6 | 3 | 2 |
| 8 | ∗6 | 7 | 2 | ∗3 | ∗4 | 5 | 1 |

For a tournament with $n$ teams, the timetable in a feasible solution of TTPPV is an $n \times n$ matrix $T$, where the first column of the matrix is enumerated from 1 to n (Table 1). An element of the matrix $T$ must satisfy the following property:[1]

$$1 \leq i \leq n,\ 2 \leq j \leq n,\ 1 \leq k \leq n,\ T_{ij} = k \Longleftrightarrow T_{kj} = i \qquad (1)$$

where $T_{ij}$ is an opponent variable which means that team $i$ has to play against the team assigned to variable $T_{ij}$ in round $j$: Index $j$ starts at 2 because the first column $(j = 1)$ consists of fixed values $\{1..n\}$. Property 1 states that the opponent of $i$ in round $j$ is $k$ implies that the opponent of $k$ in round $j$ must be $i$ (i.e. team 7 is the opponent of team 1 in the first round and team 1 must be the opponent of team 7 in the same round (Table 1)). Furthermore, each row of $T$ takes on distinct values from $\{1..n\}$ because no team would play against another team more than once, which is given by:

$$1 \leq i \leq n,\ 1 \leq j < j' \leq n,\ \forall j, j',\ T_{ij} \neq T_{ij'} \qquad (2)$$

We denote the HAP table of a timetable as an $n \times (n-1)$ matrix $H$. An element of HAP is denoted by $H_{ij}$, $H$ has the following property:

$$1 \leq i \leq n,\ 1 \leq j' \leq n-1,\ H_{ij'} \in \{0,1\},\ H_{ij'} \oplus H_{T_{i(j'+1)}j'} = 1 \qquad (3)$$

The above property means that if team $i$ has to play against team $T_{i(j'+1)}$ away in round $j' + 1$, then team $T_{i(j'+1)}$ is playing against team $i$ at home in the same round, and vice versa. For instance, team 3 is playing against team 5 away in the first round; hence, team 5 has to play against team 3 at home in the same

---

[1] In the present paper, the index of an array starts from 1.

round (Table 1). Please note that in a feasible solution the HAP table must overlap the timetable by starting at its second column; therefore, the number of columns of HAP is $n - 1$. The HAP table of a feasible solution must meet two conditions: First, the number of home games and the number of away games must be equal or differ by one for each team, which is the *balance condition* for TTPPV; Second, the *consecutive condition* is that the number of consecutive away games or home games for each team cannot exceed a fixed value (refer to [2]). Table 1 depicts a feasible solution satisfying the two conditions.

The traveling distance of a team is counted in the following way: First, for a single away game, the team travels to and from the venue of the opponent; Second, for a sequence of consecutive away games, the team travels from the venue of one opponent to that of the next, without returning home. Following [1], the distance between any two team $i$ and $j$ is calculated as:

$$\forall i,j, \ i \geq j, \ d_{ij} = d_{ji} = min(i - j, j - i + n) \tag{4}$$

The rest of the paper is organized as follows: Sect. 2 gives a short introduction to the basic notions used in this paper, Sect. 3 gradually describes the first CP model and its parallelization with empirical results. Afterwards, in Sect. 4, we present the second model, how to run this model in parallel and the experimental results by comparing models. Next, we discuss and analyze the experimental results in Sect. 5. Finally, we conclude in Sect. 6.

## 2    Preliminaries

Constraint programming (CP) is a powerful technique to tackle combinatorial problems, generally NP-complete or NP-hard. It employs constraint propagation interleaved with backtracking search. The problem to be solved is expressed through a formal model by using constraints from a rich set of modeling primitives. A constraint network $\mathcal{R}$ or constraint satisfaction problem (CSP) is a triple $\langle X, D, C \rangle$, which consists of:

- a finite set of variables $X = \{x_1, \ldots, x_n\}$, where $n$ is the number of variables in $\mathcal{R}$,
- a set of respective finite domains $D = \{D(x_1), \ldots, D(x_n)\}$, where $D(x_i)$ is the domain of the variable $x_i$, and
- a set of constraints $C = \{c_1, ..., c_t\}$, where a constraint $c_j$ is a relation $R_j$ defined on a subset of variables $S_j$, $S_j \subseteq X$.

A constraint optimization satisfaction problem $\langle X, D, C, f \rangle$ (COSP) is defined as a CSP with an optimization function $f$ that *maps each solution to a numerical value* [4,5]. Generally, a COSP problem is to search a solution $T$ in which $f(T)$ must be either the maximum value or minimum value.

The **table** constraint is one of the most frequently-used constraints in practice. Theoretically, any constraint can be represented as **table** constraint, though this may result in a space and time explosion [6]. For an ordered set of variables

$X_o = \{x_i, ..., x_j\}$ of a constraint network $\mathcal{R}$, a positive (negative) **table** constraint defines that any solution of $\mathcal{R}$ must (not) be explicitly assigned to a tuple in the tuples that consists of the allowed (disallowed) combinations of values for $X_o$. In most constraint solvers (e.g., Choco [7]), the **table** constraint can be specified with different types of consistency algorithms such CT+, STR2+, MDD+, etc. For a detailed introduction to these algorithms, please refer to [8], Chap. 5.

## 3   Modeling the TTPPV Based on Perfect Matching (The First Model)

In this section, we present and compare our first model with another model from the literature [9] in an empirical approach. In the present paper, all the models were implemented in Choco Solver 4.0.6 [7] with JDK version 9.0.4 and all experiments were performed on a computer with an Intel i7-3720QM CPU, 2.60 GHz and 8 GB DDR3 memory running Ubuntu 17.10.

A CP model for TTPPV problem can be directly derived from its problem definition as we have stated in the introduction. Thereby, in studies [9,10], Properties 1 and 3 are guaranteed by the **element(v,T,i)** constraint, which ensures that value $v$ is assigned to the $i$-th variable in an array of variables $T$. Because the value of $T_{ij}$ cannot be determined when modeling, one must employ the **ifThen** constraint or the **reified** constraint combined with the **element** constraint to express Property 1. Similarly, to ensure Property 3, the **element** constraint and the **reified** constraint may be used together again since Property 3 depends on Property 1. However, our observation on Choco solver shows that these constraints are likely to slow down the resolution process of CSPs. Thus, we present an alternative modeling approach to avoid using these constraints.

### 3.1   A Model for Perfect Matching

In order to bypass the **ifThen** constraint and the **element** constraint, we use another model to help generate the potential combination of values of columns of $T$. Besides, the potential combination of values of every column is the same. The variables of this model are defined as a $\frac{n}{2} \times 2$ matrix $P$. The model can be expressed as:

$$1 \leq i \leq i' \leq \frac{n}{2}, \ 1 \leq j \leq j' \leq 2, \ \forall i \neq i' \vee j \neq j', \ P_{ij} \neq P_{i'j'} \tag{5}$$

$$\forall (i < i' \wedge j = j' = 1) \vee (i = i' \wedge j < j'), \ P_{ij} < P_{i'j'} \tag{6}$$

Constraint 5 guarantees all elements in $P$ are pairwise distinct, which can be implemented by the **allDifferent** constraint. Then, Constraint 6 ensures that both the first column and each row of $P$ must be in ascending order, which can be enforced by the **arithm** constraint. With $n = 8$ we exemplarily show 3 solutions generated by this model depicted on the left side of every arrow in

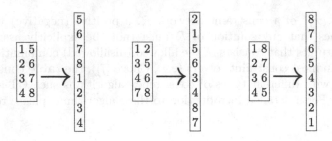

**Fig. 1.** A conversion from solutions generated by the model to the potential values of columns of $T$, the number of teams is 8.

Fig. 1 (the overall number of solutions generated by this model for 8 teams is 105).

The above model essentially generates all possible games ensured by Constraint 5, and rules out all the isomorphisms realized through Constraint 6, which is a *static symmetry breaking constraint*. If we treat every row of a solution of the model as an edge of a graph and the two values in each row as two vertices, each solution of the model can be viewed as a perfect matching for the complete graph with $n$ vertices. Thus, the number of solutions of the model is equal to the number of perfect matchings for a complete graph with $n$ vertices, which can be calculated as $N_p = \Pi_{k=1}^{n/2} \binom{2k}{2}/n/2!$, where $n$ must be even. Nevertheless, the solutions of the model cannot be used directly as the potential values of columns of $T$. Therefore, we convert each solution of the model to an array of length $n$, as shown in Fig. 1. The transformation rule for a solution of the model to the array can be stated as:

$$1 \leq i \leq \frac{n}{2}, \ \forall i, \ A_{P_{i1}} = P_{i2}, \ A_{P_{i2}} = P_{i1} \tag{7}$$

where $A$ is the array starting at 1 to $n$. For each solution of the model, the transformation assigns $P_{i2}$ ($P_{i1}$) to the element with index $P_{i1}$ ($P_{i2}$) in the array $A$ that is a potential solution of columns of timetable $T$. For example, for the leftmost solution in Fig. 1, $A[1] = 5$, $A[5] = 1$, and $A[2] = 6$ etc. Afterwards, an element of array $A$ is the opponent of the team which is the index of the element. Finally, all solutions of the model (e.g. 105 for $n = 8$) are stored into tuples denoted with $TP$.

## 3.2   A Model for Timetable

After obtaining the tuples ($TP$) filled with all arrays converted from the perfect matchings, the constraint imposed on each column of the matrix $T$ can be stated as:

$$\{(T_{1j}, T_{2j}, ..., T_{nj}) \mid 2 \leq j \leq n\} \subseteq TP \tag{8}$$

Constraint 8 and Property 2 can codetermine the feasible solutions of the timetable without the involvement of constraints imposed by Property 1.

The implementation of the model utilizes the **table** constraint specified with $TP$ to limit possible combinations of values for each column of $T$ other than the first column.

## 3.3 Experimental Results

Before elaborating the entire model for TTPPV, we would like to first compare the part of our model completed so far with the corresponding parts of the model presented in [9,10]. Both models are used to generate timetables for $n$ teams, which must satisfy Properties 1 and 2. Please note that there is no HAP table being generated in this comparison; therefore, it is not problem specific and requires neither predefined venues nor distances between these predefined venues.

Table 2 reports the execution times for generating 15,724,800 timetables from $n = 8$ to $n = 14$. Our model outperformed the model presented in [9] for all listed instances. Moreover, the advantage becomes more obvious with the increase in the size of the instance. The number of nodes in the search tree traversed per second decreased in both models with the instance becoming larger and larger. Furthermore, nodes/s of the model from [9] declined even faster than nodes/s of our model.

**Table 2.** The comparison between our timetable model and the timetable model presented in [9]. The total number of solutions for instance 8 is 15,724,800. For the larger instances, the total number of instances are much greater than 15,724,800, we still use it for the convenience of comparing two models. The data in parentheses separated by commas were calculated by our model (left) and the model of [9] (right) respectively.

| Instances | Solutions | Time (s) | Nodes/s |
|---|---|---|---|
| n = 8 | 15,724,800 | (147, 2062) | (214521, 15671) |
| n = 10 | 15,724,800 | (193, 3863) | (163849, 9037) |
| n = 12 | 15,724,800 | (238, 7326) | (133194, 4928) |
| n = 14 | 15,724,800 | (314, 17470) | (101161, 2035) |

## 3.4 The Complete Model

We are now going to present the complete model for TTPPV. According to the number of perfect matchings $N_p$, we can easily derive the upper bound of the overall search space for the complete model, which is given by $(N_p/n-1)^{n-1}/2$. Nevertheless, this upper bound is not tight enough because each row of the timetable must take on the distinct values from $\{1...n\}$, required by Property 2. Moreover, if the variables representing timetable and HAP table are tied together and evaluated simultaneously, restrictions imposed on the HAP table can also rule out some unqualified timetables. For instance, the timetable which results in a HAP table with more than 3 consecutive away games are filtered out.

The predefined venues and the round information (values assigned to a column of the timetable) together determine the home-away pattern for the round, and both of them are available after executing the model that generates all perfect matchings presented in Sect. 3.1. Therefore, we are able to construct the potential values of columns composed of the round information and its home-away pattern together for the complete model.

In light of these considerations, we define the decision variables of the complete model as an $2n \times (n-1)$ matrix $C$ with integer variables, where the first $n$ rows of the matrix represent the timetable, each of which has domain $\{1, .., n\}$ and the last $n$ rows of the matrix represent the HAP table, each of which has domain $\{0, 1\}$.

We have elaborated how to generate the potential values of columns for timetable matrix $T$ in Sect. 3.1. For the complete model, we also generate the potential values of columns for the matrix $C$. For instance, potential values of a column for the matrix $C$ for 8 teams could be $\{2\ 1\ 6\ 5\ 4\ 3\ 8\ 7\ 0\ 1\ 1\ 1\ 0\ 0\ 0\ 1\}$ in which the first 8 elements are the opponents of teams $\{1..8\}$ in a round and the last 8 elements are the home-away assignments for the corresponding games. Since the first $n$ rows of the matrix $C$ stands for a timetable, we use the solutions generated by the perfect matching model and the transformation rule defined in Eq. 7 to obtain the potential values of the first $n$ rows of the columns for the matrix $C$. We rewrite Eq. 7 since the length of the array is changed, given by:

$$1 \leq i \leq n, \ \forall i, \ A'_{P_{i1}} = P_{i2}, \ A'_{P_{i2}} = P_{i1} \tag{9}$$

where the length of the array $A'$ is $2n$. In addition, the last $n$ rows of the columns for the matrix $C$ are home-away assignments with the corresponding teams decided by Eq. 9 and predefined venues. The last $n$ elements of the array $A'$ are calculated by:

$$n \leq j \leq 2n, \ \forall j, \ A'_j = PV_{(j-n)A'_{j-n}} \tag{10}$$

where $PV$ is the predefined venue table (e.g., Fig. 2) in which each element at row $i'$ and column $j'$ is a home-away assignment (0/1) for team $i'$ and team $j'$. Hence, any last $n$ element $A'_j$ is the home-away assignment for the team $A'_{j-n}$ and team $j - n$ which are calculated by Eq. 9.

Having Eqs. 9 and 10, all solutions of the perfect matching model are converted to arrays of length $2n$ with round information and home-away assignments and these arrays are stored into tuples denoted with $TPC$. As with the Constraint 8 for the timetable model, the constraint imposed on each column of the matrix $C$ can be stated as:

$$\{(C_{1j}, C_{2j}, ..., C_{nj}) \mid 1 \leq j \leq n-1\} \subseteq TPC \tag{11}$$

As a result of Constraint 11, Property 1 and 3 can be satisfied simultaneously and the **ifThen** constraint and the **element** constraint are avoided.

|    | 1 | 2 | 3 | 4 | 5 | 6 | 7 | 8 |
|----|---|---|---|---|---|---|---|---|
| 1  | -1| 0 | 1 | 1 | 0 | 0 | 1 | 0 |
| 2  | 1 | -1| 1 | 0 | 1 | 0 | 1 | 0 |
| 3  | 0 | 0 | -1| 1 | 0 | 1 | 0 | 1 |
| 4  | 0 | 1 | 0 | -1| 1 | 1 | 0 | 1 |
| 5  | 1 | 0 | 1 | 0 | -1| 1 | 1 | 0 |
| 6  | 1 | 1 | 0 | 0 | 0 | -1| 1 | 1 |
| 7  | 0 | 1 | 1 | 1 | 0 | 0 | -1| 0 |
| 8  | 1 | 1 | 0 | 0 | 1 | 0 | 1 | -1|

|    | 1 | 2 | 3 | 4 | 5 | 6 | 7 | 8 | 9 | 10|
|----|---|---|---|---|---|---|---|---|---|---|
| 1  | -1| 1 | 0 | 0 | 1 | 1 | 0 | 1 | 0 | 1 |
| 2  | 0 | -1| 1 | 1 | 1 | 0 | 1 | 0 | 0 | 0 |
| 3  | 1 | 0 | -1| 0 | 0 | 1 | 1 | 0 | 1 | 0 |
| 4  | 1 | 0 | 1 | -1| 0 | 0 | 1 | 1 | 0 | 1 |
| 5  | 0 | 0 | 1 | 1 | -1| 0 | 0 | 1 | 1 | 1 |
| 6  | 0 | 1 | 0 | 1 | 1 | -1| 0 | 1 | 1 | 0 |
| 7  | 1 | 0 | 0 | 0 | 1 | 1 | -1| 0 | 1 | 0 |
| 8  | 0 | 1 | 1 | 0 | 0 | 0 | 1 | -1| 1 | 0 |
| 9  | 1 | 1 | 0 | 1 | 0 | 0 | 0 | 0 | -1| 1 |
| 10 | 0 | 1 | 1 | 0 | 0 | 1 | 1 | 1 | 0 | -1|

**Fig. 2.** Examples of the predefined venue data for $n = 8$ and 10. The values $1$, $0$, and $-1$ denotes home game, away game, and no game respectively. For example, on the left side table, the element at the second row and the third column is 1 and the element at third row and the second column is 0, which means that whenever team 2 encounters team 3 and vice-versa, the game is always held at team 2's home.

Additionally, since a feasible solution and its reversed solution have the same cost function value, we can shrink the search space through static symmetry breaking by adding a simple constraint, given by:

$$C_{11} < C_{1(n-1)} \tag{12}$$

The denominator of the upper bound of the search space also implies the search space halved by means of static symmetry breaking.

For the consecutive condition required by the HAP table, the regular language membership (**regular**) constraint is used here to impose on the last $n$ rows of $G$. We also use the small DFA presented in [9] as the input of the **regular** constraint to filter out the set of bit strings that contain more than two consecutive 0 or 1 for the last $n$ rows of $C$.

In summary, the complete model is composed of Constraint 11, 12, the **regular** constraint mentioned in this Section, and the constraints imposed by Property 2.

### 3.5   Executing the Complete Model in Parallel

*Embarrassingly Parallel Search* (EPS) [11] in constraint programming indicates no communication requirement during solving process. Moreover, an embarrassingly parallel workload distribution also implies that the independent constraint solver is working on distinct data using the same constraint programming model. EPS is well suited for solving the TTPPV problem in parallel since disjoint partial solutions can be easily obtained before constraint solving and then mapped to different workers. There are two basic kinds of EPS in terms of the mapping method for parallel computing. The static decomposition method implies that a few subproblems for EPS are generated. In contrast, the dynamic decomposition method splits the problem into a large number of subproblems during evaluation, which ensures each worker has equivalent activity time [11].

We use EPS with static decomposition to accelerate the solving process of TTPPV. The generic procedure can be summarized as follows:

1. A subset of the decision variables of the model is selected.
2. All the partial assignments over selected variables in the subset are generated, which can be extended to a feasible solution of the TTPPV problem.
3. The partial assignments are mapped to the workers so that each worker can work on its own independent search space by using its own constraint solver.
4. The last step is to merge the results calculated by each worker.

In order to run this model in parallel, we can obtain all candidate partial assignments before the problem-solving process. For $n$ teams, we generate all possible permutations of the set $\{2, ..., n\}$ in which the first element is less than the last element due to the static symmetry breaking, as the partial assignments for the first row of its decision variable matrix $C$. Then each worker receives the same number of partial assignments, and also utilizes the **table** constraint with the received partial assignments as its input tuples. By doing so, each worker can work on its own search space by using the same model presented in Sect. 3.4, and therefore *data-level parallelism* is achieved.

### 3.6  Experiment

In this section, we give results of our experiments on the complete model described in Sect. 3.4 with different number of workers. The comparison of the complete model and other models will be presented in Sect. 4.3.

Before running the models in parallel, we investigated the most suitable algorithms for the **table** constraints, including the constraints that are used to partition the search space and the constraints belonging to the complete model. The result shows that (FC, CT+) was the best among all candidates algorithms on instance n = 8, 10, and 12 for all numbers of workers.

**Table 3.** The experimental results on instance 10. The data formatting in the parentheses of each cell, in turn, are the number of feasible solutions, the average speed of processing nodes (nodes/s), and the optimal value gained in the corresponding execution time.

| Time (m) | Workers | | | |
|---|---|---|---|---|
| | 1 | 2 | 4 | 8 |
| 1 | (7.48e4,20982,166) | (1.65e5,22409,166) | (3.78e5,20390,162) | (5.08e5,12511,162) |
| 10 | (1.16e6,20512,162) | (2.68e6,21166,156) | (5.19e6,17719,156) | (6.48e6,10458,156) |
| 100 | (1.46e7,20665,156) | (2.72e7,19333,154) | (4.96e7,16582,154) | (6.25e7,10081,152) |
| 1000 | (1.61e8,20324,154) | (3.14e8,19231,154) | (5.51e8,16044,152) | (7.31e8,10438,152) |

Table 3 shows that the theoretical speedup can be achieved when running 2 or 4 workers in parallel in terms of the number of nodes processed. Moreover, the optimal values for the travel distance were improved with additional workers involved.

# 4   An Advanced Modeling Approach for Larger Instances (The Second Model)

In this section, we first present another model dedicated for larger instances ($n \geq$ 14). Afterwards, we also parallelize the model to gain speedup. The experimental results are also given.

## 4.1   An Advanced Model

The model presented in Sect. 3.4 works well for small instances ($n < 12$) since it sacrifices memory space to improve efficiency. However, it suffers from memory usage explosion for large instances such as $n \geq 20$. We propose an improved model based on the ideas presented in [9,10]. Roughly speaking, this model is also logically equivalent to the Properties 1, 2, and 3 in which Property 3 must rely on Property 1 as discussed previously. In study [9], however, the **element** and **reified** constraints are employed with an additional $n \times n$ matrix $V$ giving the venue of each game. Nevertheless, this approach does not take full advantage of predefined venues when constructing a timetable. Since we have already known predefined venue tables beforehand (e.g., Fig. 2), we can determine the set of $k$ consecutive values that are allowed for $k$ consecutive variables for each team. Any allowed $k$ consecutive values are composed of $k - i$ values taken from *away set* and $i$ values taken from *home set*, where $1 \leq i \leq k-1$, and away set consists of all away games for the team, otherwise home set. For instance, on the left side of Fig. 2, team 1 has to play against teams $\{2,5,6,8\}$ away, $\{3,4,7\}$ at home, thus the sets $\{2,5,3\}$, $\{6,8,7\}$, $\{8,4,7\}$ etc. are the allowed values when $k = 3$. If every $k$ consecutive variables in each row (team) of matrix $T$ (timetable) is assigned to allowed values, the timetable satisfies the consecutive condition automatically.

Algorithms 1 and 2 depict how $k$ consecutive allowed values for each team are generated and added to an array of Tuple. In lines 3–7 of Algorithm 1, *list_AwaySet* and *list_HomeSet* are created and added to the away set and home set for each team. In line 8, Algorithm 1 invokes the method described in Algorithm 2 which recursively adds the sets into *sets_AllowedSet*, each of which contains exactly $k$ elements that are allowed for $k$ consecutive variables. Afterwards, all permutations of each element in *sets_AllowedSet* are obtained and stored by *sets_Permutations* in line 9. Finally, these permutations are added to the tuple corresponding to the row (team) in line 11.

Algorithm 2 is a recursive method in which the sets consisting of $k - i$ values taken from away set and $i$ values taken from home set are generated and added to *sets_AllowedSet* in line 7 within each recursive call. When the base case is reached in line 1, *sets_AllowedSet* includes all allowed set containing exactly $k$ elements taken from both away set and home set.

Having the set of allowed values for each team generated by Algorithm 1, the constraints imposed by the consecutive condition can be expressed as:

$$\{(T_{ij}, T_{i(j+1)}, ..., T_{i(j+k-1)}) \mid 1 \leq i \leq n, \; 2 \leq j \leq n-k\} \subseteq AL_i \qquad (13)$$

---

**Algorithm 1.** Generate an array of allowed tuples

---

    **Input** : $n, k$, $arr2\_Predefined Venue$
    **Output:** Tuples[] $arr\_Tuples$
1 Create lists $list\_AwaySet, list\_HomeSet, sets\_Permutations$ and
    $sets\_AllowedSet$;
2 **for** $i \leftarrow 1$ **to** $n$ **do**
3     **for** $j \leftarrow 1$ **to** $n$ **do**
4         **if** $arr2\_Predefined Venue[i][j]==0$ **then**
5             add $j$ to $list\_AwaySet$;
6         **if** $arr2\_Predefined Venue[i][j]==1$ **then**
7             add $j$ to $list\_HomeSet$;
8     getAllAllowedSets($k, 1, list\_AwaySet, list\_HomeSet, sets\_AllowedSet$);
9     getPermutations($sets\_AllowedSet, sets\_Permutations$);
10     **forall** $permutation \in sets\_Permutations$ **do**
11         add the $permutation$ to $arr\_Tuples[i]$;
12     clear $list\_AwaySet, list\_HomeSet, sets\_AllowedSet$,
13     $sets\_Permutations$;
14 **return** $arr\_Tuples$;

---

**Algorithm 2.** getAllAllowedSet(k,i,list_AwaySet,list_HomeSet,sets_AllowedSet)

---

    **Input** : $i, k$, $list\_AwaySet, list\_HomeSet, sets\_AllowedSet$
1 **if** $i==k$ **then**
2     **return**;
3 $sets\_SubsetAway = $ getAllSubsets($list\_AwaySet, k - i$);
4 $sets\_SubsetHome = $ getAllSubsets($list\_HomeSet, i$);
5 **forall** $set\_Away \in sets\_SubsetAway$ **do**
6     **forall** $set\_Home \in sets\_SubsetHome$ **do**
7         add $set\_Away \cup set\_Home$ to $sets\_AllowedSet$;
8 getAllowedSet($k, i + 1, list\_AwaySet, list\_HomeSet, sets\_AllowedSet$);

---

where $AL_i$ stands for all the sets of $k$ allowed consecutive values for team $i$, which is stored in $arr\_Tuples[i]$ in Algorithm 1. Note that in the above constraint $j$ starts at 2 because the first column of any feasible solution of TTPPV always contains the fixed values $\{1..n\}$ in our model.

Constraint 13 can be implemented by the **table** constraint with allowed tuples defined on every $k$ consecutive elements of each row of the matrix $T$. Incidentally, the implementation with the positive **table** constraint is not the only choice in theory. We have two other options at least. First, we could use the **table** constraint with disallowed tuples, thus Algorithm 1 should generate the list of sets whose member contains exactly $k$ elements which cannot occur in a feasible timetable. However, the performance of the negative **table** constraint falls behind the positive **table** constraint in our case. Furthermore, the **table** constraint with allowed tuples supports more algorithms than disallowed tuples in the Choco solver, some of which might lead to an increase in performance.

Second, we could construct a big deterministic finite automaton (DFA) so that the **regular membership** constraint can be used instead of the **table** constraint. There are two reasons preventing us from using DFA. One reason is that the performance decreased in the experiment when comparing these two approaches, another reason is that constructing a DFA for a larger instance such as $n = 16$ resulted in a prohibitively high memory usage.

Additionally, as already pointed out in [9], we also add *implied constraints* [12] to accelerate resolution process but these implied constraints do not change the set of solutions of the model. The implied constraints for the model can be stated as:

$$1 \leq i < i' \leq n, \ 2 \leq j \leq n, \ \forall i, i', \ T_{ij} \neq T_{i'j} \tag{14}$$

Obviously, these implied constraints are the instances of the **allDifferent** constraint. As with the first model (Sect. 3.4), the static symmetry breaking constraint is also introduced:

$$T_{12} < T_{1n} \tag{15}$$

In summary, Constraints 13, 14 and 15, together with constraints entailed by Properties 1 and 2, form the model used to tackle large instances ($n \geq 12$). With a balanced predefined venue table, a solution of the model is a feasible solution of TTPPV.

## 4.2   Solving the Model in Parallel for Larger Instances

In Sect. 3.5, we have presented the approach to partition the overall search space for the TTPPV problem. However, that approach cannot be applied to the large instances model because of the following factors. First, it is impossible to generate all the possible first rows for a large instance in a reasonable execution time (e.g., $(18 - 1)!$ when $n = 18$). Second, it is impossible to store all the possible first rows in memory because out of memory exceptions would occur. Hence, we generate all possible assignments for elements starting at index 2 to $k + 1$ in the first row of $T$ instead of the entire first row. Since Algorithm 2 is already used to generate $k$ consecutive allowed values for every $k$ consecutive variables in each row, it does not require another algorithm to partition the search space. For each worker, the $k$ elements starting at index 2 to $k + 1$ in the first row can be calculated as:

$$\{(T_{12}, T_{13}, ..., T_{1(k+1)}) \mid P_i, i \bmod NW = id, T_{12} \neq n\} \tag{16}$$

where $NW$ stands for the number of workers to be used, and $id$ whose domain is $\{0, .., NW - 1\}$ is the unique ID of each worker. Besides, we denote *sets_Permutations* in Algorithm 1 by $P$. The set with iterator $i$, where $i \bmod NW = id$, is allocated to worker $id$ after iterating over sets $P$. To satisfy the static symmetry breaking constraint, the variable $T_{12}$ cannot be equal to $n$.

### 4.3  Experimental Results on the Large Instance Model

We first conducted a comparison of our first model (the model presented in Sect. 3.4), the large instances model (the second model) and the model presented in [9].

**Table 4.** Comparison of the three models on different size of instances. The data in parentheses separated by commas were calculated by the first model, the second model, and the model of [9] respectively. N/A indicates that our first model cannot handle the instance.

| Instances | Time(s) | Solutions | Optimum value | Speed(n/s) | Nodes |
|---|---|---|---|---|---|
| $n = 8$ | (9,42,115) | (80822,80822,80822) | (76,76,76) | (36946,8739,4820) | (3.56e5,3.69e5,5.59e5) |
| $n = 10$ | (300,300,300) | (4.55e5,3.45e5,5.98e4) | (162,164,168) | (20675,6734,3796) | (6.20e6,2.02e6,1.14e6) |
| $n = 12$ | (300,300,300) | (7.21e4,3.57e5,1.00e5) | (312,296,292) | (15718,4758,1964) | (4.72e6,7.13e5,5.89e5) |
| $n = 14$ | (300,300,300) | (2.85e3,1.01e5,1.93e4) | (508,490,502) | (9883,3316,1795) | (2.96e6,9.95e5,5.38e5) |
| $n = 16$ | (N/A,300,300) | (N/A,3.3e4,2.79e3) | (N/A,752,780) | (N/A,2855,1658) | (N/A,8.56e5,4.98e5) |
| $n = 18$ | (N/A,300,300) | (N/A,4.05e4,8.18e3) | (N/A,1140,1162) | (N/A,1643,977) | (N/A,4.93e5,2.93e5) |
| $n = 20$ | (N/A,300,300) | (N/A,874,777) | (N/A,1640,1566) | (N/A,1085,929) | (N/A,3.25e5,2.79e5) |

Table 4 shows the experimental results calculated in 5 min by three models from instance size $n = 8$ to $n = 20$, where the exceptional instance $n = 8$ could be finished in a shorter time by all models.

Since the parallelized large instance model relies on the **table** constraints, we also carried out the experiment to select the best algorithms specified in the **table** constraints for partitioning search space and the **table** constraints for $k$ consecutive variables. The best results were selected based on the sum of the number of feasible solutions of all workers. We obtained (MDD+, GAC3rm), (FC, GAC3rm), and (FC, GAC3rm) for 2, 4, and 8 workers respectively, where the first algorithm was specified in the **table** constraint for partitioning the search space and the second one is for the **table** constraint used for $k$ consecutive allowed values.

Table 5 reports the results of parallel execution when using 2, 4, and 8 workers as well as the serial execution. We observed that the number of solutions and the speed of processing nodes declined approximately by half when the number of workers doubled from 4 to 8 (See the first and second columns of the tuple when the number of workers is 4 and 8). To confirm the validity of our parallel approach, we simulated the parallel execution again by means of executing each task received by the workers sequentially where each worker operated on the tuples (data) that are the same as its parallel execution counterpart.

Table 6 shows that the increase of the number of solutions and the speed of processing nodes remained stable as the number of workers increases. Moreover, we experienced the improvement of the optimal values when using the same number of workers compared with results in Table 5.

**Table 5.** The experimental results for 18 teams. The data formatting in the parentheses of each cell, in turn, are the computed number of feasible solutions, the average speed of processing nodes (nodes/s), and the optimal value gained in the corresponding execution time.

| Time (m) | Workers | | | |
|---|---|---|---|---|
| | 1 | 2 | 4 | 8 |
| 1 | (7545,1711,1154) | (8026,1576,1130) | (8856,1131,1130) | (4652,685,1116) |
| 10 | (7.60e4,1717,1138) | (9983,2114,1128) | (70702,1229,1104) | (34213,595,1100) |
| 100 | (9.65e5,1562,1128) | (2.05e5,1866,1104) | (2.51e5,1248,1102) | (7.03e5,661,1084) |
| 1000 | (8.90e6,1636,1110) | (3.3e6,1700,1098) | (6.41e6,1153,1096) | (3.89e6,652,1078) |

**Table 6.** The results of simulation parallel executions by execution in sequential way.

| Time (m) | Workers | | |
|---|---|---|---|
| | 2 | 4 | 8 |
| 1 | (2024,2279,1132) | (9021,2310,1130) | (23648,2187,1082) |
| 10 | (17961,2292,1122) | (89174,2188,1118) | (2.07e5,2273,1080) |
| 100 | (5.40e5,2068,1120) | (5.68e5,2222,1104) | (1.75e6,2260,1066) |
| 1000 | (1.64e6,2328,1096) | (8.14e6,2300,1096) | (2.03e7,2216,1066) |

## 5 Discussion

Table 4 summarizes the results of comparing our first model (Sect. 3.4), second model (Sect. 4.1), and the model of [9] on the same predefined venue data sequentially for the different size of instances. The first model achieved the best performance on the instance $n = 8$ due to its shortest execution time. Recall that the number of variables of the second model is $n \times n$, besides both the first model and [9]'s model are $2n \times (n-1)$. In addition, the domain of the variables of the timetable in three models is the same. It is interesting to observe that the first model has the least total number of search nodes among the three models, which may not adhere to our intuition. We speculate this is because the first model does not use the **ifThen** constraint in our implementation; by contrast, the other two models must consider all the possible values of each variable by using **ifThen** constraints in both two implementations due to the requirement of the **element** constraint. Especially, the model in [9] has to use the **element** constraint with **ifThen** constraint (or **reified** constraint) again to assign the venue of each game. Therefore, in other words, the model of [9] has the largest search space among the three models. For $n = 10$, the first model was still the best among the three models because of the maximum number of nodes and the smallest optimum value, followed by the second model. The first model was not the best for the instance $n = 14$ based on the performance reported in Table 4 even if timetable part of the first model outperformed other models. This is because even though more feasible timetables could be generated, the overall performance was subject to the constraint imposed by the consecutive conditions.

From the perspective of seeking the optimal value, the parallel execution was better than the serial execution. Generally, the more workers were involved, the better optimal value we attained. For example, using 8 workers always attained the best optimal value compared with the relatively less number of workers in the same amount of time. The improvement on the optimal value due to the parallel execution is because the overall search tree is split into the number of independent subtrees. Therefore, even if some workers fall into local minima because of its subtrees, other workers might work on the subtrees that could result in better optimal values, and of course there are more feasible solutions generated in the same amount of time, which also might lead to better optimal values. One example that supports our view is that the optimal value attained in 1000 min by serial execution (Table 5) is worse than the optimal value attained in 1 min by parallel execution with 8 workers (Table 6). Admittedly, the results reported in Table 6 are obtained by simulating the execution of multi workers on a single worker. The reasons could be the effect from the shared cache of a multi-core processor and the limitation hyperthreading. Since our modeling approach does not require communication, there is reason to believe that we will obtain the same performance as the simulation if we run the parallel model on a computer with much more cores or a cluster.

## 6    Conclusion

We have presented two distinct models for different scale TTPPV problems, as well as utilizing data-level parallelism to execute models in parallel. On the same instances of realistic size, our models outperformed the previous model under their own best search strategy. The advantage of our models is decided by the strategy that trades time for space. Specifically, the search space is reduced by predefined tuples with the possible combinations of values. In addition, we have also explored the approach about executing models in parallel, which can often lead to a better optimal value. We have shown this experimentally by comparing the serial version with the parallel version through different size of instances.

Much has yet to be tried with our models and we believe there is still a lot of potential to improve the performance of our approach. In particular our search strategy requires focus since it is currently only selected from search strategies predefined by Choco solver. Although it has performed well, search strategies tailored to the problem should perform even better. Furthermore, local search an incomplete method for finding an optimal solution, could be combined with our models to enhance the effectiveness of the search. Finally, we plan to employ large-scale parallel computers to solve the large realistic problem and it might be a new benefit of CP approach in the real world sports scheduling.

# References

1. Pesant, G.: CSPLib: a problem library for constraints. Accessed 08 Apr 2018
2. Melo, R.A., Urrutiá, S., Ribeiro, C.C.: The traveling tournament problem with predefined venues. J. Sched. **12**(6), 607–622 (2009)
3. Kendall, G., Knust, S., Ribeiro, C.C., Urrutia, S.: Scheduling in sports: an annotated bibliography. Comput. Oper. Res. **37**(1), 1–19 (2010)
4. Tsang, E.: Foundations of Constraint Satisfaction. Academic Press, Boston (1995)
5. Rossi, F., Van Beek, P., Walsh, T.: Handbook of Constraint Programming. Elsevier, New York (2006)
6. Lecoutre, C.: STR2: optimized simple tabular reduction for table constraints. Constraints **16**(4), 341–371 (2011)
7. Prud'homme, C., Fages, J.-G., Lorca, X.: Choco Documentation. TASC - LS2N CNRS UMR 6241, COSLING S.A.S. (2017)
8. Lecoutre, C.: Constraint Networks: Techniques and Algorithms. Wiley, Hoboken (2009)
9. Pesant, G.: A constraint programming approach to the traveling tournament problem with predefined venues. In: Practice and Theory of Automated Timetabling, pp. 303–316 (2012)
10. Zanarini, A., Pesant, G.: More robust counting-based search heuristics with alldifferent constraints. In: Lodi, A., Milano, M., Toth, P. (eds.) CPAIOR 2010. LNCS, vol. 6140, pp. 354–368. Springer, Heidelberg (2010). https://doi.org/10.1007/978-3-642-13520-0_38
11. Régin, J.-C., Rezgui, M., Malapert, A.: Embarrassingly parallel search. In: Schulte, C. (ed.) CP 2013. LNCS, vol. 8124, pp. 596–610. Springer, Heidelberg (2013). https://doi.org/10.1007/978-3-642-40627-0_45
12. Smith, B.M.: Modelling. In: Foundations of Artificial Intelligence, vol. 2, pp. 377–406. Elsevier, Amsterdam (2006)

# Predicative Vagueness in Lung Metastases in Soft Tissue Sarcoma Screening

José Neves[1]([⊠])[iD], Almeida Dias[2][iD], Ana Morais[3][iD],
Francisca Fonseca[3][iD], Patrícia Loreto[3][iD], Victor Alves[1][iD],
Isabel Araújo[2][iD], Joana Machado[4][iD], Bruno Fernandes[1][iD],
Jorge Ribeiro[5][iD], Cesar Analide[1][iD], Filipa Ferraz[1][iD],
João Neves[6][iD], and Henrique Vicente[1,7][iD]

[1] Centro Algoritmi, Universidade do Minho, Braga, Portugal
{jneves, valves, analide}@di.uminho.pt,
bruno.fmf.8@gmail.com, filipatferraz@gmail.com,
[2] CESPU, Instituto Universitário de Ciências da Saúde, Gandra, Portugal
a.almeida.dias@gmail.com, isabel.araujo@ipsn.cespu.pt
[3] Departamento de Informática, Escola de Engenharia,
Universidade do Minho, Braga, Portugal
{a70484, a71702, a71934}@alunos.uminho.pt
[4] Farmácia de Lamaçães, Braga, Portugal
joana.mmachado@gmail.com
[5] Escola Superior de Tecnologia e Gestão, ARC4DigiT – Applied Research
Center for Digital Transformation, Instituto Politécnico de Viana do Castelo,
Viana do Castelo, Portugal
jribeiro@estg.ipvc.pt
[6] Mediclinic Arabian Ranches, PO Box 282602, Dubai, United Arab Emirates
joaocpneves@gmail.com
[7] Departamento de Química, Escola de Ciências e Tecnologia,
Centro de Química de Évora, Universidade de Évora, Évora, Portugal
hvicente@uevora.pt

**Abstract.** *Soft Tissue Sarcomas* (*STSs*) pose a potential risk for the development of lung metastases, which in turn results in a negative prognosis for patients. Presumptions about the occurrence of these abnormalities during *STSs* treatment would have countless implications for both patients and healthcare professionals as they could increase the efficacy of the treatment and improve overall survival. Prediction is based on a creative *Logic Programming, Case Based Reasoning* approach to problem solving, that is complemented with an unusual approach to *Knowledge Representation and Reasoning*, as it takes into consideration not only the data items entropic states but introduces the concept of *Vague's Predicate Extension*.

**Keywords:** Soft Tissue Sarcoma · Magnetic Resonance Imaging
Logic Programming · Knowledge Representation and Reasoning
Case Based Reasoning · Entropy · Predicative Vagueness

© Springer Nature Switzerland AG 2018
A. Groza and R. Prasath (Eds.): MIKE 2018, LNAI 11308, pp. 80–89, 2018.
https://doi.org/10.1007/978-3-030-05918-7_8

# 1 Introduction

*Soft Tissue Sarcoma (STS)* is a type of cancer that develops from soft tissues such as fat, muscle, nerves, blood vessels or fibrous tissues [1]. *STS* may occur anywhere in the body, but its extremities are the most common site of origin [2]. According to the classification of the *Memorial Sloan-Kettering Cancer Centre*, there are more than 70 types of *STSs*, which are classified depending on where in the body the tumour arose. However, *STSs* can also be present on more than one type of body tissue, or even have no clear origin. These are the cases in which *synovial sarcomas* and undifferentiated *STSs* are included [3]. For *STSs* of the extremities, the lungs are the main site of metastases and the prognosis of patients who develop lung metastases is generally bad [4]. Considering that an accurate diagnosis of pulmonary metastases significantly affects patient's outcome, treatment and prognosis, the early detection of such metastases is of vital importance [5]. On the other hand, *Magnetic Resonance Imaging (MRI)*, even though it is associated with operational high costs, is one of the imaging modalities more suitable for *STS'* diagnosis [6].

# 2 Theoretic Fundamentals

## 2.1 Predicative Vagueness

*Knowledge Representation and Reasoning (KRR)* aims to understand the complexity of the information and the associated inference mechanisms. In this study, a data item is to be understood to be slightly smaller in the interior, when it disassembles something, i.e., it is formed mainly of different elements, namely its *Entropic State Range* (*ESR*), *ESR's Quality-of-Information* (*QoI*) and *Degree-of-Confidence* (*DoC*), and the *Potential of Empowerment Range* (*PER*). These are just a set of over an endless items number. Indisputably, you can do practically anything you can imagine when you combine different elements, or in other words, viz.

- What happens when one splits a data item? The broken pieces become data item for another element, a process that may be endless; and
- Can a data item be broken down? Basically, it is the smallest possible part of an element that still remains the element.

and put in terms of a set of predicates that elicit the universe of discourse, whose extensions are given as productions of the type, viz.

$$
\begin{aligned}
\{ \\
&\neg p \leftarrow not\, p,\, not\, exception_p \\
&p \leftarrow p_1, \cdots, p_n, not\, q_1, \cdots, not\, q_m \\
&?(p_1, \cdots, p_n, not\, q_1, \cdots, not\, q_m)(n,\ m \geq 0) \\
&\quad exception_{p_1}, \cdots, exception_{p_j}\ (0 \leq j \leq k), \quad being\ k\ an\ integer\ number \\
\} &:: entropic\ state
\end{aligned}
$$

where "?" is a domain atom denoting falsity and $p_s$ and $q_s$ are makings of the kind, viz.

$$\bigwedge_{1 \leq i \leq n} predicate_i - clause_j((ESR_{x_1}, QoI_{x_1}, DoC_{x_1}, PER_{x_1}), \cdots$$
$$\cdots, (ESR_{x_m}, QoI_{x_m}, DoC_{x_m}, PER_{x_m})) :: ESR_j :: QoI_j :: DoC_j :: PER_j$$

where $n$, $\Lambda$ and $m$ stand for, respectively, the cardinality of the predicates' set, logical conjunction, and predicate's argument cardinality. The items $ESR_j$ $QoI_j$, $DoC_j$ and $PER_j$ show the way to data item dissection [7, 8], i.e., a data item is to be understood as having an atomic structure. It consists of identifying not only all the sub items that make up an item, but also to investigate the rules that oversee them, i.e., how $ESR_j$, $QoI_j$, $DoC_j$ and $PER_j$ are kept together and how much added value is created. This establish what we called the *Vague Predicate Extension* (*VPE*) paradox; indeed, the uncertainty principle leads to all sorts of ironies, like the particles being in more than one place at once, which is the case in the present situation. *Vagueness* is used in the sense that it is not known which are the terms that make a predicate extension, i.e., which are the ones that either may or not may be in the form, viz.

$$exception_{p_1}, \cdots, exception_{p_j} (0 \leq j \leq k), \text{ being } k \text{ an integer number}$$

or which are the terms' arguments that are of type *unknown*, taken from a *set* or *interval*, or even be *self-contradictory*.

## 2.2  Qualitative Data Items in Terms of Its Quantitative Counterparts

The present study contains both qualitative and quantitative data. With the aim of quantifying the qualitative part and facilitating process monitoring, it will be presented in graphic form [9]. Taking as an example a group of 3 (three) questions on a particular topic, where there are 3 (three) possible options, namely low, medium, high, it is itemized as a unitary range divided into 3 (three) slices. The markings in the axis correspond to each of the possible options (Fig. 1), viz.

## 2.3  Case-Based Reasoning

The problem-solving *CBR* (*Case Based Reasoning*) method was developed to solve new problems by reusing the knowledge gained by working out similar ones. This technique may be particularly useful in areas where much information is gotten through experience, and related cases may have comparable solutions, even if they have different backgrounds [10, 11]. The main limitation of using existing CBR, however, relates to its monolithic form, either in terms of program or data, i.e., modularity is missing. Undeniably, modularity is desirable because it not only supports the reuse of parts of the application or the data logic, but also facilitates maintenance. To allow *CBR* systems to process unknown, incomplete or even conflicting data/information, an extended *CBR* cycle is proposed in terms of the metrics referred to above (Fig. 2).

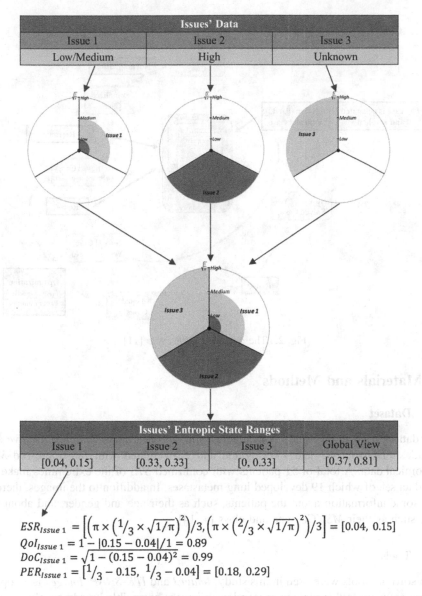

$$ESR_{Issue\ 1} = \left[\left(\pi \times \left(^1/_3 \times \sqrt{1/\pi}\right)^2\right)/3, \left(\pi \times \left(^2/_3 \times \sqrt{1/\pi}\right)^2\right)/3\right] = [0.04, 0.15]$$

$$QoI_{Issue\ 1} = 1 - |0.15 - 0.04|/1 = 0.89$$

$$DoC_{Issue\ 1} = \sqrt{1 - (0.15 - 0.04)^2} = 0.99$$

$$PER_{Issue\ 1} = \left[^1/_3 - 0.15, \ ^1/_3 - 0.04\right] = [0.18, 0.29]$$

**Fig. 1.** Going from *Qualitative* to *Quantitative* data items.

There are many examples in the literature about the use of *CBR* as a problem-solving methodology in Medicine. Different researchers have reviewed more than thirty CBR systems/projects [12, 13] revealing that CBRs have been widely employed in the medical domain, including disease diagnosis, classification, treatment and management.

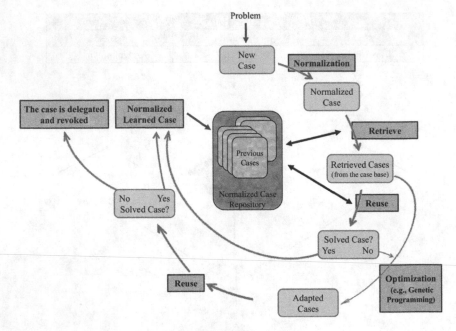

**Fig. 2.** The extended *CBR cycle* [11].

## 3    Materials and Methods

### 3.1    Dataset

The dataset used in this study is available online at the *Cancer Imaging Archive* and includes *FDG-PET/CT* and *T1*-weighted and *T2*-weighted with fat-suppressed *MRI* anatomical data. A total of 51 patients with confirmed *STS* of the extremities make up this data set, of which 19 developed lung metastases. In addition to the images, there is also some information about the patients, such as their age and gender, and about the *STS*, such as their *MSKCC* type and class [4, 14].

### 3.2    Tools

Two software tools were used in this study, *ImageJ* and *ITK-SNAP*. *ImageJ* is an open-source software tool for image processing. It is very extensible by adding plugins and scripts that perform more specific tasks [15]. *ITK-SNAP* is an open-source software application focused on the segmentation of *3D* medical images, offering a range of tools for this purpose, including a semi-automatic segmentation one [16].

# 4 Case Study

The features that make up the attribute vector have been selected as specified in the literature. The patient's characteristics and sarcoma findings were obtained to fit the data set used [4, 17–19] (Fig. 3), viz.

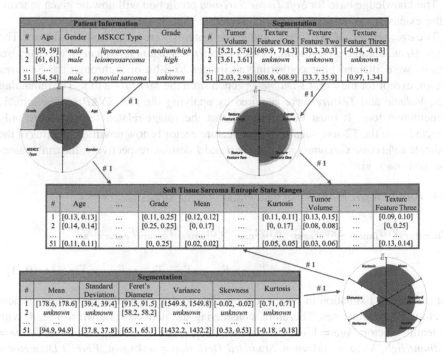

**Fig. 3.** Fragment of the knowledge base for *Soft Tissue Sarcoma* prediction.

- Age – patient's age;
- *Gender* – patient's gender;
- *MSKCC type* – *STS's* type according to the *MSKCC* classification;
- *Grade* – *STS's* grade;
- *Mean* – average gray value of the *Region of Interest* (*RoI*). In this feature and in those applied to a *RoI*, the *RoI* has been defined in the axial section in which the *STS* appears larger;
- *Standard Deviation* – Standard deviation of the gray values for the determination of the mean one;
- *Feret's Diameter* – The longest distance between two points in the boundary of the *RoI*;
- *Variance* – the second order moment over the *RoI*'s mean. Measures the variation of intensity around a mean value;
- *Skewness* – the third order moment over the *RoI's* mean. Measures the image's symmetry;

- *Kurtosis* – the fourth order moment over the *RoI's* mean. Measures the flatness of an image's histogram;
- *Volume* – the *STS's* volume; and
- *Texture features* – *ITK-SNAP* has the ability to generate texture features from a volume, in this case the *STS's* volume.

The knowledge base for *Soft Tissue Sarcoma* prediction will now be given in terms of the extensions of tables/relations presented in Fig. 3, viz.

The *age, gender, MSKCC type*, and *grade* features were taken from the dataset. The *Image Mean, Standard Deviation, Feret's Diameter, Variance, Skewness*, and *Kurtosis* features were attained after converting all images to 8-bit ones through the *FeatureJ plug-in*, except for the *Feret's Diameter* gotten from the *Measure*'s tool. The remaining ones, *Volume* and *Texture* were acquired by applying the *ITK-SNAP* semi-automatic segmentation tool. It must be mentioned that the image-related features were only extracted from the *T2-weighted MRI*. The feature vector is now rewritten in terms of the predicate *soft tissue sarcoma (sts)* (where *0* and *1* denote, respectively, the truth values *false* and *true*), viz.

$$sts: Age, Gen_{der}, MSKCC, Gra_{de}, M_{ean}, S_{tandard}D_{eviation}, Feret's$$

$$D_{iameter}, Var_{iance}, Skew_{ness}, Kurt_{osis}, Vol_{ume}, T_{exture}F_{eature}O_{ne},$$

$$T_{exture}F_{eature}T_{wo}, T_{exture}F_{eature}T_{hree} \rightarrow \{0, 1\}$$

that stands for a situation in which it is possible to diagnose whether or not a patient develops lung metastases. Therefore, considering the *new case* shown in Fig. 4, with the feature vector: *Age* = [50, 60], *Gender* = *Male*, *MSKCC* = *liposarcoma Grade* = *Medium/High, Mean* = *unknown, Standard Deviation* = *unknown, Feret's Diameter* = 57.6, *Variance* = *unknown, Skewness* = *unknown, Kurtosis* = *unknown, Volume* =[7.45, 7.82], *Texture Feature One* = *unknown, Texture Feature Two* = *unknown, Texture Feature Three* = *unknown* one may have, viz.

Assuming that every attribute has equal weight for the sake of presentation, the *sim(imilarities)* between *sts_{newcase}* and *sts_{#1}*, given in terms of its *Entropic States Ranges (ESR)*, may be computed as follows, viz.

$$effective\ sim_{sts_{\#1}}^{\substack{sts\ new\\case}} = 1 - (|0.13 - 0.098| + \cdots + |0.09 - 0|)/14 = 0.64$$

$$potential\ sim_{sts_{\#1}}^{\substack{sts\ new\\case}} = 1 - (|0.13 - 0.13| + \cdots + |0.10 - 0.25|)/14 = 0.92$$

i.e., overlapping the areas in bold (*effective dissimilarity*) and grey (*potential dissimilarity*) for both *sts_{new case}* and *sts_{#1}*. || is one's notation for *absolute value*, i.e., the distance of a number from 0 (zero). This approach allows for the definition of *effective similarity, distance* or *potential similarity* measures for *VPEs* and proposed some formulas to calculate them. This computational technique is now applied to the

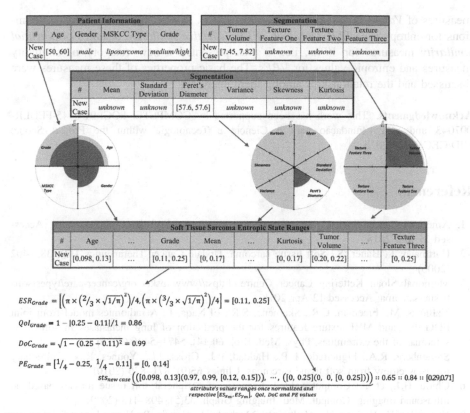

**Fig. 4.** Laying down *New Case* as a clause of *sts* predicate's extension in terms of its *QoI, DoC, PER* valuations for argument's *Grade*.

remaining retrieved cases in order to obtain the most similar ones, either in terms of *effective similarity, distance* or *potential similarity* measures for the *New Case*, which may stand for the possible solutions to the problem.

A set with 51 records was used and 20 (twenty) experiments were applied in all tests. The model correctly classified [46, 48] of a total of 51 cases, with an accuracy ranging between 90.0% and 94.1%. The accuracy of the proposed model is slightly higher than the *CBR* approach reported in literature for mental health problems [20], and similar to the fuzzy ontology-based semantic *CBR* system related to semantic understanding of medical concepts in diabetes diagnosis [21].

## 5  Conclusions and Future Work

This work presents a *Logic Programming* (*LP*) approach for the development of a decision support system to predict whether it is likely for a patient with *STS* of the extremities to develop lung metastases, based on patient's information and *MRI* features, under a *CBR* approach to computing. The discussion has focus on the uncertainty measures of *Vague Predicate's Extensions* (*VPEs*). It was proposed axiomatic definitions for entropy (i.e., *ESR, QoI, DoC, PER*), *effective similarity*, *distance* or *potential similarity* measures for *VPEs*, i.e., it was presented a new category of similarity measures and entropic values for *VPEs*. The basic properties of these measures were discussed and the relationships among them analysed.

**Acknowledgments.** This work has been supported by COMPETE: POCI-01-0145-FEDER-007043 and FCT – Fundação para a Ciência e Tecnologia within the Project Scope: UID/CEC/00319/2013.

# References

1. American Cancer Society. https://www.cancer.org/cancer/soft-tissue-sarcoma.html. Accessed 21 Mar 2018
2. Hartmann, J., Bauer, S.: Soft tissue sarcoma. Update Cancer Therapeutics **1**(3), 385–402 (2006)
3. Memorial Sloan Kettering Cancer Centre. https://www.mskcc.org/cancer-care/types/soft-tissue-sarcoma. Accessed 12 Apr 2018
4. Vallières, M., Freeman, C.R., Skamene, S.R., El Naqa, I.: A radiomics model from joint FDG-PET and MRI texture features for the prediction of lung metastases in soft-tissue sarcomas of the extremities. Phys. Med. Biol. **60**(14), 5471–5496 (2015)
5. Sardenberg, R.A., Figueiredo, L.P., Haddad, F.J., Gross, J.L., Younes, R.N.: Pulmonary metastasectomy from soft tissue sarcomas. Clinics **65**(9), 871–876 (2010)
6. Chiou, H.J., et al.: Computer-aided diagnosis of peripheral soft tissue masses based on ultrasound imaging. Comput. Med. Imaging Graph. **33**(5), 408–413 (2009)
7. Fernandes, F., Vicente, H., Abelha, A., Machado, J., Novais, P., Neves J.: Artificial neural networks in diabetes control. In: Proceedings of the 2015 Science and Information Conference (SAI 2015), pp. 362–370. IEEE Edition (2015)
8. Ramalhosa, I., et al.: Diagnosis of alzheimer disease through an artificial neural network based system. In: Cassenti, Daniel N. (ed.) AHFE 2017. AISC, vol. 591, pp. 162–174. Springer, Cham (2018). https://doi.org/10.1007/978-3-319-60591-3_15
9. Fernandes, A., Vicente, H., Figueiredo, M., Neves, M., Neves, J.: An evaluative model to assess the organizational efficiency in training corporations. In: Dang, T.K., Wagner, R., Küng, J., Thoai, N., Takizawa, M., Neuhold, E. (eds.) FDSE 2016. LNCS, vol. 10018, pp. 415–428. Springer, Cham (2016). https://doi.org/10.1007/978-3-319-48057-2_29
10. Silva, A., et al.: Length of stay in intensive care units – a case base evaluation. In: Fujita, H., Papadopoulos, G.A. (eds.) New Trends in Software Methodologies, Tools and Techniques, Frontiers in Artificial Intelligence and Applications, vol. 286, pp. 191–202. IOS Press, Amsterdam (2016)
11. Neves, J., et al.: A deep learning approach to case based reasoning to the evaluation and diagnosis of cervical carcinoma. In: Sieminski, A., Kozierkiewicz, A., Nunez, M., Ha, Q.T. (eds.) Modern Approaches for Intelligent Information and Database Systems. SCI, vol. 769, pp. 185–197. Springer, Cham (2018). https://doi.org/10.1007/978-3-319-76081-0_16
12. Begum, S., Ahmed, M.U., Funk, P., Xiong, N., Folke, M.: Case-based reasoning systems in the health sciences: a survey of recent trends and developments. IEEE Trans. Syst. Man Cybern. Part C (Appl. Rev.) **41**, 421–434 (2011)

13. Blanco, X., Rodríguez, S., Corchado, J.M., Zato, C.: Case-based reasoning applied to medical diagnosis and treatment. In: Omatu, S., Neves, J., Rodriguez, J.M.C., Paz Santana, J. F., Gonzalez, S.R. (eds.) Distributed computing and artificial intelligence. AISC, vol. 217, pp. 137–146. Springer, Cham (2013). https://doi.org/10.1007/978-3-319-00551-5_17

14. Clark, K., et al.: The cancer imaging archive (TCIA): maintaining and operating a public information repository. J. Digit. Imaging **26**(6), 1045–1057 (2013)

15. ImageJ. https://imagej.net/. Accessed 25 July 2018

16. ITK-SNAP. http://www.itksnap.org/. Accessed 11 June 2018

17. Selvaraj, D., Dhanasekaran, R.: A review on tissue segmentation and feature extraction of MRI brain images. Int. J. Comput. Sci. Eng. Technol. **4**(10), 1313–1332 (2013)

18. ImageJ User Guide. https://imagej.nih.gov/ij/docs/menus/analyze.html. Accessed 14 Feb 2018

19. FeatureJ: Statistics. https://imagescience.org/meijering/software/featurej/statistics/. Accessed 02 May 2018

20. Janssen, R., Spronck, P., Arntz, A.: Case-based reasoning for predicting the success of therapy. Expert Syst. **32**(2), 165–177 (2015)

21. El-Sappagh, S., Elmogy, M., Riad, A.M.: A fuzzy-ontology oriented case-based reasoning framework for semantic diabetes diagnosis. Artif. Intell. Med. **65**(3), 179–208 (2015)

# Expert Intelligence: Theory
# of the Missing Facet

Jabez Christopher[1], Rajendra Prasath[2], and Odelu Vanga[1(✉)]

[1] Department of Computer Science and Information Systems,
BITS-Pilani (Hyderabad Campus), Medchal District,
Hyderabad 500078, Telangana, India
{jabezc,odelu.vanga}@hyderabad.bits-pilani.ac.in
[2] Department of Computer Science and Engineering,
Indian Institute of Information Technology Sri City,
Chittoor 517646, Andhra Pradesh, India
rajendra.prasath@iiits.in

**Abstract.** This article sheds light on various less-explored areas, such as knowledge, intelligence, expertise, knowledge representation, skill acquisition and intelligent systems. It also proposes a missing facet, namely, Expert Intelligence (EI). Artificial Intelligence (AI) based systems such as expert systems and decision support systems were meant to substitute the expertise of human experts. However, in reality, these so-called intelligent systems are used as an aid for decision-making or only as a second choice of opinion in the absence of an expert. During the design of an intelligent system, a knowledge engineer encodes the knowledge of a domain expert into the system. The design and architecture of the system is meant to manipulate on the knowledge of the domain expert but his intelligence is neither acquired nor manifested. Furthermore, poor knowledge acquisition and knowledge representation schemes penalize the performance of these systems. Intelligent systems require more of an experts intelligence rather than his knowledge. Expert Intelligence attempts to bridge this gap. The notion of this article is not to provide an experimental analysis; the principle contribution of this work includes the dogma of Expert Intelligence and future directions for a paradigm-shift from knowledge-based AI approach to an intelligence-based EI approach.

**Keywords:** Intelligence · Expertise · Knowledge
Artificial Intelligence · Cognitive modeling · Expert Systems

## 1 Introduction

Artificial Intelligence (AI) is generally supposed to have started at a conference in July 1956 when John McCarthy first used the phrase. The logical syntax and formal rules developed by Russell are still the basis for automatic theorem proving systems as well as the theoretical foundations of Artificial Intelligence [1]. By the end of the 1940s there were considerable improvements in the electronic sector which provided memory and processing power required for developing

© Springer Nature Switzerland AG 2018
A. Groza and R. Prasath (Eds.): MIKE 2018, LNAI 11308, pp. 90–101, 2018.
https://doi.org/10.1007/978-3-030-05918-7_9

computing systems. Ever since a lot of inter-disciplinary research work is being carried out in psychology, computer science and human-computer interaction areas in order to model the human brain [2–5]. Psychologists propose various theories of intelligence whereas computer scientists and mathematicians modelled it [6]. This has led to the formation of various sub-disciplines of AI such as game playing, automated reasoning, expert system-design, machine learning, and semantic modelling. Intelligent frameworks and expert systems are pervasive in various fields of engineering, science, medicine, business, accounting and finance for applications such as signal processing, control systems, medical diagnosis and prognosis, stock prediction and weather forecast [6–8].

The Philosophy of Artificial Intelligence [9] and Intelligent systems have created a considerable interest in the AI research community, but the analysis on the psychology of judgement (prediction) and their application to these systems is yet to improve [10,11]. Engineers and developers have made note-worthy progress in the design and development of these systems [12]; however, studies on the core processes that catalyze the efficiency of these systems are still at initial stages. Although a plethora of theoretical ideas exist in literature, there still exists a breach in concepts related to intelligence, expertise, intelligent systems and knowledge-based systems. The intent of this paper is not to present an in-depth review of theories and concepts of intelligence; rather, it highlights the drawbacks of knowledge-based systems such as expert system, decision support system, and thereby present key ideas on how intelligence can be blended with knowledge to improve the performance of these systems. Finally this paper outlines a novel facet of intelligence namely Expert Intelligence.

## 2 An Overview of Expert Systems and Expert Knowledge

An expert is a person who demonstrates expertise in a particular field [13]. An expert has deep knowledge and skills, which a common person may not possess. An expert system is a software that endeavors to model the knowledge of a human expert, and moreover solve domain-specific problems in the same way like a human expert. Knowledge refers to the understanding and comprehension of facts possessed by an expert about that field. Expert systems are constructed with the aim to act similar to that of a human expert. Hence, an expert system too needs to have the knowledge concerning the domain of application. Figure 1 shows the architecture of a expert system from which it can be understood that the quality of knowledge is an important factor that influences the performance of a traditional expert system. Knowledge refers to the facts, information, and skills acquired by a person through experience or education. Collection of raw facts is termed data; in Informatics, knowledge is the collection of needed information and facts. Though several definitions are available in literature, no single definition of knowledge can be deemed to be complete. Some trivial types of knowledge include: Declarative knowledge, which represents facts and assertions; Procedural knowledge, the knowledge of knowing how to do something or of how things are done; Inferential knowledge refers to information obtained through logical reasoning and inference; Relational knowledge refers to knowing facts that are represented in tabular or relational format; Heuristic knowledge is defined as knowing approaches that are likely to work or knowing properties that are likely to be true; Explicit knowledge is what an individual holds openly and also known to others; Tacit knowledge refers to unwritten, unspoken, and unseen knowledge held practically by every normal human being, based on his experience, insights, perception, observations and internalized information; and finally Uncertain Knowledge, which refers to the knowledge where validity and truth of facts may change over time.

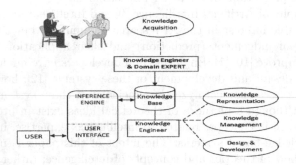

**Fig. 1.** Traditional expert system architecture.

Knowledge Base is "a collection of facts, relationships and rules which embody current expertise in a particular area" [14]. In order to construct a Knowledge Base of an expert system, the knowledge needs to be engineered. The knowledge engineering process in this context comprises of two steps: Knowledge Acquisition and Knowledge Representation. The efficacy of acquisition depends on the knowledge engineer and the domain expert; however, representation, manipulation and management of the acquired knowledge is the sole responsibility of the knowledge engineer. Knowledge acquisition is a process whereby an expert provides the necessary information about the domain through a discussion with the knowledge engineer or by means of practical, observable demonstrations. The engineer encodes the information into the Knowledge Base of the Expert System. The main ways of acquiring knowledge from domain experts can be one or a combination of the following approaches: Explanation - The human expert describes verbally, or in a document format, how he performs a certain task; Observation - The domain expert demonstrates observable examples in his domain of expertise and the knowledge engineer keenly observes his actions and encodes it using an appropriate knowledge representation scheme [15–17]. Moreover, to construct an efficient Knowledge Base, the acquired knowledge needs to be represented in a way that fits a symbol-manipulation mechanism of a computing system [18]. Knowledge representation is the symbolic way by which the acquired knowledge is expressed and structured in order to be dealt-with in a meaningful manner by a machine [19]. In an expert system, knowledge is usually represented by rules or semantic nets [16,20]. Knowledge that is acquired from an expert is encoded in an appropriate representation and is used by a manipulator known as the Inference Engine. This engine is "the reasoning core of the system which infers logical conclusions from the Knowledge Base" [14]. Generally, there is a separation between the declarative knowledge (semantics) stored in the Knowledge Base and the procedural knowledge activated by the Inference Engine. This gap between declarative and procedural aspects of an intelligent system enhances modularity, flexibility and transparency. However, this gap often widens due to inefficient knowledge acquisition and representation methods, which eventually affects the performance of the system. Hence intelligent systems require intelligence rather than sheer knowledge.

# 3 Intelligence

Intelligence is an abstract entity that is beyond all formal definitions and still remains open for interpretation. AI is considered to be centred on two goals: to understand the human mind and to achieve artifacts that exhibit human-like intelligence. There are different theories about intelligence none of which agrees fully with each other. Every approach comes up with a new wave of thoughts, assumptions and perceptions, which contradicts with at least with one of the earlier theories. This section presents a few definitions and theories of intelligence and moreover expounds some ideas from psychology, which were used for the construction and formulation of the theories of artificial intelligence and cognitive architectures. Some of the popular and well-referenced definitions of intelligence are listed as follows:

- Intelligence is the capacity to acquire and apply knowledge [21].
- Intelligence is that facet of mind underlying our capacity to think, to solve novel problems, to reason and to have knowledge of the world [22].
- Intelligence is a fundamental faculty; the alteration or the lack of which, is of the utmost importance for practical life. This faculty is judgment, otherwise called good sense, practical sense, initiative, the faculty of adapting ones self to circumstances [23].
- Intelligence is the ability of an organism to solve new problems [24].
- Intelligence is the ability to learn, exercise judgment, and be imaginative, and also the ability to adapt oneself adequately to relatively new situations in life [25].

For a detailed review of definitions and formal proofs, readers may refer to the works presented in [26].

## 3.1 Theories of Intelligence

Faculty theory of intelligence states that the mind is made up of different faculties for various functions like memory, reasoning, discrimination and imagination.

One Factor or Uni-factor theory considers intelligence to be a single, global capacity of the mind. This single capacity is common sense or general intelligence.

Since an individual has different abilities, both domain-specific and generic, this theory failed to make a stamp when other theories were proposed. Spearmans two-factor theory proposes that intellectual abilities comprises of two factors: general ability or common ability known as G factor and group of specific abilities known as S factor [27]. The former represents general problem-solving, inferencing and mathematical ability and the latter refers to domain-specific abilities. Thorndikes multi-factor theory attempts to define intelligence as a set of factors that are highly correlated. The number of factors cannot be explicitly specified for any domain or individual. Thorndike proposed and used the CAVD test; C Sentence Completion, A Arithmetic Reasoning, V Vocabulary and D Following Directions. Each of the sub-tests measured the capacity of a person for the above mentioned abilities and aspects of Abstract Intelligence or general intelligence. Significant positive correlations were found between these abilities thus indirectly giving the g factor. Thurstones Group factor theory denied the existence of innumerable factors, as that of Thorndike, and the presence of a general factor that pervades all mental activities. Group factor theory proposes that, in all, there are seven groups which cover the entire range of mental abilities [28]. Each of these primary factors is independent of others. These groups or the primary mental abilities are as follows: word fluency, verbal comprehension, spatial visualization, number facility, associative memory, reasoning, and perceptual speed. Based on the above factors Thurstone constructed an intelligence testing and measuring scheme known as 'Test of Primary Mental Abilities (PMA)'. Cattell's theory of fluid and crystallized intelligence: As the word emphasizes, so is the theory. Crystallized intelligence refers to the static form of intelligence indicated by a person's depth and breadth of general knowledge. Fluid intelligence highlights the use of logical thinking, abstract reasoning and problem-solving ability on the acquired knowledge, which is crystallized, at novel instances [29]. Gardeners theory of Multiple Intelligence differentiates intelligence into specific "modalities", rather than seeing it as dominated by a single general ability [30]. Gardner initially chooses eight abilities, namely, spatial, bodily-kinesthetic, musical, linguistic, logical-mathematical, interpersonal, intrapersonal, and naturalistic ability. He states that intelligence of a person is concerned with how he or she brings out these abilities. Sternberg proposed the Triarchic theory which is more of a cognitive approach rather than the psychometric approach [31]. He mentions intelligence as a mental activity directed towards purposive adaptation to selection and shaping of real-world environments. He proposed the Triarchic theory under three parts: componential, experiential, and practical components. In the field of intelligence these parts are also considered as considers this as Analytical Intelligence, Creative Intelligence and Practical Intelligence respectively. Analytical intelligence deals with problem solving and reasoning ability. Creative Intelligence is the ability to imagine, innovate and originate things. Practical intelligence refers to the efficacy of the process of doing actions but not the knowledge about the process (practical knowledge).

Eysenck, in his structural theory [32] postulates the neurological correlates of intelligence. He identified three correlates of intelligence i.e. reaction time, inspection time and average evoked potential. First two are observed behavior. Third behavior is a description of mental waves. From the above definitions and theories of intelligence it can be inferred that there are subtle relationships and differences between knowledge and intelligence. Knowledge is just a static collection of facts and information but intelligence involves dynamic application of knowledge for problem-solving and reasoning.

# 4 Intelligent Systems and Knowledge-Based Systems

Newwell proposed an approach for achieving intelligence into a computational device, what has been termed as "weak and strong methods" [33]. The earliest successful AI programs utilized weak reasoning and problem-solving methods that were drawing descriptions on human thought processes. Newell in fact deems Artificial Intelligence as the "science of weak methods". Weak methods are portable, generalizable and not dependent on the particular content or substance of the domain of problem-solving. Weak methods are less capable of finding solutions. Strong methods are more heavily dependent on rich knowledge of the problem-solving area and an understanding of what kinds of operations are likely to be successful in encountered situations. They are domain specialists, experts, and not generalists. Knowledge-based systems right from the initial expert system [34,35] till today utilize strong methods. It is typically a knowledge-based choice of decision-alternatives.

## 4.1  The Gap Between Expertise and Knowledge-Based Systems

Expertise is yet another ill-defined concept [36]. Expertise is responding well at challenging situations [37]. In the context of knowledge-based expert systems, dealing with unexpected input is a challenging task. A non-trivial situation cannot be handled by machines. Though there are probabilistic methods to deal with randomness, and fuzzy methods to deal with vagueness and uncertainty, there exists a breach between the approach of a human expert and all machine learning methods. Experts prove their expertise at such critical situations. If a machine is trained to handle such acute outliers and critical situations, then it is prone to be over-trained. The cost and the complexity of the system needs to be compromised for this cause.

In practice, expertise is gained due to the deliberate practice [38]. Trivial experience does not bring forth expertise. Experts are domain specific [39]. Focused work on specific aspects, with the help of a teacher, in a dedicated environment, with opportunities for reflection, exploration of alternatives and problem-solving makes consequent performances resource-consuming and more intelligent. Though contradictions exist along this line of thought [40] from a system-development viewpoint, expert systems are usually not trained for specific situations; they are developed with software and computing methods that enable them to generalize like human beings, which sometimes make systems to crash or yield disgraceful results. Expertise is a long-term development process, resulting from rich experience and practice. Expertise is not transferable [41]. Expertise is limited in its scope and elite performance does not transfer [37]. Knowledge is important to attain expertise. Domain-specific skills and knowledge have an impact on basic abilities. The transfer of high-level proficiency from one domain, to proficiency in another domain, is very less even when the domains seem very similar. An expert system designed for diagnosis of cancer cannot be used for diagnosis of stomach disorders, though both come under the umbrella of medical diagnosis.

## 4.2   Expertise and Knowledge Representation

Experts' superior ability to encode information from their domain of expertise should be reflected in the design and implementation of the Knowledge Base in the expert system. For example, an experienced geologist may remember an image based on its physical features whereas another geologist might remember based on its colours. The manner in which the geologists encode, store and retrieve images in their brain should be replicated while designing the knowledge base. The representation of a problem by experts, in their domain, is deeper, more principled and organized than a knowledge engineer or perhaps the expert system itself. They acquire techniques to develop complex representations and outlier detections that allow them to access information relevant to the demands efficiently. These techniques can account for their superior performance at critical situations too [42].

Chase and Ericsson characterized experts efficient use of long term memory in terms of three principles, popularly known as the skilled memory theory [43]. The first – meaningful encoding principle – states that experts encode information in terms of well-organized body of concepts and semantics in Long Term Memory. This enables experts to form more elaborate and accessible memory representations than beginners and novices. The second principle – the retrieval structure principle – states that experts develop and use memory mechanisms called retrieval structures to facilitate the recovery of information from long term memory. The organized and logical methods experts apply to temporarily maintain such information in an easily accessible state is reflected in their performance. Skilled memory theory's third principle – the speed up principle – states that encoding and retrieval operations in the long term memory speed-up due to practice. At a certain stage the speed and performance-accuracy of the long term memory almost equals the short term memory. Although the above listed principles have concrete analogies in computing systems and expert system architecture, very less importance is given to such ideologies during the process of expert system design.

## 4.3   Expertise and Automation

Expertise involves automation of fundamentals. Repetition of some fundamental tasks or preparatory stages for any activity by an expert leads to improved fluency, confidence and ease of doing those tasks. The more they do it, the better they become at it. Furthermore, the time required for doing these tasks diminishes gradually. For instance, assume a doctor analyzes ten symptoms for diagnosing a disease. Every day he gets to diagnose many patients for that disease and in due course the doctor comes to a state where he is able to predict the disease just by analyzing few symptoms in lesser time duration. This scenario is analogous to the inferencing mechanism of an expert system. Though the expert system gets trained in due course of time with some supervised machine learning techniques, the process of inferencing and the time taken for inferencing remains unaltered. Furthermore, automation of fundamentals leads to release of cognitive resources which enables an expert to fine tune his activities and perform better. A resemblance to this statement cannot be observed in any expert system. An expert system should require less resource and time for processes repeated consecutively at definite or indefinite intervals; this would enhance the efficiency of the system in terms of resource-utilization and time complexity. Expertise involves automation, and automation involves efficient utilization of time and resources.

## 4.4   Knowledge Representation and Reasoning

Knowledge-based systems and Machine Learning (ML) frameworks experience many issues with knowledge transfer and extrapolation. Recent models such as deep learning, though seem to be successful in various real-world application domains, require a lot of data, lacks an interface for knowledge transfer and moreover cannot make open inference about the world [44]. Reasoning systems that infer from logic are easily apprehensible, and logical rules are easy to chain and transfer between systems; but inductive logic is sensitive to noise. A few drawbacks of inductive reasoning are as follows: it cannot prove its conclusions always; it assumes uniformity of nature to prevail at all situations in the universe; it relies on observation for information collection. In order to arrive at conclusions for a larger number of cases from smaller ones, it has to be assumed that nature works the same everywhere. While most of the observations has confirmed this assumption, there would be situations which will not behave as assumed, particularly when it is generalized from a limited perspective. It is also not known how much of the perception of uniformity is based on the mechanisms of observation.

## 5   Expert Intelligence

From the analysis made from literature, principles of psychology, and its analogy to expert systems, it can be understood that the term Expert System is a misnomer; it neither incorporates the expertise of an expert nor the intelligence of an expert. A system needs more of the expert's intelligence rather than his knowledge. This paper brings to light a missing facet called Expert Intelligence (EI). Expert Intelligence would render environment-adaptable and more meaningful expert systems. The dogma of EI is stated below:

- An expert is a person who has a vast knowledge about a domain, works with intelligence and portrays expertise.
- EI is a blend of an expert's knowledge, intelligence and expertise.
- EI is the ability to quickly react at critical and adverse situations.
- EI is the facet of mind underlying the capacity to examine, identify non-trivial problems, and provide novel solutions.
- EI supports proficient utilization of resources for repeated procedures at various levels of abstraction.

EI should be associated with a unique knowledge representation scheme which cannot be precisely modelled by typical knowledge acquisition and representation methods. Consider a supervised Machine Learning framework where EI can be incorporated in the Knowledge Discovery process; the intelligence of an expert can be used during the training phase in the data preprocessing module and in the data mining module. This would improve the quality of the data; the data would be more domain-relevant. Moreover, rather than going for long, interactive optimization approaches, EI can be used to modify and tune the parameters of a classifier at various folds of validation which may significantly reduce the time taken for the training phase.

## 5.1   Characteristic Features of an EI-Based System

AI systems may be designed to be adaptive [10]. However, intelligent systems developed using principles of AI, and layered with techniques and methods from machine learning and soft computing, have their own limitations. Systems developed using EI, adhering to the EI dogma, will incorporate new features and dimensions in the development process which would catalyze the performance of these systems. The characteristic features are highly desirable, and moreover they do exist in different facets of computing and engineering. However, development of systems with EI principles will make their manifestation even more explicit, which would eventually enhance the efficiency and efficacy of the systems. EI-based systems reveal the experts intelligence. During the development of the system, the machine learning techniques and the adaptation methods used in the system, grasp the experts tuning methods rather than his sheer knowledge. All the activities of the expert are recorded and stored. These actions are later triggered by the EI-based system only at critical junctures. The knowledge acquisition phase in a AI-based system is blended with the acquisition of intelligence too. This would enable the system to process and deliver meaningful results with a higher precision in a specific domain. An EI-based system ensures that the extent of system-usage for a specific task is inversely proportional to the resources-usage of the system for that task. For example, consider a knowledge-based system in which knowledge is encoded in the form of IF-THEN rules; the system is programmed to accomplish its purpose with a set of rules. Whereas, an EI-based system would gradually minimize the number of rules during its operation thereby minimizing the resources (memory) used to store the rules and moreover the time taken to scan the rules too. EI exhibits a form of expertise that supports proficient utilization of resources by releasing of resources. Using fewer resources for fundamental tasks and automating frequent trivial tasks would eventually minimize the total turnaround time of the system. The knowledge engineering process and the representation of knowledge is quite different in EI. Rather than the trivial rule-based approach and ontology approach of knowledge representation, EI-based systems should contain novel, built-in, hybrid approaches. These approaches should not only encode knowledge but also have methods and mechanisms to capture, store, manipulate and manifest intelligence. Unlike the AI-based systems, EI systems will be more versatile and robust in handling peculiar and critical instances.

## 6 Conclusion

The discussions and research directions outlined in this paper are intended as an effort towards a conceptual understanding of EI. Intelligence in various facets such as Artificial Intelligence, Business Intelligence, Collective Intelligence, Computational Intelligence and Swarm Intelligence [45–48] have made their impact to be felt in diverse streams of engineering, science and management. Their principles, theories and concepts have indeed stirred up researchers in psychology, cognitive modelling and logic programming. In addition to these, the ideas and concepts outlined in this paper complement a missing facet to intelligence which would certainly bring about a wave of changes in the design and modelling of intelligent systems. Expert Intelligence, a blend of expert-knowledge, expertise and intelligence is a novel paradigm of intelligence which is at its initial stages of development. Development of memory structures, architectures and frameworks based on the dogma of EI would certainly yield true expert systems. Works related to capturing and representing expertise in machine-understandable form is still a less-explored area of research [49,50]. Hybrid systems, logics, knowledge engineering processes, and intelligence representation-cum-manipulation methods are required to realize and appreciate the paradigm-shift from AI to EI.

## References

1. Russell, B.: Mathematical logic as based on the theory of types. Am. J. Math. **30**(3), 222–262 (1908)
2. Keravnou, E.T., Washbrook, J.: Deep and shallow models in medical expert systems. Artif. Intell. Med. **1**(1), 11–28 (1989)
3. Giuse, D.A., Giuse, N.B., Miller, R.A.: Towards computer-assisted maintenance of medical knowledge bases. Artif. Intell. Med. **2**(1), 21–33 (1990)
4. Baum, E.B.: Toward a model of intelligence as an economy of agents. Mach. Learn. **35**(2), 155–185 (1999)

5. Boegl, K., Adlassnig, K.-P., Hayashi, Y., Rothenfluh, T.E., Leitich, H.: Knowledge acquisition in the fuzzy knowledge representation framework of a medical consultation system. Artif. Intell. Med. **30**(1), 1–26 (2004)

6. Reed, S.K., Pease, A.: Reasoning from imperfect knowledge. Cogn. Syst. Res. **41**, 56–72 (2017)

7. Biundo, S., Bercher, P., Geier, T., Müller, F., Schattenberg, B.: Advanced user assistance based on ai planning. Cogn. Syst. Res. **12**(3–4), 219–236 (2011)

8. Zhong, N., Liu, J., Sun, R.: Intelligent agents and data mining for cognitive systems. Cogn. Syst. Res. **3**(5), 169–170 (2004)

9. Müller, V.C.: Introduction: philosophy and theory of artificial intelligence. Minds Mach. **22**, 67–69 (2012)

10. Wang, P.: Analogy in a general-purpose reasoning system. Cogn. Syst. Res. **10**(3), 286–296 (2009)

11. De Kamps, M.: Towards truly human-level intelligence in artificial applications. Cogn. Syst. Res. **14**(1), 1–9 (2012)

12. Liao, S.-H.: Expert system methodologies and applicationsa decade review from 1995 to 2004. Expert Syst. Appl. **28**(1), 93–103 (2005)

13. Wai, J.: What does it mean to be an expert? Intelligence **45**, 122–123 (2014)

14. Meadows, A.J.: The Origins of Information Science, volume 1. Taylor Graham and the Institute of Information Scientists, London (1987)

15. Hart, A.: Knowledge acquisition for expert systems. In: Göranzon, B., Josefson, I. (eds.) Knowledge, Skill and Artificial Intelligence, pp. 103–111. Springer, Boston (1988). https://doi.org/10.1007/978-1-4471-1632-5

16. Walker, A.: Knowledge systems: principles and practice. IBM J. Res. Develop. **30**(1), 2–13 (1986)

17. Scott, I., Gronow, S.: Valuation expertise: its nature and application. J. Val. **8**(4), 362–375 (1990)

18. Minsky, M.: A framework for representing knowledge (1974)

19. Kaur, H., Jyoti, Y.J., Arora, A., Dolly, L.A.: Artificial intelligence: bringing expert knowledge to computers. Discov. J. **2**, 4–7 (2012)

20. Takashima, Q.: Characteristics and technical challenges of current expert systems. In: Proceedings of the Technology Assessment and Management Conference of the Gottlieb Duttwiler Institute, Rüschlikon, Zürich, Switzerland, pp. 31–48 (1985)

21. Mifflin, H.: The American Heritage Dictionary of the English Language. American Heritage, New York (2000)

22. Anderson, M.: Intelligence and Development: A Cognitive Theory. Blackwell Publishing, Oxford (1992)

23. Binet, A., Simon, T.: Méthodes nouvelles pour le diagnostic du niveau intellectuel des anormaux. L'année Psychologique **11**(1), 191–244 (1904)

24. Bingham, W.V.: Aptitudes and Aptitude Testing. Harper, New York (1937)

25. Sternberg, R.J.: Handbook of Intelligence. Cambridge University Press, New York (2000)

26. Legg, S., Hutter, M.: A formal measure of machine intelligence. arXiv preprint cs/0605024 (2006)

27. Spearman, C.: The theory of two factors. Psychol. Rev. **21**(2), 101 (1914)

28. Thurstone, L.L.: Primary Mental Abilities. University of Chicago, Chicago (1938)

29. Cattell, R.B.: Abilities: Their Structure, Growth, and Action. Houghton Mifflin, Boston (1971)

30. Howard, G.: Frames of Mind: The Theory of Multiple Intelligences. Basics, NY (1983)

31. Sternberg, R.J., Sternberg, R.J.: Beyond IQ: A Triarchic Theory of Human Intelligence. CUP Archive, Cambridge (1985)
32. Eysenck, H.J.: The Structure of Human Personality (Psychology Revivals). Routledge, New York (2013)
33. Newell, A.: Heuristic programming: Ill-structured problems. In: Aronofsky, J. (ed.) Progress in Operations Research III, pp. 360–414. Wiley, New York (1969)
34. Buchanan, B., Sutherland, G., Feigenbaum, E.A.: Heuristic DENDRAL : A Program for Generating Explanatory Hypotheses in Organic Chemistry. Stanford University, Stanford (1968)
35. Lindsay, R.K., Buchanan, B.G., Feigenbaum, E.A., Lederberg, J.: Dendral: a case study of the first expert system for scientific hypothesis formation. Artif. Intell. 61(2), 209–261 (1993)
36. Hoffman, R.R.: How can expertise be defined? implications of research from cognitive psychology. In: Williams, R., Faulkner, W., Fleck, J. (eds.) Exploring Expertise, pp. 81–100. Palgrave Macmillan, London (1998)
37. Feltovich, P.J., Prietula, M.J., Ericsson, K.A.: Studies of expertise from psychological perspectives. In: Ericsson, K.A., Hoffman, R., Kozbelt, A., Williams, A.M. (eds.) The Cambridge Handbook of Expertise and Expert Performance, pp. 41–67. Cambridge University Press, Cambridge (2006)
38. Ericsson, K.A., Krampe, R.T., Tesch-Römer., C.: The role of deliberate practice in the acquisition of expert performance. Psychol. Rev. 100(3), 363 (1993)
39. Ericsson, K.A., Lehmann, A.C.: Expert and exceptional performance: evidence of maximal adaptation to task constraints. Ann. Rev. Psychol. 47(1), 273–305 (1996)
40. Campitelli, G., Gobet, F.: Deliberate practice: necessary but not sufficient. Current Dir. Psychol. Sci. 20(5), 280–285 (2011)
41. Lesgold, A., Rubinson, H., Feltovich, P., Glaser, R., Klopfer, D., Wang, Y.: Diagnosing x-ray pictures, Expertise in a complex skill (1988)
42. Herbig, B., Glöckner, A.: Experts and decision making: first steps towards a unifying theory of decision making in novices, intermediates and experts (2009)
43. Chase, W.G., Ericsson, K.A.: Skill and working memory. Psychol. Learn. Motiv. 16, 1–58 (1982)
44. Bottou, L.: From machine learning to machine reasoning. Mach. learn. 94(2), 133–149 (2014)
45. Sternberg, R.J.: Intelligence, wisdom, and creativity: three is better than one. Educ. Psychol. 21(3), 175–190 (1986)
46. Beni, G.: From swarm intelligence to swarm robotics. In: Şahin, E., Spears, W.M. (eds.) SR 2004. LNCS, vol. 3342, pp. 1–9. Springer, Heidelberg (2005). https://doi.org/10.1007/978-3-540-30552-1_1
47. Hämäläinen, R.P., Saarinen, E.: Systems intelligence: a key competence in human action and organizational life. Systems intelligence in leadership and everyday life, pp. 39–50 (2007)
48. Grasso, A., Convertino, G.: Collective intelligence in organizations: tools and studies. Comput. Support. Coop. Work (CSCW) 21(4–5), 357–369 (2012)
49. De Groot, A.D.: Thought and Choice in Chess, vol. 4. Walter de Gruyter GmbH & Co KG, Berlin (2014)
50. Ericsson, K.A., Charness, N.: Expert performance: its structure and acquisition. Am. Psychol. 49(8), 725 (1994)

# A Comprehensive Methodology to Implement Business Intelligence and Analytics Through Knowledge Discovery in Databases

Fernando Paulo Belfo[1]([✉]) and Alina Banca Andreica[2]

[1] Polytechnic Institute of Coimbra,
ISCAC Coimbra Business School, Coimbra, Portugal
fpbelfo@gmail.com
[2] Faculty of European Studies, Babes-Bolyai University of Cluj-Napoca,
Cluj-Napoca, Romania
alina.andreica@ubbcluj.ro

**Abstract.** Business intelligence is used by companies for analysing business information, providing not only historical or current views on business operations, but also providing predictions about the business. Consequently, knowledge discovery in databases can support the implementation of business intelligence solutions, especially in order to deal with the reality of big data, using diverse data mining techniques that can help to better prepare the data and to create improved models. The current paper proposes a methodology to implement business intelligence and analytics solutions, based on the CRISP-DM methodology, where the application of simplification and equivalence algorithms in modelling data representations can be used for improving the process of business management. This promising approach can boost business intelligence and analytics by using alternative techniques for discovering and presenting new knowledge about the business. The application of simplification and equivalence algorithms within the business context enables finding the most comprehensive or relevant knowledge, represented for instance as association rules, and bringing a real competitive advantage for the stakeholders.

**Keywords:** Business intelligence · Knowledge discovery in databases
Data mining · Equivalence algorithm · Canonical representation

## 1 Introduction

Data mining is one of the steps that compose the process of knowledge discovery in databases (KDD). Data mining can be defined as the nontrivial process of identifying valid, novel, potentially useful, and ultimately understandable patterns in stored data within structured databases. The most important problem addressed by the KDD process is the one of mapping low-level data (usually too big to easily understand) into other forms that might be more compact [1, 2].

Various economic activities have increasingly developed projects of knowledge discovery in databases to solve different problems or to provide them with previously unknown opportunities of finding solutions. Among such economic areas, we can

© Springer Nature Switzerland AG 2018
A. Groza and R. Prasath (Eds.): MIKE 2018, LNAI 11308, pp. 102–111, 2018.
https://doi.org/10.1007/978-3-030-05918-7_10

highlight examples from the financial area [3], the insurance area [4], the accommodation and catering [5], the academic area [6] or the medical field [7]. These knowledge discovery techniques helped the organizations which developed such projects to define strategies that contributed to increasing their performance.

Data mining applications are vast and implementing such techniques in business gains more and more impact. Furthermore, data mining techniques can be combined with business intelligence and analytics (BI&A).

Business intelligence (BI) encompasses the technologies and strategies that are used by companies for the data analysis of business information, providing not only historical or current views of business operations, but also providing prediction about the business. Business intelligence commonly uses technologies like data mining, text mining, process mining or complex event processing. Since the 1990's, business intelligence and analytics and the related field of big data analytics have also become increasingly important and have consequently evolved [8].

The conjunction of these two areas (data mining and business intelligence and analytics) continues to be promising. Data mining allows discovering patterns within data, like association, prediction, segmentation or sequential relationships.

Each type of these datamining tasks may use several types of techniques and popular algorithms. For example, discovering association rules (link analysis) is usually performed using an algorithm like the popular Apriory. For instance, imagine that there is a datamining project with the goal of determining certain association rules among customers, rules which contribute to better defining customer credit. In this respect, a sample of customers of a commercial bank is used. One possible association rule derived from the sample of customers used is represented below and has a confidence of 100% and a support of 36%.

$$IF\ competence\ =\ high\ AND\ personality\ =\ good\ THEN\ credit\_history\ =\ good \quad (1)$$

Yet, traditional association rules are somewhat rigid because they are anchored on the specific instances of attributes and their relations within the available business databases. Simplification and equivalence algorithms bring a more flexible perspective within the businesses realities.

The motivation behind this paper is that equivalence algorithms and canonical representation can present an interesting alternative way to help discovering and presenting more comprehensive knowledge, like enhanced association rules among businesses data. They can contribute to discovering common customer similar (and not necessarily equal) behaviours or characteristics. These operations may be performed using structured content, organized in the database management systems of companies (BI&A 1.0) or by searching web-based content, typically an unstructured content (BI&A 2.0) or by using mobile and sensor based content (BI&A 3.0) [8].

The current paper proposes the application of simplification and equivalence algorithms in modelling data representations for improving business management either at an operational, or at a tactical or strategic level. This promising approach could boost business intelligence and analytics by using alternative techniques for discovering and presenting business knowledge. We propose a specific application of equivalence algorithms within the business context in order to find the most comprehensive knowledge, like association rules, and to represent them for the stakeholders.

## 2   A Methodology to Implement Business Intelligence and Analytics

Based on the CRISP-DM methodology, an acronym for "Cross-Industry Standard Process for Data Mining" [9], we propose a methodology for implementing business intelligence and analytics that is represented on Fig. 1. Our proposal of business intelligence and analytics (BI&A) implementation has a dynamic perspective. It is based on the idea that advanced BI&A may have a model (or several models) to support the creation of novel and powerful views of business operations. This model (or models) that support the BI&A system may be implemented with the support of a KDD process (or several processes if several models are necessary). This section will explain it better.

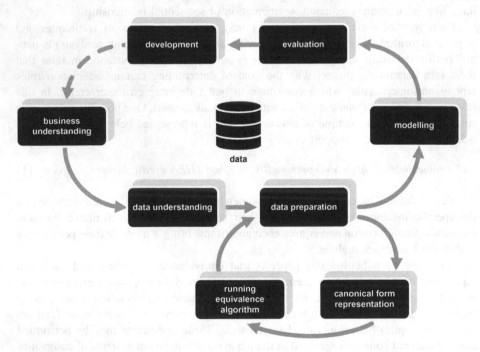

**Fig. 1.** Proposed methodology to implement business intelligence and analytics.

### 2.1   From Business Understanding to Development

Based on the CRISP-DM methodology, an acronym for "Cross-Industry Standard Process for Data Mining" [9], we propose the following methodology for implementing business intelligence and analytics - see Fig. 1. Business intelligence and analytics may be viewed as a sequence of processes including: business understanding, data understanding, capture and preparation, determining the canonical form representation and running the equivalence algorithms, data mining modelling and development, testing and evaluating the results – see Fig. 1.

As proposed within CRISP-DM methodology [9], the initial phase of this methodology focuses on understanding the project objectives and requirements from a business perspective. As this new methodology intends to support the implementation of advanced business intelligence solutions, it proposes the conversion of the knowledge into a data mining problem definition.

The second phase is the data understanding phase. It starts with an initial data collection and proceeds with activities that will help to better know the data, to identify potential quality problems within it, to discover first perceptions on data and formulate initial hypotheses.

The data preparation represents the third phase. It covers all the activities to construct the final dataset that will feed the modelling tool. Data preparation tasks are usually performed several times, whenever they are needed. The data preparation phase includes tasks like the selection of tables, records and attributes, as well as transformation and data 'cleaning'. Our methodology proposes the application of canonical representation and equivalence algorithms as a mean of obtaining improved data, which will allow obtaining enriched models. These two steps will be further explained.

The modelling phase is the next phase and uses several techniques, as further described. These techniques are selected and applied, while their parameters are calibrated to optimal values. After the data mining problem type has been defined, one or more tasks and techniques can be selected among the candidates for that type of problem. The main tasks are classification, segmentation, prediction or association. Then, one algorithm from the set of available ones should be chosen in order to perform the modelling. Usually, data preparation has to be improved, therefore, often the process should resume to that previous phase.

After building the model (or the models), it (they) should be evaluated. Within this phase it is important to carefully assess the model. The steps executed prior to the construction of the model can be reviewed in order to ensure that the business objectives are properly achieved. The main output of this phase concerns a decision regarding the use of the data mining results. If these results are satisfying, they can be further used in the development of the business intelligence solution. If not, the algorithm goes back to the modelling phase, or sometimes, even to the beginning of the project, reformulating the preliminary phases as well.

The last phase of the process is the development of the business intelligence and analytics solution. The process only ends after the knowledge that was discovered is organized and presented in a way that the customer can use it. This is the final goal of business intelligence. There are many types of organizing the way in which the data is presented to the user. It may involve applying "live" models within an organization's decision making processes, for example aggregating real-time analysis of customers' behaviour or presenting real-time and predictive analytics for the operational activity of a factory's shop floor. The choice of an adequate visualization technique is very important. For example, if the business intelligence is supported on the exploration of association rules, there are some innovative ways of doing it [10]. Figure 2 presents one of these examples.

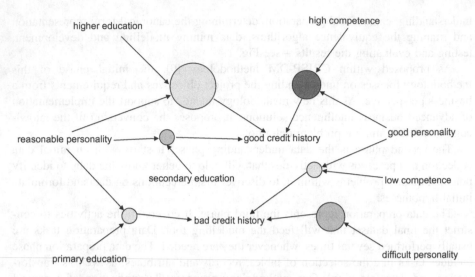

higher education

high competence

reasonable personality → good credit history

good personality

secondary education

low competence

bad credit history

primary education

difficult personality

**Fig. 2.** Graph-based visualization with items and rules as vertices.

Although the proposed methodology is inspired from the CRISP-DM, main differences concern the data preparation and the development phases of the BI&A solution. The data preparation is the step that provides this methodology with a more comprehensive approach. Data preparation will be supported by canonical form representation and running the equivalence algorithm. The development phase involves specific aspects related to the construction of an artefact like a business intelligence and analytics solution.

## 2.2 Deepening the Data Preparation and Modelling

The data mining phase consists of choosing data mining tasks and corresponding algorithms. Its tasks may belong to predictive or descriptive types. Predictive (or supervised) activities learn decision criteria in order to be able to classify unknown cases (future trends) using the knowledge acquired from a set of samples which belong to already known classes. Descriptive (or unsupervised) activities work with a set of data that does not have a given output class seeking to identify common unknown patterns in these data. The most important predictive tasks are classification, prevision and tendency analysis, while the most important descriptive tasks are clustering, association, summarization and visualization [11–14].

Let's look again at the association rule example that was previously presented in Sect. 1. Within this rule, we can observe that if the bank customer has a high competence and if the customer's personality is good, then, most probably (with a confidence of 100% and a support of 36%), this would mean that he customer has a good credit history.

Within a traditional KDD project, conducted under the CRISP-DM model, it is common that the data preparation phase includes tasks like new data construction. Yet, this construction is usually composed by very simple and direct procedures. For example, the creation of a new attribute for the age, computed using the customer's date of birth.

Within the previously presented example, the customers of the commercial bank could be previously classified with a specific personal competence that could be low, medium or high. This classification is traditionally already performed before the KDD project starts. After the data preparation phase, there should be a unique table where the chosen algorithm, for example, the Apriori algorithm, will run and using the necessary attributes.

Instead of previously defining a customer as having a high competence, the canonical form representation and the equivalence algorithm may help evaluating it. This computation will be performed within the data preparation phase, specifically within the step of constructing new data. The canonical form representation defines entities' equivalences that can help to classify old and new objects. After the canonical form representation is computed, the equivalence algorithm will run and help to define the personal competence of bank customers as low or high.

## 2.3    Canonical Form Representation

Within this section we overview the methods we propose [15, 16] for implementing equivalence algorithms at the database level for various entities and entity classes, including hierarchical structures, the entities being retained in database tables. This solution is very useful, since the volume of data that has to be processed is often very large, being consequently retained in databases.

The equivalence algorithms we have implemented are based on the theoretical framework given in [17] and the principles for representing) and processing hierarchical are presented in [16].

We have implemented post order type n-ary tree algorithms using the pointer tree representation [16] in order to parse the hierarchy of entities. We proved that the function implementing the equivalence test for two entities based on the property that they have the same canonical representative is much more efficient than the one using the definition [16].

The categories of entities and the principles for implementing equivalence algorithms on these categories are also described in [15, 16]. Intuitively, the canonical set of a category of entities may be obtained by "flattening" its category sub-tree and computing the union set of all canonical sets if its descendant leaf entities. In the case of categories of entities, the canonical representative is recursively computed [18].

In many practical cases, entity equivalences or even canonical elements have to be mapped, sometime with user assistance. In [18, 19], we address mappings and pattern matching issues. We overview here the principles proposed in this respect.

We designed pattern matching rules for equivalent entities by reducing the mapping between two elements, belonging to the two equivalence classes that are to be mapped, to mapping their canonical representatives [18, 19]. The formalization is given in [18, 19].

Intuitively, instead of dealing with the equivalence of any elements between two classes, we reduce the problem to the simpler one of dealing with the equivalence of the two classes' representatives – see Fig. 3.

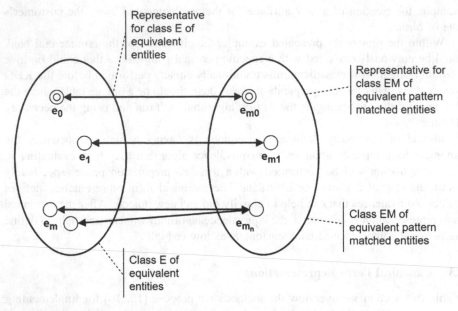

**Fig. 3.** Pattern Matching scheme for Equivalence classes [18].

The canonical set of a category of entities or events may be achieved by "flattening" its category sub-tree and computing the union set of all canonical sets of its descendant leaf entities. The process of obtaining the canonical representative of categories of entities or events is recursively computed [18, 20].

## 2.4    Principles for Building Associations and Running Equivalence Algorithm

We have previously addresses the topic of building the cloud database representation in [18, 19]. Within this section, we describe the way in which we can use a canonical for in order to perform associations within the database that is processed.

Let us suppose that in the database we have $S_1$ and $S_2$ equivalent sets of data with the canonical representation S and $S_2$ and $S_3$ equivalent sets of data that have also been mapped into the same canonical representation S, then sets $S_1$ and $S_3$ do not have to be further checked if they are equivalent, since they have the same canonical representative S. The mapping and equivalence association scheme is graphically represented in Fig. 4 [18].

Instead of using specific instances that exist on each attributes, equivalence algorithms allow to combine detailed cases on to several types of entities or events. The principles behind implementing equivalence algorithms on categories of entities [15, 16] may also be used to implement equivalence on categories of any types of information objects as entities, like customers or products, or events, like travels or purchases.

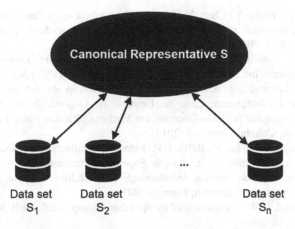

**Fig. 4.** Building the associations with the canonical representation

# 3   Conclusions

A project of knowledge discovery in databases is usually triggered by challenges or opportunities from the business environment and, to be truly effective, the business field must properly support and be supported by the information technology tools, based on the fundamental principle of business alignment with information [21, 22]. In fact, KDD projects are good examples of initiatives based on good business alignment with information technology, one of the major concerns of information technology managers in companies in recent years [23]. The equivalence algorithms and the canonical representation give the necessary flexibility to define new business concepts which can be used in order to capture more comprehensive knowledge, like enhanced association rules comparatively to the traditional approach.

The simplification and equivalence algorithms represent an opportunity of boosting business intelligence and analytics through an adequate process of knowledge discovery in databases. This paper presents a methodology to implement business intelligence and analytics solutions using the approach of knowledge discovery in databases processes and incorporating the advantages of canonical form representation and of the equivalence algorithms. Using the proposed methodology, the implementers of BI&A solutions may better prepare the data that will be used in the modelling phase and that supports the BI&A system.

# References

1. Fayyad, U., Piatetsky-Shapiro, G., Smyth, P.: From data mining to knowledge discovery in databases. AI Mag. **17**(3), 37 (1996)
2. Fayyad, U.M., Piatetsky-Shapiro, G., Smyth, P., Uthurusamy, R.: Advances in Knowledge Discovery and Data Mining. Springer, Heidelberg (1996). https://doi.org/10.1007/978-3-319-93040-4

3. Ngai, E., Hu, Y., Wong, Y., Chen, Y., Sun, X.: The application of data mining techniques in financial fraud detection: a classification framework and an academic review of literature. Decis. Support Syst. **50**(3), 559–569 (2011)
4. Azadmanesh, S., Tarokh, M.J.: Labeling customers using discovered knowledge case study: automobile industry. Int. J. Manag. Value Supply Chain. (IJMVSC) **3**(3), 13–24 (2012)
5. Loureiro, A., Lourenço, J., Costa, E., Belfo, F.: Indução de Árvores de Decisão na Descoberta de Conhecimento: Caso de Empresa de Organização de Eventos. In: VI Congresso Internacional de Casos Docentes em Marketing Público e Não Lucrativo. ISCAC Business School, Coimbra, Portugal (2014)
6. Pimenta, C., Ribeiro, R., Sá, V., Belfo, F.P.: Fatores que Influenciam o Sucesso Escolar das Licenciaturas numa Instituição de Ensino Superior Portuguesa. In: 18ª Conferência da Associação Portuguesa de Sistemas de Informação (CAPSI 2018) Associação Portuguesa de Sistemas de Informação: Santarém, Portugal (2018)
7. Cios, K.J., Moore, G.W.: Uniqueness of medical data mining. Artif. Intell. Med. **26**(1–2), 1–24 (2002)
8. Chen, H., Chiang, R.H., Storey, V.C.: Business intelligence and analytics: from big data to big impact. MIS Q. **36**, 1165–1188 (2012)
9. Chapman, P., et al.: CRISP-DM 1.0: Step-By-Step Data Mining Guide. SPSS, CRISP-DM Consortium: U.S.A (2000)
10. Hahsler, M., Chelluboina, S.: Visualizing association rules: introduction to the R-extension package arulesViz. R project module, pp. 223–238 (2011)
11. Galvão, N.D., Marin, H.D.F.: Data mining: a literature review. Acta Paulista de Enfermagem **22**(5), 686–690 (2009)
12. Berry, M.J., Linoff, G.: Data Mining Techniques: For Marketing, Sales, and Customer Support. Wiley, New York (1997)
13. Fu, Y.: Data mining: tasks, techniques, and applications. IEEE Potentials **16**(4), 18–20 (1997)
14. Kivikunnas, S.: Overview of process trend analysis methods and applications. In: ERUDIT Workshop on Applications in Pulp and Paper Industry. Citeseer (1998)
15. Andreica, A., Stuparu, D., Miu, C.: Design techniques in processing hierarchical structures at database level. In: Proceedings of Iadis Information Systems, pp. 483–488 (2010)
16. Andreica, A., Stuparu, D., Miu, C.: Applying mathematical models in software design. In: 2012 IEEE International Conference on Intelligent Computer Communication and Processing (ICCP). IEEE (2012)
17. Buchberger, B., Loos, R.: Algebraic simplification. In: Buchberger, B., Collins, G.E., Loos, R., Albrecht, R. (eds.) Computer Algebra, pp. 11–43. Springer, Vienna (1982). https://doi.org/10.1007/978-3-7091-7551-4_2
18. Andreica, A.: Designing uniform database representations for cloud data interchange services. In: Proceedings of CLOSER 2017 - 7th International Conference on Cloud Computing and Services Science, pp. 554–559 (2017)
19. Andreica, A.: Applying Equivalence Algorithms in Solving Pattern Matching Problems. Case Study for Expert System Design, p. 255. ICT, Society, and Human Beings (2016)
20. Andreica, A., Belfo, F.: Building cloud data interchange services for E-learning systems: applications on the moodle system. In: Proceedings of the 8th International Conference on Cloud Computing and Services Science (CLOSER 2018), pp. 565–572 (2018)

21. Reich, B.H., Benbasat, I.: Measuring the linkage between business and information technology objectives. MIS Q. **20**(1), 55–81 (1996)
22. Belfo, F., Sousa, R.D.: Reviewing business-IT alignment instruments under SAM dimensions. Int. J. Inf. Commun. Technol. Hum. Dev. **5**(3), 18–40 (2013)
23. Kappelman, L., et al.: The 2016 SIM IT Issues and Trends Study. MIS Q. Exec. **16**(1), 47–80 (2017)

# Categorical Modeling Method of Intelligent WorkFlow

Daniel-Cristian Crăciunean[1]([⊠]) and Dimitris Karagiannis[2]

[1] Computer Science and Electrical Engineering Department,
Lucian Blaga University of Sibiu, Sibiu, Romania
daniel.craciunean@gmail.com
[2] Faculty of Computer Science, University of Vienna, Vienna, Austria
dk@dke.univie.ac.at

**Abstract.** A category as well as a model is a mixture of graphical information and algebraic operations. Therefore, category language seems to be the most general to describe the models. It can provide us with the features that must characterize both the DSL language and the Modeling Method concept.

The theory of categories works with patterns or forms in which each of these forms describe different aspects of the real world. Category theory offers both, a language, and a lot of conceptual tools to efficiently handle models.

An important aspect of modeling is building complex functions from a given set of simple functions, using different operations on functions such as composition and repeat composition. Category theory is exactly the right algebra for such constructions.

The category theory creates the premises for the development of intelligent workflow modeling tools equipped with advanced analysis tools and automated learning mechanisms adapted to analyze and improve processes. The model allows on-line process information extraction, automatic learning from these data and self-improvement.

**Keywords:** Modeling method · Metamodel · Intelligent WorkFlow
Category theory · Categorical modeling method

## 1 Introduction

In principle, WorkFlow [12, 13] process models visually describe how organizations work. For this they use a graphical language. The grammar of the language specifies the syntax and semantics of graphical elements in a process model and the rules of combining atomic elements to obtain WorkFlow processes. Atomic graphical elements typically include at least activities, connector events, and logical flow control elements. The grammar of the modeling language specifies how atomic elements can be composed to model real-world domains in such a language [10, 12].

In this paper we will use the language provided by the category theory to formalize the modeling method [2, 3] concept appropriately adapted to the WorkFlow models. The category theory provides a graphical language as a metametamodel to specify metamodels.

© Springer Nature Switzerland AG 2018
A. Groza and R. Prasath (Eds.): MIKE 2018, LNAI 11308, pp. 112–126, 2018.
https://doi.org/10.1007/978-3-030-05918-7_11

Using such a formalism to specify the concept of modeling method has a number of major advantages. First, formalization requires a precise definition without ambiguity, contradictions or uncertainties. Defining models as functors in category theory allows the definition of some functors to translate them from one metamodel to another. Also, formalism specifies all metamodels in the same metametamodel and thus creates the prerequisites for the unitary integration of all specified metamodels. This is closely related to the fact that the metametamodel allows the sharing of mechanisms and algorithms by the metamodels (for performance analysis, for example, as well as for logical verification).

Due to the very large diversity of real world processes, it is impossible for an existing metamodel of a process to be well aligned in all cases. This problem is often solved by endlessly adding new facilities to existing metamodels to cover the modeling requirements of processes that were not foreseen in the initial phase. Obviously, these additions lead to complicated metamodels, difficult to understand and difficult to learn by those who are going to use them.

Hence the need to build specific metamodels for each domain that are totally compatible with the specific processes of a given field. In order to keep up with the expectations of information technology, appropriate modeling tools are needed, so that processes can be clearly defined and analyzed. Unambiguous definition of WorkFlow processes when designing, provides a very important guarantee that they will work correctly.

A process consists of a set of tasks that need to be fulfilled if certain conditions that determine the order of accomplishment of tasks are met. The developing and the diversity of software systems makes it impossible to manage all the processes involved in an organization's activity with a single software system. To manage all of the organization's specific activities, a variety of systems from a variety of vendors is needed, complemented by customized subsystems.

Therefore, there is a need for an explicit level of the system that assembles the system components and directs the objects (documents) that need to be processed from one workplace to another. This explicit level is called WorkFlow [12, 13]. A meta-model of this level relies heavily on graphical features offered to define WorkFlow.

The definition of a WorkFlow is divided into two important parts: defining the process and allocating resources. In addition to tools for defining workflows, we also often have analytical tools available in the context of WorkFlow management. In principle, we can distinguish three types of tools: process definition tools, resource allocation tools, and analysis tools. In a series of workflow management systems, these three tools are integrated into a single workflow definition and analysis tool [12, 13].

## 2   Theoretical Foundations and Notes

**Definition 1.** [5, 7] A category $C$ is defined as follows: We consider a collection of objects A, B, .. X, Y, Z, ... which we denote by ob($C$) and we call it the set of objects of $C$. For each pair of objects (X, Y) of $C$, we consider a set of arrows from X to Y denoted by $C$(X, Y). On the set of arrows we consider a composing operator denoted by ∘, which attaches to each pair of arrows (f, g) of the form: f:X→Y, g:Y→Z a morphology g∘f: X→Z and respecting the axioms 1 and 2.

1. The composition is associative:

$$\text{If } f:X→Y, g:Y→Z \text{ şi } h:Z→W \Rightarrow (h∘g)∘f=h∘(g∘f):X→W.$$

2. For each object X, there is the identity arrow $id_X:X→X$ with the property that $id_X ∘ f = f$, $g ∘ id_X = g$ for all pairs of arrows $f : X → Y$ and $g : U → X$.

**Definition 2.** [7, 9] Let $\mathcal{C}$ and $\mathcal{D}$ be two categories, a functor $\phi$ from $\mathcal{C}$ to $\mathcal{D}$ consists of the functions: $\phi_{ob} : ob(\mathcal{C}) → ob(\mathcal{D})$, and for each pair of objects A, B of $\mathcal{C}$ we have the functions: $\phi_{A,B} : \mathcal{C}(A,B) → \mathcal{D}(\phi(A), \phi(B))$ which fulfills the following conditions:

$$\phi(1_A)=1_{\phi(A)}, \phi(fg) = \phi f \phi g \text{ if } A_1 \xrightarrow{f} A_2 \xrightarrow{g} A_3.$$

Typically, all functions $\phi_{ob}$, $\phi_{A,B}$ are denoted by the $\phi$ symbol, for simplicity.

Categories and functors are a category, Cat. In Cat, categories are objects and functors are arrows (functions).

**Definition 3.** [7, 9] Let $\phi$, $\psi$ be functors from category $\mathcal{C}$ to category $\mathcal{D}$. A morphism from $\phi$ to $\psi$, also called natural transformation, is a family of arrows in $\mathcal{D}$: $\tau A:\phi A→\psi A$ (A∈ $\mathcal{C}$). So, for any arrow f:A → B in $\mathcal{C}$, we have $(\psi f)∘\tau A = \tau B∘(\phi f)$. This condition is called the naturality condition.

The concept of graph is a precursor to the category concept itself: a category is a graph in which paths can be composed. We notice that there are no compositions in graphs. This is the essential difference between graphs and categories. But, having a graph $\mathcal{G}$, we can form a category generated by $\mathcal{G}$ called the free category on $\mathcal{G}$. Free category objects are the same as $\mathcal{G}$. Arrows from object A to object B are arched paths from A to B with appropriate domains and codomains. The composition is the concatenation of the paths. Identities are the void path.

**Definition 4.** [7, 8] Let $\mathcal{P}$ and $\mathcal{G}$ be two graphs. A diagram in graph $\mathcal{G}$ of the graph $\mathcal{P}$ is a graph homomorphism D:→$\mathcal{G}$. $\mathcal{P}$ is called the shape graph of the diagram D.

A graph homomorphism extends uniquely to a functor between the free categories generated by the two graphs, so diagrams in the sense of graph homomorphisms generate diagrams in the sense of functors. In this idea for simplifying the approach, we will use the term functor also when its domains are graphs.

**Definition 5.** [7, 8] Let $\mathcal{P}$ and $\mathcal{G}$ be two graphs. A diagram in $\mathcal{G}$ of the $\mathcal{P}$ graph is a functor: D : $\mathcal{P} → \mathcal{G}$. $\mathcal{P}$ is called the shape graph of the diagram D.

**Definition 6.** [7, 8] Let $\mathcal{G}$ be a graph and $\mathcal{C}$ a category. Let D:→$\mathcal{C}$ be a diagram in $\mathcal{C}$ with the form $\mathcal{G}$ and $\Delta\mathcal{C}:\mathcal{G}→\mathcal{C}$ be a constant functor (which maps all objects in C and all arcs in idC). A commutative cone with base D and vertex C is a natural transformation p:$\Delta$C → D.

**Definition 7.** The set of cones along with the morphisms between them form a category that we call the category of cones.

The categorical product of two objects is a limit of a diagram generated by a simple shape with two vertices and no arcs. The terminal object of a category is the limit of a diagram with an empty base.

The limit in Set of the diagram $A \xrightarrow{f} C \xleftarrow{g} B$ is the pullback of set A with set B over set C. We have the following useful result for modeling: A morphism f:A $\rightarrow$ B is a monomorphism if and only if the pullback of f and f exists and it is A.

**Definition 8.** [7, 8] Let $\mathcal{G}$ be a graph and $\mathcal{C}$ a category. Let D: $\mathcal{G} \rightarrow \mathcal{C}$ be a diagram in $\mathcal{C}$ with the shape $\mathcal{G}$ and $\Delta_C$: $\rightarrow \mathcal{C}$ constant functor (which maps all objects in C and all arcs in id$_C$). A commutative cocone with base D and vertex C is a natural transformation p:D $\rightarrow \Delta_C$.

**Definition 9.** The set of cocones along with the morphisms between them form a category we call the category of cocones.

**Definition 10.** An initial object (cocone) in the category of cocones, if any, is called colimit of diagram D. This colimit is also called the universal cocone.

The coproduct of two objects in the Set category is a colimit of a simple diagram with two vertices and no arcs.

The colimit of the diagram $A \xleftarrow{f} C \xrightarrow{g} B$ is the pushout of A with B over C. Pushout is the dual concept of pullback and can characterize epimorphisms. A morphism f: A $\rightarrow$ B is an epimorphism if and only if the pushout of f and f exists and is B.

**Definition 11.** [7, 8] A sketch $S = (\mathcal{G}, \mathcal{D}, \mathcal{L}, \mathcal{K})$ consists of a graph $\mathcal{G}$, a set $\mathcal{D}$ of diagrams in $\mathcal{G}$, a set $\mathcal{L}$ of cones in $\mathcal{G}$, and a set $\mathcal{K}$ of cocones in $\mathcal{G}$. The graph arrows of a sketch are often called sketch operations.

**Definition 12.** [7, 8] A model of a sketch $S = (\mathcal{G}, \mathcal{D}, \mathcal{L}, \mathcal{K})$ is a functor M from $\mathcal{G}$ to Set that takes each diagram from $\mathcal{D}$ to a commutative diagram in Set, each cone from $\mathcal{L}$ to a cone limit and every cocone from $\mathcal{K}$ to a colimit cocone.

We will denote with numbers the nodes of the shape graph, with lowercase letters the nodes of the graph of sketches and with uppercase letters, the objects of the categories.

# 3 Categorical Sketch of the WorkFlow Modeling Method

A modeling method is a concept [1, 3] that consists of two components: (1) a modeling technique, which is divided in a modeling language and a modeling procedure, and (2) mechanisms & algorithms working on the models described by a modeling language. The modeling language contains the elements with which a model can be described. The modeling procedure describes the steps applying the modeling language to create results, i.e., models. Algorithms and mechanisms provide functionality to use and evaluate models described by a modeling language. Combining these functionalities enables the structural analysis, as well as simulation of models. The formal specification of the modeling method concept inevitably involves the concept of multilevel modeling.

So, essentially, a graphic model of a WorkFlow is a graph in which we have as vertices (objects) different concepts (activities, tasks, connectors, gateways) and the arcs indicate the routing of the cases modeled by the process in question [4].

A workflow model is essentially a graph $G = (X,\Gamma,\sigma,\theta)$ where X is a set of objects representing the vertices of the graph, $\Gamma$ is a set of arcs and $\sigma$ and $\theta$ are functions $\sigma,\theta : \Gamma \to X$ which assigns to each arc $r \in \Gamma$ the source and target objects $\sigma(r),\theta(r) \in X$.

We will see that the sketch is an easy mechanism in category theory for specifying metamodels. In fact, category theory has all the facilities necessary to organize and hierarchize structures. Sketches are not designed as a notation, but as a mathematical structure that incorporates an exact formal syntax and semantics [7, 8].

Not any graph that has the nodes made of activities, events and gateways is a correct WorkFlow model. For example, the graph must be connected and may not have more than one arc between two elements, etc.

From our point of view, the static part of a WorkFlow model is a graph with some syntactic restrictions. These restrictions will then be introduced into the sketch of a modeling method metamodel based on mechanisms specific to the category theory such as commutative diagrams, limits and colimits.

**Example 1.** We consider a modeling method SMM (Simple Modeling Method) that has the following concepts:

A deposit $W_1$ where we can store one type of part:
Notation: circle Attributes: stock, capacity.
A deposit $W_2$ where we can store two type of parts:
Notation: rectangle; Attributes: stock1, stock2, capacity1, capacity2.
A processing or transfer activity from $W_1$ to $W_2$:
Notation: arrow; Attributes: Stock1Out, Stock2Out, StockIn.
A processing or transfer activity from $W_2$ to $W_1$:
Notation: arrow different from the previous arrow; Attributes: Stock1In, Stock2In, StockOut.

By the end of the paper we will build a modeling tool for such WorkFlow processes. We start by defining the metamodel: A SMM model is a directed graph $G = (X,\Gamma,\sigma,\theta)$ that satisfies the following properties:

1. G is a bipartite graph: $X = W_1 \cup W_2$ ;
2. $\Gamma$ is a set of arcs partitioned into two subsets $\Gamma = \Gamma_{12} \cup \Gamma_{21}$;
3. $\sigma,\theta : \Gamma \to X$ are functions that associate to an arc, a source and a target. We will use the following notations: $\sigma_{12} = \sigma/\Gamma_{12}$, $\sigma_{21} = \sigma/\Gamma_{21}$, $\theta_{12} = \theta/\Gamma_{12}$, $\theta_{21} = \theta/\Gamma_{21}$;
4. G is a connected graph
5. There is only one arc between any two vertices.

Let's build the sketch corresponding to SMM. We obviously start from the general sketch corresponding to a directed multigraph with loops (Fig. 1) and introduce the restrictions in the SMM definition from above.

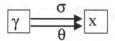

**Fig. 1.** Multigraph sketch

1. G is a bipartite graph: $X = W_1 \cup W_2$. That is, the set of objects X is the disjoint union of two subsets of object $W_1$ and $W_2$. This means that X is the coproduct of a discrete diagram formed by two nodes and with the vertex X, which in Set will become the colimit of this discrete diagram. This discrete diagram is reflected in the graph of the sketch as in Fig. 2.
2. $\Gamma$ is a set of arcs divided into two subsets $\Gamma = \Gamma_{12} \cup \Gamma_{21}$. Therefore, the set of arcs $\Gamma$ is the disjoint union of the two subsets of arcs $\Gamma_{12}$ and $\Gamma_{21}$. This means that $\Gamma$ is the coproduct of a discrete diagram formed by two nodes. Thus the sketch will contain the subgraph from Fig. 3.
3. $\sigma, \theta : \Gamma \to X$ are functions that associate to an arc, a source and a target. The additional notations $\sigma_{12}$, $\sigma_{21}$, $\theta_{12}$ and $\theta_{21}$ will also be reflected in the graph of the sketch because they are operators of the sketch. The sketch will contain Fig. 4.
4. G is a connected graph. For this we will put the condition that the pushout of s with t to be a terminal object in the Set category. That is, the colimit of the diagram from Fig. 5. is a terminal object in Set.
5. There is only one arc between any two nodes. To impose this constraint we will build the $X \times X$ product. This is the limit of a discrete diagram formed by two nodes. The graph of the sketch must contain the subgraph from Fig. 6. The condition that is required in this commutative diagram to have no more than one arc between any two nodes is that the function $\mu$ becomes a monomorphism in Set. But $\mu$ is a monomorphism if and only if the pullback of $\mu$ with $\mu$ exists and is equal to $\Gamma$. That is, the diagram from Fig. 7. is a pullback diagram.

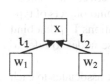

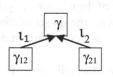

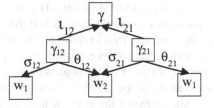

**Fig. 2.** Object classification diagram

**Fig. 3.** Arc classification diagram

**Fig. 4.** Additional notations diagram

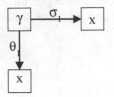

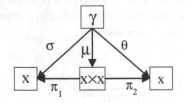

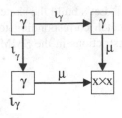

**Fig. 5.** Pushout of $\theta 1$ with $\sigma 1$

**Fig. 6.** Commutative diagram

**Fig. 7.** Pullback diagram

We have seen that a sketch $S = (\mathcal{G}, \mathcal{D}, \mathcal{L}, \mathcal{K})$ consists of a graph $\mathcal{G}$, a set $\mathcal{D}$ of diagrams in $\mathcal{G}$, a set $\mathcal{L}$ of cones in $\mathcal{G}$, and a set $\mathcal{K}$ of cocones in $\mathcal{G}$. We have presented the graph in several images to be more suggestive, but it can be presented as a common graph as in Fig. 8. A model of this graph in the Set category is a functor that maps the graph nodes in sets and the arcs in functions (sketch operators).

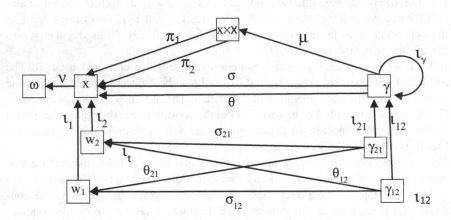

**Fig. 8.** The graph of SMM sketch

Graph $\mathcal{G}$ has 8 nodes and 15 arrows. These will be interpreted in a model as follows: (1) x - all X in a SMM model; (2) $w_1$ - all objects $W_1$ in a SMM model; (3) $w_2$ - all objects $W_2$ in a SMM model; (4) x × x - the cartesian product of the set X with X; (5) $\omega$ represents a terminal object in Set; (6) $\gamma$ - represents all relations $\Gamma$ between the objects of the model; (7) $\gamma_{12}$ - represents the subset of the relations $\Gamma_{12}$ that bind objects of type $w_1$ with objects of type $w_2$; (8) $\gamma_{21}$ - represents the subset of the relations $\Gamma_{21}$ that bind objects of type $w_2$ with objects of type $w_1$. We have numbered these nodes to refer to them in the shape graph of the diagrams.

The arrows of the graph will be interpreted as follows: $\sigma:\Gamma \rightarrow X$ associates to each relation the source node; $\theta:\Gamma \rightarrow X$ associates to each relation the target node; $\iota_\gamma:\Gamma \rightarrow \Gamma$ represents the identity function on the set $\Gamma$; $\iota_2:W_2 \rightarrow X$ inclusion of $W_2$ in X; $\iota_1:W_1 \rightarrow X$ inclusion of $W_1$ in X; $\sigma_{12}:\Gamma_{12} \rightarrow W_1$ associates to each relation from $\Gamma_{12}$ the source node from $W_1$; $\theta_{12}:\Gamma_{12} \rightarrow W_2$ associates to each relation from $\Gamma_{12}$ the target node from $W_2$; $\sigma_{21}:\Gamma_{21} \rightarrow W_2$ associates to each relation from $\Gamma_{21}$ the source node from $W_2$; $\theta_{21}:\Gamma_{21} \rightarrow W_1$ associates to each relation from $\Gamma_{21}$ the target node from $W_1$; $\iota_{12}:\Gamma_{12} \rightarrow \Gamma$ is the inclusion of $\Gamma_{12}$ in $\Gamma$; $\iota_{21}:\Gamma_{21} \rightarrow \Gamma$ is the inclusion of $\Gamma_{21}$ in $\Gamma$; $\mu:\Gamma \rightarrow X \times X$ associates to each relation from $\Gamma$ a pair of objects from the Cartesian product $X \times X$; $\pi_1:X \times X \rightarrow X$ projection of $X \times X$ after the first component; $\pi_2:X \times X \rightarrow X$ projection of $X \times X$ after the second component; $\nu:X \rightarrow \omega$ associates to each object in $X$ its class of equivalence in Set.

The constraints will be imposed by commutative diagrams, cones and cocones [7] as follows.

1. The sketch will contain the following commutative diagrams:

The condition that a model does not contain more than one arrow between two objects is ensured by the injectivity of a function $\mu:\Gamma \rightarrow X \times X$. Defining the function $\mu$ can be done by the commutativity of the diagram $D_1$ defined in Fig. 6. The shape graph of this diagram is in Fig. 9. The functor $d_1$ is defined as follows: $d_1(6) = \gamma$; $d_1(1) = x$; $d_1(4) = x \times x$; $d_1(1') = x$; $d_1(\sigma) = \sigma$ ; $d_1(\theta) = \theta$; $d_1(\mu) = \mu$; $d_1(\pi_1) = \pi_1$; $d_1(\pi_2) = \pi_2$.

2. The set L of cones consists of the following:

The node denoted by $x \times x$ in the graph of the sketch will have to become the Cartesian product $X \times X$ in the Set category. For this, it will have to be the limit of the discrete diagram with the shape graph given by nodes 1 and 1'. The functor $l_1$ corresponding to this diagram will be defined as: $l_1(1) = x$; $l_1(1') = x$, and $X \times X$ will be the limit of this discrete diagram, i.e. the Cartesian product $X \times X$.

The node denoted with $\omega$ in the graph will become the limit of a cone with an empty base, i.e. a terminal object from Set.

At point (v) the pullback of $\mu$ with $\mu$ is the limit of the diagram from Fig. 7. The shape graph of this diagram is in Fig. 10 and the functor $l_2$ corresponding to this diagram is defined as: $l_2(6) = \gamma$; $l_2(6') = \gamma$; $l_2(4) = x \times x$; $l_2(\mu) = \mu$. The limit of this diagram in the Set category will have to be $\Gamma$.

3. The set of cocones consists of the following:

At point (i) $X = W_1 \cup W_2$, i.e. X is the colimit of the discrete diagram formed by the nodes $w_1$ and $w_2$. The shape graph of this diagram is made up of nodes 3 and 2 and the functor $k_1$ corresponding to this diagram is defined as: $k_1(3) = w_1$; $k_1(2) = w_2$. Therefore, the node denoted with x in the graph of the sketch will become in the Set category the set X of all objects involved in the model and will be the colimit to this discrete diagram, i.e. the disjunctive union of the $W_1$ and $W_2$ sets.

At point (ii) $\Gamma = \Gamma_{12} \cup \Gamma_{21}$, i.e. X is the colimit of the discrete diagram formed by nodes $\Gamma_{12}$ and $\Gamma_{21}$. The shape graph of this diagram is made up of nodes 7 and 8 and the functor $k_2$ corresponding to this diagram is defined as: $k_2(7) = \gamma_{12}$; $k_2(8) = \gamma_{21}$. Therefore, the node denoted with $\gamma$ in the graph of the sketch will become in the Set category the set $\Gamma$ which will be the colimit of this discrete diagram.

At point (iv) the pushout of $\sigma$ with $\theta$ is the colimit of the diagram from Fig. 5. The condition that this colimit is a terminal object in Set assures us that the graph G is connected. The shape graph of this diagram is in Fig. 11 and the functor $k_3$ corresponding to these diagram is defined as follows: $k_3(6) = \gamma$; $k_3(1) = x$; $k_3(1') = x$; $k_3(\sigma) = \sigma$; $k_3(\theta) = \theta$.

So we've got the sketch of a SMM, we denote it with $L^1(\text{SMM}) = (\mathcal{G}, \mathcal{D}, \mathcal{L}, \mathcal{K})$.

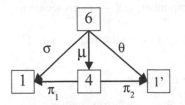

**Fig. 9.** The shape graph of the commutative diagram

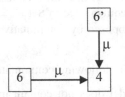

**Fig. 10.** The shape graph of the pullback diagram

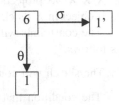

**Fig. 11.** The shape graph of the pushout diagram

## 4   The Metamodel

A model M of a sketch $L^1 = (\mathcal{G}, \mathcal{D}, \mathcal{L}, \mathcal{K})$ in the Set category is a functor from $\mathcal{G}$ to Set that takes each diagram in $\mathcal{D}$ to a commutative diagram, each cone in $\mathcal{L}$ to a cone limit and each cocone in $\mathcal{K}$ to a cocone colimit. From the way we constructed the sketch $L^1(\text{SMM})$, it follows that any sketch $L^1(\text{SMM})$ in Set is a SMM, and any SMM can be represented by a model of this sketch. The sketch is the formal object that specifies a metamodel and contains all the necessary semantics for expressing the syntax restrictions from the definition of the metamodel.

The sketch $L^1$ is the basic sketch of a modeling method. The nodes of this sketch represent the types of objects that can be defined in this modeling method as well as the types of relations that can be defined between these objects in this modeling method and the arcs are the sketch operators.

Therefore these concepts will have to be represented in the modeling tool on PaletteDrawers to be used when visually building a model. Therefore we consider a model $\phi$ of the sketch $L^1$, $\phi : L^1 \rightarrow$ Sets which associates to each class (node) from $L^1$ with an instance of that class. These objects will be put into PaletteDrawers for use when visually building a model. In PaletteDrawers are only the necessary entities for use when visually building a model.

**Example 2.** For Example 1, in sketch $L^1(\text{SMM})$ the basic concepts that will be put in the PaletteDrawers for use when visually building a model will have the type indicated by the vertex of the sketch from Fig. 8. PaletteDrawers will contain only the following entities: $\phi(w_1)$, $\phi(w_2)$, $\phi(\gamma_{12})$ and $\phi(\gamma_{21})$. Therefore, PaletteDrawers will be populated with four elements, one instance of each node of the $L^1$ sketch.

Any model of the sketch $L^1 = (\mathcal{G}, \mathcal{D}, \mathcal{L}, \mathcal{K})$ is a concrete model that complies with the conditions imposed by the sketch $L^1$. To construct such a model, it is sufficient to consider a model $H^2 : L^1 \rightarrow$ Sets that associates the classes (nodes) in the sketch $L^1$ with sets of extensions of these classes.

**Example 3.** For Example 1, the model $H^2 : L^1 \to$ Sets becomes: $H^2(w_1) = W_1$ is the set of all extensions of type $w_1$ in a SMM model; $H^2(w_2) = W_2$ is the set of all extensions of type $w_2$ in a SMM model; $H^2(\gamma_{12}) = \Gamma_{12}$ represents the subset of relations $\Gamma_{12}$; $H^2(\gamma_{21}) = \Gamma_{21}$ represents the subset of relations $\Gamma_{21}$; The other objects and arcs of the sketch are useful for imposing constraints on the model. The arrows of the graph will be interpreted as functions with the same name as the domains corresponding to the model image $H^2$.

Let $H_i^2$ and $H_j^2$ be two models of the sketch $L^1$ defined as above. Then we can define a natural transformation $\tau : H_i^2 \to H_j^2$. It is obvious that there isn't always a natural transformation between two models and it is equally obvious that there are models among which we have such transformations.

Therefore, the set of models $H_k^2$, $k \geq 0$ together with the natural transformations between models form a category that we call the modeling method category. Each object in this category is a modeling method. The next level of refining leads to instances of these models that can be executed (see Sect. 6).

## 5 The Metametamodel

The sketch $L^1$ will be constructed as a model of a metametamodel represented by the sketch $L^0$ from Fig. 12. We now define a model $H^1 : L^0 \to$ Sets that associates classes (nodes) in $L^0$ with sets of extensions of these classes. The model $H^1$ is composed of two applications $H_0^1$ and $H_1^1$ and has as image of $H_0^1$ a pair of sets $E_R^1$, $E_C^1$ and as image of the application $H_1^1$ two functions $s^1$ and $t^1$ defined as follows: $H_0^1(R) = E_R^1$; $H_0^1(C) = E_C^1$; $H_1^1(t) = t^1$; $H_1^1(s) = s^1$;

**Example 4.** For Example 1, the model $H^1 : L^0 \to$ Sets becomes: $E_C^1 = \{x, w_1, w_2, x \times x, \gamma, \gamma_{12}, \gamma_{21}, \omega\}$ is a set of extensions of class C, and $E_R^1 = \{\sigma, \theta, \iota_p, \iota_t, \sigma_{12}, \theta_{12}, \sigma_{21}, \theta_{21}, \iota_{12}, \iota_{21}, \mu, \pi_1, \pi_2, \nu, \iota_\Gamma\}$ is a set of extensions of class R.

The function $s^1$ associates each extension of type R with an extension of type C called source and the function $t^1$ associates each extension of type R with an extension of type C called target: $s^1(\sigma) = \gamma$, $t^1(\sigma) = x$; $s^1(\theta) = \gamma$, $t^1(\theta) = x$; $s^1(\iota_2) = w_2$, $t^1(\iota_2) = x$; $s^1(\iota_1) = w_1$, $t^1(\iota_1) = x$; $s^1(\sigma_{12}) = \gamma_{12}$, $t^1(\sigma_{12}) = w_1$; $s^1(\theta_{12}) = \gamma_{12}$, $t^1(\theta_{12}) = w_2$; $s^1(\sigma_{21}) = \gamma_{21}$, $t^1(\sigma_{21}) = w_2$; $s^1(\theta_{21}) = \gamma_{12}$, $t^1(\theta_{21}) = w_1$; $s^1(\iota_{12}) = \gamma_{12}$, $t^1(\iota_{12}) = \gamma$; $s^1(\iota_{21}) = \gamma_{21}$, $t^1(\iota_{21}) = \gamma$; $s^1(\mu) = \gamma$, $t^1(\mu) = x \times x$; $s^1(\pi_1) = x \times x$, $t^1(\pi_1) = x$; $s^1(\pi_2) = x \times x$, $t^1(\pi_2) = x$; $s^1(\nu) = x$, $t^1(\nu) = \omega$; $s^1(\iota_\gamma) = \gamma$, $t^1(\iota_\gamma) = \gamma$.

If we consider $E_C^1$ and $E_R^1$ as a set of arcs then the $H^1$ model can be represented as a graph that has as nodes extensions of class C and as arcs extensions of class R, i.e. exactly sketch $L^1$. The graph of the sketch is that from Fig. 8.

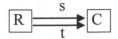

**Fig. 12.** The sketch of the metametamodel

## 6  The Dynamic Behavior of a WorkFlow Model

The dynamic behavior of a WorkFlow model over time is accomplished by executing the component activities. The simulation begins with a message which initializes the process with the data describing its initial state. The dynamics of the process is accomplished through the succession of activities being executed.

The behavior of the model is based on the state idea, determined by the values of the variables. The resulting values influence the execution of the commands, which in turn will lead to changes in the state.

All of these relations are transition relations or transition systems, where variables are states and relations express transitions or state changes. Thus, in the model of the transition systems, if we replace the states with state vectors of the system and the atomic actions with set of activities, we obtain the modeling from the WorkFlow.

The transitions will look like $(V^1, p, V^2)$ where $V^1$ is the state vector of the system before the transition, $V^2$ is the state vector of the system at the end of the transition, and p is a set of activities to be executed. In practice, we also use transitions of the form $(E^1, p, E^2)$ where p represents a set of functions as above, $E^1$ is a set of events that trigger the execution of the functions p and $E^2$ is a set of events produced by the execution of these functions.

On the other hand, executing a set of activities changes an instance of the model by turning it into another instance. As a result, we will use transitions of the form $(\mathfrak{I}^1, p, \mathfrak{I}^2)$ where $\mathfrak{I}^1$ is the instance of the model before the execution of the functions p and $\mathfrak{I}^2$ is the instance of the same model after executing the functions p.

Let $H^2$ be a model of the sketch $L^1$, defined as above, i.e. an object of the modeling method category. We denote with $L^2$ this model $L^2 = H^2(L^1)$. The $L^2$ model represents a concrete system. The object X of this model is a set of concepts of the concrete system. The object $\Gamma$ is a set of types of relations that can be defined between these entities. That is, $L^2$ contains all types of objects specific to the considered metamodel. The syntactic constraints imposed on the model are contained in the other components of the $L^1$ sketch, i.e. the commutative diagrams, the cones and the cocones.

**Example 5.** Referring to Example 1, to create the instances of the model $L^2$, it is sufficient to limit ourselves to the elements in the subsketch which contain all the necessary information to use the model and which are: $W_1, W_2, \Gamma_{12}$ and $\Gamma_{21}$. The other objects and arcs of the sketch are useful for imposing the syntactic constraints on the model.

If in the above model we have: $W_1 = \{W_{11}, W_{12}, W_{13}\}; W_2 = \{W_{21}, W_{22}\};$ $\Gamma_{12} = \{\Gamma_{12}^1, \Gamma_{12}^2\}; \ \Gamma_{21} = \{\Gamma_{21}^1, \Gamma_{21}^2, \Gamma_{21}^3\}; \ \sigma_{12} : \Gamma_{12} \to D_1$ where $\sigma_{12}(\Gamma_{12}^1) = D_{11};$ $\sigma_{12}(\Gamma_{12}^2) = D_{12}; \theta_{12} : \Gamma_{12} \to D_2$ where $\theta_{12}(\Gamma_{12}^1) = D_{22}; \theta_{12}(\Gamma_{12}^2) = D_{22}; \sigma_{21} : \Gamma_{21} \to$ $D_2$ where $\sigma_{12}(\Gamma_{21}^1) = D_{21}; \ \sigma_{12}(\Gamma_{21}^2) = D_{21}; \ \sigma_{12}(\Gamma_{21}^3) = D_{22}$ and $\theta_{21} : \Gamma_{21} \to D_1$ where $\theta_{12}(\Gamma_{21}^1) = D_{11}; \theta_{12}(\Gamma_{21}^2) = D_{12}; \theta_{12}(\Gamma_{21}^3) = D_{13}$ then the SMM model is like in Fig. 13.

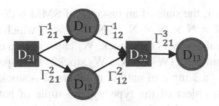

**Fig. 13.** SMM Example

We consider an instance functor $\phi$ defined on such a model with values in the Set category: $\phi : L^2 \to$ Sets, which associates to each set of classes in $L^2$ a set of instances, that is, each class will be replaced by one instance of it. The instances differ from one another by the values of the attributes, i.e. by the state of each instance.

If we have two models $\phi, \psi : L^2 \to$ Sets then we can define a natural transformation $\tau : \phi \to \psi$. The set of all instances together with all the natural transformations between them form a category that we call the category of instances and natural transformations of the model $L^2$ and we denote it with CIT. We notice that in this case, natural transformations become functors, i.e. transform objects into objects and arcs into arcs while retaining the structure.

The execution semantics of the WorkFlow models are defined based on execution rules assigned to each atomic construct of the language. The state of a WorkFlow model is characterized by the values of the attributes. The dynamic behavior of a system is represented by state changes caused by the execution of activities according to the model control flow based on execution rules specific to each type of object. The WorkFlow model semantics specifies the execution rules for different atomic entities for each WorkFlow node type.

If the state $V'$ is obtained from $V$ by applying the execution rules of the model, then we say that between $V$ and $V'$ there is a simple derivation relation from $V$ to $V'$ and we denote this with $V \Rightarrow V'$. The reflexive and transitive closure of this relation is denoted with $V \overset{*}{\Rightarrow} V'$.

If we now consider that each instance has a global state specified by the vector $V_k$, then an execution of the WorkFlow model is a path in the CIT category, i.e. a sequence of natural transformations of the form: $\mathfrak{I}_0 \overset{\tau^0}{\to} \mathfrak{I}_1 \overset{\tau^1}{\to} \dots \mathfrak{I}_n \overset{\tau^n}{\to} \dots$, where for every step $\mathfrak{I}_k \overset{\tau^k}{\to} \mathfrak{I}_{k+1}$, where $\mathfrak{I}_k$ has the global state $V_k$ and $\mathfrak{I}_{k+1}$ has the global state $V_{k+1}$, there is a simple derivation relation $V_k \Rightarrow V_{k+1}$. In other words, the natural transformation $\tau^k$ is equivalent to the execution of a set of entities of the model.

An execution of a model is a path in CIT and it can be defined as a functor as follows. We consider the category $\Omega$ which looks like this: $\Omega : 0 \overset{\alpha_0}{\to} 1 \overset{\alpha_1}{\to} \dots k \overset{\alpha_k}{\to} \dots$ Then there is a functor $\Phi : \Omega \to$ CIT defined as follows: $\Phi(i) = \mathfrak{I}_i$ for all $i \geq 0$; $\Phi(\alpha_i) = \tau^i$ for all $i \geq 0$; Therefore, an execution of a model is a functor $\Phi : \Omega \to$ CIT.

The CIT category represents the admissible routes of a process. As a result, the CIT category allows for the timely retrieval of information from process routing, extracting value from these data, and then using it to make forecasts or automate process improvement [11].

**Example 6.** In Example 1, the state of an instance of SMM is defined by a function V: $X \cup \Gamma \to N \times N \cup N \times N \times N \times N \cup N \times N \times N$ which assigns to each object of type $w_1$ a pair of natural numbers ($W_1$.stock, $W_1$.capacity), to each object of the type $w_2$ a 4-tuple of natural numbers ($W_2$.stock1, $W_2$.stock2, $W_2$.capacity1, $W_2$.capacity2), to each object of type $\gamma_{12}$ a 3-tuple of natural numbers ($\Gamma_{12}$.stock1Out, $\Gamma_{12}$.stock2Out, $\Gamma_{12}$.stockIn) and to each object of the type $\gamma_{21}$ a 3-tuple of natural numbers ($\Gamma_{21}$.stock1In, $\Gamma_{21}$.stock2IN, $\Gamma_{21}$.stockOut).

If we order the objects entirely by their identifiers such as $[W_{11}, W_{12}, W_{13}, W_{21}, W_{22}, \Gamma_{12}^1, \Gamma_{12}^2, \Gamma_{21}^1, \Gamma_{21}^2, \Gamma_{21}^3]$ then V = $[D_{11}$.State, $D_{12}$.State, $D_{13}$.State, $D_{21}$.State, $D_{22}$.State, $\Gamma_{12}^1$.State, $\Gamma_{12}^2$.State, $\Gamma_{21}^1$.State, $\Gamma_{21}^2$.State, $\Gamma_{21}^3$.State].

Therefore, a functor $\phi : L^2 \to$Sets will create an instance of $L^2$ that will have a certain state represented by such a vector V.

The SMM metamodel was implemented in MM-DSL then translated and executed in ADOxx. In Fig. 14. we can see a screen capture from the SMM modeling tool (the metamodel of Example 4) in which we built the graphic model in Example 5 (Fig. 13) that we executed and it works.

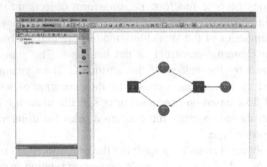

**Fig. 14.** Screen capture from the SMM modeling tool

# 7   Conclusions

Universal constructs in category theory are the basis for implementing a package of mechanisms and algorithms in a modeling method. In fact, the categories theory constructs, provide us with a package of universally valid results that could be implemented in modeling method and which would be valid in any model built according to category theory.

In many ways it is important to represent, for the most part, the semantics of the models in the metamodel. If we consider the model based on category theory then the constructions in the category theory can be implemented at the metamodel level as a package of mechanisms and algorithms that will work coherently in all the specified models.

Thus, the modeling process can support a lot of relatively independent components without too much communication between them, and yet they will work together perfectly. In addition, maintenance will be sensibly simplified because it can change or replace some of the components without affecting the others.

Software development based on such algorithms increases productivity. In modeling based on mechanisms and algorithms contained in the metamodel, the functionality of the models is assured mainly by assembling the existing reusable algorithms, and less by creating new algorithms that obviously provides increased productivity in contrast to modeling from scratch every time. Such modeling promotes the reuse of existing software components and not reinventing the wheel in every new model.

In the category theory, models are functors that map the sketches into the Set category that leads to a lot of important features on simulation, analysis, and process improvement.

Based on these functors, important issues such as model migration and model equivalence can be solved. The difficult problem of Database Migration can also be solved.

The paths from the CIT category represent, in fact, the admissible execution rules on which real-time deviations can be reported to be corrected.

The CIT category arrows that represent natural transformations are objects that can have attributes that dynamically sustain a series of data such as the trace of the process, the frequency of execution of the activities, the estimated time, the estimated cost, the probability that an activity will be executed by a certain resource, etc.

Also, on the basis of some information from the CIT category, it is possible to give indications to the activities to be executed and make recommendations on the most favorable route based on criteria such as minimizing the cost, minimizing the time until the case completion, etc.

Therefore, category theory creates the premise for developing intelligent workflow modeling tools with advanced analysis tools and automated learning mechanisms tailored to analyze and improve processes.

# References

1. Karagiannis, D., Kühn, H.: Metamodelling platforms. In: Bauknecht, K., Tjoa, A.M., Quirchmayr, G. (eds.) EC-Web 2002. LNCS, vol. 2455, p. 182. Springer, Heidelberg (2002). https://doi.org/10.1007/3-540-45705-4_19
2. Karagiannis, D., Visic, N.: Next generation of modelling platforms. In: Grabis, J., Kirikova, M. (eds.) BIR 2011. LNBIP, vol. 90, pp. 19–28. Springer, Heidelberg (2011). https://doi.org/10.1007/978-3-642-24511-4_2
3. Karagiannis, D., Mayr, H.C., Mylopoulos, J.: Domain-Specific Conceptual Modeling Concepts, Methods and Tools. Springer, Switzerland (2016). https://doi.org/10.1007/978-3-319-39417-6
4. Karagiannis, D., Junginger, S., Strobl, R.: Introduction to business process management systems concepts. In: Scholz-Reiter, B., Stickel, E. (eds.) Business Process Modelling. Springer, Heidelberg (1996). https://doi.org/10.1007/978-3-642-80317-8_5
5. Manes, E.G., Arbib, M.A.: Algebraic Approaches to Program Semantics. Springer, New York (1986). https://doi.org/10.1007/978-1-4612-4962-7
6. Fowler, M., Parsons, R.: Domain Specific Languages, 1st edn. Addison-Wesley Longman, Amsterdam (2010)

7. Barr, M., Wells, C.: Category Theory For Computing Science- Reprints in Theory and Applications of Categories, No. 22 (2012)
8. Barr, M., Wells, C.: Toposes, Triples and Theories, November 2002
9. Walters, R.F.C.: Categories and Computer Science, Cambridge Texts in Computer Science. In: Cooke, D.J. (ed.) Loughborough University (2006)
10. Weske, M.: Business Process Management - Concepts, Languages, Architectures, 2nd Edn., pp. I–XV, 1–403. Springer, Heidelberg (2012). https://doi.org/10.1007/978-3-642-28616-2, ISBN 978-3-642-28615-5. (2012)
11. Glynn, W.: Topics in Concurrency Lecture Notes, April 2009
12. van der Aalst, W.M.P.: Process Mining Discovery, Conformance and Enhancement of Business Processes. Springer, Heidelberg (2011). https://doi.org/10.1007/978-3-642-19345-3
13. van der Aalst, W.M.P., van Hee, K.M.: Workflow Management: Models, Methods, and Systems. MIT press, Cambridge (2004)

# Classification of Dengue Serotypes Using Protein Sequence Based on Rule Extraction from Neural Network

Pandiselvam Pandiyarajan[1](✉)
and Kathirvalavakumar Thangairulappan[2]

[1] Department of Computer Science, Ayya Nadar Janaki Ammal College,
Sivakasi 626124, Tamilnadu, India
pandiselvam.pps@gmail.com
[2] Research Centre in Computer Science, V.H.N.Senthikumara Nadar College,
Virudhunagar 626001, Tamilnadu, India
kathirvalavakumar@yahoo.com

**Abstract.** Dengue virus is a growing problem in tropical countries. It serves disease, especially in children. Some exiting clinical methods CIMSiM, DEN-SiM, ELISA, SPSS, SARIMA, PCR and RT-PCR need a volume of blood cells which cannot be obtained from children. Meanwhile, some existing machine learning algorithms are used to diagnose the dengue infection based on the date of dengue fever, days, current temperature, white blood cell count, joint muscles, metallic taste in mouth, appetite, abdomen pain, hemoglobin, mild bleeding, vomiting, headaches, rainfall, and relative humidity attributes. These methods are used to diagnose the dengue in later stages. Sometimes these methods could not identify the correct results. To overcome these problems, this paper proposes the stable method of classifying dengue serotypes based on amino acids in the protein sequences. It needs only skin cells or hair or nail which can be easily obtained from any person including children also. The proposed method classifies dengue serotypes using entropy-based feature selection and rule extracted from the neural network. Results of the experiments show that the proposed method for classifying dengue fevers with its serotypes.

**Keywords:** Dengue diagnosis · Protein sequence · Neural network
Classification · Rule extraction

## 1 Introduction

Dengue is a man-killed disease transmitted by an Ades aegypti mosquito in several regions. It spreads through tropic countries. It serves diseases, especially in children. Dengue infections can be difficult to differentiate from other viral infections. It can be identified as an undifferentiated fever, Dengue Fever (DF), Dengue Hemorrhagic Fever (DHF) and Dengue Shock Syndrome (DSS) and referred as serotypes DENV I, DENV II, DENV III and DENV IV [19]. Generally, serotype refers to the subdivision of a virus that divided based on their surface antigen [20]. Each serotype has its own characteristics and is unique. Recovery from infection provides lifelong immunity

© Springer Nature Switzerland AG 2018
A. Groza and R. Prasath (Eds.): MIKE 2018, LNAI 11308, pp. 127–137, 2018.
https://doi.org/10.1007/978-3-030-05918-7_12

against that particular serotype. Subsequent infections by other serotypes increase the severity of dengue. DF, with the symptoms increasing body temperature, fever, headache, pain in muscle and itching, is identified within 2–7 days after the bite of the Ades aegypti mosquito. DHF, with the symptoms decreasing body temperature, minor bleeding from the nose, gums and skins, is identified within 3–7 days after the patient is affected by DF. DSS is identified within 2–3 days after the patient is affected by DHF, it is with the symptoms fluctuating body temperature, vomiting with the flow of minor blood. These are the stages of dengue infection from the initial stage to critical stages [8]. Few clinical diagnostic methods are available to diagnose the later stages of Dengue infections. These methods are based on the detection of IgG and IgM anti-bodies in the blood. After the infection, IgM cannot be recognized between 30 to 90 days. The recognition of IgG alone is not enough to confirm the dengue infection without the presence of IgM. The global problem of dengue is misclassification by clinical tests and treatments [19]. The classification of dengue serotypes plays a major task in the world. This paper suggests a reliable method for recognizing dengue ser-otypes from day 1 of infection. The paper is structured as follows: Sect. 2 describes the review of the literature, Sect. 3 presents the classification process using Entropy-based feature selection, feedforward neural network and Extraction of rule from the neural network and Sect. 4 describes the experimental results.

## 2 Literature Review

The number of different diseases prediction models are used in medical diagnosis systems which are using data mining and machine learning techniques [1, 5] like Bayesian classification, decision tree [14], regression model [10], neural network [3], single best model and ensemble model. Different machine learning techniques (su-pervised, semi-supervised, unsupervised, deep learning and reinforcement) and clas-sification algorithms [2] (Decision tree, kNN, Artificial Neural Network [4]) are used in diagnosing different diseases such as Heart, dengue and cancer.

Hanirex et al. [6] have identified dominating amino acids for DENV I using TDTR (Two Dimensional Transactions Reduction) approach based on an apriori and FP growth algorithm. The utilized dataset hold only 777 amino acids of DENV I which was obtained from GenBank: AAB27904.1. They have identified that Leucine (L), Phenylalanine (F), Lysine (K), Serine (S) and Glycine (G) are the dominating amino acids in DENV I. Changing of climate condition plays a vital role in the spreading of viral diseases. Karim [9] has analyzed the climate changes in Pakistan and the spread of diseases during the period 2010–2015. This dataset is with the attributes temperature, date, hour, time, wind speed, dew point, wind direction, relative humidity, wind chill and standard pressure. The Backpropagation algorithm is used to analyze these attri-butes and predict the climate changes. The result of this system is used to know the probable spread of diseases including dengue, yellow fever and malaria in Pakistan.

Tate et al. [11] have developed a web/mobile based application for the prediction of a particular disease using Random Forest algorithm and this prediction system involves swine flu, diabetes and dengue. They have classified the patients with their symptoms. As per the prediction system, if the patient has a sudden high fever, severe headaches, severe joint and muscle pain, pain behind the eye, fatigue, nausea, vomiting, skin rash and mild bleeding symptoms then the system set that particular patient is belonging to dengue. They have constructed yes tree for all the attributes. If maximum yes occurs then the system produces the result as positive otherwise negative.

Sandhu et al. [12] have proposed an effective framework for finding patients suffering from dengue using keyword domain thesaurus, case-based reasoning method and text mining [7, 13]. They have used ontology domain thesaurus technique and have used RAKE (Rapid Automatic Keyword Extraction) algorithm for extracting the list of keywords (Symptoms, fever treatments, medications, location, causes, environment, family/friends and others) from raw text information. This framework is also used to create the synthetic dataset and case base and used to find similar cases and also used to identify dengue outbreaks with the references of users' information based on queries.

Sahil et al. [15] have applied classification algorithms in weka for identifying dengue patients and used to classify the dengue based on Pid, date of dengue fever, days, current temperature, WBC (White Blood cell Count), joint muscles, metallic taste in mouth, appetite, abdomen pain, nausea, diarrhea and hemoglobin. Dengue dataset has been applied to different algorithms such as Naïve Bayes, J48, SOM (Self Organizing Map) and Random forest and assessed the performances of different algorithms working on the same data set using accuracy measures like root mean square error, relative absolute error and correctly classified instances. As per the accuracy measures, they have suggested Naïve Bayes and J48 are working well in dengue dataset.

Some of the Clinical methods named as SPSS (Statistical Package for Social Science), mRNA (Messenger RNA analysis), SARIMA (Seasonal Auto Regressive Integrated Mixing Average) Models, PCR (Polymerase Chain Reaction) and Mathematical approach are used for prediction of dengue diseases [20, 23].

Rocha et al. [21] have studied that DENV I serotype was more prone to present with several clinical and laboratory features as compared with DENV IV patients together with spontaneous bleeding (DENV I: 33.0% and DENV IV: 20.0%), intense abdominal pain (DENV I: 29.7% and DENV IV: 14.1%), neurological symptoms (DENV I: 6.7% and DENV IV: 2.2%) and thrombacy topenia (DENV I: 33.7% and DENV IV: 18.2%). The immune status measurement of DENV I and DENV IV are the same for 202 patients. They have shown that DENV I and DENV IV are more or less the same in an antibody response patterns and severity of the diseases.

Munasinghe et al. [22] have applied artificial neural network for dengue prediction system using Climate/weather dataset with attributes temperature, rainfall, relative humidity. They have applied hidden Markov model for selecting the most significant features from the dengue dataset then the selected features are trained to predict dengue diseases. Focks et al. [24] have used CIMSiM (Container – Inhabiting Mosquito Simulation Model) and DENSiM (Dengue Simulation Model) tool to predict dengue disease based on weather data from the Caribbean, Central America, South America and Southeast Asia.

## 3  Proposed Method

The proposed method has four segments (i) preprocessing (ii) feature selection (iii) classification of dengue serotypes using the neural network and (iv) Rule extraction.

### 3.1  Numerical Representation of Biological Sequences

The biological sequences as signals are to be encoded into a suitable format for data analysis and data mining tools. This is usually achieved by assigning numeral to each symbol that forms the biological sequences. There are two fundamental kinds of biological sequences namely DNA nucleotide sequences and protein sequences relevant to dengue diagnosis. EIIP value of amino acid is a physical quantity that denoting the mean energy of valence electron [17] and also used to find the protein-coding regions (hotspots of protein). The EIIP values of amino acids are calculated by Eqs. (1, 2) [17]. In the proposed method, the energy contribution of each amino acid in the protein sequence is found and is used for classifying dengue serotypes. The first protein sequence is converted to EIIP indicator sequence using the energy contribution value (Q) of each amino acid by Eq. (3). Q value is calculated using EIIP value (W) of amino acids which are represented in Table 1.

**Table 1.**  EIIP Value (W) of amino acids

| Amino acids | Single letter symbol | EIIP value (W) |
|---|---|---|
| Alanine | A | 0.0373 |
| Arginine | R | 0.0959 |
| Asparagine | N | 0.0036 |
| Aspartic Acid | D | 0.1263 |
| Cysteine | C | 0.0829 |
| Glutamine | Q | 0.0671 |
| Glutamic Acid | E | 0.0058 |
| Glycine | G | 0.0050 |
| Histidine | H | 0.0242 |
| Isoleucine | I | 0.0000 |
| Leucine | L | 0.0000 |
| Lysine | K | 0.0371 |
| Methionine | M | 0.0823 |
| Phenylalanine | F | 0.0946 |
| Proline | P | 0.0198 |
| Serine | S | 0.0829 |
| Threonine | T | 0.0941 |
| Tryptophan | W | 0.0548 |
| Tyrosine | Y | 0.0516 |
| Valine | V | 0.0057 |

$$W = 0.25 \frac{Z^* \sin(1.04\pi Z^*)}{2\pi} \tag{1}$$

$$Z^* = \frac{1}{N} \sum_{i=1}^{m} n_i z_i \tag{2}$$

where $Z^*$ is the average quasi valence number, $Z_i$ is the valence number of $i^{th}$ atomic component, $n_i$ is the number of atoms of $i^{th}$ component, m is the number of atomic components in the molecule and N is the total number of atoms.

$$Q_i = \frac{C_i}{T} W_i \tag{3}$$

where $c_i$ represents a number of particular amino acid in the protein sequence, T represents the total number of amino acids in the protein sequence and $W_i$ represents an EIIP value of particular amino acids.

## 3.2 Feature Selection

Feature selection is the process of selecting unique features from the dataset to improve the quality of the classification process. An entropy-based method is used for selecting the features. This method selects the amino acids which are used to classify different serotypes of dengue virus. Before applying the feature selection method, the amino acids with the EIIP value as 0 are to be eliminated. Entropy (E) is calculated for the Q values of amino acids in the protein sequence using Eq. (4).

$$E = - \sum_{i=1}^{m} p_i \log p_i \tag{4}$$

where $p_i$ represents the probability of $Q_i$ and m represents a total number of amino acids in the protein sequence. E value of amino acids ranges between 0 and 1. The Binary value R1 is set based on the E value of particular amino acids using Eq. (5). R1 is set to 1 if E has positive value otherwise R1 is set to 0. The amino acids with R1 value as 1 are selected as features.

$$R1 = \begin{cases} 1 & if \ E > 0 \\ 0 & otherwise \end{cases} \tag{5}$$

The selected features are used for training the neural network.

## 3.3    Classification of Dengue Serotypes

Single hidden layer feedforward neural network is considered to classify the dengue serotypes into DENV I, DENV II, DENV III and DENV IV. The sigmoidal activation function is used in the hidden layer. The linear activation function is used in the output layer. $X = [x_1 \ldots\ldots\ldots x_n, 1]$ is the input pattern to the network where 1 represents the bias value. W is a weight matrix connecting an input layer and the hidden layer. Z is a weight matrix connecting the hidden layer and an output layer. H and Y are vectors that represent the output of the hidden and output layer.

$$net_h = \sum XW, \qquad net_o = \sum HZ \tag{6}$$

$$H = f(net_h), \qquad Y = f(net_o) \tag{7}$$

$$f(net) = \frac{1}{1 + e^{-net}} \tag{8}$$

Backpropagation algorithm is used to train the single hidden layer feedforward network. This algorithm is learned by samples and backpropagate the error from the output layer. Weights are adjusted according to the deviation of errors.

## 3.4    Rule Construction

A data range matrix in Fig. 1 specifies the required data range of each significant attribute $I_i$ to classify the data in a particular class $C_k$. The required data range of each significant attribute for classifying the data as the target serotype class is derived as follows.

| | $C_1$ | $C_2$ | $C_k$ | $C_n$ |
|---|---|---|---|---|
| $I_1$ | $[L_{11}, U_{11}]$ | $[L_{12}, U_{12}]$ | $[L_{1k}, U_{1k}]$ | $[L_{1n}, U_{1n}]$ |
| $I_2$ | $[L_{21}, U_{21}]$ | $[L_{22}, U_{22}]$ | $[L_{2k}, U_{2k}]$ | $[L_{2n}, U_{2n}]$ |
| $I_3$ | $[L_{31}, U_{31}]$ | $[L_{32}, U_{32}]$ | $[L_{3k}, U_{3k}]$ | $[L_{3n}, U_{3n}]$ |
| $I_i$ | $[L_{i1}, U_{i1}]$ | $[L_{i2}, U_{i2}]$ | $[L_{ik}, U_{ik}]$ | $[L_{in}, U_{in}]$ |
| $I_m$ | $[L_{m1}, U_{m1}]$ | $[L_{m2}, U_{m2}]$ | $[L_{mk}, U_{mk}]$ | $[L_{mn}, U_{mn}]$ |

**Fig. 1.**  Data range matrix

$L_{ik}$ and $U_{ik}$ are selected from the trained neural network. The minimum and maximum values of $I_i$ of the patterns those falls under $C_k$ are considered as $L_{ik}$ and $U_{ik}$. $L_{ik}$ and $U_{ik}$ are the minimum and maximum value of $Q_i$ of $i^{th}$ amino acid for the target class k respectively. The rules for each target class can be constructed using the non-zero data available in the corresponding column k of DM. In general, rules can be written as

*If( (data($I_1$)≥$L_{11}$ ∧ data($I_1$)≤$U_{11}$) ∧ (data($I_2$)≥$L_{21}$ ∧ data($I_2$)≤$U_{21}$) ∧......∧ data($I_m$)*
*≥ $L_{m1}$ ∧ data($I_m$)≤$U_{m1}$)) then Class = $C_1$*
*Else If( (data($I_1$)≥$L_{12}$ ∧ data($I_1$)≤$U_{12}$) ∧ (data($I_2$)≥$L_{22}$ ∧ data($I_2$)≤$U_{22}$) ∧......∧*
*data($I_m$) ≥ $L_{m2}$ ∧ data($I_m$)≤$U_{m2}$)) then Class = $C_2$*
*Else If ..............*
*Else If( (data($I_1$)≥$L_{1n-1}$ ∧ data($I_1$)≤$U_{1n-1}$) ∧ (data($I_2$)≥$L_{2n-1}$ ∧ data($I_2$)≤$U_{2n-1}$)*
*∧......∧ data($I_m$) ≥ $L_{mn-1}$ ∧ data($I_m$)≤$U_{mn-1}$)) then Class = $C_{n-1}$*
*Else*
*Class =$C_n$*

The rules can be restructured in the descending order in terms of a number of attributes required for classification [18].

## 4 Results and Discussion

The proposed method has been implemented by Matlab 13. The protein sequences of 70 patients are taken from an NCBI (National Centre for Bio-Informatics) [16]. Among 70 patients, protein sequences of 25 patients are randomly considered for training. Among these sequences, 6 patients are affected with DENV I, 6 patients are affected with DENV II, 8 patients are affected with DENV III and 5 patients are affected with DENV IV. Generally, a single protein sequence contains plenty of 20 different amino acids (A, R, N, D, C, Q, E, G, H, I, L, K, M, F, P, S, T, W, Y, V) at frequent intervals. Similarly, each protein sequence of dengue patients is having more than **10563** amino acids. These sequences are converted into an EIIP indicator sequence using EIIP values of amino acids listed in Table 1. The EIIP value of amino acids Leucine (L) and Isoleucine (I) are 0. Hence these two amino acids are eliminated from the processing. The Q values for the remaining 18 amino acids are calculated using Eq. (3). The resultant Q value is represented in a matrix of size $18 \times 1$ for a patient. It becomes 18 $\times$ 25 for the 25 patients. Entropy value (E) is calculated for the computed value Q of the amino acids. The binary value R1 is computed based on the value of E. The Amino acids with R1 value of 1 are considered as features for further processing which are shown in Table 2. It shows that the seven amino acids Alanine (A), Arginine (R), Aspartic Acid (D), Methoionine (M), Proline (P), Serine (S) and Threonine (T) are selected as features for identifying dengue serotypes. The selected amino acids are used for training the neural network. The number of input, hidden and output neurons considered for training the neural network is 7, 20 and 4 respectively. The feedforward neural network is trained for classifying the dengue serotypes DENV I, DENV II, DENV III and DENV IV. The network is trained with different learning parameters ($\lambda$) and epochs. It has been identified that when $\lambda$ takes 0.083331 the network gives a good accuracy of 95.7%. For improving classification performances of the proposed work, the rule is extracted from the trained neural network. The most significant amino acids are selected based on EIIP values for extracting the rule. Alanine (A), Arginine (R), Aspartic Acid (D), Methoionine (M), Proline (P), Serine (S) and Threonine (T) have EIIP values 0.0373, 0.0959, 0.1263, 0.0823, 0.0946, 0.0829 and 0.0941 respectively. From the experiments it has been identified that when the amino acids with the EIIP values greater than 0.09 it gives good accuracy. Here 4 amino acids Arginine (R), Aspartic Acid (D), Proline (P) and Threonine (T) are selected for rule extraction as it follows the above condition. The following is the generated Rule.

**Table 2.** Q, Entropy and R1 of dengue patients

| Amino acids | Q values | | | Entropy values | | | R1Value |
|---|---|---|---|---|---|---|---|
| | Patient I | Patient II | Patient III | Patient I | Patient II | Patient III | |
| A | 0.002592 | 0.002475 | 0.002704 | 0.03952 | 0.016681 | 0.041872 | 1 |
| R | 0.005478 | 0.005571 | 0.005125 | 0.830367 | 0.860735 | 0.654552 | 1 |
| N | 0.000131 | 0.000145 | 0.000149 | −0.06939 | −0.07408 | −0.07355 | 0 |
| D | 0.005504 | 0.004991 | 0.005198 | 0.839007 | 0.671089 | 0.676768 | 1 |
| C | 0.001465 | 0.001393 | 0.001477 | −0.12998 | −0.13636 | −0.13382 | 0 |
| Q | 0.002154 | 0.001999 | 0.002288 | −0.03986 | −0.06433 | −0.03162 | 0 |
| E | 0.000376 | 0.000412 | 0.000403 | −0.12647 | −0.13176 | −0.12829 | 0 |
| G | 0.000411 | 0.000398 | 0.000436 | −0.13159 | −0.12978 | −0.13286 | 0 |
| H | 0.000527 | 0.000478 | 0.000543 | −0.14493 | −0.13992 | −0.14449 | 0 |
| K | 0.00225 | 0.002363 | 0.002507 | −0.02363 | −0.00395 | −0.00561 | 0 |
| M | 0.003126 | 0.003131 | 0.003109 | 0.154365 | 0.155129 | 0.124417 | 1 |
| F | 0.002953 | 0.000584 | 0.000596 | −0.11509 | −0.14962 | −0.14889 | 0 |
| P | 0.009667 | 0.004101 | 0.004387 | 2.465417 | 0.404748 | 0.440681 | 1 |
| S | 0.004955 | 0.004767 | 0.004557 | 0.660539 | 0.60119 | 0.488243 | 1 |
| T | 0.007121 | 0.007215 | 0.007919 | 1.419613 | 1.454331 | 1.616 | 1 |
| W | 0.001533 | 0.001438 | 0.001599 | −0.12331 | −0.13246 | −0.12259 | 0 |
| Y | 0.001124 | 0.001111 | 0.001157 | −0.15394 | −0.15456 | −0.15438 | 0 |
| V | 0.000391 | 0.000365 | 0.000401 | −0.12878 | −0.12472 | −0.12805 | 0 |

*If R<=0.005478 ^ R>=0.004486 ^ D<=0.005504 ^ d>=0.004311 ^ P<=0.000626 ^ P>=0.00081 ^ T<=0.007151 ^ T>=0.007121 then Class =DENV I.*
*Else If R>=0.005571 ^ R<=0.005983 ^ D>=0.004991 ^ D<=0.005318 ^ P>=0.007548 ^ P<=0.004279 ^ T>=0.007548 ^ T<=0.007564 then Class=DENV II*
*Else If R =0.004894 ^ D>=0.004992 ^ D<=0.005067 ^ P=0.004242 ^ T>=0.007606 ^ T<=0.007633 then Class= DENV III*
*Else If R=0.006061 ^ D=0.005875 ^ P=0.004552 ^ T=0.008151 then class=DENV IV.*

The classification result of a neural network is compared with the NCBI result. The classification result obtained from rule extraction is tabulated in Table 3 with the result of NCBI. The protein sequences of 25 patients used for training the neural network are correctly classified in terms of their serotypes as per the extracted rule. The extracted rules are tested with another 45 protein sequences of dengue affected patients. Among them, 97.7% of the patients are correctly classified based on the extracted rule. This result is compared with the NCBI result and is shown in Fig. 2. The proposed method takes less amount of time for classifying the dengue serotypes as it involves the only rule.

**Table 3.** Obtained and NCBI results after Rule Extraction

| Patient ID | R | D | P | T | Obtained result | NCBI result |
|---|---|---|---|---|---|---|
| 1 | 0.005478 | 0.005504 | 0.00081 | 0.007121 | DENV I | DENVI |
| 2 | 0.005478 | 0.005504 | 0.00081 | 0.007121 | DENV I | DENV I |
| 3 | 0.004486 | 0.004311 | 0.000626 | 0.007151 | DENV I | DENV I |
| 4 | 0.005983 | 0.005318 | 0.004279 | 0.007564 | DENV II | DENV II |
| 5 | 0.005571 | 0.004991 | 0.004101 | 0.007548 | DENV II | DENV II |
| 6 | 0.005635 | 0.005109 | 0.00405 | 0.007557 | DENV II | DENV II |
| 7 | 0.004894 | 0.004992 | 0.004242 | 0.007606 | DENVIII | DENV III |
| 8 | 0.004894 | 0.004992 | 0.004242 | 0.007606 | DENV III | DENV III |
| 9 | 0.004894 | 0.005067 | 0.004242 | 0.007633 | DENV III | DENV III |
| 10 | 0.004894 | 0.005067 | 0.004342 | 0.007633 | DEN V III | DENVIII |
| 11 | 0.006061 | 0.005875 | 0.004552 | 0.008151 | DENV IV | DENV IV |
| 12 | 0.006061 | 0.005875 | 0.004552 | 0.008151 | DENV IV | DENV IV |
| 13 | 0.006061 | 0.005875 | 0.004552 | 0.008151 | DENV IV | DENV IV |
| 14 | 0.006061 | 0.005875 | 0.004552 | 0.008151 | DENV IV | DENV IV |
| 15 | 0.005478 | 0.005504 | 0.00081 | 0.007121 | DENV I | DENV I |
| 16 | 0.005571 | 0.004991 | 0.004101 | 0.007548 | DENV II | DENV II |
| 17 | 0.005571 | 0.004991 | 0.004101 | 0.007548 | DENV II | DENV II |
| 18 | 0.004894 | 0.004992 | 0.004242 | 0.007606 | DENV III | DENV III |
| 19 | 0.004894 | 0.004992 | 0.004242 | 0.007606 | DENV II | DENV III |
| 20 | 0.005478 | 0.005504 | 0.00081 | 0.007121 | DENV I | DENV I |
| 21 | 0.005635 | 0.005109 | 0.00405 | 0.007557 | DENV II | DENV II |
| 22 | 0.004894 | 0.004992 | 0.004242 | 0.007606 | DENV III | DENV III |
| 23 | 0.004894 | 0.004992 | 0.004242 | 0.007606 | DENV III | DENV III |
| 24 | 0.005478 | 0.005504 | 0.00081 | 0.007121 | DENV I | DENV I |
| 25 | 0.006061 | 0.005875 | 0.004552 | 0.008151 | DENV IV | DENV IV |

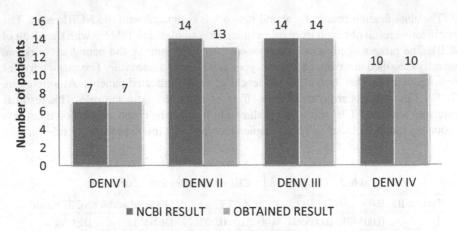

Fig. 2.  Obtained and NCBI results of test data set

## 5    Conclusion

Classification framework with a rule is provided for classifying dengue serotypes into DENV I, DENV II, DENV III and DENV IV based on entropy values of EIIP indicator sequence and rule extraction from the neural network. The comparative results shown in Figures and Tables shows the proposed methods yield good results. The results obtained from the extracted rule give good accuracy than the accuracy of a neural network. The procedure can be easily applied for even the children as it needs only hair or nail or skin cells instead of blood cells.

## References

1. Thitiprayoonwongre, D., Suriyaphol, P., Soonthornphisaj, N.: Data mining of dengue infection using decision tree. Lat. Adv. Info. Sci. Appl., 154–159 (2017). The 12th WSEAS International Conference on Applied Computer Science, ISBN 978-1-61804-092-3
2. Rahim, N.F., Taib, S.M., Abidin, A.I.Z.: Dengue fatality prediction using data mining. J. Fundam. Appl. Sci. **9**, 671–683 (2017)
3. Ahmed, N., Ishaq, A., Shoaib, M., Wahab, A.: Role of expert systems in identification and overcoming oof dengue fever. Int. J. Adv. Comp. Sci. Appl. **8**, 82–89 (2017)
4. Gambhir, S., Malik, S.K., Kumar, Y.: PSO ANN based diagnostic model for the early detection of dengue disease. New. Hori. Trans. Med **4**, 1–8 (2017)
5. Fatima, M., Pasha, M.: Survey of machine learning algorithms for disease diagnostic. J. Intell. Learn. Syst. Appl. **9**, 1–16 (2017)
6. Hanirex, D.K., Kaliyamurthie, K.P.: An adaptive transaction reduction approach for mining frequent item sets: a comparative study on dengue virus type -1. Int. J. Pharm. Bio. Sci. **6**, 336–340 (2015)
7. Kowia, T., Ohwada, H.: Extraction of disease related genes from pubmed paper using word2vec. In: CSBio'17 8th International Conference on Computational Systems Biology and Bioinformatics, pp. 46–49 (2017)

8. Iqbal, N., Islam, M.: Machine learning for dengue outbreak prediction: an outlook. Int. J. Adv. Res. Comp. Sci. **8**, 93–102 (2017)
9. Karim, S.: Learning from experience in context of climate prediction in Pakistan using data mining techniques avidence from computer research in Pakistan. Pak. J. Eng. Technol. Sci. **6**, 81–93 (2016)
10. Freeze, J., Erraguntla, M., Varma, A.: Data integration and predictive analysis system for disease prophylaxis: Incorporating dengue fever forecasts. In: The Proceedings of the 51st Hawaii International Conference on System Sciences, pp. 913–922 (2018)
11. Tate, A., Gavhane, V., Pawar, J., Rajpurohit, B., Deshmwch, G.B.: Prediction of dengue diabetes and swine flu using random forest classification algorithm. Int. R. J. Engg. Tech. **4**, 685–690 (2017)
12. Sandhu, R., Kaur, J., Thapar, V.: An effective framework for finding similar cases of dengue from audio and text data using domain thesaurus and case base reasoning. Enterprise. Info. Sys. **12**, 155–172 (2017)
13. Villanes, A., Griffiths, E., Rappa, M., Healey, C.G.: Dengue fever surveillance in India using text mining in public media. Am. J. Trop. Med. Hyg. **98**, 181–191 (2018)
14. Saravanan, N., Gayathri, V.: An performance and classification evaluation of J48 algorithm and Person's based J48 algorithm PNJ48. Int. J. Adv. Res. Comp. Sci. Manag. Stu. **6**, 22–32 (2018)
15. Sakil, K.A., Anis, S., Alam, M.: Dengue disease prediction using weka data mining tool (2017)
16. National Center for Biotechnology Information. http://www.ncbi.nlm.nih.gov/genomes/virusvariation/database/nphselect.cgi
17. Inbamalar, Sivakumar: Filtering Approach to DNA Signal Processing. In: IACSIT Coimbatore Conferences IPCSIT 28. IACSIT Press, Singapore (2012)
18. Augasta, M.G., Kathirvalavakumar, T.: Reverse engineering the neural networks for rule extraction in classification problems. Neural. Process. Lett. **35**, 131–150 (2011)
19. Pandiselvam, P., Kathirvalavakumar, T.: Classification of dengue gene expression using entropy based feature selection and pruning on neural network. Ad. Intell. Sys. Comp. **736**, 519–529 (2018)
20. World Health Organization, Dengue: Guidelines for Diagnosis, Treatment, Prevention and control. New edition, Geneva (2009)
21. Rocha, B.A.M., et al.: Dengue specific serotype related to clinical severity during the 2012/2013 epidemic in centre of Brazil. Inf. Dis. Poverty **6**, 2–11 (2017)
22. Munasinghe, A., Premaratne, H.L., Fernando, M.G.N.A.S.: Towards an early warning system to combat dengue. Int. J. Comput. Sci. Elect. Engg. **1**, 252–256 (2013)
23. Shamala, D.S.: Laboratory diagnosis of dengue: a review. Int. Med. J. Malaysia **14**, 17–28 (2015)
24. Focks, D.A., Alexander, N., Villegas, E.: Multicounty Study of Aedes Aegypti Pupil Productivity Survey Methodology: Findings and Recommendations, pp. 1–56. World Health Organization, Geneva (2006)

# Orienting Social Event Streams
# as Data Stories

Ammar Rashed, Abdullah İhsan Seçer, Abdurrahman Aboudakika,
and Ahmet Bulut[✉]

İstanbul Şehir University, Dragos, 34865 İstanbul, Turkey
{ammarrashed,abdullahsecer,talaataboudakika}@std.sehir.edu.tr,
ahmetbulut@sehir.edu.tr

**Abstract.** We study the evolution of our university's social networks
over time, capturing direct, contextual, and latent changes in these networks. With the assumption of our university's social dynamics being
embodied in the networks we construct, we continuously monitor these
networks in order to gain an understanding of the changes they go
through and their evolution. Our system has three main components:
(i) crawling the web for collecting data, (ii) networked data analysis,
and (iii) data storytelling. Our goal is to render the social development
of our university as a community in a lucid and insightful manner.

**Keywords:** Social network analysis · Data science · Data visualization

## 1 Introduction

The digital ecosystem has experienced an exponential growth with billions of
people and machines creating online content. Fueled by the proliferation of e-
commerce and social media, the digital data revolution has necessitated the
understanding of ever growing and large volumes of heterogeneous data for
extracting key business insights and for gaining competitive advantage in order
to survive in the age of data. Many institutions face an existential threat lest
they fail to adapt to the impending data revolution. Irrespective of the scale of
the institution and its business sector, data driven decision-making has become
the heartbeat of business operations.

The data revolution has attracted a significant body of researchers to work
on different aspects of social media from e-commerce to sociology, and to computer science. In this work, we focus on designing an intelligent system for social
media. Our main goal is to create living and interactive stories off of the social
media traces of any online community. The collected data is projected on to a
live dashboard for monitoring the heartbeat of the community continuously. The
dashboard is expected to expose key insights such as what excites the individual
members of the community and who collectively moves them. Wu et al. built
a system for visually exploring in multiple facets the digital footprint of events
with high impact using social media streams [10]. The relationships between

© Springer Nature Switzerland AG 2018
A. Groza and R. Prasath (Eds.): MIKE 2018, LNAI 11308, pp. 138–147, 2018.
https://doi.org/10.1007/978-3-030-05918-7_13

seemingly unrelated social media events were studied by Lu et al. in order to answer questions such as whether positive tweets about a product proceed positive reviews about that product [6]. However, these recent studies mostly focus on synthesizing the media content and do not address how to visualize the social co-evolution of a network of individuals.

The structure of a network with its nodes and edges between pairs of nodes is a valuable conduit that enables us to study various population dynamics from how quickly new ideas spread through the network to where these ideas are adopted first if at all. Additionally, we can use the social media data of the users in the network to learn more about their interests and their general sentiment towards particular events that affect the community.

We identify and validate the members of a given community using its official social media accounts. Then, we periodically crawl the social media data of those members from select media outlets and ingest them into the backend datastore for network analysis. We identify micro communities in the community network and then study how they evolve over time, possibly changing the overall character of the macro or the parent community. We can further inspect the parent network and its micro communities in terms of their capacity for introversion (or extraversion) from coarse to finer grain using multi-modal data.

Note that the rendering and the encapsulation of the digital context of a given online community may be computationally infeasible simply because there are more things that we do not measure compared to what we actually measure about that community. This is partly due to the lack of means to accurately and thoroughly measure the objective as well as the subjective characteristics of a social context. Because of the inherent lack of data, any computational model we build may not fully represent the society we aim to model. However, even if each subtle yet possible data point may not be fully captured, we might still draw meaningful conclusions from the aggregate behavior of the individual members of the society and shed light onto how a certain call for change spawns and diffuses into the network to finally become visible in the aggregate. Therefore, we still resort to capturing as much data as possible that pertain to the intrinsic workings and the societal fabric of that community.

In the rest of the paper, we present the technical details of our system, which is currently under development. While developing the core parts of the system, we focused on our university and its community, i.e., our students, academics, and administrative personnel. We are designing it for monitoring the social media event streams of our university in order to orient its life-changing events as vivid data stories to tell. Currently, our data storytelling capacity is primitive: it corresponds to the visualization of the network and the synthesis of a case study we conducted on the network.

## 2   Methodology

### 2.1   Definitions

A network is a graph $G = (U, V)$ defined on a set of nodes $V$ and a set of edges $E$. For two nodes $u, v \in V$, if there is an edge $e \in E$ between them, it is denoted as $e = \{u, v\}$ for an undirected graph, and as $e = (u, v)$ for a directed graph. If the nodes of a given network are users exclusively, then it is called a social network. If the nodes are affiliations only, then it is called an affiliation network. However, if the nodes can be users as well as their affiliations, e.g., academic departments and social clubs, then this richer network is called a social-affiliation network [3]. Each edge in a social-affiliation network corresponds to either a user-to-affiliation relationship or a user-to-user relationship: on Twitter, a user can follow another user, and on Facebook, a user can join a group. In such affiliation-rich communities as universities, it is important to capture a diverse set of affiliations in order to gain deeper insights into the intrinsic workings of the community.

### 2.2   System Overview

Figure 1 depicts the complete data pipeline. The pipeline consists of three main stages as data collection, network analysis, and data storytelling. Next, we discuss each stage in detail.

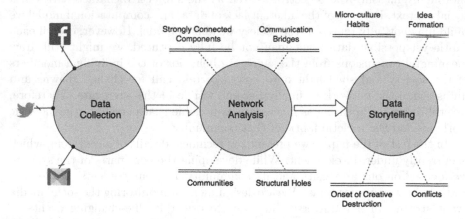

**Fig. 1.** End-to-end data analysis pipeline consisting of data collection, network analysis, and data storytelling.

**Data Collection.** Using Twitter API, we retrieve Twitter users of interest and their connections (the identities of followers and followees). After retrieval, we use our email directory, which contains user profiles for proper identification, in order to validate Twitter users in our community. For this purpose, we compute a text-based membership score based on Levenshtein distance, the value of which ranges from 0% to 100% [7]. All information retrieved from Twitter for each user along with this computed score is stored in a relational datastore. The score is used in order to filter out all accounts with membership scores below a predetermined threshold $\tau$. The default value of $\tau$ is 90%.

---

**Algorithm 1.** Crawler for identifying Twitter accounts from a given community.

**Input:** ego_nodes initialized with known accounts.

1: crawl_pool ← ego_nodes;
2: **while** crawl_pool is not empty **do**
3:     node ← pop node from the head of the pool;
4:     retrieve user_info, followers, followees of node from Twitter;
5:     **for** follower in node.followers **do**
6:         follower[membership] ← compute the membership score;
7:     **end for**
8:     node.followers ← {follower | follower[membership] $\geq \tau$};
9:     write node into the database;
10:    crawl_pool ← crawl_pool + node.followers;
11: **end while**

---

Similar to how ego networks are built, we begin our crawl starting from a select set of institutional Twitter accounts as ego nodes[1], which we know with utmost certainty that they belong to our university. These ego nodes are the main Twitter account, the Twitter accounts for all academic departments and graduate programs, and the Twitter accounts for all known student clubs. The followers of each ego node are added to the crawl pool for further exploration. The exploration is recursive with a cap on recursion depth. Once all nodes are explored in the crawl pool, the crawling terminates. The complete algorithm is given in Algorithm 1. For each node explored, its data profile including the connections, i.e., who follows the user (followers), and whom the user follows (followees) is written to the database for downstream analysis. The data exchange that occurs between the web services involved during a crawling session is depicted in Fig. 2.

Each time we run the crawler, new community members as of the last run would be identified since the chances are higher for them to follow either one of the institutional accounts or at least follow an existing user who has already been explored and added into our database. The existence of a connection between a pair of nodes is a volatile entity: it may get added indicating the start of a relationship, and later on it may get deleted indicating the end of a relationship. And the number of state changes a relationship goes through could be arbitrary for any given pair of nodes. For simplicity and efficiency, we maintain the state of a connection as a binary piece of information, i.e., as being either present or absent. However, the evolution of the relationship can still be studied using the snapshots of the network, which are taken on different times.

---

[1] Node, account, and user all refer to the same entity in this context.

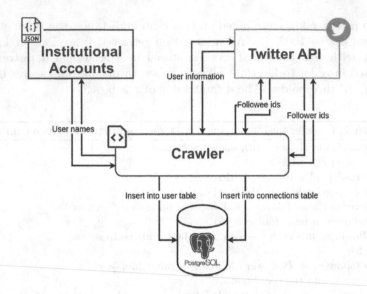

**Fig. 2.** The data collection from Twitter using its public API.

**Network Analysis.** Each individual has a distinct set of personal character-istics. Each of us individually engage in a set of behaviours and activities that would drive the formation of links within the network, occasionally leading us to specific friendships that may defy any "norm". However in aggregate, links in a social network tend to form between people that are similar to one another [8]. That is, there are factors that exist outside the nodes and edges of a network (the network's structure), and that affect how the network's structure evolves. The compatibility of two individuals can strongly influence whether a link forms between them. This tendency is called homophily. Furthermore, shared activi-ties between two individuals create an increased chance of an interaction between them, which would lead to the formation of a relationship between them in the future. Examples such of shared activities include working for the same com-pany, living in a certain suburb, frequenting a particular pub, and playing golf in close proximity. These activities are "focal points of social interaction (foci)", i.e., social, psychological, legal, or physical mediums around which shared activ-ities are organised [4]. In our setting, all of our institutional accounts constitute the set of foci. In order to assess whether homophily is prevalent in our univer-sity and how it manifests itself, we chose to study the natural language used in our community. The reason for this choice is two-fold: (i) we can determine the language of choice objectively and (ii) each language subject to our assessment is adopted by a sufficiently large number of users in the community.

Distinct closure processes drive the formation of individual links in a given network. There are three closure processes as shown in Fig. 3. Membership clo-sure (also known as social influence) is the tendency of a person to alter her behaviour in order to align it with those of her friends, who influence her socially.

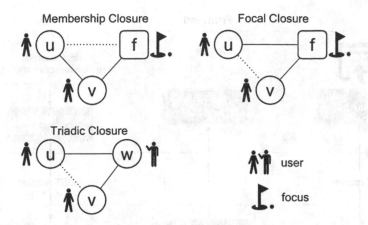

**Fig. 3.** There are three closure processes that operate on a network. In the drawings, the nodes $u$, $v$, and $w$ represent distinct users while the node $f$ represents a focus. Social influence drives membership closure; selection drives focal closure; trust and gravity drives triadic closure.

Focal closure (also known as selection) is the tendency of a person seeking out to form friendships with people that are similar and compatible with herself. Triadic closure is the tendency of two people, who share a common friend, becoming friends due to the trust being established transitively and the facilitation of their friendship by the mutual friend.

The edges in a social-affiliation network are between two users, or between a user and a focus[2]. An edge $\{u, v\}$ is a focal edge if either $u$ or $v$ is a focus. The formation of a focal edge $\{u, f\}$ between a user $u$ and a focus $f$ at time $t$ is because of the membership closure if there existed two edges before $t$, one of which is an edge between $u$ and another user $v$, and a focal edge between user $v$ and focus $f$. The formation of an edge $\{u, v\}$ between two users at time $t$ is because of the focal closure if there existed a focus $f$ with edges $\{u, f\}$ and $\{v, f\}$ being present before time $t$. The formation of an edge $\{u, v\}$ between two users $u$ and $v$ at time $t$ is because of the triadic closure if there existed edges $\{u, w\}$ and $\{v, w\}$ before time $t$ where $w$ represents a user.

**Data Storytelling.** We used Django as our web development framework for creating a dynamic and interactive dashboard [2]. A network, which is represented in javascript object notation (json) data format, defines the granularity of data exchanged between the network analysis layer and the data storytelling layer. Data scientists can use the interactive widgets provided in the dashboard in order to select nodes and edges of interest, which defines a new network to render as shown in the right hand side of Fig. 4. We used a popular javascript

---

[2] It is possible to have an edge between two foci in Twitter because the institutional accounts are maintained by human beings, who may also be "regular" users in the network.

**Frontend**

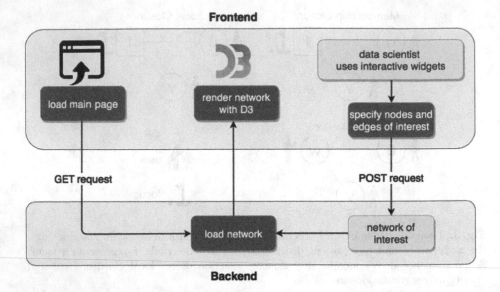

**Backend**

Fig. 4. The interface between the front-end and the back-end of our system.

library called data driven documents known as $d3$ for rendering the network within a browser as depicted in the left hand side of Fig. 4 [1].

We used Girvan-Newman network partitioning algorithm in order to identify communities within the network and annotate user nodes with the communities they are associated with [5]. User nodes in the same community are displayed with the same color. When specifying the nodes and edges of interest, data scientists can use appropriate levers, which are added on during the structural analysis of the network. For example, one can filter nodes by their clustering coefficient in order to disclose tightly-knit regions, or cliques. The range of possible values can be used to specify the size of each node. For instance, a node with a high degree can be depicted larger than a node with a lower degree.

Each time the crawler is run, it takes a snapshot of the network. We run the crawler periodically so that we can study the evolution of the network. For this purpose, we added a scrollbar in the dashboard, which is used to access and render the state of the network over the snapshot timeline. Furthermore, the dashboard allows zooming in on a specific user node. Using a search query, data scientists can search for specific user/s of interest, and the rendering responds automatically. The matching set of user nodes to the query are highlighted with a higher opacity and a bigger size than the rest of the network. The network is centered automatically around one of the selected nodes (if there exists any).

# 3   Findings and Discussion

In this section, we present our initial findings on the social-affiliation network and the social network of our university.

## 3.1   Network Structure Analysis

We studied the structural properties of each network using a popular network analysis tool called NetworkX [9]. We computed graph modularity, graph diameter, and clustering coefficient per node. According to the snapshot taken on May $24^{th}$, 2018, our networks have the "aggregate" properties (mean values) as shown in Table 1.

**Table 1.** The mean structural properties of the social-affiliation network and the social network of our university computed using the data snapshot taken on May $24^{th}$, 2018.

|                          | Social-affiliation network | Social network |
|--------------------------|----------------------------|----------------|
| Total number of nodes    | 1041                       | 554            |
| Total number of edges    | 2286                       | 951            |
| Node degree              | 4.39                       | 3.43           |
| Clustering coefficient   | 0.306                      | 0.113          |
| Modularity               | 0.4535                     | 0.619          |
| Graph diameter           | 7                          | 8              |

The social-affiliation network, which contains both users and their foci as nodes and the corresponding edges between these nodes, has a smaller diameter compared to the social network, which only contains users as nodes and the edges between different users. This is expected since the distance between two arbitrary users will be shorter when we include the possibly overlapping affiliations in the network as well. Similarly, the network with affiliations is more clustered having denser communities compared to the less clustered social network, which is devoid of any affiliations. The social-affiliation network is less modular with a higher average clustering coefficient and a smaller diameter compared to the social network, which confirms that it contains both dense and large communities.

## 3.2   Studying Homophily by Language

Between two snapshots taken on May $8^{th}$ and May $24^{th}$ respectively, we found that there was a total of 638 new focal closures. We define an edge $e = \{u, v\}$ between users $u$ and $v$ as heterogenous if their language of choice on Twitter is different. That is, $u$ and $v$ use different natural languages majorly to tweet. On the other hand, if $u$ and $v$ have adopted the same language, then an edge between them is considered as homogenous.

The degree of heterogeneity of a whole network is the ratio of heterogenous edges among all edges. We can compare the degree of heterogeneity "observed" to the theoretical level of heterogeneity "expected". This can be done by first computing the language distribution over the users in the actual network. Then, for any edge $e = \{u, v\}$, the languages adopted by its endpoints $u$ and $v$ are randomly assigned using the underlying language distribution. Assume that there are two possible languages $L_1$ and $L_2$ used in the community. Let the ratio of users that adopt $L_1$ be $p$, and the ratio of users that adopt $L_2$ be $q$. Then, homogenous edges in a theoretical network occur with a ratio of $p \times p = p^2$ and $q \times q = q^2$ for $L_1$ and $L_2$ respectively. An heterogenous edge $e = \{u, v\}$ in a theoretical network occur with a ratio of $p \times q + q \times p = 2pq$, where the first term on the left hand side of the equation represents $u$ adopting $L_1$ and $v$ adopting $L_2$, and the second term on the left hand side of the equation represents $u$ adopting $L_2$ and $v$ adopting $L_1$. The value of $2pq$ is the ratio of heterogenous edges expected in a network with an underlying language distribution parameterized by $p$ and $q$. We compute the ratio $r$ of heterogeneous edges in the actual network, and compare this empirical value to the theoretical limit $2pq$. If $r$ is significantly less than $2pq$, then this observation constitutes an evidence for the presence of homophily in the community, for which the network stands for.

Table 2 summarizes the results we obtained on our community. As can be seen from the results, the ratio of heterogeneous edges in both networks we constructed are above their corresponding theoretical limits. This is an indication of a multi-cultural ambience being prevalent in our university. Note that the institutional accounts seem to have a more homogenous distribution weighing on one particular language, thereby reducing the ratio of heterogeneous edges in the social-affiliation network to 0.48 in comparison to the social network, which does not have any institutional Twitter accounts, and which has a higher degree of heterogeneity with the corresponding ratio being 0.52.

**Table 2.** The study of homophily by language of choice in our networks. The observed ratios are compared with the theoretical limits. The results indicate that there is no homophily present in the cultural attribute we studied.

| Network studied | Ratio of heterogeneous edges | Theoretical limit = $2pq$ |
|---|---|---|
| Social-affiliation network | 0.48 | 0.38 |
| Social network | 0.52 | 0.39 |

## 4    Conclusions

Working with the right context data, we captured valuable subjective characteristics of our university as a community. By taking into account the time dimension and the focal dimension, we were able to study the onset and the dynamics of implicit phenomena, such as the tendency of individuals to selectively seek out new relationships. We studied homophily by the spoken and written language, and observed that there is no language barrier specifically before a true multi-cultural interaction and integration in our university.

In the future, we plan to enrich the data storytelling capability and capacity of our system. We have already started to work on how to adjust the level of resolution on the network with smart overlays, which hopefully could help us first detect certain calls for change in the community, and then monitor their progression. In order to synthesize the network in multi-resolution, the strongly connected components of the network will be identified; the directed acyclic graph will be overlaid on the components so as to better visualize the flow of influence and change. At the peripheries of micro communities, we plan to isolate the local bridges with a sufficiently large span, study the individual characteristics of their endpoints, and visualize what parts of the network they interconnect.

# References

1. Bostock, M., Ogievetsky, V., Heer, J.: D3 data-driven documents. IEEE Trans. Vis. Comput. Graph. **17**(12), 2301–2309 (2011)
2. Burch, C.: Django, a web framework using Python: tutorial presentation. J. Comput. Sci. Coll. **25**(5), 154–155 (2010)
3. Easley, D., Kleinberg, J.: Networks, Crowds, and Markets: Reasoning About a Highly Connected World. Cambridge University Press, New York (2010)
4. Feld, S.L.: The focused organization of social ties. Am. J. Sociol. **86**(5), 1015–1035 (1981)
5. Girvan, M., Newman, M.E.J.: Community structure in social and biological networks. Proc. Natl. Acad. Sci. **99**(12), 7821–7826 (2002). https://doi.org/10.1073/pnas.122653799
6. Lu, Y., Wang, H., Landis, S., Maciejewski, R.: A visual analytics framework for identifying topic drivers in media events. IEEE Trans. Vis. Comput. Graph. **24**(9), 2501–2515 (2018)
7. Miller, F.P., Vandome, A.F., McBrewster, J.: Levenshtein Distance: Information Theory, Computer Science, String (Computer Science), String Metric, Damerau? Levenshtein Distance, Spell Checker, Hamming Distance. Alpha Press, Orlando (2009)
8. Moody, J.: Race, school integration, and friendship segregation in America. Am. J. Sociol. **107**(3), 679–716 (2001)
9. Schult, D.A.: Exploring network structure, dynamics, and function using NetworkX. In: Proceedings of the 7th Python in Science Conference (SciPy), pp. 11–15 (2008)
10. Wu, Y., et al.: StreamExplorer: a multi-stage system for visually exploring events in social streams. IEEE Trans. Vis. Comput. Graph. **24**(10), 2758–2772 (2018)

# Software Driven Optimal Design
# for Maintenance Man Hour

Antony Gratas Varuvel[1](✉) and Rajendra Prasath[2]

[1] Aeronautical Development Agency, Ministry of Defence, Government of India,
Post Box No. 1718, Vimanapura Post, Bangalore 560017, Karnataka, India
vaagratus@jetmail.ada.gov.in
[2] Indian Institute of Information Technology, Sri City, Sathyavedu Mandal,
Chittoor 517646, Andhra Pradesh, India
rajendra.prasath@iiits.in

**Abstract.** Cost of ownership of a capital item, increases exponentially, as the age of the equipment increases. Maintenance efforts involved in optimally maintaining the item procured, is determined predominantly by the Mean Time Between Failure [MTBF], Mean Time to Repair [MTTR] in addition to the required Man Hours. Knowing the faults and prognostics prior to failures will result in significant reduction in down time and the cost of maintenance. Software plays vital role in this regard, along with the required instrumentation in capturing and forecasting the anticipated failures and inform well in advance the maintenance requirements of the particular item. This paper describes in detail about designing an item, with the perspective of optimizing the maintenance efforts and cost, by using software techniques as one of the design parameters. MMH/OH is one among the terminologies used to describe, the amount of efforts required in terms of time, to operate a system [fly an aircraft/drive a car] for an hour in the normalized scale. Starting with the allocation of MMH/OH target, to systems, subsystems and LRUs [Line Replaceable Unit], realization of the target MMH/OH is dealt with, in detail, using software enabled control and communication. The proposed model and technique has been validated with a typical fighter aircraft.

**Keywords:** Availability · LRU · MMH/FH · MMH/OH · MSF
MTBF · MTTR · Scheduled maintenance · Unscheduled maintenance
Reliability

## Abbreviation Acronyms

| | |
|---|---|
| *BD* | Base Depot |
| *BIT* | Built In Test |
| *D* | Depot |
| *DC* | Duty Cycle |
| *DfM* | Design for Maintenance |
| *DMU* | Digital Mock Up |
| *EMTBF* | Effective Mean Time Between Failure |

© Springer Nature Switzerland AG 2018
A. Groza and R. Prasath (Eds.): MIKE 2018, LNAI 11308, pp. 148–167, 2018.
https://doi.org/10.1007/978-3-030-05918-7_14

| $EMTTF$ | Effective Mean Time to Failure |
|---|---|
| $FH$ | Flight Hour |
| $FT$ | Fault Tolerance |
| $FTF$ | Fault Tolerance Factor |
| $GSE$ | Ground Support Equipment |
| $IVHM$ | Integrated Vehicle Health Management |
| $IVR$ | Immersive Virtual Reality |
| $LCC$ | Life Cycle Cost |
| $LRU$ | Line Replaceable Unit |
| $MDT$ | Mean Down Time |
| $MMH$ | Maintenance Man Hour |
| $MSF$ | Maintenance Significant Factor |
| $MTBF$ | Mean Time Between Failure |
| $MTTF$ | Mean Time to Failure |
| $OH$ | Operational Hour |
| $PHM$ | Prognostics Health Management |
| $pdf$ | Probability Density Function |
| $R\&M$ | Reliability and Maintainability |
| $RAMS$ | Reliability, Availability, Maintainability and Safety |
| $RSF$ | Reliability Significant Factor |
| $SCM$ | Scheduled Maintenance |
| $USCM$ | Unscheduled Maintenance |
| $VR$ | Virtual Reality |

# 1   Introduction

Availability of an item assumes at most importance, as that of functionality, when the life cycle of the item is sufficiently large enough to maintain the item, than discarding or replacing. The two important pivotal points, Reliability and Maintainability, of availability are hence play vital role, in determining the effectiveness of the item for the user, for operational readiness. In order to ensure that, an item is available on demand, it is imperative to design an item with Reliability and Maintainability Trade-offs duly weighed, against each other. For an aircraft, the operational effectiveness is expressed in terms of MMH/FH, a normalized time expressing the amount of time an aircraft is on-ground, so as to fly for an hour. This means that, there are essential activities which are required to be carried out on an aircraft, so as to ensure a safe and reliable flight. For any capital items, the same is expressed in MMH/OH. In order to maintain any items with optimal maintenance tasks and high availability, it needs to be designed with MMH/OH as one of the requirements, in addition to the other essential requirements. Achieving the required MMH is also required to be treated as one of the design parameter. This paper aims at demonstrating the allocation model of MMH/OH to the lower indenture levels applicable, followed by the methodology by which the allocated values of MMH/OH are reduced using software techniques. An allocation technique of MMH/FH for an aircraft has already been published in [8]. This forms the basis of the present paper, orienting the approach towards realization of the same through design iterations, with higher availability fixed at the focal point. Refer Fig. 1.

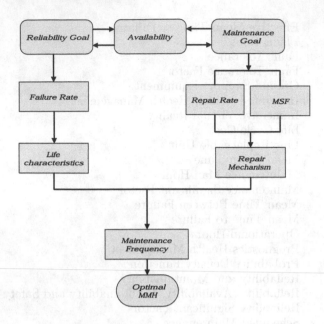

**Fig. 1.** Optimal MMH

## 2    Availability and MMH/OH

Availability is often determined by the inherent Reliability and Maintainability characteristics of the item. For the case of an aircraft [commercial/military], the availability is one of the critical parameters, which would eventually quantify the operational effectiveness, for the intended usage. Functionality requirements would be superseded, by availability requirements, if the criticality of the item under consideration is predominant or the down time plays an adverse role in degrading the usefulness of the item to the custodian.

Typically in a war scenario, any fighter aircraft is required to be readied with in short span of time and the same is required to be modified or rectified for the reported failures, when the aircraft is in queued in the line for flight. The time allowable to join the combat team is very limited and narrow, beyond which the aircraft would not meet the intended operational requirements. MMH of capital items is expected to be the lowest so as to enhance the on-demand availability. Whilst, availability is determined by R and M, the MMH/OH is also a function of R and M. However, sole R and M alone does not fully quantize MMH/OH. Mean Down Time [MDT], which is inclusive of Inherent MTTR and other significant factors of influence, called as MSF [Maintenance Significant factors] plays significant role towards achieving the required availability. Refer Fig. 1. Administrative, logistics and other delays are ignored in the approach, due to the fact that, those are minimized or even zeroed, when the maintenance team is prepared for the purported maintenance action a-priori, with the help of the on-board software and other resources.

# 3   MMH/OH Allocation

MMH/OH is the statistical average of the total hours the equipment is in idle/inoperable state and the total man hours spent in bringing back the system into operational state. Practical method of maintainability allocation was explained in Ref [1]. In general, MMH accounts for all the activities and the man hours until over haul. In the case of the aircraft, all intermediate maintenance tasks, such as cleaning, repairs, inspection, lubricating, adjusting, replenishing and minor disassembly/assembly are accounted for. Given a target value of MMH/OH, the realization plan should eventually include, initially, the allocation of the target into lower indenture levels . Allocation of the desired MMH/OH of any complex system of systems [typically an aircraft, or a heavy industrial equipment or smart car] to the lower indenture levels could be achieved by bifurcating the MMH/OH into two major tasks, such as,

– MMH/OH for Scheduled Maintenance
– MMH/OH for Unscheduled Maintenance

**Fig. 2.** Design for MMHFH

At any given instant of time of servicing of any complex system, there could be both scheduled, as well as unscheduled maintenance activities. Scheduled maintenance activities are determined by the life characteristics of the item under consideration, while the latter is assumed to be fully dominated by randomness of occurrence of faults. Although Maintenance scheduling for critical parts of aircraft is explained in Ref [2], the practical application is extremely untenable. Allocation of the target MMH/FH to the constituent systems are undertaken, while concentrating on both the types of maintenance elaborated above. The VAAG allocation technique for MMH/FH presented in [8], is reproduced below, by modifying the Flight Hour into Operational Hour, as applicable for any domain, including consumer automotive system/capital items.

$$\left[\frac{MMH}{OH}\right]_i = \left[\frac{MMH}{OH}\right]_t \left(\frac{\dfrac{\dfrac{\theta_{Ui}}{EMTBF_i} \cdot \alpha_i}{\sum\limits_{i=1}^{n} \dfrac{\theta_{Ui}}{EMTBF_i}} + \dfrac{\beta_i \cdot \theta_{Si}}{\sum\limits_{i=1}^{n} \theta_{Si}}}{\sum\limits_{i=1}^{n} \dfrac{\dfrac{\theta_{Ui}}{EMTBF_i} \cdot \alpha_i}{\sum\limits_{i=1}^{n} \dfrac{\theta_{Ui}}{EMTBF_i}} + \dfrac{\beta_i \cdot \theta_{Si}}{\sum\limits_{i=1}^{n} \theta_{Si}}}\right) \tag{1}$$

where,

$$\left[\frac{MMH}{OH}\right]_i : \text{MMH/OH for system/item } i$$

$$\left[\frac{MMH}{OH}\right]_t : \text{Target MMH/OH}$$

The MMH/OH target of the platform under consideration would get allocated to the constituent systems, as per the above model. The resultant numerical value consists of two targets, such as,

(i) MMH/OH goal for Scheduled Maintenance, for system $i$
(ii) MMH/OH goal for Unscheduled Maintenance, for system $i$

Having allocated the overall target MMH/OH to the lower level, this paper will further emphasize the methodology by which the allocated targets would be met. Special emphasis has been given for using software techniques, with the intention to reduce the maintenance efforts and time. It is essential to clearly understand the maintenance requirements of each of the item under consideration, so as to effectively optimize the duration as well as man powers. In the model developed, the skilled manpower is assumed, without attaching any reference or linking to the variability of skillset.

## 4   Levels of Maintenance

Various approaches for aircraft maintenance was elaborated in Ref [4]. For a specific system, both/any of the above mentioned activities would be carried out. MMH required to execute any task decreases linearly initially due to,

(i) Decreasing infant mortality failures
(ii) Increase in the development of skillset

However, the tasks and the frequency increases exponentially during the later life cycle of the system, due to

(i) Ageing of the components
(ii) introduction of new technology

The same is depicted in a curve, named as *Spoon-shaped Curve* as referred in [3]. For simplicity of representation, a similar curve is reproduced in Fig. 3, by including the skillset of the manpower.

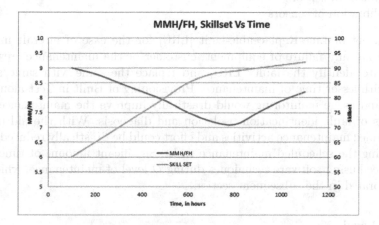

**Fig. 3.** Variation of MMH/FH over time

The [scheduled and unscheduled] maintenance tasks/activities which are required to be executed could broadly be categorized as,

(i) O-level
(ii) I-Level
(iii) D-Level

depending on the capabilities on fault diagnosis, isolation, repair/replacement characteristics.

In some cases BD level of maintenance is also undertaken, based on the user requirement and priorities, and technical capabilities of the team. This is an additional level of maintenance, wherein having known the root cause of the problems at hand, the technical team would be able to replace the components. However, *BD* level of maintenance may be carried out, only for some selected items, which does not call for specialized and sophisticated analysis, repair and replacement facility. Reference is made to [6].

### 4.1   O Level

*O level* defines the tasks, which could be carried out, without any assistance from the third party or any special equipment, within very short span of time. The MTTR of these cases are to be lowest to the possible extent. In other words, items which exhibits high failure rate are to be ensured, to have less MTTR. *O-level* signifies that, the user can easily carryout activities, without visiting the repair shop/manufacturing facility. Typical examples are,

- Upgrading of system firmware
- Resetting of system state to default state
- Error-logging & Error recovery
- Alignment of sensors
- Recalibration of sensors

The concept of Line-Replaceable-Unit [LRU] for the case of aircraft industry argues that, any failure of equipment, customer or the maintenance crew shall be able to identify the faulty LRU, and replace the same with same/similar LRU, with lesser time of maintenance. Provisioning of Built in Test along with health and usage monitoring would drastically improve the maintenance effort in terms of fault identification, isolation and diagnosis. With the aid of this, unscheduled maintenance activities and effort could be drastically reduced, while optimizing the scheduled maintenance tasks. Significant amount of time could be reduced using software techniques during $O$ level of maintenance, which will be elaborated in the subsequent section.

### 4.2  I Level

The next level of maintenance, called as *I-level*, is usually imply, fault removal activities which cannot be carried out immediately, upon failure. But suitably be postponed/scheduled at a later point in time, which necessitates the aircraft to be brought out of the flying line and more detailed activities would be carried out to bring the system up. Those faults necessitate the user to bring the system to the repair shop, so as to diagnose the fault reported, trouble shoot and identify the cause of the fault. Special types of tools and skillset are required to facilitate this task, and hence these activities would not, in general, be carried out by the user. Usage of software tools and techniques at this stage also amounts to reduction of maintenance time. But, not as significant as in the case of $O$ level.

### 4.3  D Level

Further examination of the faulty items would be carried out at the premises of the manufacturer, where in-depth investigation of the faults reported will be carried out. The items which enter this phase are treated as '*As Good as new*'. When the trouble shooting of a problem identifies the root cause as the basic failure behaviour of the component, then further investigation or repair need to be carried out by the manufacturer of the item. Design expertise is required to troubleshoot and repair the component, and hence this activity cannot be carried out by the repair/overhaul shop. Time required to repair the defective item in the manufacturing facility is usually ignored in the MMH calculation, as the same is rectified by replacement, rather than repair, to meet the availability requirement of the capital item. Thorough investigation including physics of failure analysis may be carried out by the manufacturer to exactly pin point on the failure mode, so that the same could be eliminated from re occurring.

# 5 Design for MMH

The MMH [could be normalized by Flight Hour [FH] or Operating Hours [OH] based on the platform for which it is intended] is influenced critically by the following Maintenance Significant Factors, termed as *MSF*.

– Accessibility
– Complexity
– Diagnostics/Prognostics
– Fault Tolerance

Flow of activities which are essential in achieving the target MMH/OH, for both scheduled and unscheduled categories of maintenance tasks are depicted pictorially and given below in Fig. 3. In order to ensure that, the system is designed for MMH/OH, it is required to instil the maintenance oriented design from the drawing board through optimization and to realization. Every factor listed above play a vital role in effectively reducing the maintenance time. It is also the fact that, all the factors listed above could not be considered to have equal weightage and it is improbable/impractical to assign the best MSF to all the items of the systems. These factors are to be considered in addition to the inherent Reliability and Maintainability features such as MTBF/MTTF and MTTR. Following subsections deal with various MSF, which play major role in determining the effectiveness of maintenance apart from inherent MTBF/MTTF & /MTTR. Ignoring these MSF in the initial stages of platform design, would greatly affect the RAMS, characteristics negatively, impacting total availability and Life Cycle Cost.

  While every MSF is described in detail in the following subsections, the usage and salient advantages of utilizing the software based tools in optimization of each MSF is also elaborated.

## 5.1 DMMH for Accessibility

Accessibility is one of the prime factors which would significantly affect the duration with which an item could be accessed for the purposes of diagnostics/prognostics/removal/replacement. Maintenance would be ineffective, if the item under consideration is not adequately accessible. Any item, whose failure frequency is more in relative terms, is required to be provisioned in an area or location, where effortless access is ensured, to access and diagnose the same. Installation and removal of these items shall not warrant removal of any other items in the vicinity. Conversely, an item with higher reliability may be positioned suitably, even without any accessibility. Hence, the following parameters of accessibility are considered crucial, for ease of maintenance, and thereby improving/reducing the MMH.

– Hand(s) Accessible
– Tool(s) Accessible
– Ground Support Equipment Accessible
– Vision Accessible

The above parameters exclude human engineering factors (anthropometry) and the exposure/skill set of the maintenance crew/personnel. It is assumed that, these parameters are analysed and evaluated prior to deployment of the maintenance crew team, to meet the stated maintenance activities. Accessibility, being expressed with subjectivity, is proposed here to be expressed in percentage. The MSF-Accessibility, $MSF\text{-}A$, is expressed in weighted average scale and is given as,

$$A_i = \frac{\sum\limits_{j=1}^{m} X_j}{m}.w_A \tag{2}$$

where,

$X_{(j)}$ : Percentage accessibility of chosen parameter $j$
$m$ : Total number of accessibility parameters
$w_{(a)}$ : Maximum scale factor chosen for accessibility

GSE enables easy maintenance using which an item under maintenance is accessed, removed, and positioned, for further diagnosis, repair and replacement. Influence of availability of GSE for the required maintenance tasks is ignored, and assumed that GSE is readily available, on-demand, for the required maintenance task. From the experience of maintenance tasks relating to a typical fighter aircraft, the trend of accessibility with respect to the amount of time required to access the item is known to be as given below, Typical influence of accessibility on the maintenance time, as observed practically is represented below in Fig. 4. Catering for simple and common parts, such as same types of mounting

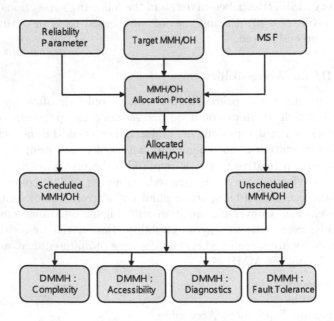

**Fig. 4.** Design for MMHFH

scheme, screws, fasteners across all the panels would significantly improve the maintainability.

Advancement in DMU (using the tools like CATIA) with specialized tools and techniques improvised the accessibility studies, which otherwise required detailed imaginative powers or the actual item to be available for the accessibility studies. Iterations on the mock up are easily carried out to cater for conflicting demands and trade-off. Added to these features, IVR, which is software intensive, plays a vital role in experiencing the real world maintenance or operational interactions with man-in-loop, with the help of immersive sensors and electronics. Refer to Figs. 2 and 6.

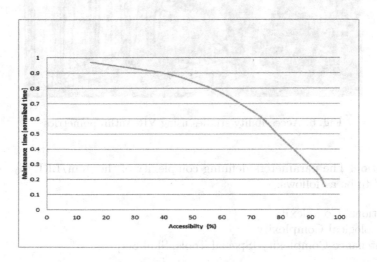

**Fig. 5.** Accessibility

## 5.2   DMMH for Complexity

Complexity of the item under consideration for maintenance and the efforts in maintenance, are linearly related. This has been validated using data available within the aircraft industry, especially the fighter aircraft domain. Higher the complexity of the item, higher would be the maintenance time and efforts involved in rectifying the maintenance task reported. Though the state-of-the art technology would be adopted for maintenance of the state-of-the art item, the training required to facilitate the maintenance personnel would be higher while in comparison with the same required for a simple item, by design. Hence, the MMH required to maintain an item with highly advanced technology, is expected to be more. However, with advanced techniques, the troubleshooting would be simpler and fault-free. More complexity involves more sensors for IVHM and complex processing algorithms to find out the present state of the fault and its

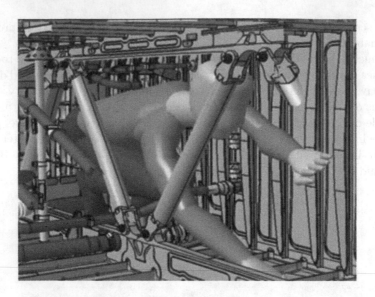

**Fig. 6.** Accessibility studies using VR-Anthropometrics

propagation. The parameters defining complexity of the item/LRU/System are assumed to be as follows:

– Functional Complexity
– Technological Complexity
– Maintenance Complexity [Special Tools, Skill Set]

Expressed mathematically the above, while ignoring the troubleshooting techniques adopted, the *MSF-C* is given by:

$$C_i = w_C \cdot f(C_i) \tag{3}$$

$$C_i = \frac{\sum\limits_{j=1}^{m} Y_j}{m} \cdot w_C \tag{4}$$

where,

$Y_j$ : Percentage complexity of Item/LRU/System $j$
$m$ : Total number of complexity parameters
$w_C$ : Maximum scale factor chosen for complexity

The curve indicating the relationship among the complexity, which is a subjective parameter, against the time required for maintenance in normalized scale is given in the plot below (Fig. 7).

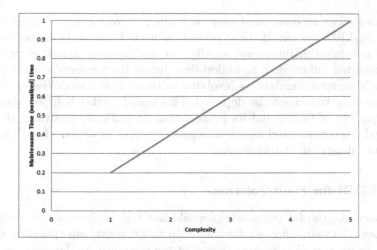

**Fig. 7.** Complexity

## 5.3   DMMH for Diagnostics

Design capability to diagnose the fault leads to reduced maintenance time and efforts. Meaning, the amount of time required on-ground to troubleshoot and isolate the fault would greatly be reduced, if diagnostics feature is built within the item/system. Introduction of Built-In-Test [BIT] enables, the identification of the fault upon occurrence, and masking the fault, so that the fault would not be allowed to propagate to the boundary of the failure state. In the course, the maintenance efforts are reduced significantly, as trouble shooting and isolating the fault reported consumes major and sizeable pie of the maintenance time. The diagnostics capabilities define the *MSF-D* as given below:

$$D_i = \begin{cases} 1 & \text{if } x < 10\% & (5a) \\ 2 & \text{if } 10\% < x < 40\% & (5b) \\ 3 & \text{if } 40\% < x < 70\% & (5c) \\ 4 & \text{if } 70\% < x < 100\% & (5d) \\ 5 & \text{if } x = 100\% & (5e) \end{cases}$$

Where $x$ is the percentage capability of the BIT to detect the faults resident within the item/LRU/System. Ideal would be 100% leading to a factor of 5.

Incorporation of the state-of-the art technologies warrants for higher skillset required to maintain an item. Integrated Vehicle Health Monitoring System [IVHM] or the Prognostics Health Management [PHM] would entail opportunity to know the health of the system and its expected duration of fault free, yet acceptable level of operation, before the fault propagation exceeds the critical limit. Though the prognostic feature would enable early detection of the potential failure modes and occurrence, the effect of the same is not considered, as it is treated as an on-ground exercise leading to forecasting of latent failures of the item/LRU/system. If the expected failure is found to be higher than the time for scheduled maintenance activity, the maintenance activities pertaining to the predicted failure shall be undertaken during the previous scheduled maintenance. Numerous simulations involving software based modelling on the life behaviour of systems could be depicted. This would further help in characterizing the pattern of failure and its propagation, by critically analysing the data. Unwanted down times and maintenance are avoided by effectively utilizing the algorithms aboard an IVHM system.

## 5.4  DMMH for Fault Tolerance

Acceptance of graceful degradation would not only enhances the availability but reduces the maintenance efforts also. In this context, incorporation of fault tolerant features enable postponement of maintenance to the next scheduled maintenance period, according to the types of fault encountered and the severity level of the fault in meeting the overall objective of the item. Functional classification and the criticality of those identified functions are to be addressed well in advance to cater for fault tolerant design and the associated maintenance tasks. There are two types of fault tolerant design. Among the two, software based fault tolerance is more rewarding than the hardware based fault tolerant system.

IVHM plays a crucial role in minimizing the MMH to a possible extent. Both Fault Tolerance and IVHM Capability are treated synonymously here, owing to their impact on scheduled maintenance activities primarily, and unscheduled maintenance activities secondarily. IVHM or PHM aids in forecasting the health of mechanical systems, which otherwise could be provided with Diagnostics/BIT capability. Remaining useful life of those items could also be predicted in advance using the trend of the data. Accordingly, preventive maintenance activities could be initiated at appropriate time, as determined by the maintenance personnel. Generally, the level of fault tolerant could be categorized as follows, based on the experience with the aerospace domain:

$$
FT_i = \begin{cases}
1 & \text{No fault Tolerance} & \text{(6a)} \\
2 & \text{Degraded, Minimum Capability} & \text{(6b)} \\
3 & \text{Fail Safe, More work load} & \text{(6c)} \\
4 & \text{Fail Operational, Partial Capability} & \text{(6d)} \\
5 & \text{Fail Operational, Full Capability} & \text{(6e)}
\end{cases}
$$

The same could be applied to automotive or any safety critical applications. Incorporation of IVHM or PHM culminated into enormous improvements in terms of reduction in down time, and the same is modelled in [7].

# 6   D-MMH/FH: Scheduled Maintenance

The scheduled maintenance of any item is dominated and determined by the inherent characteristics of the items and its failure modes. Based on the life characteristics over time, the maintenance frequency would be arrived at. The maintenance frequency increases as the age of the item increases. Scheduled maintenance is often applied to items which are having moving parts/fluids/brushing. Refer [2]. Based on the MMH/FH model developed by [8], the MMH/OH for scheduled maintenance would be arrived at:

$$
\left[\frac{MMH}{OH}\right]_{Si} = \left[\frac{MMH}{OH}\right]_{i} \left( \frac{\dfrac{\beta_i \cdot \theta_{Si}}{\displaystyle\sum_{i=1}^{n} \theta_{Si}}}{\dfrac{\dfrac{\theta_{Ui}}{EMTBF_i} \cdot \alpha_i}{\displaystyle\sum_{i=1}^{n} \dfrac{\theta_{Ui}}{EMTBF_i}} + \dfrac{\beta_i \cdot \theta_{Si}}{\displaystyle\sum_{i=1}^{n} \theta_{Si}}} \right)
\tag{7}
$$

where,

$\left[\dfrac{MMH}{OH}\right]_{Si}$ :MMH/OH for SCM for item $i$

$\left[\dfrac{MMH}{OH}\right]_{Ui}$ :MMH/OH for UNSCM for item $i$

$\left[\dfrac{MMH}{OH}\right]_{t}$ :Target MMH/OH for item $i$

$EMTBF_i$ :Effective MTBF for item $i$

$DC_i$ :Duty cycle for item $i$, ranging from 0 to 1

$MTBF_{(i)}$ :MTBF of item $i$

$SCM$ :Scheduled Maintenance

$UNSCM$ :Unscheduled Maintenance

$UF$ :Uncertainty Factor

$MF$ :Maintenance Frequency

$T$ :Total duration of operation, prior to SCM

$t_i$ :Total duration of maintenance of an item $i$, during T

$M$ :Total calendar time of operation, prior to SCM

$m_i$ :ETTR in calendar time of item $i$, during M

$\beta_i$ :Constant of proportionality for item $i$
i.e., Maintenance Frequency

$n$ :Total number of items in the system

$\theta_{Si}$ :MSF for item $i$, for SCM

$FT_i$ :1, for SCM [No fault tolerance]

$\alpha_i$ :Constant of proportionality for UNSCM for $i$
i.e., Uncertainty [Risk] Factor

$\theta_{Si}$ :Maintenance Significant Factor for $i$

$C_{(i)}$ :Complexity factor of item $i$

$A_{(i)}$ :Accessibility factor for of item $i$

$D_{(i)}$ :Diagnostics factor for item $i$

$FT_{(i)}$ :Fault Tolerant factor of item $i$

---

For calendar based maintenance,

$$\beta_i = \frac{t_i}{T} \tag{8}$$

For usage based maintenance,

$$\beta_i = \frac{m_i}{M} \tag{9}$$

$$EMTBF_i = \frac{MTBF_i}{DC_i} \tag{10}$$

$$\theta_{Si} = \frac{C_i}{A_i . D_i} \tag{11}$$

It is clearly evident from the equation that, software plays significant roles in each of the MSF, which in turn used for designing a system for MMH.

# 7   D-MMH/OH: Unscheduled Maintenance

Unlike scheduled maintenance, the unscheduled maintenance is predominantly determined by the failure phenomena, which is often described by the *probability density function* of the failure events. This type of maintenance is applicable for electronics based systems, where in the failure modes are expected to occur randomly in most of the cases, and with determinism in some cases, where electromechanical design in embodied. Ref [5]. The proportion of unscheduled maintenance of MMH/OH of an item, would be more for electronics based design, due to the very nature and the randomness of occurrence of faults. The proportion of MMH/OH of unscheduled maintenance of the total maintenance for an item $i$ is derived from the original MMH/FH model and presented below:

$$\left[\frac{MMH}{OH}\right]_{Ui} = \left[\frac{MMH}{OH}\right]_{i} \left( \frac{\dfrac{\dfrac{\theta_{Ui}}{EMTBF_i} \cdot \alpha_i}{\displaystyle\sum_{i=1}^{n} \dfrac{\theta_{Ui}}{EMTBF_i}}}{\dfrac{\dfrac{\theta_{Ui}}{EMTBF_i} \cdot \alpha_i}{\displaystyle\sum_{i=1}^{n} \dfrac{\theta_{Ui}}{EMTBF_i}} + \dfrac{\beta_i \cdot \theta_{Si}}{\displaystyle\sum_{i=1}^{n} \theta_{Si}}} \right) \tag{12}$$

$$\theta_{Ui} = \frac{C_i}{A_i . D_i . FT_i} \tag{13}$$

In order to absorb the uncertainty of the occurrence, a risk factor $\alpha$ is introduced in the above model, and is restricted to a maximum of 50%. Based on the system architecture and design, the factor $\alpha$ is determined (Figs. 8 and 9).

**Fig. 8.** Accessibility studies using VR

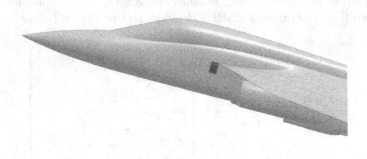

**Fig. 9.** Maintenance terminal

## 8    Software Intensive Maintenance Terminal

In order to effectively incorporate software based maintenance trouble shoot-ing and display, it is proposed to incorporate a active display device on the aircraft or any capital item, so as to indicate the system logs and health sta-tus of the constituent components. It is envisaged that, any fault logs/error codes/diagnostic data/prognostics data are stored, analysed and displayed to the maintenance crew through the display. Required maintenance actions would be initiated appropriately, with the cues obtained from this display terminal, called Maintenance Terminal. This would improve the on-demand availability of the capital item, and reduce down time. The display terminal is expected to be software intensive with the capability to display the current status of the items and forecast future behaviour of the components based on the captured data. The data are analysed using suitable algorithms, which can predict and characterize the life the components based on the trend of the captured data.

## 9    Validation

In order to validate the proposed technique, sample data from typical fighter aircraft has been taken up after masking. It is assumed that, the fighter aircraft considered consists of 10 systems. Each system can have any to many number of subsystems. The MTBF of the systems are obtained from *Reliability Allocation Method*, derived from user requirements on the target Reliability for the aircraft. Other factors derived are given in the table below:

To derive the factors in the above Table 1, it is essential to quantify all the MSFs in the same numerical scale chosen [it is 5, in the present case]. The accessibility factor is given below, in Table 2

In the similar lines, the MSF-Complexity is also represented in the numerical scale for all the systems of the aircraft, and is given in Table 3.

The other two significant MSFs, viz., $D_i$ and $FT_i$ are given in Table 1. Using all the MSFs and MTBF, the system level targets could be set, categorizing into

**Table 1.** Parameters determining MMH

| Systems | Given MTBF | MSF : $D_i$ | MSF : $FT_i$ | USCM : $\theta_{Ui}$ | UF : $\alpha_i$ | SCM : $\theta_{Si}$ | MF : $\beta_i$ |
|---|---|---|---|---|---|---|---|
| Airframe | 10000 | 1 | 1 | 0.5 | 0.2 | 0.5 | 0.2 |
| Flight Control | 1500 | 4 | 4 | 0.0833 | 0.5 | 0.333 | 0.2 |
| Avionics | 900 | 4 | 5 | 0.0667 | 0.5 | 0.333 | 0.1 |
| Propulsion | 700 | 3 | 1 | 0.5 | 0.2 | 0.5 | 0.4 |
| Environmental Control | 1200 | 2 | 1 | 0.5 | 0.3 | 0.5 | 0.7 |
| Electrical Power | 1800 | 4 | 2 | 0.1875 | 0.5 | 0.375 | 0.1 |
| Hydraulics Power | 2500 | 2 | 2 | 0.25 | 0.3 | 0.5 | 0.7 |
| Fuel Sytem | 1400 | 2 | 1 | 0.5 | 0.3 | 0.5 | 0.8 |
| Safety System | 1700 | 1 | 1 | 0.667 | 0.1 | 0.667 | 0.4 |
| Landing System | 1300 | 1 | 1 | 0.8 | 0.3 | 0.8 | 0.8 |

**Table 2.** MSF-Accessibility

| Systems | Hand accessible | Tool accessible | GSE accessible | Vision accessible | MSF-$A_i$ |
|---|---|---|---|---|---|
| Airframe | 90 | 80 | 70 | 80 | 4 |
| Flight Control | 75 | 70 | 40 | 55 | 3 |
| Avionics | 70 | 60 | 50 | 60 | 3 |
| Propulsion | 50 | 40 | 30 | 40 | 2 |
| Environmental Control | 80 | 70 | 40 | 50 | 3 |
| Electrical Power | 60 | 40 | 20 | 40 | 2 |
| Hydraulics Power | 70 | 70 | 40 | 60 | 3 |
| Fuel Sytem | 70 | 60 | 50 | 60 | 3 |
| Safety System | 70 | 60 | 40 | 70 | 3 |
| Landing System | 100 | 100 | 100 | 100 | 5 |

**Table 3.** MSF-Complexity

| Systems | Functional complexity | Technology complexity | Maintenance complexity | MSF-$C_i$ |
|---|---|---|---|---|
| Airframe | 40 | 30 | 0.5 | 2 |
| Flight Control | 70 | 70 | 1 | 4 |
| Avionics | 70 | 70 | 1 | 4 |
| Propulsion | 60 | 70 | 0.5 | 3 |
| Environmental Control | 60 | 70 | 0.5 | 3 |
| Electrical Power | 40 | 40 | 1 | 3 |
| Hydraulics Power | 50 | 80 | 0.5 | 3 |
| Fuel Sytem | 70 | 60 | 0.5 | 3 |
| Safety System | 40 | 30 | 0.5 | 2 |
| Landing System | 100 | 90 | 0.5 | 4 |

two major components of maintenance, such as, MMH for Scheduled maintenance and MMH for unscheduled maintenance for a given system. the result is tabulated in Table 4. The MMH/FH has been obtained for the sample data, as the data are pertaining to an aircraft.

**Table 4.** Validation

| Systems | System Total Target : $\left[\frac{MMH}{FH}\right]_i$ | System SCM Target : $\left[\frac{MMH}{FH}\right]_{Si}$ | System USCM Target : $\left[\frac{MMH}{FH}\right]_{Ui}$ |
|---|---|---|---|
| Airframe | 0.31031 | 0.26562 | 0.04469 |
| Flight Control | 0.30121 | 0.17708 | 0.12413 |
| Avionics | 0.25405 | 0.08854 | 0.16551 |
| Propulsion | 1.16965 | 0.53124 | 0.63841 |
| Environmental Control | 1.48827 | 0.92967 | 0.55861 |
| Electrical Power | 0.33236 | 0.09961 | 0.23275 |
| Hydraulics Power | 1.06373 | 0.92967 | 0.13407 |
| Fuel Sytem | 1.67187 | 1.06245 | 0.60939 |
| Safety System | 0.88357 | 0.70832 | 0.17525 |
| Landing System | 2.52498 | 1.69996 | 0.82502 |

## 10   Conclusion

The main objective of the present paper is to draw a methodology by which the MMH could be implanted into the design of the systems and realization of the designed systems appropriately on the platform, with the objective of reducing the maintenance efforts, and hence the cost, thereby improving the on-demand availability of the item, throughout its life cycle. The design for MMH process presented utilized MSF, which are determined by the application of software tools and techniques. The MMH/OH allocation technique has been proposed, and elaborated with validation, by using a typical fighter aircraft data. From the user defined goal of Reliability and MMH, this paper provide an approach, using which the user requirements are further allocated to system/subsystem/LRU level. All the relevant and required MSFs have been incorporated in the proposed model and the means of achieving the same has been detailed, by carefully deciding on the MSFs, which plays major role in maintenance, apart from the R & M factors.

**Acknowledgment.** This research work was executed in Aeronautical Development Agency, Bangalore-INDIA.

# References

1. John, S., Chipchak, A.: Practical method of maintainability allocation. IEEE Trans. Aerosp. Electron. Syst. **AES–7**(4), 585–589 (1971)
2. Fard, N.S., Melachrinoudis, E.: Maintenance scheduling for critical parts of aircraft. In: Proceedings Annual Reliability and Maintainability Symposium (1991)
3. Yanjie, Q., Zhigang, L., Bifeng, S.: New concept for aircraft maintenance management. In: Proceedings Annual Reliability and Maintainability Symposium, pp. 401–405 (2001)
4. Dupuy, M.J., Wesely, D.E., Jenkins, C.S.: Airline fleet maintenance: trade-off analysis of alternate aircraft maintenance approaches. In: Proceedings of 2011 IEEE Systems and Information Engineering Design Symposium, 29 April 2011
5. Zhang, A., Cui, L., Zhang, P.: Advanced military aircraft of study on condition-based maintenance. In: 2013 International Conference on Information Technology and Applications (2013)
6. Rau, C.-G., Necas, P., Boscoianu, M.: Review of maintainability and maintenance optimization methods for aviation engineering systems. Sci. Mil. **6**(2), 54 (2011)
7. Holzel, N.B., Schilling, T., Gollnick, V.: An aircraft lifecycle approach for the cost-benefit analysis of prognostics, and condition-based maintenance based on discrete-event simulation. In: Proceedings Annual Conference of the Prognostics and Health Management Society (2014)
8. Varuvel, A.G., Prakash, R.: An allocation technique of MMH/FH for an aircraft. In: Prasath, R., Gelbukh, A. (eds.) MIKE 2016. LNCS (LNAI), vol. 10089, pp. 93–104. Springer, Cham (2017). https://doi.org/10.1007/978-3-319-58130-9_10

# Modeling Trajectory Data as a Directed Graph

Ali Korkmaz, Ferdi Elik, Furkan Aydin, Mertcan Bulut, Seda Kul[(✉)],
and Ahmet Sayar

Computer Engineering Department, Kocaeli University, 41380 Izmit, Turkey
alikorkmaz1923@gmail.com, elik.ferdi@gmail.com,
aydofurkan25@gmail.com, canmertbulut@gmail.com,
{seda.kul,ahmet.sayar}@kocaeli.edu.tr

**Abstract.** In the last decade, usage of personal smartphones has tremendously increased. Almost everyone is using cell phones, which are communicating with location-aware devices. A large amount of trajectory data is produced from these devices and can be used for information services. One of the key elements in the mining of GPS or mobility data is the stay point recognition. A stay point is described as a location where a person frequently visits or stay for a long time period. In this work, we first introduce an algorithm to define a stay point for a person whose trajectory data is recorded with a smartphone. Later, with another algorithm, we define a graph model representing a person's moving characteristics, which is built upon our stay point's algorithm.

**Keywords:** GPS · Trajectory · Stay point

## 1 Introduction

Nowadays people are using Global Positioning System (GPS) systems for their location information. People use real-time location sharing information systems like "Glympse" and "Locale" for determining changed behavior in the different locations, "Where" for location recommendation and "NeverLate" for defining changing time to go to the other locations. These systems collect trajectory data and use many trajectory-mining analyses [1, 2].

In this paper, we are focusing on a defining and calculating Stay-Points for trajectories [3, 4]. We want to add a new perspective to the common approaches regarding the stay point calculation. To do so, we first calculate stay points and from them, we define directed graphs.

A place of interest is defined as a place where a user usually goes and stays for a while. In this work, we can find the user's place of interest from their stay points. Place of interests can help us to learn about the user's lifestyle, life standard etc. If a person goes to a library every day and stays there for a long time, then that library is marked as a stay point. If a library is a user's stay point then we can say that the user studies a lot. Therefore, it gives us a hint about the user's life. Users can be a hardworking person or they like to read a lot, or they like silent places. Those are sample analyses drawn from trajectory data and stay point analyses.

© Springer Nature Switzerland AG 2018
A. Groza and R. Prasath (Eds.): MIKE 2018, LNAI 11308, pp. 168–176, 2018.
https://doi.org/10.1007/978-3-030-05918-7_15

In this work when we take a place of interests of a person and insert it into our graph-based approach it will make a time based directional graph. The graph will show us the user's place of interest in a timely order. In the graph, we can find the stay points that the user often goes to and we can find out what points the user circulates most.

In business life, this information about people can be very useful. For example, it can be used in the advertising industry. If you know where a person will go or where he/she usually stays, you can make billboards on his/her way. Nowadays people matching apps are so popular. These companies can use graph-based approach for matching people. If two people have the similar pattern in their graphs, we can match them. If two people have similar stay points, we can match them. Therefore, a user will match people look like each other. Matched people are going to similar places and stay there same time with similar timelines so they will be similar to each other. Briefly, the user can find people having the similar interests and enjoying spending time from similar things. It can be also used as a security system for the kids or elderly people. If a person that you are tracking produces a new stay point, you will have a notification about it. By this way, you can know if that person is in danger.

In this article, we aim to classify trajectory data based on their time attributes and intensity characteristics. Since GPS technologies is not so sensitive, multiple nearby stay points are clustered as a single point. The naming of stay points and the decision if the point is going to be saved or not is left to the users. After having defined stay point determination algorithm, we introduce an algorithm to model stay points as a graph. Graph definition of stay points for each user enable us to use graph data mining tools to drive useful information about the users' mobility characteristics. In the graph model, edges are drown in varying thickness sizes and with directional format. Thickness of the edges represent the magnitude of the traffic between any two nodes. If there is an edge from node-1 to node-2, that means when a user in stay point node-1, that user most frequently goes to stay point represented as node-2.

The paper is organized as follows. Section 2 presents related works. The proposed stay point algorithm and graph modelling algorithms are given in Sects. 3 and 4 respectively. Section 5 concludes the paper.

## 2 Related Works

There are some related works on determining a stay point. We list them as follows.

Xiao [4] uses taxi trajectory data to determine the stay points. In this work, they use noise filtering for obtaining more successful stay points. Stylianou [5] uses curve extrema for the stay point identification. They demonstrate the potential of a geometry-based method for stay-point extraction. This is accomplished by transforming a user's trajectory path to a two-dimensional discrete time series curve that in turn transforms the stay-points to the local minima of the first derivative of this curve. Montoliu et al. [6] in their article proposes a new framework to discover places-of-interest from multimodal mobile phone data. Pérez-Torres et al. [7] propose and validate the feasibility of having an alternative event-driven mechanism for stay points detection that is executed fully on-device, and that provides higher energy savings by avoiding communication costs. Their solution is encapsulated in a sensing middleware for Android smartphones, where a stream of GPS location updates is collected in the background, supporting duty cycling schemes, and incrementally analyzed following an event-driven paradigm for stay points detection. In the work presented in this paper, we focus mainly on stay points detection. After that, we introduce an algorithm to create a directed weighted graph from the previously determined stay points. This two process together enable trajectory data analysts to mine moving patterns of the system users. We use Microsoft's Geolife [8] (Zheng 2007) data to prove the proposed algorithms work. Awada et al. [9] proposed a simplified deterministic channel model for user mobility investigations in 5G networks. He says that current models lack the accuracy in capturing spatial correlation. For this purpose, they propose a simplified deterministic channel model. The result that they obtained shows that signal degradation due to obstruction is faster for higher carrier frequency and user velocity, and slower for higher diffraction angle. Lv et al. [10] proposed a hidden Markov model (HMM) and a spatiotemporal predictor and a next-place predictor. They say that continuously transmit GPS information can cause low battery and lack of privacy.

## 3 Stay Point Algorithm

The most important thing in determining stay-points for a user is to record the users' locations. The locations are recorded in a pre-defined time interval. The value of time interval is very important in defining stay-points. If it is defined as higher or lower than some threshold values, then the collected data might be very high or very low respectively. This situation might end up with unsuccessful results.

The second threshold value which is key to the success of the algorithm is distance value. It helps in making a decision about if a recently determined point is going to be included into the existent stay-point or a new stay point needs to be defined from that point. If the newly determined point is close enough to one of to an existent stay-point, then, that means there is no need to introduce another stay point.

First, we need to forecast these two threshold values. In the proposed stay-point algorithm, threshold values are pre-defined and static. The threshold values depend on the raw data we have. We need to initialize them if we want to find stay points of trajectories. Here are our stay point algorithm steps.

We loop in all trajectory data. For example, we take first element of the loop then we open new loop so we can roam every element in trajectory data. This roaming will continue until exceeding of threshold values. The point at which threshold values are passed is marked as stay point. If threshold values never passed then we don't have any stay points.

---

**Algorithm-1: Find Stay Points in Trajectory**

---

**Input :** Trajectory (Location, Date) List, distance threshold dt, time threshold tt
**Output:** a set of stay points as SP

1. **while** i < trajectory size -1
2.     Point pI = trajectory index of i
3.     Create new region list that contains Location and Dates
4.     j = i + 1
5.     **while** j < trajectory size
6.         Point pJ = trajectory index of j
7.         distance = calculate distance between pI and pJ
8.         add pj to region list
9.         **if** distance > dt
10.             time = last element of region date - first element of region date
11.             **if** time > tt
12.                 remove pJ from region
13.                 newLocation = computeMeanCoordinates from region list
14.                 arrivalDate = first element of region date
15.                 leaveDate = last element of region date
16.                 add (newLocation , arrivalDate , leaveDate) to SP
17.             clear region list
18.             i=j
19.             break
20.         **else if** j == trajetory size -1
21.             i = j
22.         j = j + 1
23. **return** SP

---

After having defined the stay point algorithm (Algorithm-1), we introduce a new algorithm (Algorithm 2) to create a directed graph from the stay points produced by Algorithm 1. The graph algorithm is given in the following section.

# 4   Creating Directional Weighted Graph from a Set of Stay-Points

The purpose of this work is to make stay points to be easily utilized in many applications about data mining and data analyses. By creating a graph model from trajectory datasets we can utilize many ready to use graph databases and graph analyze tools. For example, we can see complicated things simpler in graph-based systems and they will be more systematic. In this approach, we can see similarities of stay points belonging to different users, we can classify the movement characteristics of the users whose trajectory data is recorded. There are vast amounts of applications which are not mentioned here.

Figure 1 is raw trajectory data [11, 12] plotted on a map showing an area nearby of Pekin in China. This data is obtained from Microsoft's trajectory data research. When we apply to stay point algorithm (Algorithm 1) on this data, we obtain a set of stay point determined as shown in Fig. 2. The red dots show the stay points for a specific user whose trajectory data is given in Fig. 1. Stay points can be a restaurant where the user ate something or it can be school, house or work.

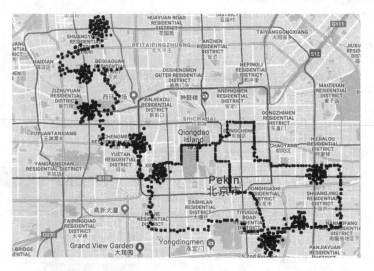

**Fig. 1.** Raw trajectory data (Color figure online)

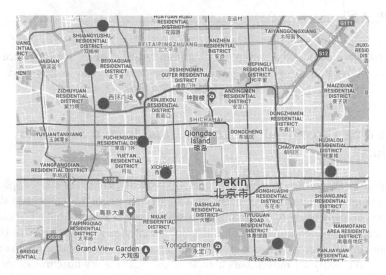

**Fig. 2.** Raw trajectory data

In the following section, we define the proposed graph generating algorithm in which stay points are given and moving characteristics of a specific user is created as a directed graph. Figure 3 illustrate the outcome of the proposed graph algorithm with sample stay points.

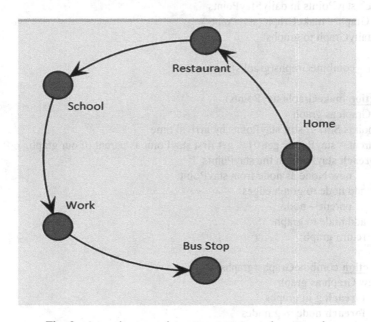

**Fig. 3.** A user's stay point pattern represented as a graph

## 4.1   Graph Algorithm

Directed Graph algorithm takes the stay points, make them nodes and introduces edges between the couples of edges. Nodes are connected each other with directed edges. Connections were established in a sequence. This sequence is established with time parameters. For example, let's look at the sample input data given as below for the sample illustration given in Fig. 3:

- Home -> 11 PM–7.30 AM
- Restaurant -> 9 AM–10 AM
- School -> 11 PM–4 PM
- Work -> 5 PM–9 PM
- Bus Stop -> 9.30 PM–10 PM

In stay point algorithm we define time threshold: 30 min, distance threshold: 200 m. Figure 4 is a general description of our algorithm

## Algorithm-2: Stay Point Graph Relation Algorithm

Input : Stay Point List as stayPoints
Output: Graph
1. foreach stayPoints in dailyStayPoints
2. dailyGraph = makeGraph (stayPoints)
3. add dailyGraph to graphs

4. graph = combineGraphs(graphs)

5. **Function** makeGraph(stayPoints)
6. new Graph as graph
7. staypoints.Sort  // sort stayPoints by arrival time
8.     parent = stayPoints.get(0) // get first stayPoint as parent of our graph
9.     **foreach** stayPoint in the stayPoints
10.        new Node as node from stayPoint
11.        add node to graph.edges
12.        parent = node
13.        add node to graph
14.        return graph;

15. **Function** combineGraphs(graphs)
16.     new Graph as graph
17.        **foreach** g in graphs
18.        **foreach** node in g.nodes
19.           addOrUpdate(node)
20.        **foreach** edge in g.edges
21.              addOrUpdateEdgeWeight(edge)
22.     return graph;

23. **Function** addOrUpdate(node)
24.     **foreach** n in graphNodes
25.        if node.stayPoint likeSame n.stayPoint  // if close to each other 1000 meters
26.           n.stayPoint update location as mean of the node.stayPoint location and
n.stayPoint location
27.        else
28.           add node.stayPoint as new Node to graphNodes

29. **Function** addOrUpdateEdgeWeight(edge)
30.     if edge exist before
31.        increase weight of the edge
32.     else
33.        add edge  as new Edge

Stay points are drawn according to daily trajectory data. The points for each day checked to see if they are the same as the previous stay points. If the newly determined stay point is geographically close enough to the one of the existed stay points, then it will be merged to the already existed one. If it is not close enough to any existed staypoint, then this point will be defined as a new stay point node.

A sample output of graph algorithm is given in Fig. 5. Figure 5 is produced from set of stay points given in Fig. 4 by running Algorithm 2. As you realize the thickness of the edges differ. The proposed algorithm (Algorithm 2) not only introduces edge between the nodes but also calculates their thickness. Between any two nodes, the bigger the thickness, the higher the number of movement activation. This property gives a lot of information about the trajectory data for a specific user. The thicknesses of the edges show the frequency of usage of the path between any two nodes. An application scenario is illustrated in Fig. 4.

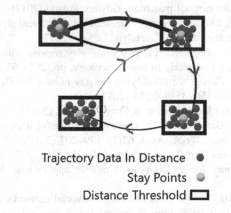

Trajectory Data In Distance ●
Stay Points ◐
Distance Threshold ▭

**Fig. 4.** Visual explanation of stay point algorithm

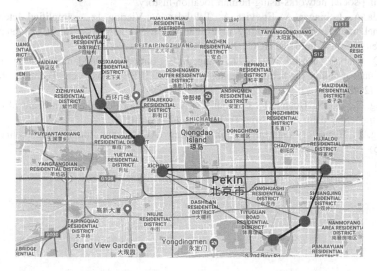

**Fig. 5.** Directional weighted graph example

## 5  Conclusion

Increased usage of smart phones in our daily life and increased usage of sensors and their increased data collection force the application developers to create analyses tools specifically for trajectory data sets. In this paper, we introduce a novel two-step algorithm first creating stay points and second producing directed graph from a trajectory data. Creating graph model from a trajectory data set enabled us to use advanced graph tools such as Neo4 J, and algorithms such as shortest path in advanced trajectory data analytics.

## References

1. Bakkal, F., Eken, S., Savaş, N.S., Sayar, A.: Modeling and querying trajectories using Neo4j spatial and TimeTree for carpool matching, Gdynia, Poland (2017)
2. Savaş, N.S., Bakkal, F., Eken, S., Sayar, A.: Evaluation of different algorithms for measuring the similarities of trajectory datasets, Antalya, Turkey (2017)
3. Damiani, M.L., Issa, H., Cagnacci, F.: Extracting stay regions with uncertain boundaries from GPS trajectories: a case study in animal ecology, pp. 253–262 (2014)
4. Xiao, H., Wang, W.J., Zhang, X.: Identifying the stay point using GPS trajectory of Taxis. Appl. Mech. Mater. **353–356**, 3511–3515 (2013)
5. Stylianou, G.: Stay-Point Identification as Curve Extrema (2017)
6. Montoliu, R., Blom, J., Gatica-Perez, D.: Discovering places of interest in everyday life from smartphone data. Multimed. Tools Appl. **62**(1), 179–207 (2012)
7. Pérez-Torres, R., Torres-Huitzil, C., Galeana-Zapién, H.: Full on-device stay points detection in smartphones for location-based mobile applications. Sensors **16**(10), 1693 (2016)
8. Zheng, Y., Xie, X., Ma, W.-Y.: GeoLife: building social networks using human location history. GeoKife, 26 July 2018. https://www.microsoft.com/en-us/research/project/geolife-building-social-networks-using-human-location-history/
9. Awada, A., Lobinger, A., Enqvist, A., Talukdar, A., Viering, I.: A simplified deterministic channel model for user mobility investigations in 5G networks. In: IEEE International Conference on Commerce (ICC), May 2017
10. Lv, Q., Qiao, Y., Ansari, N., Liu, J., Yang, J.: Big data driven hidden Markov model based individual mobility prediction at points of interest. IEEE Trans. Veh. Technol. **66**, 5204–5216 (2017)
11. Luong, C., Do, S., Hoang, T., Deokjai, C.: A method for detecting significant places from GPS trajectory data. J. Adv. Inf. Technol. **6**, 44–48 (2015)
12. Zheng, Y.: Trajectory data mining: an overview. ACM Trans. Intell. Syst. Technol. **6**, 29 (2015)

# Connected Cars Traffic Flow Balancing
# Based on Classification and Calibration

Ioan Stan[✉] and Rodica Potolea

Computer Science Department, Technical University of Cluj-Napoca,
Cluj-Napoca, Romania
{ioan.stan,rodica.potolea}@cs.utcluj.ro

**Abstract.** Most of the vehicular traffic flow challenges happens because of the roads infrastructure or route planning process in a navigation system. This results in longer time spent in traffic by many people in the world.

In this paper we classified and synthesized comprehensive traffic scenarios in order to improve drivers daily experience thorough connected cars navigation model calibration. The proposed solution systematically calibrates connected cars parameters in order to balance the traffic flow in a simulated connected cars ecosystem based on real map data.

The experimental results and measurement metrics prove that our classification and synthesis of comprehensive traffic scenarios is a favorable infrastructure that supports connected cars navigation model calibration for efficiently balance the vehicular traffic flow in urban areas.

**Keywords:** Connected cars · Calibration · Traffic flow · Balancing Metrics

## 1 Connected Cars Traffic Service

Most of the existing navigation solutions are using traffic information when provide a route between starting and destination points. Some of the solutions only uses the traffic data as an informative layer on the map but doesn't consider it during route planning process. This aspect makes the planned route to be inaccurate in terms of estimated time of arrival (ETA) because the traffic delays are not considered (see [1]). The solutions that are using traffic services during route planning process proved to be more useful for drivers that wants to have a more accurate estimated time of arrival at the destination [2].

On top of navigation solutions, nowadays, the Internet of Things (IoT) ecosystem is a promising environment that can combine and control different technologies and data in order to obtain better results in different domains. Intelligent Transportation System is such a domain that orchestrate the collaboration between infrastructure and entities in the infrastructure through the communication channels (e.g. wireless technologies, sensors, cameras, etc.)

Different classification and studies were done regarding Intelligent Transportation Systems development, communication and design in [3], [4] and [5]).

© Springer Nature Switzerland AG 2018
A. Groza and R. Prasath (Eds.): MIKE 2018, LNAI 11308, pp. 177–188, 2018.
https://doi.org/10.1007/978-3-030-05918-7_16

One very important aspect of an Intelligent Transportation System is the connection and information sharing between vehicles, this being known as Connected Cars concept. One main part of the Connected Cars infrastructure is the Navigation System that, as mentioned above, uses traffic as a service.

As is shown in [5], information sharing and communication between vehicles inside an Intelligent Transportation System can improve the services that are used by the vehicles. Therefore, in a Connected Cars ecosystem the traffic service used during route planning and navigation, can be highly improved through data sharing between the connected cars.

In this paper we proposed a solution that analyzed, synthesized and modeled comprehensive vehicular traffic scenarios in order to improve drivers experience in the context of Connected Cars. First, we classified and synthesized traffic scenarios based on their context. In the next section, we presented different parameters and metrics as a model for Connected Cars Navigation System and proposed the most important one to be calibrated in a way that improves vehicular traffic flow of a Connected Cars ecosystem. The proposed solution was validated and discussed in the experiments and measurements section. In the last two sections we discussed the related work and proposed future improvements based on our conclusions.

## 2   Traffic Scenarios Classification and Synthesis

Depending on the planned route, each driver can meet different traffic scenarios during the driving period. In this section we classified comprehensive traffic scenarios based on their context in terms of length of the planned routed and areas where the route is.

In general, most of the traffic congestion happens in urban areas on unique roads that link different areas. Moreover, the traffic behavior and experience depends on the requested route length (distance between start and destination points). Urban traffic depend on the population size because the number of cars/commuters increases with the population. On the other hand, in general cities with higher population have higher number of streets and therefore can support more alternative routes for drivers. In these regards we classified and discussed different traffic scenarios based on the length of the planned route and also on the route navigation environment infrastructure (urban and non-urban areas).

Before starting our classification, we define the urban areas based on their population as follows:

- **Small City** is a city with a population less than 100.000 people.
- **Medium City** is a city with a population between 100.000 to 500.000 people.
- **Big City** is a city with a population greater than 500.000 people.

Also, based on the length of the route we define the following route categories:

- **Short Route** is a route that has the length less than 1 km for the fastest planned route between start and destination points.

- **Medium Route** is a route that has the length between 1 and 5 km for the fastest planned route between start and destination points.
- **Long Route** is a route that has the length more than 5 km for the fastest planned route between start and destination points.

Note: The planned routes used in this paper are supposed to be requested for fastest mode.

## 2.1   Short Routes in Small/Medium/Big Cities

A short planned route in an urban area follows most of the time the straight forward path between start and destination points. Two main reasons of this aspect are the following:

- navigating through a route that avoids traffic jam can have a much longer distance than the initial planned route and reaching the destination will result in a higher navigation time even in case the traffic jam is avoided.
- usually the infrastructure of a small/medium size cities doesn't support route alternatives for routes shorter than 1 km.

Having above limitations such a scenario can't be resolved using Connected Cars data.

## 2.2   Medium Routes in Small Cities

Knowing that in general small cities doesn't have infrastructure to provide route alternatives a medium route will follow the most straight forward path between start and destination points and also will use the main roads of a small city. In such a case the vehicular traffic flow is only influenced by the number of cars that passes the city at a specific moment because most of them will use the main roads of the city. Therefore, we found that any traffic challenges in such a scenario can't be approached by using Connected Cars ecosystem advantages.

## 2.3   Medium Routes in Medium/Big Cities

A medium route in general contains more segments than a smaller route. Having the context of a medium/big city with more roads than in a smaller city, a medium length route can be planned more efficient in order to improve the vehicular traffic flow and therefore, avoid traffic congestion. One solution for traffic congestion avoidance was proposed in [6]. Using such an approach the medium routes in medium/big size cities can be planned in a way that traffic is balanced on all the streets in the cities.

## 2.4   Long Routes in Small Cities

As for small and medium length routes, the long routes that passes a small city doesn't have alternatives since they are following the straight forward path and are using the only existing roads of the small city. In case of a traffic congestion the only solution that can be found is to avoid the small city if possible but, this comes with more navigation time than in the initial planned route. A solution that tries to find alternatives routes in a small city is not feasible since our problem is reduced to short/medium route in a small city because a long route usually passes entire city.

## 2.5   Long Routes in Medium/Big Cities

More than in the case of medium length planned routes in medium/big size cities, in this scenario it is easier to avoid traffic congestion because of the high probability to find many alternative routes that can balance the traffic on the roads without increasing significantly navigation time.

The work in [6] simulates a connected car context in which the cars are supposed to follow short/medium/long length planned routes in a medium size city (Cluj-Napoca in Romania). They proved that traffic congestion can be avoided in urban areas by sharing connected cars information through an efficient data structure.

## 2.6   Short/Medium Routes in Non-Urban Areas

The infrastructure of non-urban areas usually doesn't provide route alternatives for short planned routes and therefore, traffic congestion in these areas can't be avoided for such scenarios. Moreover, cars that follow a short route will just increase the traffic in their navigation area.

In general, as in the case of short routes in urban areas, the medium planned routes in non-urban areas can have the same problem of few/no route alternatives for their navigation distance.

Planned routes in non-urban areas shorter than 20 km are exceptions and therefore, it is not the scope of this paper to analyze such scenarios.

## 2.7   Long Routes in Non-Urban Areas

As mentioned in the previous subsection, planned routes measuring less than 20 km in non-urban areas are exceptional cases and therefore, for non-urban areas we consider that a **Long Route** has more than 20 km.

If the infrastructure supports different route alternatives, the traffic congestion problem can be solved for long routes in non-urban areas using the same approach as in case of long routes in medium/big cities.

## 2.8   Core Traffic Scenario

The above analysis on traffic scenarios was done in order to provide a comprehensive and clear overview of the traffic behavior and challenges in the connected cars ecosystem. As was shown, there are situations in which the problems can't be solved because of the physical infrastructure limitations of the roads.

Synthesizing the above traffic scenarios analysis, we can conclude that the vehicular traffic flow in a connected cars ecosystem can be improved in case of medium/long length routes request in medium/big size cities and also in case of long routes in non-urban areas.

Supposing that most of the traffic issues happen in urban areas in the following part of the paper we will focus to solve vehicular traffic flow challenge for medium/long length route requests in medium/big size cities. We name such a scenario **Core Traffic Scenario**.

On top of work done in [6] where is described a novel approach for traffic information representation in order to avoid traffic congestion in a connected cars context, in this paper we classified and synthesized comprehensive traffic scenarios in order to balance the traffic flow through connected cars navigation model calibration.

Note: All the above scenarios are considering that traffic is used during route calculation process. In case there are no traffic events/flows that influences the planned route's ETA the fastest route is only influenced by the geometry of the route.

## 3   Connected Cars Navigation Model

In a non-connected cars ecosystem the traffic is provided by traffic services based on road data measurements and can't be influenced by any other parameters used during route planning process.

Traffic evolution can be controlled only in a system in which a route that has to be planned depends on the previous planned routes and on the state of the context (cars on the roads). This means that cars and infrastructure share data. In [6] were described two route computation algorithms and their parameters in a connected cars context. Starting from this, we will analyze and detail some of the concepts, parameters and factors that are used to compute a route in a connected cars context so that the vehicular traffic flow in urban areas can be balanced in a systematic way:

- $p(x, y)$ - GPS point represented by x and y coordinates
- $p_s$ - starting point of a planned route
- $p_d$ - destination point of a planned route
- $R(p_s, p_d)$ - fastest planned route between starting point $p_s$ and destination point $p_d$
- **carID** - connected car represented by an ID. It corresponds to a route $R(p_s, p_d)$
- **segID** - map segment represented by an ID

- **turn$_i$** - turn costs that have a fixed value for a specific turn type (e.g. right turn, slight right turn, left turn, etc.). Having many turns in a planned route reduces the speed of the connected car that follows the route and therefore assist the traffic congestion.
- **S$_{limit}$(segID)**) - default speed limit of a segment. A higher speed limit for a segment allows more connected cars to pass the segment in a time interval
- **C$_{map}$(segID)** - map cost value of a segment ID based on map geometry (e.g. euclidian distance, turn costs, speed limit on the segment, etc.)
- **C$_{cars}$($\rho$(segID, t))** - cost factor corresponding to predicted car density on a segment at a specific time
- $\theta$ - car density threshold value that indicates traffic congestion on any segments. In case the threshold is reached on a segment the route generation algorithm in [6] will try to generate routes that avoids that segment.

Besides the above presented factors that are used to plan a route in a connected cars ecosystem below is described a comprehensive set of metrics used to measure and improve the traffic flow. Many of the below metrics were used in [6] to predict and measure traffic congestion in order to generate routes in such a way in which the congestion is avoided as much as possible.

- **T(segID, t)** - predicted traffic on a segment at a specific time
- **C$_{traffic}$(traffic(segID, t))** - cost factor corresponding to predicted traffic on a segment at a specific time
- **lanesCount(segID)** - number of lanes on a segment used for car density computation
- **carsCount(segID, t)** - predicted number of cars on a segment at a specific time used for car density computation
- **S$_{avg}$(segID, t)** - average speed on segments at a specific time
- **ETA(carID)** - Estimated time of arrival for each route request represented by a carID. This is equivalent with computed route driving time.
- **speed(carID)** - average speed of a specific car corresponding to a generated route
- **length$_{Route}$(carID)** - length of a planned route represented by the carID
- **length(SegID)** - length of a segment from a planned route
- **carsCount(segID)** - total number of connected cars that navigates through a specific segment on the map
- **averageCarLength** - the average length of a car. In this work we considered to be 7 meters
- predicted car density on a segment at a specific time

$$\rho(\textbf{segID}, \textbf{t}) = \frac{\textbf{carsCount}(\textbf{segID}, \textbf{t}) \cdot \textbf{averageCarLength}}{\textbf{length}(\textbf{SegID}) \cdot \textbf{lanesCount}(\textbf{segID})}$$

In order to balance the vehicular traffic flow in a connected cars ecosystem we analyzed the above parameters and found that the most appropriate and clean solution is to calibrate traffic congestion threshold value ($\theta$) used by the connected cars routing algorithm in [6] in such a way in which the vehicular traffic flow balance is proved through a subset of the above described metrics.

# 4    Balanced Traffic Flow Measurements and Experiments

Traffic evolution in a specific zone depends on the planned routes that passes that zone. This means that traffic flows can be balanced by equally distributed planned route segments in the specific zone. The main goal of our proposal and experiments is to prove that the vehicular traffic flow in a connected cars ecosystem can be balanced through a connected cars parameter calibration ($\theta$). In this regards we simulated connected cars traffic in a city and discussed some of the connected cars metrics in order to prove the correctness of our solution.

## 4.1    Measurements Platform and Metrics

We found the most appropriate base platform for our proposal is the one developed in [6].

To achieve our purpose, we calibrated traffic congestion threshold parameter $\theta$ (described in a section above) in such a way in which the simulated vehicular traffic flow in an urban area is balanced. We proved the traffic flow balancing correctness using below metrics:

- length$_{Route}$(carID)
- length(SegID)
- carsCount(segID)

## 4.2    Urban Traffic Flow Experiments and Discussion

For our measurements we generated 10.000 route requests to simulate traffic in a connected cars ecosystem. A connected car is supposed to follow a planned route resulted from a route request. The start and end points of each route request are randomly generated in 6 main districts from Cluj-Napoca (see Fig. 3) so that the length of a planned route varies between 1 and 20 km in order to fulfill the scenario of a medium/long routes in a medium/big size city (Cluj-Napoca city in Romania is having around 500.000 people.)

Figure 1 represents the lengths of the randomly generated routes distribution in the city of Cluj-Napoca. We can observe that the figure is almost a Gaussian distribution for a range of 1 to 20 km having $\mu = 5.7$ km and $median = 6.7$ km.

In the following we'll denote navigated segments the segments on the maps that are used by at least one simulated connected car to navigate on it.

Figure 2 shows the lengths of the navigated segments. The spikes represent the longer segments on the main roads in Cluj-Napoca (see most visible roads in Fig. 3).

The total length of the navigated segments is about 332 km. Considering that a car occupies 7 meters (usually is less) all 10.000 cars occupies at worst 21% of the sum of navigated segments' lengths. This is a good distribution of the connected cars on the navigated segments.

Figure 4 represents the 10.000 cars distribution on the segments of the planned routes generated by the connected cars routing algorithm in [6] having traffic congestion threshold $\theta$ calibrated at 0.5. This value was found after

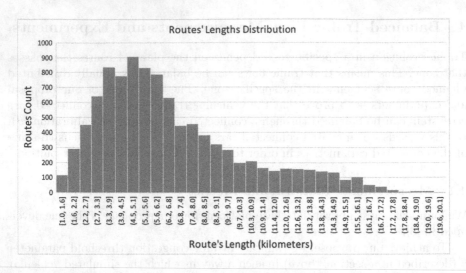

**Fig. 1.** Routes' Lengths Distribution

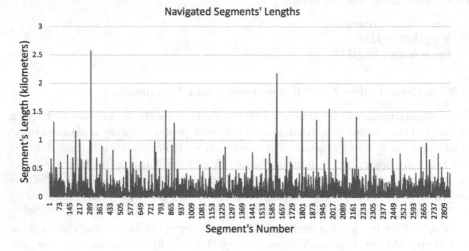

**Fig. 2.** Lengths of Navigated Segments

many manual tests that generated routes in Cluj-Napoca. The results in the Fig. 4 confirms the found value (0.5) for $\theta$ parameter by showing that the cars distribution on the segments is well-balanced and therefore, ensures a balanced traffic flow in the context of 10.000 connected cars that run on planned routes in Cluj-Napoca.

It can be observed that first segments are not navigated by so many cars because they correspond to the first set of planned routes representing the connected cars that didn't covered much space on the navigated segments in the beginning.

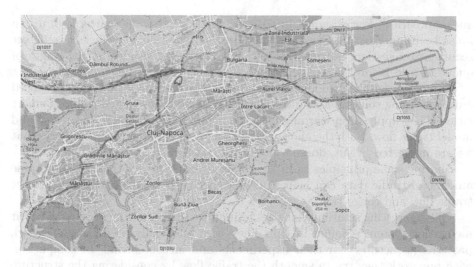

**Fig. 3.** Cluj-Napoca Open Street Map

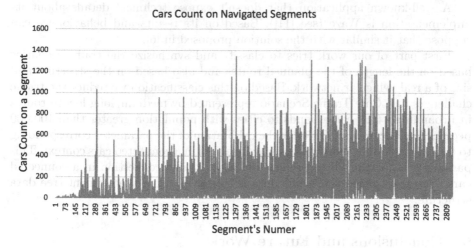

**Fig. 4.** Cars Distribution on Navigated Segments

Besides our experiment, it is worth mentioning that tests like the ones discussed have to be customized accordingly in case of larger cities (e.g. London, New York, Tokyo, Beijing) because in such cases the traffic flow is influenced by other parameters (e.g. public transportation).

## 5 Related Work

The traffic prediction challenges were approached by many that tried to improve navigation solutions in order to provide efficient routes for end users. This resulted in different strategies and measurements based on many technologies and approaches. For example, in [7] it is tried to find traffic patterns in urban areas by using Floating Car Data (FCD). Their solution was efficient to detect recurrent congestion, bottleneck locations, and to get an idea on the length of queue formed before the bottlenecks.

A little closer to our domain of interest is the work in [8] where is proposed a deep learning solution for route calculation based on predicted traffic in smart cities. They apply deep learning on large scale GPS taxi traces to predict and model traffic flow. Both the above-mentioned papers approach some aspects that we are interested in but, doesn't align with the goals we targeted in our work.

Sharing some principles as in [8], the work in [9] proves that a considerable amount of traffic data can help to detect specific patterns in order to predict traffic flow and congestion.

One interesting solution that tries to improve traffic flow in a cooperative car navigation system is found in [10]. They used and analyzed different network patterns (structures) for their experiments and measurements. In comparison with our work they try to smooth the traffic flow by considering the structure of a simulated vehicular network instead of real map data.

A well-known application that doesn't expose technical details about its implementation is Waze (see [11]). Based on its results and behavior we can suppose that it similar with the solution proposed in [6].

First part of our work tries to classify and synthesize the traffic scenarios based on the length of the planned routes and also based on the structure and size of a real vehicular network. Based on this classification we reduce the traffic challenges to a Core Traffic Scenario represented by medium/long length routes in urban areas that corresponds to cities with population greater than 100.000 people. The key of our solution is the calibration of the parameter corresponding to the threshold that indicates traffic congestion in a connected cars context. This parameter is used in [6] to predict and avoid traffic congestion in a connected cars context in which the traffic data is stored by using the segment tree data structure.

## 6    Conclusions and Future Work

In this paper we classified and synthesized a set of comprehensive traffic scenarios corresponding to connected cars navigation systems by using the length of the planned routes, type of the areas of the planned routes (urban and non-urban) and size of the urban areas in terms of population. This classification helped us to compile a Core Traffic Scenario challenge that can be solved through connected cars navigation system model calibration.

In order to balance the traffic flow in the Core Traffic Scenario (medium/long length routes in a city with more than 100.000 people) we analyzed some parameters and metrics of a connected cars navigation system that are used to predict and improve traffic flow. A subset of the described parameters and metrics proved to be very favorable for traffic flow balancing problem and were used, analyzed and discussed in the experiments.

For our experiments and measurements we simulated 10.000 routes in Cluj-Napoca using a real map (OpenStreetMap). The results and metrics analysis confirmed our solution by showing that a proper calibration of the traffic congestion threshold value ($\theta$) can balance the traffic flow in a connected car ecosystem by using only 21% of the connected cars navigated segments space.

The achievement in this paper proves that connected cars ecosystem provides promising mechanisms (through parameters and metrics in our case) that can balance the traffic flow in order to improve the time spent in cars.

Comparing with other research proposals, our solution has the advantage of calibrating a connected cars navigation model used by the solution presented in [6] that tries to avoid traffic congestion simulated on real map data.

We manually calibrated the main parameter $\theta$ and it took some time to run so many experiments with different values. An immediate improvement in the future is to use machine learning in order to adapt the value of $\theta$ automatically based on more aspects regarding connected cars ecosystem (number of route requests, length of the routes and cities' population).

In terms of experiments the next thing to do is to run the existing setup on more urban areas and with different number of route requests. It can be valuable to analyze the behaviour of our solution in non-urban areas. Comparison with other existing solution can be also considered in future.

From data representation perspective, in future we can analyze and compare different data structures used to represent connected cars information, especially traffic, in order to find which is the most efficient for our Core Traffic Scenario.

# References

1. Shcherb, V.: OsmAnd: maps and GPS navigation. https://osmand.net/
2. Nzouonta, J., Rajgure, N., Wang, G., Borcea, C.: Vanet routing on city roads using real-time vehicular traffic information. IEEE Trans. Veh. Technol. **58**(7), 3609–3626 (2009)
3. Figueiredo, L., Jesus, I., Machado, J.A.T., Ferreira, J.R., de Carvalho, J.L.M.: Towards the development of intelligent transportation systems. In: 2001 IEEE Intelligent Transportation Systems, ITSC 2001, Proceedings (Cat. No. 01TH8585), pp. 1206–1211 (2001)
4. Papadimitratos, P., Fortelle, A.D.L., Evenssen, K., Brignolo, R., Cosenza, S.: Vehicular communication systems: enabling technologies, applications, and future outlook on intelligent transportation. IEEE Commun. Mag. **47**(11), 84–95 (2009)
5. Martinez, F.J., Toh, C., Cano, J., Calafate, C.T., Manzoni, P.: Emergency services in future intelligent transportation systems based on vehicular communication networks. IEEE Intell. Transp. Syst. Mag. **2**(2), 6–20 (2010)
6. Stan, I., Toderici, D., Potolea, R.: Segment trees based trac congestion avoidance in connected cars context. In: IEEE 14th International Conference on Intelligent Computer Communication and Processing (2018)
7. Altintasi, O., Tuydes-Yaman, H., Tuncay, K.: Detection of urban traffic patterns from Floating Car Data (FCD). In: 19th EURO Working Group on Transportation Meeting, Transportation Research Procedia, EWGT 2016, 5–7 September 2016, Istanbul, Turkey, vol. 22, pp. 382–391 (2017). http://www.sciencedirect.com/science/article/pii/S235214651730193X

8. Niu, X., Zhu, Y., Cao, Q., Zhang, X., Xie, W., Zheng, K.: An online-traffic-prediction based route finding mechanism for smart city. Int. J. Distrib. Sens. Netw. **11**(8), 970256 (2015). https://doi.org/10.1155/2015/970256
9. Wang, J., Mao, Y., Li, J., Xiong, Z., Wang, W.-X.: Predictability of road traffic and congestion in urban areas. PLOS ONE **10**(4), 1–12 (2015). https://doi.org/10.1371/journal.pone.0121825
10. Yamashita, T., Izumi, K., Kurumatani, K., Nakashima, H.: Smooth traffic flow with a cooperative car navigation system. In: Proceedings of the International Conference on Autonomous Agents, pp. 478–485, January 2005
11. Routing server - Waze GPS Navigation Software. https://wiki.waze.com/wiki/Routing_server

# Identification and Control of a Car Speed Dynamics Using Artificial Intelligence

Vlad Muresan$^{(\boxtimes)}$, Valentin Sita, Iulia Clitan, and Adrian Barstan

Technical University of Cluj-Napoca, 400414 Cluj-Napoca, Romania
Vlad.Muresan@aut.utcluj.ro

**Abstract.** The paper proposes an original solution to identify and control the speed dynamics of a car, using neural networks. The neural network which models the car speed is trained based on experimental input-output data sets which were obtained from a real car. In this purpose, during the experiment, all the signals which are important for the car dynamics are measured. Based on the determined neural reference model of the car dynamics, a car speed control strategy is proposed. In the paper, the simulations of the car dynamics, both in open and in closed loop, are presented, the efficiency of the applied methods being proved.

**Keywords:** Car speed · Neural network · Control structure · Reference model
Artificial intelligence · Simulation

## 1 Introduction

The subject of cruise control systems represents an important and an actual problem in control system science [1]. The improvement of the mathematical models of the cars dynamics and, also, the tuning of speed controllers in order to generate much better performances represent the main targets in this research field. Another important target imposed to the cars control systems is the minimization of the fuel consumption, through the usage of better control strategies.

The main aims of this paper are to determine a mathematical model which describes a car dynamics, based on experimental data, respectively, using the obtained model to tune a speed controller for the considered car. In this context, the application of the artificial intelligence methods, based on the neural networks usage [2], due to their multiple advantages in data processing, become a viable solution.

An important stage in the treated research subject approach is represented by the data acquisition during the experiment. During this stage, the obtaining of consistent sets of experimental data is necessary. Next, the experimental data acquisition procedure is described. The data was acquired using a VAG-COM 409.1 OBD2 Diagnostic Scanner, which is a USB to CAN cable converter. For interfacing and acquire parameters from a car, the VAG-COM cable can be used with the VCDS software, produced by Ross-Tech, LLC/Uwe M. Ross. When the VCDS application is installed, also the USB drivers of the specific VAG-COM interface are installed, but the COM port must be selected from the Options menu. The main screen of the VCDS application is presented in Fig. 1. In the parameters list we select every item that we want to

© Springer Nature Switzerland AG 2018
A. Groza and R. Prasath (Eds.): MIKE 2018, LNAI 11308, pp. 189–204, 2018.
https://doi.org/10.1007/978-3-030-05918-7_17

log by selecting the specific check boxes. A very important feature of the application is the fact that the data from the Measuring Blocks screen can be recorded and saved to a . CSV file. In our case we logged the following parameters: Engine Speed - - (G28), Engine Load, Vehicle Speed, Fuel Consumption - Signal, Fuel Consumption - Equivalent, Acceleration Pedal Position - Sensor 1 (G79).

**Fig. 1.** VCDS application main screen.

The "Turbo" button can be used to increase the sample rate. To start logging data, the "Log" button must be selected, too. After we want to finish the logging data, we select the "Stop" button. When we finish logging all the data that we want, we select the "Done, Close" button. The .CSV file is generated automatically. When logging data, the cruise control can be used to record constant parameters or to record data with linear acceleration. This aspect can be done by selecting a specific speed and the car will automatically accelerate to that speed. Using the acceleration pedal manually, the signals form will be atypical ones, but the obtained experimental data will be more consistent for their usage in the car movement model identification procedure.

## 2 Experimental Data Processing

In order to model the car movement, the acceleration pedal position is considered as the input signal, being notated with u(t) and the car speed is considered as the output signal, being notated with v(t). The signal u(t) is measured in [%] (100% signifies the fact that the acceleration pedal is totally actuated and 0% signifies the fact that the acceleration pedal is not actuated) and the signal v(t) is measured in [km/h]. As it can be remarked, the two signals are functions which depend on time (t) and their values which are used in order to determine the car movement mathematical model, are experimentally obtained using the method presented in the previous paragraph. The experiment made for the data acquisition can be briefly presented as follows: the acquisition system is set in working mode; the driver pushes the acceleration pedal to certain positions; as consequences of the driver actions, the sensors transmit the values of the two main signals (u(t) and (v(t)), values which are stored in a data base. During the experiment, the driver tried to apply to the acceleration pedal consecutive positive-negative step type position variations. These types of variations are considered consistent for the car movement model identification. In the same time, other signals are measured (as examples: the selected gear, the engine speed, the fuel consumption), but their usage in the modeling procedure is not necessary. Due to the automatic gear changing, the car movement modeling can be made without considering the gear variation. The experimental data are presented in Fig. 2.

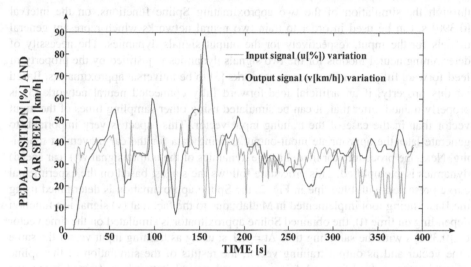

**Fig. 2.** The data obtained during the experiment, associated to u(t) and v(t) signals. (Color figure online)

A main problem in processing the data presented in Fig. 2, is represented by the fact that the sensors are not synchronized between them and, in order to obtain a consistent set of input-output data for the car movement model learning, the mathematical models of the u(t) and v(t) signals have to be determined. In Table 1, an example of two data subsets of the two signals is presented, in order to highlight their value deviation in relation to time.

**Table 1.** Example of two data subsets, experimentally obtained.

| Signal | Values |
|---|---|
| Time1 (t [s]) | 7.06 8.6 10.18 11.72 13.3 14.84 16.42 17.96 19.54 21.08 |
| Input signal (u(t) [%] | 14.8 22.3 30.1 24.6 34 37.9 37.1 32.8 35.2 34 |
| Time 2 (t [s]) | 6.61 8.15 9.73 11.27 12.85 14.39 16.03 17.51 19.09 20.63 |
| Output signal (v(t) [km/h] | 0 0 0 4 5 10 15 19 21 24 |

From Table 1, it results that we cannot make a consistent input-output data pair (for example at the moment t = 13.3 s, u(t) = 34 km/h, but for v(t) we do not have the corresponding value – we only have the value v(t) = 5 km/h for t = 12.85 s). Due to this analysis, the conclusion that we need to determine the mathematical models of the two signals, results, and after that, we need to simulate them using the same sampling time in order to eliminate the previous presented inconsistency. The primary solution is the approximation of the two signals presented in Fig. 2, using Spline functions. After the initial fitting (through interpolation), the two obtained approximating Spline functions are simulated using the same sampling time $\Delta t = 0.1$ s, resulting a consistent (synchronized) input-output pair of data. Secondary, the two sets of data obtained through the simulation of the two approximating Spline functions, on the interval [0,390] s, can be used in order to train two neural networks which represent general models for the input, respectively for the output signals dynamics. The necessity of determining neural models for the two signals dynamics is justified by the property of feed-forward fully connected neural networks [3] to be universal approximators. Based on this property, if an artificial feed-forward fully connected neural network [3] is properly trained, after that, it can be simulated using other sampling times of the input vector than in the case of the training input vector. This aspect is very important, to generate later the appropriate input-output training data for the car movement modeling. Next, the procedure for modeling the dynamics of the output signal v(t) (car speed) dynamics is exemplified. This procedure follows the stages: based on the experimental curve presented with blue line in Fig. 2, the Spline approximation is determined using the Basic fitting tool implemented in Matlab; due to the fact that (v) signal is a function depending on time (t), the obtained Spline approximator is simulated on the time vector $t \in [0,390]$ s with the sampling time $\Delta t = 0.1$ s; using as training input vector the same time vector and as output training vector, the results of the simulation of the Spline approximator, a feed-forward fully connected neural network is trained using the Levenberg-Marquardt learning algorithm [4] (we have imposed that the training is stopped after 10000 epochs and the model is considered enough accurate if, after the training, the quality indicator (the Mean Square Error – MSE) has the value smaller than 0.1 km/h). The trained neural network is, as it was previously mentioned, a feed-forward fully connected one, having one hidden layer which contains 250 nonlinear neurons with hyperbolic tangent as activation function (the nonlinear neurons are used due to the strong nonlinear variation of the v(t) signal highlighted in Fig. 2). Also, the output layer contains only one linear neuron (the neuron has linear activation function). The comparative graph between the experimental curve v(t), the output signal generated by the Spline approximating function and the response of the neural model, is presented in Fig. 3.

The large number of neurons (250) from the hidden layer is justified due to the necessity of using a considerable computation power, in order to learn with precision the behavior of the strong nonlinear signal v(t). Also, the number of neurons from the structure of the hidden layer was determined iteratively through simulation, having as objective the minimization of the quality indicator (MSE) final value. The output signal from the neural model of v(t) signal, is given by:

$$v(t) = W_2 \cdot tanh[(W_1 \cdot t + B_1)] + b_2 \tag{1}$$

where $W_1$ with the size $[250 \times 1]$ represents the vector of the input weights, $B_1$ with the size $[250 \times 1]$ represents the vector of the bias values of the neurons from the hidden layer, "tanh" represents the hyperbolic tangent function (the bipolar sigmoid function), $W_2$ with the size $[1 \times 250]$ represents the vector of the weights which

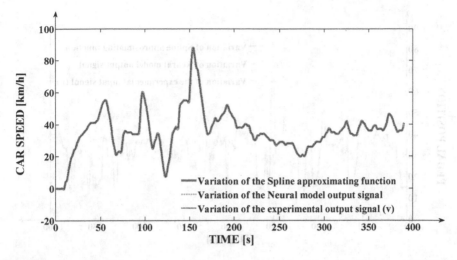

**Fig. 3.** The comparative graph between the experimental curve v(t), the Spline approximating function response and the response of the neural model.

connect the hidden layer with the output layer and finally, $b_2$ represents the bias value of the output neuron. The values of the previously presented vectors and coefficients result as the training solutions. The Mean Square Error between the Spline function output and the Neural Model output, computed on 3901 pair of samples, is MSE1 = 0.0769 km/h, error smaller than the maximum imposed limit of 0.1 km/h, fact which proves the fact that we have obtain a very accurate model. This aspect is, also, proved by the fact that the three curves from Fig. 3 are practically superposed (the differences between them cannot be distinguished with the eye; the Spline function, obviously approximates with high accuracy the experimental curve, the corresponding MSE value being equal cu 0 km/h if we compute it considering the experimental samples).

The procedure for modeling the dynamics of the output signal u(t) (pedal position) dynamics is similar as in the case of the v(t) signal. In this context, we use the same neural structure for learning the u(t) signal behavior. The comparative graph between the experimental curve u(t), the associated output signal generated by the Spline approximating function and the response of the associated neural model, is presented in Fig. 4.

The conclusions regarding the obtained neural model accuracy are the same as in the case of Fig. 3 and the Mean Square Error between the Spline function output and the Neural Model output, in this case, computed on 3901 pair of samples, is MSE2 = 0.0182% (error smaller than the maximum imposed limit of 0.05%, fact which proves the fact that we have obtain a very accurate model, too).

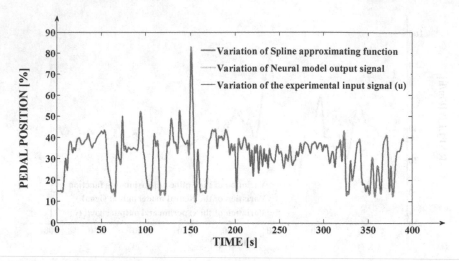

**Fig. 4.** The comparative graph between the experimental curve u(t) and the associated responses of Spline approximating function, respectively of the neural model.

## 3 Car Dynamics Modeling (Process Modeling)

The car dynamics modeling consists in the determining the functional dependency between the input signal u(t) and the output signal v(t). In this purpose, we take as example the mathematical modeling of the car dynamics, only in speed increasing regime. Analyzing Fig. 3, it can be remarked that on the first 47 s of the experiment, as consequence of the input signal u(t) application, the output signal (car speed) is increased from 0 km/h to 55 km/h. The experimental curve on this time interval is presented in Fig. 5. It can be remarked that the initial position of the acceleration pedal, before the gear change from neutral point to gear 1, was at 14.8%. Also, the small decrease of the car speed under the value 0 km/h (highlighted with an ellipse on the Fig. 5) is due to a small error given by the approximation using Spline functions. But this small error has an insignificant value and does not influence in a negative manner the modeling procedure. Also, this error could be physically assimilated to the case when the car starts on a ramp, with very small inclination.

Due to the long duration of the car speed increase presented in Fig. 5, relative to the entire experiment duration (390 s), the pair of signals from Fig. 5 is considered consistent in order to determine an accurate model of the car dynamics. The forms of the signals u(t) and v(t) presented in Fig. 5 differ from the standard forms of the signals used by classical identification methods (for example the u(t) signal form differs significantly from the ideal step type signal form). Consequently, the classical identification methods cannot be applied for the car dynamics modeling. A viable identification solution, applicable for the treated process is based on neural networks usage (neural networks which can be used to learn complex mathematical transfers between signals of non-standard forms). Even considering this advantage of neural networks usage, their training is difficult in the context of the treated process due to the fact that the experimental input signal u(t) is not a white noise one (the typical input

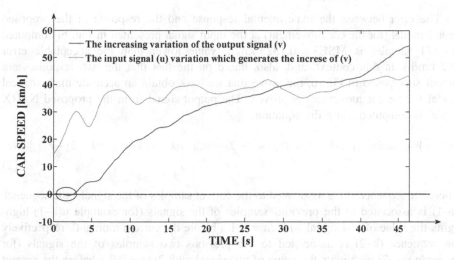

**Fig. 5.** The first increasing evolution of the experimental v(t) signal and the evolution of the experimental u(t) signal which generated the v(t) increase.

signal used for dynamic neural networks training). The neural structure proposed for learning the car movement dynamics is the NARX model (Nonlinear Autoregressive fully connected neural network with exogenous inputs) [3]. The NARX structure has one hidden layer containing 12 nonlinear neurons (having as activation function the hyperbolic tangent), one linear neuron in the output layer and two delay lines both on the input and on the output signals (used to memorize the previous two samples of the signals). The number of the delay lines was chosen in order to model the car dynamics as a second order process (with the purpose of finding the most simple solution). Also, the neurons from the hidden layer are nonlinear, due to the fact that the modeled process is a strong nonlinear one (using a totally linear neural structure, the process modeling was not possible). The number of the neurons from the hidden layer was fixed to 12, a value which is enough small to imply a fast convergence of the learning algorithm, but in the same time is enough big to imply a sufficient computing power for processing the experimental signals. The proposed neural structure is trained using as input vector the u(t) signal presented in Fig. 5 and as output vector the v(t) signal presented in Fig. 5, using the Levenberg-Marquardt learning algorithm and imposing the training stop after 50000 epochs. The used sampling time is $\Delta t = 0.1$ s, practically the input-output vector containing the first 471 samples of the neural networks (presented in the previous paragraph) responses presented in Fig. 4, respectively in Fig. 3. Also, the obtained model is considered enough accurate if the quality indicator (Mean Square Error) has the value smaller than 0.2 km/h. The comparative graph between the experimental curve and the response of the neural model of the car movement (obtained after training) at the input signal from Fig. 5, is presented in Fig. 6 (in Fig. 6, the input signal is, also, highlighted with red line).

The error between the experimental response and the response of the proposed neural model (for the car movement) at the input signal presented in Fig. 5, computed on 471 samples is MSE3 = 0.1323 km/h, value lower than the acceptable error (0.2 km/h). In this context, and, also, based on the fact that the two responses are almost superposed in Fig. 6, the prove that we have obtain an accurate mathematical model for the car movement is proved. The output signal from the proposed NARX model is computed using the equation:

$$v(k) = W_{HL} \cdot tanh[(W_{I1} \cdot u(k-1) + W_{I2} \cdot u(k-2) + W_{O1} \cdot v(k-1) + W_{O2} \cdot v(k-2) + B_{HL})] + b_O$$

(2)

where the sequence (k) is associated to the current samples of the signals, the sequence (k–1) is associated to the previous samples of the signals (for example u(k–1) high-lights the value of u(t) signal with $\Delta t = 0.1$ s before the current moment), respectively the sequence (k–2) is associated to the previous two samples of the signals (for example v(k–2) highlights the value of v(t) signal with $2 \cdot \Delta t = 0.2$ s before the current moment). The usage of the past values of v(t) output signal in Eq. (2), signifies the fact that the proposed neural model presents feedback from the output signal.

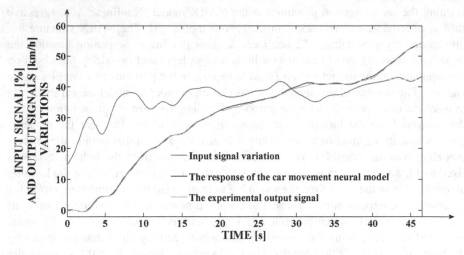

**Fig. 6.** The comparative graph between the experimental curve and the response of the neural model of the car movement. (Color figure online)

Also, the vectors from Eq. (2) which are obtained as training solutions, are: $W_{I1}$ with the size [12 × 1] represents the vector of the input weights which connect the u (k–1) signal with the hidden layer, $W_{I2}$ with the size [12 × 1] represents the vector of the input weights which connect the u(k–2) signal with the hidden layer, $W_{O1}$ with the size [12 × 1] represents the vector of the feedback weights which connect the v(k–1) signal with the hidden layer, $W_{O2}$ with the size [12 × 1] represents the vector of the feedback weights which connect the v(k–2) signal with the hidden layer, $B_{HL}$ with the size [12 × 1] represents the vector of the bias values of the neurons from the hidden layer, $W_{HL}$ with the size [1 × 12] represents the vector of the weights which connect the hidden layer with the output layer and finally, $b_O$ represents the bias value of the output neuron.

Having the previously determined neural model for the car movement, the possibility to simulate the car dynamics for other types (forms) of input signals (besides the input signal used in the identification procedure), occurs. An interesting aspect is represented by the car speed evolution for step types input signals. In Fig. 7, the comparative graph between the proposed neural model responses is presented, for 3 step type signals having the steady state values: $u_1(t) = 36\%$, $u_2(t) = 37\%$ and $u_3(t) = 42\%$ (in all three cases, the initial values are 0%). In the context of the approached process, the step type input signal can be assimilated with a very fast commutation of the acceleration pedal from a position (in our example 0%) into another one. The simulations results presented in Fig. 7 are centralized in Table 2, too. From Fig. 7 and Table 2, the increasing evolution of the v(t) signal steady state value at the increase of the u(t) signal, results. This aspect is physically obvious (at the fuel supply increase, the car speed increases, too), but due to the strong nonlinear character of the car movement, the proportionality between u(t) and v(t) signals, in steady state regime, is not respected. The strong nonlinear character of the approached process can be, also, remarked through the atypical form of the curves from Fig. 7 (they significantly differ as evolution form from the curves associated to the linear processes step responses).

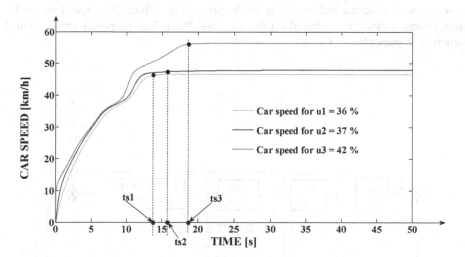

**Fig. 7.** The comparative graph between the responses of the proposed neural model for the car movement, at different input step type signals.

Another important aspect which results from Fig. 7 and Table 2, is represented by the increasing evolution of the car speed settling time at the increase of the input signal value. This phenomenon occurs due to the fact that for higher values of the input signal, the car speed presents higher variations than in the case of smaller values of the input signal. Also, this phenomenon occurs due to the nonlinear character of the process and persists for the entire domain of car speeds. The simulations presented in Fig. 7 and Table 2 represent particular examples, but due to the general character of the proposed neural model, the car speed dynamics can be simulated for any variation forms of the u (t) signal, enclosed between [0,100] %.

**Table 2.** The centralizer which contains the simulations results

| Input step signal value (u(t)) [%] | Settling time ($t_s$) [s] | Steady state value of the output signal (v(t)) [km/h] |
|---|---|---|
| $u_1(t) = 36\%$ | $t_{s1} = 13.5$ s | $v_1 = 43.2$ km/h |
| $u_2(t) = 37\%$ | $t_{s2} = 16.15$ s | $v_2 = 44.1$ km/h |
| $u_3(t) = 42\%$ | $t_{s3} = 18.4$ s | $v_3 = 56.7$ km/h |

## 4   Car Speed Control Strategy

The existence of the neural model of the car dynamics opens two important possibilities: the first one was previously presented in paragraph 3 representing the possibility of simulating the car speed evolution for any variation form of the input signal; the second one is referring to the possibility of including the car movement process in a speed control structure and implicitly to the possibility to tune [5] a speed controller (this second possibility is based on the first one, too). The proposed speed control structure is presented in Fig. 8.

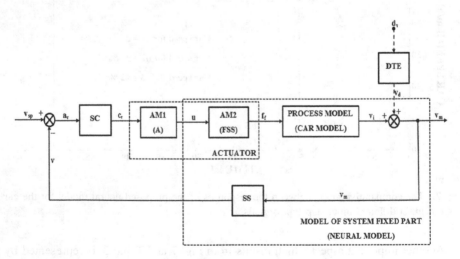

**Fig. 8.** The proposed speed control structure.

The elements from the control structure, are: the MODEL OF SYSTEM FIXED PART (the NEURAL MODEL proposed in the previous paragraph) – it makes the connection between u(t) and v(t) signals; the Speed Controller (SC); the Actuating Mechanism 1 (which is practically an Adapter A) which makes the connection between the signals $c_v(t)$ and u(t); the Disturbance Transfer Element (DTE) which models the dynamics of the disturbance signal propagation into the control system. The signals from the control structure, are: $v_{sp}$ – the setpoint signal for car speed; v – the car speed (measured by SS); $a_v = v_{sp} - v$ is the speed error; $c_v$ – control signal generated by the speed controller; u – acceleration pedal position; $f_f$ – fuel flow (the flow of fuel with which the engine is supplied); $v_i$ – the initial speed value (not affected by the disturbance signal effect); $v_d$ – disturbance signal equated in speed value; $d_v$ – primary disturbance signal (non-equated in speed value; for example a ramp); $v_m = v_i + v_d$ is the speed value affected by the disturbance effect (the measurable speed value). All the presented signals are functions which depend on time (t). As it results from Fig. 8, the MODEL OF SYSTEM FIXED PART can be decomposed in: the Actuating Mechanism 2 (AM2) – the Fuel Supplying System (FSS) of the engine; the CAR MODEL which models the transfer between $f_v$ and $v_i$ signals; the Speed Sensor (SS) which measures the car speed value. The separately modeling of the elements AM2, CAR MODEL and SS is not necessary due to the fact that in paragraph 3, we have identified their behavior as one equivalent element. Also, the elements AM1 and AM2 (serial connected) form the ACTUATOR. The Adapter AM1 has the purpose of adapting the control signal $c_v(t)$ generated by SC to the acceleration pedal position u(t) (practically, it changes the acceleration pedal position according to the $c_v(t)$ variation). The work of this element, it having a very fast dynamics, can be modeled using only a proportionality constant and is included in the controller mathematical model.

Due to the fact that the MODEL OF SYSTEM FIXED PART is a strong nonlinear one (as it was presented in paragraph 3), the tuning of SC is made using the relay method (method which is appropriate for controller tuning, in the case when the controlled process is a nonlinear one). This procedure consists in replacing SC from Fig. 8 with a relay element and, due to its action, in imposing an undamped oscillatory regime of the car speed. This procedure is applied in the context when the disturbance signal does not occur in the system ($v_d = 0$ km/h – the arrow corresponding to the disturbance signal occurs in Fig. 8 with dashed line in order to suggest the fact that, in normal working regime, the disturbance signal does not occur in the system). Using a two-position relay with hysteresis of $\pm 3$ km/h (near the setpoint signal which is set to the value of 50 km/h) and having the output signal u(t) = 37% if v(t) > 53 km/h, respectively u(t) = 42% if v(t) < 47 km/h, the response of the control system is presented in Fig. 9. As a remark, the model of the AM1 element was included into the work of the two position relay.

In Fig. 9, the fact that after the moment t = 18 s, the car speed v(t) presents oscillations with constant amplitude, can be remarked. From Fig. 9, two important parameters result: the period of the oscillations $T_{osc} = 9.5$ s; the amplitude of the oscillations $A_{osc} = 7.1$ km/h which is considered relative to the average value of the oscillations $v_{av} = 49$ km/h. The parameters $T_{osc}$ and $A_{osc}$, respectively the average value $v_{av}$ are highlighted on Fig. 9. The fact that $v_{av}$ is sensible different than the imposed setpoint speed (50 km/h) is due to the strong nonlinear character of the car

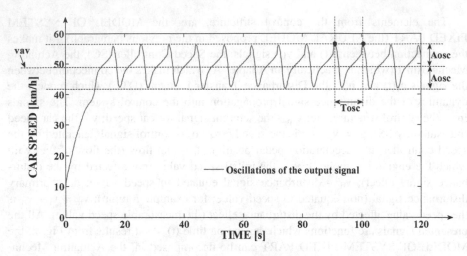

**Fig. 9.** The response of the control system in the case of using the relay, instead of the speed controller.

dynamics. Using the parameters $T_{osc}$, $A_{osc}$, respectively the relay parameters and applying the Ziegler – Nichols equations associated to the relay method [5], a PI (Proportional – – Integral) controller is computed. After the sensible adjustment of the PI controller parameters, near the initial obtained values, in order to obtain the best set of performances, the final form of the speed controller transfer function results:

$$H_{SCPI}(s) = \frac{U(s)}{A_v(s)} = K_{SC} \cdot (1 + \frac{1}{T_{SC} \cdot s}) = 0.7567 \cdot (1 + \frac{1}{5 \cdot s}) \tag{3}$$

where $K_{SC} = 0.7567\%\cdot h/km$ represents the proportionality constant of the PI speed controller and $T_{SC} = 5$ s represents the integral time constant of the controller. Also, U (s) represents the Laplace transformation of the controller output signal u(t) (the acceleration pedal position) and $A_v(s)$ represents the Laplace transformation of the controller input signal $a_v(t)$ (the speed error). It can be remarked the fact that the proportionality constant of AM1 is included in the proportionality constant of SC. After the simulation of the control system, the fact that the obtained simple PI controller does not generate the imposed set of performances was remarked. In this context, an augmented form of the PI controller is proposed, this form being presented in Fig. 10.

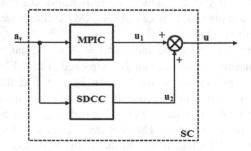

**Fig. 10.** The augmented form of the PI controller.

In Fig. 10, the MPIC (Main PI Controller), being practically the controller given by Eq. (3) (which includes the AM1 element from Fig. 8, too), generates the $u_1(t)$ control signal. The SDCC (Speed Derivative Correction Controller) element generates the $u_2(t)$ control signal. The final control signal is given by $u(t) = u_1(t) + u_2(t)$. Practically, the effect of SDCC adjusts the effect of MPIC in order to improve the control system response settling time. The transfer function of SDCC has the following form:

$$H_{SDCC}(s) = \frac{U_2(s)}{A_v(s)} = K_D \cdot \frac{s}{T_f \cdot s + 1} = 0.8975 \cdot \frac{s}{5 \cdot s + 1} \qquad (4)$$

where $U_2(s)$ represents the Laplace transformation of the correction control signal $u_2(t)$, $K_D = 0.8975\%\cdot h/km$ represents the derivative constant of the SDCC and $T_f = 5$ s represents the time constant of the first order filter attached to SDCC in order to obtain its feasible form (as it can be remarked from Eq. (4), SDCC is a derivative element with first order filter) [6]. Practically, the MPIC and SDCC control elements are parallel connected. The values of $K_D$ and $T_f$ were determined using an iterative algorithm which minimizes the value of the control system response settling time. In Fig. 11, the comparative graph between the control system responses is presented, in the case of using (the case of modified PI controller) and in the case of not using the SDCC element (the case of simple PI controller). In this simulation, the setpoint signal for the speed is set at the value $v_{sp} = 50$ km/h. From Fig. 11, the fact that in both cases, the steady state errors of the responses have the value 0 km/h (in steady state regime, the car speed reaches the setpoint value $v_{sp}$). The main advantages of using the modified PI controller, relative to the case of using the simple PI controller, are: the consistent improvement of the settling time $- t_{s5} = 12.2$ s $<< t_{s4} = 22.6$ s (as in the case of Fig. 7, the settling time is considered in the moment when the response reaches 99% from the steady state value and remains enclosed in the steady state band of $\pm 1\%$ near this value); the overshoot avoidance (in the case of using the modified PI controller, the overshoot value is 0%, respectively in the case of using the simple PI controller, the overshoot has the value 3.4%). The better control performances generated by the modified PI controller are due to the higher control effort generated on the first 11 s of car acceleration (as effect of SDCC action). This aspect is highlighted in Fig. 12 in which the comparative graph between the two control signals, associated to the curves from Fig. 11, is presented.

From Fig. 12, the much more fast variation of the blue curve (associated to the modified PI controller) after the simulation start, can be remarked.

In Fig. 13, the disturbance effect rejecting regime [6] is highlighted. The disturbance signal with the steady state value $v_d = -5$ km/h occurs (due to a ramp) in the system at the moment $t = 40$ s. From Fig. 13, it results that the effect of the disturbance is rejected with high efficiency by the controller. This affirmation is based on two aspects: firstly, in steady state regime, the car speed reaches again and very fast the setpoint value (50 km/h); secondly, the car speed variations, during the disturbance effect rejection, are smaller than $\pm 1$ km/h. In this simulation, the DTE time constant was considered at the value of 1 s (DTE is a first order element).

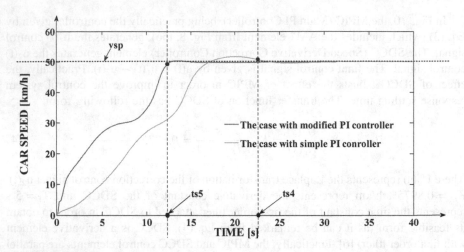

**Fig. 11.** The comparative graph between the control system responses, in the case with and in the case without using SDCC element.

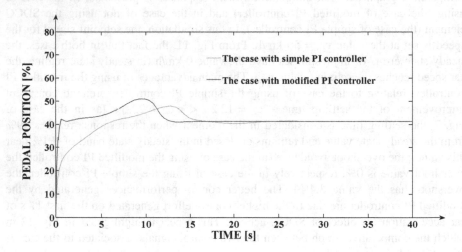

**Fig. 12.** The comparative graph between the control signals associated to the two curves from Fig. 11. (Color figure online)

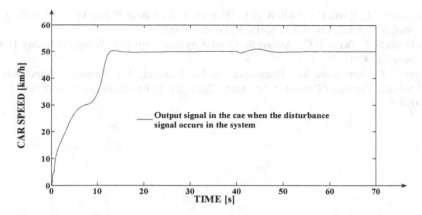

**Fig. 13.** The disturbance effect rejecting regime.

## 5 Conclusions

The paper presents an original solution to model and control a car movement process. The artificial intelligence, through the neural networks usage, is applied both to model the dynamics of the input-output signals important for the process identification and to model the car movement dynamics. Due to the fact that, after identification, a neural model of the car movement is available, the car speed can be simulated and a speed controller is tuned. In order to obtain appropriate control performances, the initial PI controller was modified to a more complex form. The neural networks are, also, used at the modified controller behavior learning in order to be implemented on a microcontroller. In this context, the same NARX structure is used as in the case of the processes modeling, but having only 9 linear neurons in the hidden layer. The controller efficiency was proved, through simulation, both in the case when the disturbance occurs or not in the system. As future work, we can exemplify: the process modeling on the entire range of speed values (on the speed decreasing regime, too); the implementation of advanced controllers; the fuel consumption minimization, through control. All the simulations from the paper are made in MATLAB/Simulink.

## References

1. Vollrath, M., Schleicher, S., Gelau, C.: The influence of cruise control and adaptive cruise control on driving behaviour – a driving simulator study. Accid. Anal. Prev. **43**(3), 1134–1139 (2011)
2. Maren, A., Harston, C., Pap, R.: Handbook of Neural Computing Applications. Academic Press, London (1990)
3. Haykin, S.: Neural Networks and Learning Machines, 3rd edn. Pearson, Upper Saddle River (2009)

4. Norgaard, M., Ravn, O., Poulsen, N.K., Hansen, L.K.: Neural Networks for Modelling and Control of Dynamics Systems. Springer, London (2000)
5. Golnaraghi, F., Kuo, B.C.: Automatic Control Systems, 9th edn. Wiley Publishing House, Hoboken (2009)
6. Coloşi, T., Abrudean, M., Ungureşan, M.-L., Mureşan, V.: Numerical Simulation of Distributed Parameter Processes. Springer, Cham (2013). https://doi.org/10.1007/978-3-319-00014-5

# Industry 4.0, Intelligent Visual Assisted Picking Approach

Mario Arbulu[1](✉)(iD), Paola Mateus[1](✉)(iD), Manuel Wagner[1](✉)(iD),
Cristian Beltran[2](✉)(iD), and Kensuke Harada[2](✉)(iD)

[1] Universidad Nacional Abierta y a Distancia (UNAD), Bogota 111511, Colombia
{mario.arbulu,paola.mateus,manuel.wagner}@unad.edu.co
[2] Graduate School of Engineering Science, Department of Systems Innovation,
Osaka University, 1-3 Machikaneyama, Toyonaka 560-8531, Japan
{beltran,harada}@sys.es.osaka-u.ac.jp
http://www.unad.edu.co
http://www.hlab.sys.es.osaka-u.ac.jp/people/harada/

**Abstract.** This work deals with a novel intelligent visual assisted picking task approach, for industrial manipulator robot. Intelligent searching object algorithm, around the working area, by RANSAC approach is proposed. After that, the image analysis uses the Sobel operator, to detect the objects configurations; and finally, the motion planning approach by Screw theory on SO(3), allows to pick up the selected object to move it, to a target place. Results and whole approach validation are discussed.

**Keywords:** Artificial intelligence · Autonomous picking
Artificial vision · Sobel · RANSAC · Screws modeling

## 1  Introduction

The Industry 4.0 challenges are directed around integrating automation process, cloud and IoT. Furthermore, robotics manipulation, and autonomy are currently improving, by artificial intelligence algorithms, [1,2]. For instance the proposed World Robotics Summit (WRS), motivate researchers around the world, in order to overcome some challenges at industrial robotics applications too, [3]. Currently, artificial vision is used to assist robotic systems, by extracting visual features from given images. Some research have been done for obtaining the necessary features, such as foreground extraction, noise removal and unnecessary objects. A proposal of color segmentation method, is detailed in [4]. A background modeling through statistical edge is given by [5]. Additionally, in [6] visual control systems had been used, which are based on images for trajectory tracking. Also, for vision pre-processing, object detection algorithms are used [7], visual tracking [8], and color intensity [9]. Some of them are conventional

Supported by UNAD, Convocatoria 007.

A. Groza and R. Prasath (Eds.): MIKE 2018, LNAI 11308, pp. 205–214, 2018.
https://doi.org/10.1007/978-3-030-05918-7_18

methods, which have limitations on objects detection; and others extract depth features, which have complex processing [10–12].

So, the object detection and features extraction, for intelligent vision assisted proposed in this work, is focused in select the interest working planes where the objects are located. After that, the Sobel [13] operator is proposed to edge detection, with morphological operations and dilatation [14,15]. And finally, regions are labeled for obtaining the interest object features as: area, position $(x, y)$, centroid and orientation angle.

## 2    Theoretical Background

In this section theoretical background will be detailed regarding: artificial vision, artificial intelligence, and motion computation; which will describe the overall approach proposed (see Fig. 1). Where the user sends a pieces set inquiry, in order to develop the manipulator intelligent picking task. This proposal will be applied in the Industrial Assembly Challenge, in the WRS, specifically in the kitting task.

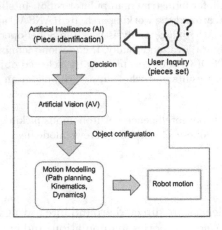

**Fig. 1.** Overall approach proposal.

### 2.1    Artificial Vision Approach

Through the Sobel algorithm [16], the horizontal and vertical edges detection is realized, (see Fig. 2(b)).

The edges detection is obtained, with a central approximation of the first derivative, as following:

$$\frac{df(x)}{dx} = \frac{f(x+1) - f(x)}{2} \tag{1}$$

with a mask $[-1/2\ 0\ 1]$ for the vertical edges, and other mask $[-1/2\ 0\ 1]^T$ for the horizontal edges.

Next, in order to remove the generated false edges, the Sobel operator is evaluated by the gradient at the $x$ and $y$ coordinates ($G_x$, and $G_y$), such as:

$$\nabla f = [G_x, G_y] \tag{2}$$

where, $G_x = \begin{bmatrix} \frac{-1}{2} & 0 & \frac{1}{2} \end{bmatrix} * \begin{bmatrix} 2 \\ 4 \\ 2 \end{bmatrix} = \begin{bmatrix} -1 & 0 & 1 \\ -2 & 0 & 2 \\ -1 & 0 & 1 \end{bmatrix}$

being $\begin{bmatrix} 2 \\ 4 \\ 2 \end{bmatrix}$ the vertical smoothing, which is proposed by the Sobel operator

and $G_y = \begin{bmatrix} \frac{-1}{2} \\ 0 \\ \frac{1}{2} \end{bmatrix} * [2\ 4\ 2] = \begin{bmatrix} -1 & -2 & -1 \\ 0 & 0 & 0 \\ 1 & 2 & 1 \end{bmatrix}$

being $[2\ 4\ 2]$ the horizontal smoothing, which is proposed by the Sobel operator.

For obtaining better pixels information on each edges previously detected, the square morphological dilatation is proposed, (see Eq. 3). It is by using the logic operator OR and selecting a 9 pixels window $I(m, n)$. With the $I(m, n)$ window, a whole image sweep is realized, thus a new image is generated which corresponds to the square dilatation, (see Fig. 2(c)).

$$W[I(m, n)] = \begin{bmatrix} I(m-1, n-1) & I(m-1, n) & I(m-1, n+1) \\ I(m, n-1) & I(m, n) & I(m, n+1) \\ I(m+1, n-1) & I(m+1, n) & I(m+1, n+1) \end{bmatrix}$$

being $m$ the coordinate in the $x$ pixel and $n$ the coordinate in the $y$ pixel.

$$Dil(m, n) = OR\{W[I(m, n)]\} = max\{W[I(m, n)]\} \tag{3}$$

In order to obtain the features, and differentiate each one of the detected objects in the image; the object labeled is developed by the mask $B_{3X3}$ (see Fig. 2(d)). That mask sweeps vertically each pixel from the skeleton, it find adjacent pixels with the value 1, and it assign a label value.

$$B_{3x3} = \begin{pmatrix} P(m-3, n-3) & P(m-3, n) & P(m-3, n+3) \\ P(m, n-3) & P(m, n) & P(m, n+3) \\ P(m+3, n-3) & P(m+3, n) & P(m+3, n+3) \end{pmatrix} \text{ where } P(m, n) \text{ is}$$

the evaluated pixel value.

Being $O_k$ each labeled $k$-th object, a rectangle which embed to each object ($ro_k$), is obtained as follows: $ro_k = \begin{bmatrix} m_k & n_k & A_K & B_k \end{bmatrix}$ k $\in$ N

Rectangle with higher left vertex in ($m_k, y_k$), height $B_k$ and width $A_k$. Thus, each object centroid $co_k$ is obtained, by the following expressions: $x_k = m_k \frac{A_k}{2}$, $y_k = n_k \frac{B_k}{2}$, $co_k = (x_k, y_k)$

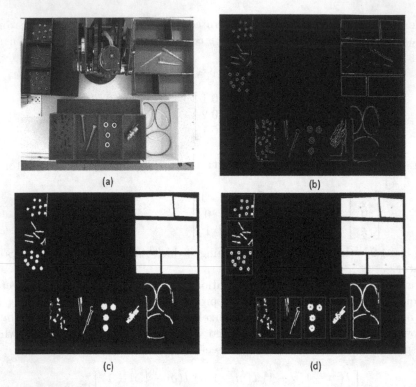

**Fig. 2.** (a) Working area image in RGB, (b) Obtained image by Sobel operator, (c) Dilatation at square shape and fills holes, (d) Objects label: bounding box is the red square, and the centroid is the red cross on each one.

## 2.2    Artificial Intelligence Approach

The method in this subsection deals with features detection; which is the workflow of extraction and correspondence, and them are saved in a features vector. This method is used to find and object, inside of working area (i.e. Fig. 3), and it is called "Random Sample Consensus" (RANSAC). Specifically, features detection is developed with "Speeded Up Robust Features" algorithm (SURF), which is based in Hessian Matrix ($H(i,j)$), where in a given point $\boldsymbol{x} = $ (i, j) in a image $\boldsymbol{I}$:

$$H(i,j) = \begin{bmatrix} L_{xx}(i,j) & L_{xy}(i,j) \\ L_{xy}(i,j) & L_{yy}(i,j) \end{bmatrix} \tag{4}$$

Where $L_{xx}(i,j)$ corresponds to convolution of second order derivative of $\boldsymbol{g(j)}$, (Gauss function) $d^2g(j)/dx^2$ with the $\boldsymbol{I}$ image in the $\boldsymbol{x}$ point, and in the similar way for the elements $L_{xy}(i,j)$ and $L_{yy}(i,j)$, [17].

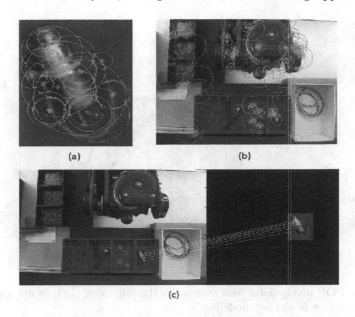

(a)     (b)

(c)

**Fig. 3.** (a) Object SURF features detection (b) Work space SURF features detection (c) Object location in the work space.

The RANSAC algorithm application removes outliers, which can produce error detection. And at first, it obtain a data set with inliers and outliers, given by:

$$\frac{\begin{bmatrix} n-o \\ s \end{bmatrix}}{\begin{bmatrix} n \\ s \end{bmatrix}} = \frac{(n-s)(n-s-1)...(n-s-o+1)}{n(n-1)...(n-o+1)}$$

Where $s$ is the set size and $n$ is the data number, [18]. These outliers set is shifted by a probabilistic values set $q$ (Desired probability for drawing an outlier free subset.), which reduces computational cost. If the probability of an inlier is $w$, so the probability of a outlier is: $\epsilon = 1 - w$. It is necessary to make at least N selections of sets, given by: $N = log(1 - q)/log(1 - w^s)$

### 2.3 Screws Modeling

In order to compute suitable manipulator motion, the screw approach theory embedded on Special Euclidean groups SO(3), [19], is detailed in this section. Being the forward kinematics of 5 DOF manipulator robot of Fig. 4, as following:

$$g_{th}(\theta) = e^{\zeta_1.\hat{\theta}_1}.e^{\zeta_2.\hat{\theta}_2}.e^{\zeta_3.\hat{\theta}_3}.e^{\zeta_4.\hat{\theta}_4}.e^{\zeta_5.\hat{\theta}_5}.g_{th}(0) \tag{5}$$

Regarding the Eq. 5, $g_{th}(0)$ is the $4 \times 4$ matrix, which describes the initial end-effector configuration (position and orientation); $g_{th}(\theta)$ is the $4 \times 4$ matrix, which

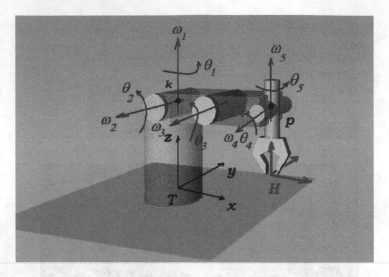

**Fig. 4.** Five DOF manipulator arm frames (T, H), joint axes ($w_i$), rotation angles $\theta_i$, $p$ and $k$ axes cross points for modeling.

describes the target end-effector configuration, where $\theta$ is the $5 \times 1$ vector of joints rotations. For the $i^{th}$ joint, the joint angle rotation is $\theta_i$; the twist is $\zeta_i$; and finally, the exponential matrix is $e^{\zeta_i \cdot \theta_i}$. The product of exponential applied to the initial end-effector configuration $g_{th}(0)$, allows to model the end-effector motion to a target configuration, through successive rotations around the free joints axes. In order to compute the inverse kinematics, the Paden-Kahan (P-K) subproblems will be applied, [20]. Thus, for solving the $\theta_3$ joint rotation, the third P-K subproblem is used, because it solve what is the rotation, around any free axis, which translates a point to a given distance:

$$||e^{\zeta_1 \cdot \hat{\theta}_1} . e^{\zeta_2 \cdot \hat{\theta}_2} . e^{\zeta_3 \cdot \hat{\theta}_3} . e^{\zeta_4 \cdot \hat{\theta}_4} . e^{\zeta_5 \cdot \hat{\theta}_5} . p - k|| = \delta \qquad (6)$$

Applying the exponential matrices from axes 1 to 5, to the cross point of axes 4 and 5 ($p$), the axes rotations $\theta_4$ and $\theta_5$ do not affect to that point (see Eq. 6).

Furthermore, the distance $\delta = ||g_{sh}(\theta) . g_{sh}(0)^{-1} . p - k||$ from the resulting rotated point $p$ to the point $k$, is not affected by exponential matrices 1 and 2. So, the $\theta_3$ joint angle rotation is solved with the third P-K subproblem, by the following simplified expression:

$$||e^{\zeta_3 \cdot \hat{\theta}_3} . p - k|| = \delta \qquad (7)$$

Next, the second P-K subproblem give us the solution, of two rotation joint angles with crossed axes; so, the first and second joint angles rotations $\theta_1$ and $\theta_2$ are given by:

$$e^{\zeta_1 \cdot \hat{\theta}_1} . e^{\zeta_2 \cdot \hat{\theta}_2} . e^{\zeta_3 \cdot \hat{\theta}_3} . e^{\zeta_4 \cdot \hat{\theta}_4} . e^{\zeta_5 \cdot \hat{\theta}_5} . p = p'' \qquad (8)$$

Evaluating the exponential matrices 1 to 5, in $p$ point (see Eq. 8), only the rotations 1 to 3 affect to $p$ point; thus, that point achieves the $p'' = g_{sh}(\theta) . g_{sh}(0)^{-1} . p$

position. As, the joint rotation $\theta_3$ has been already solved, and axes 1 and 2 are crossed at $k$ point, the joint angle rotations $\theta_1$ and $\theta_2$ could be solved with the second P-K subproblem, as next, where $p' = e^{\zeta_3.\hat{\theta}_3}.p.$:

$$e^{\zeta_1.\hat{\theta}_1}.e^{\zeta_2.\hat{\theta}_2}.p' = p'' \tag{9}$$

As the joints rotation angles $\theta_1$ to $\theta_3$ have been computed, and it is notice that, the joints axes $\omega_4$ and $\omega_5$ are crossed at $p$, following expression is obtained, through apply rotations $\theta_4$ and $\theta_5$ to point $k$:

$$e^{\zeta_4.\hat{\theta}_4}.e^{\zeta_5.\hat{\theta}_5}.k = k' \tag{10}$$

The above expression (Eq. 10) allows to solve the joints rotations $\theta_4$ and $\theta_5$, by the second P-K subproblem, being $k' = e^{-\zeta_3.\hat{\theta}_3}.e^{-\zeta_2.\hat{\theta}_2}.e^{-\zeta_1.\hat{\theta}_1}.g_{sh}(\theta).g_{sh}(0)^{-1}.k$

Furthermore, some via points have been selected in 3D space, in order to define smooth Cartesian trajectories for approaching, picking and dispatching the objects to defined targets. Those via points are obtained, as orthogonal projections from the objects (or pieces) locations, computed in the artificial vision approach previously proposed.

## 3  Results

The proposal was validated with simulation and experimental tests. After, the user inquiry, the robot can do successfully the kitting task autonomously. The RANSAC approach identifies where is the desired piece (see Fig. 5), next the image analysis compute the pieces position, by border detection with Sobel

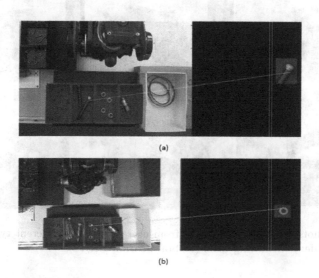

(a)

(b)

**Fig. 5.** (a) Screw detection (b) Packing ring detection.

operator, and shape dilatation. Using a *pixel* to *mm*, scale adaptation, and the reference translation to robot base; the pieces configurations (position and orientation) are obtained, as targets in Cartesian space. Those target pieces configurations are introduced to compute robot motion, with Screw theory, (see Fig. 6). The correction factor of pieces configurations, due to the image analysis precision, give us an small displacement in $y$ direction up to maximum value of 10mm.

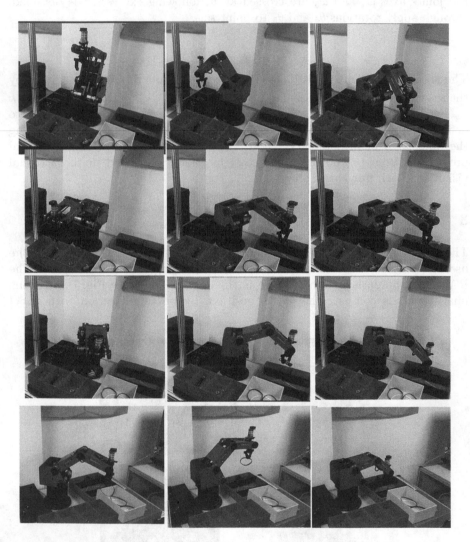

**Fig. 6.** Snapshots of intelligent picking from user inquiry, for different type of pieces, in order to achieve the kitting task. (Robot: Scorbot ER 4u)

# 4   Conclusions

The RANSAC algorithm removes outliers, which allows increase the detection probability to find an object inside the working area. The image analysis algorithm detects accurately enough, each object configuration, which allows to move the robot end-effector, for picking any object in the working area. Kinematics motion computation by screw theory, allows efficient computation of joint patterns, avoiding singularities, and with meaningful analytic description. The whole intelligent picking algorithm have been successfully tested in order to achieve the kitting tasks. Current research is focused on increase the robustness of image analysis, intelligence and motion planning.

# References

1. Indri, M., Grau, A., Ruderman, M.: Guest editorial special section on recent trends and developments in industry 4.0 motivated robotic solutions. IEEE Trans. Ind. Inform. **14**(4), 1677–1680 (2018). https://doi.org/10.1109/TII.2018.2809000

2. Wan, J., Tang, S., Hua, Q., Li, D., Liu, C., Lloret, J.: Context-aware cloud robotics for material handling in cognitive industrial Internet of Things. IEEE Internet Things J. **5**(4), 2272–2281 (2018). https://doi.org/10.1109/JIOT.2017.2728722

3. World Robot Summit 2018. http://worldrobotsummit.org/en/

4. Nieuwenhuis, C., Cremers, D.: Spatially varying color distributions for interactive multilabel segmentation. IEEE Trans. Pattern Anal. Mach. Intell. **35**(5), 1234–1247 (2013). https://doi.org/10.1109/TPAMI.2012.183

5. Rivera, A.R., Murshed, M., Kim, J., Chae, O.: Background modeling through statistical edge-segment distributions. IEEE Trans. Circuits Syst. Video Technol. **23**(8), 1375–1387 (2013). https://doi.org/10.1109/TCSVT.2013.2242551

6. Mezouar, Y., Chaumette, F.: Optimal camera trajectory with imagebased control. Int. J. Robot. Res. **22**(10–11), 781–804 (2003)

7. Guo, M., Zhao, Y., Zhang, C., Chen, Z.: Fast object detection based on selective visual attention. Neurocomputing **144**, 184–197 (2014)

8. Stalder, S., Grabner, H., Van Gool, L.: Dynamic objectness for adaptive tracking. In: Lee, K.M., Matsushita, Y., Rehg, J.M., Hu, Z. (eds.) ACCV 2012. LNCS, vol. 7726, pp. 43–56. Springer, Heidelberg (2013). https://doi.org/10.1007/978-3-642-37431-9_4

9. Zhu, W., Liang, S., Wei, Y., Sun, J.: Saliency optimization from robust background detection. In: Proceedings of CVPR, pp. 2814–2821, June 2014

10. Seo, H.J., Milanfar, P.: Static and space-time visual saliency detection by self-resemblance. J. Vis. **9**(12), 15 (2009). Art. no. 15

11. Bai, X., Sapiro, G.: A geodesic framework for fast interactive image and video segmentation and matting. In: IEEE 11th International Conference on Computer Vision, pp. 1–8 (2007)

12. Price, B., Morse, B., Cohen, S.: Geodesic graph cut for interactive image segmentation. In: IEEE Computer Society Conference on Computer Vision and Pattern Recognition, pp. 3161–3168 (2010)

13. Kanopoulos, N., Vasanthavada, N., Baker, R.L.: Design of an image edge detection filter using the Sobel operator. IEEE J. Solid State Circuits **23**(2), 358–367 (1988)

14. Chen, J., Su, C., Grimson, W.E.L., Liu, J., Shiue, D.: Object segmentation of database images by dual multiscale morphological reconstructions and retrieval applications. IEEE Trans. Image Process. **21**(2), 828–843 (2012). https://doi.org/10.1109/TIP.2011.2166558

15. Jin, X.C., Ong, S.H., Jayasooriah, A.: Domain operator for binary morphological processing. IEEE Trans. Image Process. **4**(7), 1042–1046 (1995). https://doi.org/10.1109/83.392348

16. Lim, J.S.: Two-Dimensional Signal and Image Processing, pp. 478–488. Prentice Hall, Englewood Cliffs (1990)

17. Bay, H., Tuytelaars, T., Van Gool, L.: SURF: speeded up robust features. In: Leonardis, A., Bischof, H., Pinz, A. (eds.) ECCV 2006. LNCS, vol. 3951, pp. 404–417. Springer, Heidelberg (2006). https://doi.org/10.1007/11744023_32

18. Yaniv, Z.: Random sample consensus (RANSAC) algorithm, a generic implementation. Insight J., 1–14 (2010). http://www.insight-journal.org/browse/publication/769

19. Mustafa, S.K., Agrawal, S.K.: On the force-closure analysis of n-DOF cable-driven open chains based on reciprocal screw theory. IEEE Trans. Robot. **28**(1), 22–31 (2012). https://doi.org/10.1109/TRO.2011.2168170

20. Dimovski, I., Trompeska, M., Samak, S., Dukovski, V., Cvetkoska, D.: Algorithmic approach to geometric solution of generalized PadenKahan subproblem and its extension. Int. J. Adv. Robot. Syst., 1–11 (2018). https://doi.org/10.1177/1729881418755157

# Detection and Mapping of a Toxic Cloud Using UAVs and Emergent Techniques

Marco Avvenuti, Mario Giovanni C. A. Cimino$^{(\boxtimes)}$, Guglielmo Cola, and Gigliola Vaglini

Dipartimento di Ingegneria dell'Informazione, University of Pisa,
Largo Lucio Lazzarino 1, 56122 Pisa, Italy
{marco.avvenuti,mario.cimino,gigliola.vaglini}@unipi.it,
g.cola@iet.unipi.it

**Abstract.** Unmanned aerial vehicles have gained a lot of interest in recent times, due to their potential use in several civil applications. This paper focuses on the use of an autonomous swarm of drones to detect and map a toxic cloud. A possible real-world scenario is the accidental release of hazardous gases into the air, resulting from fire or an explosion at an industrial site. The proposed method is based on the concept of swarm intelligence: each drone (agent) performs basic interactions with the environment and with other drones, without need for a centralized coordination technique. More precisely, the method combines collision avoidance, flocking, stigmergy-based communication, and a cloud exploration behavior called inside-outside. For the experiments we developed a simulator using the NetLogo environment, and tested different combinations of these emergent behaviors on two scenarios. Parameters were tuned using differential evolution and separate scenarios. Results show that the combined use of different emergent techniques is beneficial, as the proposed method outperformed random flight as well as an exhaustive search throughout the explored area. In addition, results show little variance considering two different cloud shapes.

**Keywords:** Differential evolution · Drone · Fractals · Mapping
NetLogo · Quadcopter · Stigmergy · Swarm intelligence · Toxic cloud
Unmanned aerial vehicle

## 1 Introduction

Over the last few decades, unmanned aerial vehicles (UAVs), also known as drones, have become extremely accessible thanks to the advancement in different technological areas, and their use has been proposed in an increasing number of applications [3,8]. In particular, drones can replace traditional human-operated vehicles in dangerous missions, such as monitoring a wildfire and exploring unknown or highly polluted environments.

© Springer Nature Switzerland AG 2018
A. Groza and R. Prasath (Eds.): MIKE 2018, LNAI 11308, pp. 215–224, 2018.
https://doi.org/10.1007/978-3-030-05918-7_19

The use of multiple low-cost drones is particularly effective in these scenarios, as it ensures better fault tolerance and timely accomplishment of missions. However, the simultaneous use of multiple drones also poses the challenge of finding a proper coordination strategy. In this context, approaches inspired by natural swarms (swarm intelligence) have been investigated [1,2,4]. In a swarm, each agent's behavior is characterized by simple interactions with the environment, without full awareness of the overall aim of the mission: the aim is achieved as a result of these simple behaviors (emergence of global behavior in swarm intelligence). This approach proved effective in different applications, and strongly reduces the requirements in terms of drone's processing capabilities and duration of operation.

One interesting application for UAV swarms is represented by the exploration of the environment after a disaster, such as the accidental release of toxic gases in the atmosphere from an industrial site [7,13,17]. In this scenario, a swarm could be immediately deployed to quickly detect and map the toxic cloud. This information could be paramount to take prompt measures in order to preserve public safety in the area nearby the industrial site. Recent works have proposed and evaluated different approaches, in terms of drone and sensor characteristics, to monitor the presence of chemical substances in the air [16]. These systems are also known as eNose applications [11]. A commonly used sensing technology is represented by MOSFET (chemoresistive) sensors, which offer long-term stability and fast response [15,18]. The response is caused by direct interaction with the volatile chemical, hence the use of stationary measurement systems is not a viable solution in most cases.

The swarm should adopt an effective strategy to quickly detect the presence of the pollutant in the air and then determine the area occupied by the toxic cloud. A relevant work in this field was presented in [9], which proposed a decentralized approach for a UAV swarm. This approach relied on constrained randomized behavior, and took into account restrictions regarding sensors, processing capabilities, and flight envelope. The mapping procedure was based on the inside-outside strategy: drones move straight across the cloud and then turn to repeat the procedure. A somehow similar study was presented in [10], which considered different mapping strategies (including inside-outside) to determine the contour of a toxic cloud. Both studies considered fixed-wing drones for their simulations.

In this work, we propose and evaluate a method for detecting and mapping a cloud using a swarm of quadcopters. The contribution can be summarized as follows:

- The proposed method is based on the combined use of different emergent techniques, namely flocking, stigmergy, and inside-outside cloud exploration. Drone behavior logic also includes an obstacle avoidance strategy to avoid collisions with other drones as well as with obstacles (e.g., buildings).
- The method was evaluated by means of two scenarios built in the Netlogo simulation environment. The scenarios were created using the areal view of a real incinerator and two different cloud shapes inspired by real life examples.

Clouds were represented in two dimensions for the sake of simplicity (the same approach can be easily extended to study clouds in 3D).
- The parameters of the emergent techniques were tuned using differential evolution and artificial cloud shapes, which were generated using fractals.
- The contribution of each emergent technique was evaluated in terms of time required to fulfill the mission (i.e., detect at least 95% of the cloud area).
- Results show that the adoption of each emergent technique in the combined approach is beneficial to reduce the average exploration and mapping times, as well as to reduce variance between different repetitions of the experiment. The proposed method outperforms random flight and exhaustive exploration.

The following Section presents the proposed strategy. Section 3 describes the evaluation procedure based on Netlogo. Finally, results are presented and discussed in Sect. 4.

## 2   Method

The behavior of a drone in the proposed method is shown in Fig. 1. At the beginning of a mission, each drone is in the *exploration* state, and its aim is to explore the environment in order to find the toxic cloud. In exploration, drone behavior is characterized by flocking and stigmergy (pheromone attraction). There is an emergent formation of groups of drones (flocks), which start moving randomly throughout the environment. Drones follow the rules of flocking and random flight when no pheromone is sensed, whereas they follow a pheromone trace when present. As soon as a drone detects the toxic cloud, its state changes from exploration to *mapping*. At this point, drone behavior is characterized by the inside-outside mapping strategy and stigmergy (pheromone release). The drone starts mapping the cloud without following flocks or pheromone traces released by other drones. Instead, the drone releases pheromone while inside the cloud, so as to attract other drones towards the target. Finally, a transition from mapping to exploration may occur if the drone exits the cloud as part of the mapping strategy and it is not able to re-enter the cloud within a predefined time interval.

Throughout the mission drones also observe basic rules to prevent collisions (collision avoidance). In particular, we developed a simple approach based on two

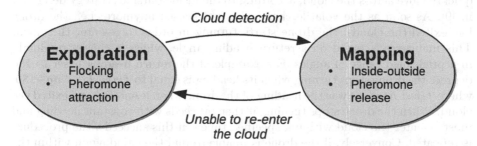

**Fig. 1.** Drone behavior as a finite state machine.

parameters – obstacle vision and obstacle vision angle – which are used to define an obstacle vision area. This is the area where the drone is capable of sensing the presence of obstacles (e.g., another drone, a tree, a building, etc.). When a drone detects an obstacle in its vision area, it reduces its speed and changes its heading to prevent a collision. It should be highlighted that this work is not focused on flight simulation, but on exploration and target discovery.

The following subsections describe flocking, stigmergy, and inside-outside mapping.

## 2.1  Flocking

Flocking is used to coordinate the movement of drones in the exploration phase and keep them in communication range. As defined in the best known work presented in [14], flocking is based on the rules of alignment, separation, and cohesion. Alignment consists in aligning the heading according to the average heading of nearby drones (flock mates). Separation ensures that a minimum distance is maintained between flock mates, so as to prevent collision and ensure effective sensing. Finally, cohesion directs each drone towards the center of the flock. These three rules are combined using specific parameters.

## 2.2  Stigmergy (Pheromone Attraction and Pheromone Release)

Digital stigmergy is a form of communication between agents, based on the release of a digital pheromone. This digital mark is characterized by radius, intensity, and linear evaporation dynamics. In our implementation, drones in the exploration state are attracted by the pheromone released by other drones (pheromone attraction): pheromone is sensed according to an olfaction radius parameter. Pheromone release is performed during the mapping phase, when a drone senses the presence of the toxic cloud.

## 2.3  Inside-Outside Mapping Strategy

After entering the cloud for the first time, the drone changes its state from exploration to mapping. In mapping, the drone keeps a constant heading to quickly move across the cloud, according to the inside-outside strategy described in [9]. As soon as the volatile chemical is not sensed anymore (i.e., the drone has exited the cloud), the drone starts turning in order to re-enter the cloud. This maneuver is based on a return heading angle, which is chosen randomly in a predefined range of angles. For example, if the return heading is set to 180 degrees the drone stops turning when its heading is equal to $fixed\_heading+180$, where $fixed\_heading$ was the heading of the drone when it entered and exited the cloud. When the drone stops turning, it then proceeds with constant heading and must re-enter the cloud within a specified time – if this succeeds, the procedure is repeated. Conversely, if the drone is unable to find the cloud again within the specified time, it returns to the exploration state.

As previously mentioned, in the mapping state the drone is not attracted by digital pheromone and it does not follow flocking rules. On the other hand, while mapping the cloud a drone is responsible for releasing pheromone to attract other drones towards the target.

## 3   Experimental Setting

We implemented all the aspects of drone behavior using Netlogo, which is a leading platform for multi-agent simulation [12]. Flight parameters were chosen according to the characteristics of common quadcopters, like the DJI Phantom 4. A relatively slow cruising speed of $\sim$4 m/s was chosen – slow speed better suits the considered scenario, as MOSFET sensors have a typical delay of a few seconds before responding to the toxic chemical.

As previously mentioned, our approach to detect and map a toxic cloud is based on flocking, stigmergy, and inside-outside mapping. Hereafter, we refer to the proposed approach as Combined, as it combines several emergent techniques. For our evaluation, we compared Combined with simpler approaches, based on a reduced subset of the emergent techniques. Considered approaches are listed and described in Table 1. This allowed us to evaluate the contribution of each technique.

Two scenarios were created for the evaluation, shown in Fig. 2b and c. Both scenarios are based on the same aerial view of an incinerator, shown in Fig. 2a. The simulation environment is divided into patches: the two scenarios are made of $200 \times 200$ patches: each patch represents a squared area of $4 \times 4$ meters in the corresponding real-world scenario. As a result, the search field corresponds to an area of 640,000 m$^2$. The above mentioned speed of 4 m/s means that a drone is capable of visiting a patch per second. Buildings and trees are represented in

**Table 1.** Evaluated approaches.

| Approach | Description |
| --- | --- |
| Random | Random flight |
| Stigmergy only | Drones are attracted by digital pheromone; pheromone is released by drones inside the cloud. Random flight when no pheromone is sensed |
| Stig. & Flocking (SF) | Stigmergic attraction and release; drones also follow the rules of flocking |
| Inside-outside only | Random flight outside the cloud; each drone, after detecting the cloud, performs mapping according to the inside-outside strategy |
| Combined | Proposed approach described in Sect. 2. Drones behave according to SF when outside the cloud. As soon as a drone finds the cloud it starts performing inside-outside mapping and it also releases pheromone while inside the cloud |

(a) Aerial view of the incinerator (source Google Earth)

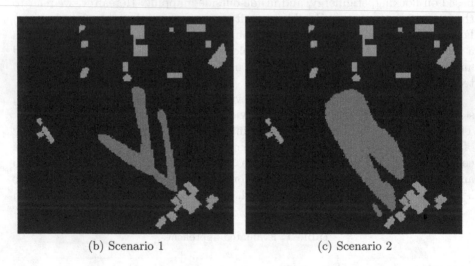

(b) Scenario 1                    (c) Scenario 2

**Fig. 2.** Aerial view and Netlogo scenarios. (Color figure online)

gray, whereas the patches containing the toxic cloud (target) are red. The two scenarios differ for the cloud shape, which was inspired by real aerial views of toxic volatile chemicals. The number of drones used in each simulation is 20 – at the beginning of the mission drones are deployed from the bottom-left corner of the scenario.

Adaptation of parameters related to flocking, stigmergy, and inside-outside emergent techniques was achieved using differential evolution [5]. In practice, it is not possible to tune the techniques to the exact cloud to be detected and mapped, but artificial cloud shapes can be used to adapt the techniques to the problem at hand as much as possible. In this study, optimization was done on

**Fig. 3.** Artificial cloud shapes used to tune parameters with differential evolution.

separate artificial scenarios, created using fractals and shown in Fig. 3. Fractals were created using the Fractint software [6].

The performance of a specific approach, among the ones listed in Table 1, was measured in terms of the time required to map 95% of the cloud area. Since all experiments were partially characterized by random behavior, each experiment was repeated 100 times to determine the average time to fulfill the mission and the respective 95% confidence interval.

For the sake of simplicity, in this preliminary study we did not consider diffusion and dispersion dynamics, as well as the effect of the wind. It was supposed that these dynamics do not affect the cloud shape significantly during the mission, which lasts less than 30 min.

**Table 2.** Results – mission duration in seconds with the different approaches.

| Approach | Scenario 1 | | Scenario 2 | |
|---|---|---|---|---|
| | Mean time | CI 95% | Mean time | CI 95% |
| R | $4665 \pm 526$ | 104 | $4560 \pm 370$ | 73 |
| S | $1756 \pm 280$ | 55 | $1634 \pm 308$ | 61 |
| SF | $1638 \pm 242$ | 48 | $1523 \pm 230$ | 46 |
| IO | $1892 \pm 343$ | 68 | $1552 \pm 182$ | 36 |
| CO | $1017 \pm 98$ | 19 | $1014 \pm 57$ | 11 |

## 4   Results and Discussion

The results obtained by the evaluated approaches are shown in Table 2. More precisely, for each approach it is shown: the average time ± the standard deviation of the time required to find 95% of the toxic cloud patches; the respective 95% confidence interval (CI). Times are expressed in simulation ticks, which correspond to seconds.

As expected, the behavior based entirely on random flight obtained the worst result, with more than 4000 s required on average to fulfill the mission in both the considered scenarios. In this simple approach, drones tend to scatter throughout the map and do not exploit any kind of communication when the cloud is found.

This does not enable prompt mapping of the cloud. Moreover, in the considered scenarios this approach would require to replace the drones during the mission, as battery duration is typically in the order of 30 min.

The use of stigmergy alone drastically improves the performance in both scenarios, with a mean time of about 1700 s. As soon as a drone finds a target (i.e., a patch containing the toxic cloud), it leaves a digital mark with specific diffusion and evaporation characteristics, which are defined by the parameters tuned with differential evolution. This digital mark attracts the drones nearby towards the cloud. As more drones reach the target, there is a substantial increase in the amount of released pheromone – this leads to a stronger and more diffused digital mark, which is capable of attracting more drones. As such, most of the drones quickly converge towards the target and explore the relevant patches.

Previous works, like [4], showed that combining stigmergy and flocking further increases the performance of a swarm of drones in target discovery. This result is confirmed by our study, as the SF approach obtains slightly better results than stigmergy alone. One possible interpretation of this result is that with flocking rules drones tend to be closer to each other, which in turn facilitates stigmergy-based communication. When a drone finds the target, thanks to flocking rules it is ensured that other drones (flock mates) are close enough to immediately sense the pheromone mark and move towards the cloud.

Before testing the approach proposed in this study, we evaluated the use of the inside-outside mapping strategy alone, without stigmergy-based communication and flocking rules. Hence, drones move randomly while searching for the cloud and do not communicate to each other when the cloud is found. Results were slightly worse than SF, especially in the first scenario, where the peculiar cloud shape increases the probability of being unable to re-enter the cloud while performing the mapping strategy. In fact, this strategy is very efficient when the drone is actually mapping the cloud, but it is clear that it must be combined with proper techniques to also deal efficiently with cloud detection and to attract drones towards the target once it has been detected.

To this end, we proposed a method that combines all of these emergent techniques. Drones exploit stigmergy and flocking to explore the environment and to quickly move towards the target when is found. At the same time, the inside-outside strategy is used by drones that have found the cloud to efficiently perform mapping. The combined approach obtained substantially better results in terms of mean time, standard deviation, and 95% CI. Notably, despite the different cloud shape, the result was very similar for both scenarios (about 1000 s), with a 95% CI below 20 s. In terms of average time, it showed a reduction of 78% if compared to the random approach, and a reduction of 36% compared to SF. Another way to evaluate this result consists in considering the time required to exhaustively explore all the patches in the scenario, without taking into account the presence of obstacles. As our scenarios are made of 40,000 patches and each of the 20 drones can visit one patch per second, the time to exhaustively visit all the patches would be 2000 ticks or seconds. That would be two times longer than the time achieved by the proposed approach.

In future work we plan to extend the promising results of this preliminary study and address its main limitations. To obtain a more realistic scenario, gas dispersion and diffusion dynamics will be considered, as well as the effect of the wind. Another important aspect to be considered, is the choice of the optimal number of drones to be deployed. To this end, we will carry out an evaluation as the number of drones is varied and consider more scenarios. In addition, we will evaluate how the discovery process evolves over time for each technique, by measuring the time required to map different percentages of the cloud area.

**Funding.** This work was carried out in the framework of the SCIADRO project, co-funded by the Tuscany Region (Italy) under the Regional Implementation Programme for Underutilized Areas Fund (PAR FAS 2007–2013) and the Research Facilitation Fund (FAR) of the Ministry of Education, University and Research (MIUR).

# References

1. Alfeo, L., Cimino, M.G.C.A., Francesco, N.D., Lazzeri, A., Lega, M., Vaglini, G.: Swarm coordination of mini-UAVs for target search using imperfect sensors. Intell. Decis. Technol. **12**, 1–14 (2018)
2. Brust, M.R., Zurad, M., Hentges, L., Gomes, L., Danoy, G., Bouvry, P.: Target tracking optimization of UAV swarms based on dual-pheromone clustering. In: 2017 3rd IEEE International Conference on Cybernetics (CYBCONF), pp. 1–8, June 2017
3. Chmaj, G., Selvaraj, H.: Distributed processing applications for UAV/drones: a survey. In: Selvaraj, H., Zydek, D., Chmaj, G. (eds.) Progress in Systems Engineering. AISC, vol. 366, pp. 449–454. Springer, Cham (2015). https://doi.org/10.1007/978-3-319-08422-0_66
4. Cimino, M.G.C.A., Lazzeri, A., Vaglini, G.: Combining stigmergic and flocking behaviors to coordinate swarms of drones performing target search. In: 2015 6th International Conference on Information, Intelligence, Systems and Applications (IISA), pp. 1–6, July 2015
5. Cimino, M.G.C.A., Lazzeri, A., Vaglini, G.: Using differential evolution to improve pheromone-based coordination of swarms of drones for collaborative target detection. In: Proceedings of the 5th International Conference on Pattern Recognition Applications and Methods, ICPRAM 2016, pp. 605–610. SCITEPRESS - Science and Technology Publications, Lda, Portugal (2016)
6. Fractint. https://www.fractint.org/. Accessed Sept 2018
7. Gallego, V., Rossi, M., Brunelli, D.: Unmanned aerial gas leakage localization and mapping using microdrones. In: 2015 IEEE Sensors Applications Symposium (SAS), pp. 1–6, April 2015
8. Hartmann, K., Giles, K.: UAV exploitation: a new domain for cyber power. In: International Conference on Cyber Conflict, CYCON 2016-Augus, pp. 205–221 (2016)
9. Kovacina, M.A., Palmer, D., Yang, G., Vaidyanathan, R.: Multi-agent control algorithms for chemical cloud detection and mapping using unmanned air vehicles. In: IEEE/RSJ International Conference on Intelligent Robots and Systems, vol. 3, pp. 2782–2788, September 2002
10. Mani, G.: Mapping contaminated clouds using UAV - a simulation study. In: IEEE India Conference (2013)

11. Nagle, H.T., Gutierrez-Osuna, R., Schiffman, S.S.: The how and why of electronic noses. IEEE Spectr. **35**(9), 22–31 (1998)
12. Netlogo. http://ccl.northwestern.edu/netlogo. Accessed Sept 2018
13. Neumann, P.P., Asadi, S., Lilienthal, A.J., Bartholmai, M., Schiller, J.H.: Autonomous gas-sensitive microdrone: wind vector estimation and gas distribution mapping. IEEE Robot. Autom. Mag. **19**(1), 50–61 (2012)
14. Reynolds, C.W.: Flocks, herds and schools: a distributed behavioral model. In: Proceedings of the 14th Annual Conference on Computer Graphics and Interactive Techniques, SIGGRAPH 1987, pp. 25–34. ACM, New York (1987)
15. Rossi, M., Brunelli, D.: Analyzing the transient response of MOX gas sensors to improve the lifetime of distributed sensing systems. In: 5th IEEE International Workshop on Advances in Sensors and Interfaces IWASI, pp. 211–216, June 2013
16. Rossi, M., Brunelli, D.: Autonomous gas detection and mapping with unmanned aerial vehicles. IEEE Trans. Instrum. Meas. **65**(4), 765–775 (2016)
17. Šmídl, V., Hofman, R.: Tracking of atmospheric release of pollution using unmanned aerial vehicles. Atmos. Environ. **67**, 425–436 (2013)
18. Yu, J., Li, J., Dai, Q., Li, D., Ma, X., Lv, Y.: Temperature compensation and data fusion based on a multifunctional gas detector. IEEE Trans. Instrum. Meas. **64**(1), 204–211 (2015)

# Convolutional Neural Networks for Multi-class Intrusion Detection System

Sasanka Potluri[✉], Shamim Ahmed, and Christian Diedrich

Institute for Automation Engineering, Otto-von-Guericke University Magdeburg,
Magdeburg, Germany
{sasanka.potluri,christian.diedrich}@ovgu.de,
shamim.ahmed@st.ovgu.de

**Abstract.** Advances in communication and networking technology leads to the use of internet-based technology in Industrial Control System (ICS) applications. Simultaneously to the advantages and flexibility, it also opens doors to the attackers. Increased attacks on ICS are clear examples for the need of developing strong security mechanisms to develop defense in depth strategies for industries. Despite several techniques, every day a novel attack is being identified and this highlights the importance and need of robust techniques for identifying those attacks. Deep learning-based intrusion detection mechanisms are proven to be efficient in identifying novel attacks. Deep learning techniques such as Stacked Autoencoders (SAE), Deep Belief Networks (DBN) are widely used for intrusion detection but the research on using Convolutional Neural Networks (CNN) is limited. In this paper, the efficiency of CNN based intrusion detection for identifying the multiple attack classes using datasets such as NSL-KDD and UNSW-NB 15 is evaluated. Different performance metrics such as precision, recall and F-measure were calculated and compared with the existing deep learning approaches.

**Keywords:** Intrusion Detection System (IDS) $\cdot$
Convolutional Neural Networks (CNN) $\cdot$ Industrial Control Systems (ICS) $\cdot$
Deep learning $\cdot$ Network security

## 1 Introduction

Wide spread internet-based communication technology brings flexibility, interoperability and many other advantages to the Industrial Control Systems (ICS). On the other side, it also brings the equivalent security related issues too. As ICS mainly handles critical infrastructure, attacks on such systems may endanger people's safety and health, damage industrial facilities and produce financial loss.

Typical network attacks on ICS include but not limited to vulnerabilities, Denial-of-Service (DoS), Probing, surfing etc. Intrusion detection is a technique to identify such malicious activities (attacks, penetrations, break-ins and other form of computer abuse) in a communication network or in a computer related system. Intrusion Detection System (IDS) detects such intruder's actions that violate the confidentiality, availability or integrity of the ICS infrastructure [1].

© Springer Nature Switzerland AG 2018
A. Groza and R. Prasath (Eds.): MIKE 2018, LNAI 11308, pp. 225–238, 2018.
https://doi.org/10.1007/978-3-030-05918-7_20

IDS are mainly classified into two types: host-based IDS (HIDS) and network-based IDS (NIDS). HIDS in general a piece of software resides on the host system or infrastructure and looks for and suspicious activities occurring at host or being invaded on the host. NIDS can be either a software or a dedicated hardware which tracks the network packets in real time or close to real time and tries to identify the malicious patterns in the network traffic [2]. Based on the needs of the individual organizations and available resources, the type of IDS is deployed in the network infrastructure for intrusion detection.

Key parameters such as performance requirement, reliability requirements, operating systems and applications, risk management goals, security architecture etc. differentiate the use of intrusion detection mechanisms from IT infrastructure to ICS infrastructure. A detailed information about the priorities and their relation to security parameters in mentioned in [3]. Due to these reasons and continuous novel attacks on ICS highlights the importance and need of research for developing IDS mechanisms to improve the defense in depth strategies. [4] also gives a detailed overview on the challenges and different scientific works in improving the security in the context of ICS.

Many IDS mechanisms exist and also uses deep learning techniques such as Stacked Autoencoders (SAE) and Deep Belief Networks (DBN). But very few researchers concentrated on the multiple attack type classification. In order to counter fight with the malicious attacks, a good knowledge on the type of attacks is necessary. This paper mainly concentrates on identifying different network attacks on ICS that mainly impact the security parameters availability and confidentiality using Convolutional Neural Network (CNN) which was underseen by many researchers in this domain.

The rest of the paper is structured as follows. Section 2 will discuss about the relevant literature related to the development of IDS using different deep learning techniques and their outcomes and drawbacks. In Sect. 3, an overview about the used datasets for evaluating the performance of the mentioned approach is discussed. Section 4 proposes the CNN based IDS architecture with detailed discussion about the pre-processing, training and testing. Section 5 discuss about the implementations and obtained results by comparing accuracy of intrusion detection with different performance metrics. Finally, Sect. 6 concludes the paper and proposes the future work needs to be done.

## 2    Related Work

With DARPA Intrusion Detection Evaluation released in 1998 and 1999 in conjunction with the MIT [5], the concept of intrusion detection and development of security mechanisms in communication systems came into main stream of research. Since then, several researchers developed intrusion detection strategies using different existing datasets like KDD, NSL-KDD etc. to evaluate the performance of the developed IDS. A detailed analysis on different datasets of intrusion detection is mentioned in [6]. The drawback of existing datasets and the need for development of NSL-KDD dataset was discussed in [7]. Despite being old, NSL-KDD dataset was used to evaluate the performance of the proposed mechanism. As many researchers used the same dataset use of same dataset makes our approach comparable with existing approaches. Due to this reason, the related work section also deals with the literature who used NSL-KDD dataset for the development of IDS.

Deep learning techniques also come under the subcategory of machine learning algorithms. But discussing about every machine learning algorithm used for development of IDS is not possible. A detailed analysis of NSL-KDD data using various machine learning techniques with Waikato Environment for Knowledge Analysis (WEKA) tool is discussed in [8]. Different deep learning techniques for IDS is discussed here.

Deep learning based studies show that it completely surpasses the traditional methods in intrusion detection. In [9], deep neural networks for flow based anomaly detection was proposed and proves that deep learning techniques can be used for anomaly detection in software defined networks. [10] uses deep learning with self-taught learning technique and benchmarks the performance using NSL-KDD dataset for network intrusion detection. Here deep learning is used to classify the normal and attack classes. Performance evaluation for multiclass classification was not performed.

In [11], Recurrent Neural Networks (RNN) are considered as a reduced-size networks. They classify the multiple attack classes and the performance looks promising. But, the dataset used for training is not complete NSL-KDD dataset, they used a part of the training dataset which makes the performance biased. They also concentrated mainly on feature grouping rather than attack classification. Unfolded RNN were used in [12], and also used the limited training dataset of NSL-KDD dataset for training against attacks. When compared to existing machine learning approaches, the detection accuracies are higher with RNN. DBN for IDS was propose by [13] and explained the efficiency of achieving higher accuracy. They performed the training operation with 20%. 30% and 40% of the NSL-KDD train dataset and tested it with the same.

Overcoming the above mentioned drawbacks, [14] uses SAE for deep feature extraction and multiclass attack classification. The results look promising and much better than the existing approaches. To overcome the drawback of long training time [15] mentioned the use of accelerated computing platform techniques to train the deep neural networks faster along with multi-class attack classification. In [16], the use of hybrid deep learning techniques a combination of deep learning and machine learning techniques were discussed. For better classification a combination of multiple detection mechanisms with ranking approach for highest detection accuracy of the individual attack classes was proposed.

Recently [17], provided a detailed multiclass class classification of NSL-KDD datasets using the DBN and SAE. They outperformed the detection accuracy when compared to other approaches by proposing the nonsymmetric deep autoencoder. They also performed a more detailed 13-class multi-class classification to evaluate the performance of their proposed approach and looks promising. Despite the results looks promising, they used the same training dataset to test and evaluate the performance of the proposed approach which leads to achieve higher detection accuracies.

As CNN are mainly performed on images, only one related work using CNN for development of IDS was found. We also used this approach as a basis for our implementation. [18] provided an effective image conversion method of NSL-KDD data set. The numerical features in NSL-KDD are normalized using min-max normalization and then different binary values are assigned to the different features of NSL-KDD data. This assigned binary values are converted to an image for training and testing of the CNN. This approach converts all the NSL-KDD features into image format. Even though they performed very structured pre-processing, the performance of IDS was analyzed using available ResNet50 and GoogLeNet architectures which are famous for image processing applications. The accuracies were not satisfactory and discussion on multi-class classification fails which led us to investigate further on the performance on CNN for multi-class classification. Another research on CNN based IDS was mentioned in [19] used 10% KDDcup 99 dataset. Despite getting better accuracies they just used 10% dataset so this research is not considered in our benchmarking.

Some common drawback from existing approaches are listed. Many approaches use the same training dataset of NSL-KDD for training and testing and it shows better detection accuracies. This is not accurate as the feature for normal and attack in NSL-KDD dataset are different in training and testing dataset. Only selected part of the training and testing dataset are used to evaluate the developed mechanism which will result in biased outputs. Very few works concentrate on the multiclass attack classification and the use of CNN for IDS is not familiar.

## 3  Datasets

Different datasets exists for evaluating the performance of the developed IDS out of which, NSL-KDD dataset is well used by researchers. As it became old, in 2015, new dataset named UNSW NB 15 dataset was developed. No research was found using this dataset for performing intrusion detection. As it has more number of attack classes and huge compared to NSL-KDD, we used this dataset also to train and test performance of the proposed approach. More information about the datasets is discussed below.

### 3.1  NSL-KDD Dataset

The inherent drawbacks in the Knowledge Discovery in Databases (KDD) cup 99 dataset [20] has been revealed by various statistical analyses and has affected the detection accuracy of many IDS modelled by researchers. NSL-KDD dataset is a refined version of its predecessor. It contains essential record of the complete KDD dataset. There is a collection of downloadable files at the disposal for the researchers.

Three main refinements done on KDD dataset were:

1. Redundant records are removed to enable the classifier to produce an un-biased result.
2. Sufficient number of records is available in the train and test datasets, which is reasonably rational and enables to execute experiments on the complete set.
3. The number of selected records from each difficult level group is inversely proportional to the percentage of records in the original KDD dataset.

In each record, there are 41 attributes unfolding different features of the flow and a label is assigned to each sample either as an attack type or as normal. The details of the attributes namely the attribute name, their description and sample data is given in [21]. The features in NSL-KDD dataset are of different data types. The features of the dataset can also be grouped into three different categories. They are basic features, traffic features and content features. Apart from normal data, records for 39 different attack types exist in NSL-KDD dataset. All these attack types were grouped into four attack classes. The summary of the attack classes and their attack types and a detailed information is available in [21].

Figure 1 gives an overview on the NSL-KDD datasets used for training and testing the developed IDS. This gives the number of data elements in the entire dataset.

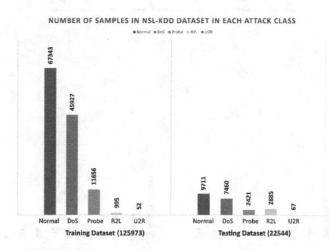

**Fig. 1.** Overview NSL-KDD dataset

## 3.2 UNSW-NB 15 Dataset

In the year 2015 [22, 23, 24], the UNSW-NB 15 data set was introduced first time by Moustafa and Slay. The data set was created in the lab of Australian Center for Cyber Security (ACCS) and the IXIA PerfectStorm tool was used to create the data set. A volume of 100 GB raw network traffic was captured using tcpdump tool to create the data set.

The main objective of creating this new dataset is to overcome the shortcomings of previously defined datasets like KDD Cup 99, NSL-KDD or DARPA 98/99. The efficiency of an IDS is entirely depended on how well it has been trained to capture intrusions and the training efficiency is depended on the dataset that contains contemporary activities of normal and attack. There are three major disadvantages of previously defined datasets [23] they are:

- Lack of knowledge on modern footprint attack fashions. E.g. the attack behaviors are changed closer to normal behavior with the time for attacks like stealthy or spy attacks.
- The defined normal traffic benchmark is not similar with the present normal traffic because these datasets were defined before two decades ago.

- The training and testing set have different distribution on attack types. For instance, the existing benchmark datasets have different data types comparing between the training and testing set.

The UNSW-NB 15 dataset includes 49 features in total and it has nine attack classes. The attack classes and the attack categories are defined in [24].

Figure 2 gives an overview on the UNSW-NW 15 dataset used for training and testing the developed IDS. This gives the number of data elements in the entire dataset.

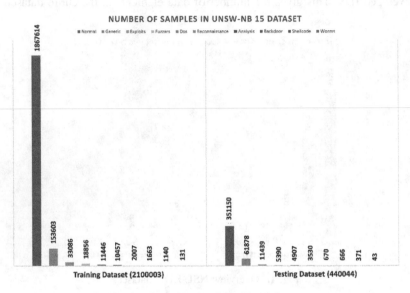

**Fig. 2.** Overview UNSW-NB 15 dataset

# 4  Convolutional Neural Networks Based IDS Architecture

## 4.1  Proposed CNN Model

The architecture of the proposed CNN based IDS architecture is depicted in following Fig. 3. The represented figure proposes the approach used for NSL-KDD dataset but the procedure is same for UNSW-NW 15 dataset too.

As said earlier, NSL-KDD/UNSW-NW 15 dataset was used for training and testing purpose of the proposed architecture. All the features are taken for pre-processing.

In pre-processing stage, all the features of the dataset are transferred to a binary vector space. We use one hot encoding principle to convert the nominal features (2, 3, 4) into binary vector. Converting the nominal values into binary format has an added advantage when compared to label encoding. Label encoding assumes that higher the categorical value, better the category is but when extracting features this may lead to confusion and misguiding of the deep learning algorithms.

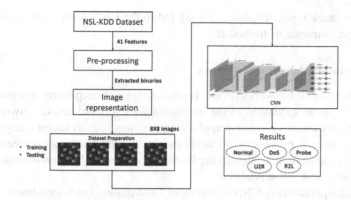

**Fig. 3.** CNN based IDS architecture

The features of numeric type include both integer and float variables. Min-Max normalization approach is used to normalize the continuous data into the range of [0, 1]. The mathematical formula for Min-Max normalization is represented in Eq. 1.

$$x_{new} = \frac{x - x_{min}}{x_{max} - x_{min}} \tag{1}$$

Where x stands for individual numeric feature value, xmin stands for the minimal value of the feature, xmax stands for the maximum value, xnew stands for the pre-processed value after normalization. After normalization, the individual value is discretized into 10 intervals with individual range increasing with 0.1. All the discretized values are again converted to binary format using one-hot encoder schema. The binary features in dataset are taken as it is. After pre-processing, each NSL-KDD network packet turns into a binary vector with 464 dimensions.

These extended binary vectors are then transferred into an 8 × 8 grayscale image in the image representation stage. Each 8 bits from the binary vector was taken individually and translated into a grayscale pixel. From binary vector, we get 58 grayscale image pixels. To make it 8 × 8 image, rest of the pixels are padded with 0's. The grayscale image of individual categories is represented in the following Fig. 4.

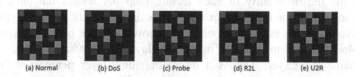

(a) Normal        (b) DoS        (c) Probe        (d) R2L        (e) U2R

**Fig. 4.** Input image 8 × 8 of different classes from NSL – KDD Dataset

The generated images from image representation stage of our framework is visible in Fig. 4. The images represented here are just a sample from the entire set of generated images. A deep insight into the image can show slight difference between the normal and different attack types. These images are fed to the CNN for training as well as for testing the performance of trained IDS.

## 4.2 Convolutional Neural Networks

Convolutional Neural Networks (CNN) is one category of deep learning algorithm and are considered as an extension to the traditional feed forward neural networks. CNN have proven very effective in many application domains such as image recognition and classification, speech processing applications etc. Its effectiveness has been successfully proven in tasks such as identifying faces, objects and traffic sign detection mainly used in robotics and self-driving cars.

Four main operations of CNN comprise of Convolution layer, non-linear activation function such as ReLu, pooling layer, and fully connected layer (classification).

- Convolution Layer: As the name itself indicates, the CNN got its name from convolution operations. The main task of convolution is to extract features from the input image. Convolution operation preserves the spatial relationship between pixels by learning image features using filter or a kernel. The output image out of convolution operation is termed as 'Activation Map' or 'Convolved Feature' or 'Featured Map'. The values of the filter or Kernel are updated automatically during the training process of CNN to learn the features of an image in a better way. The size of feature map is controlled by depth (corresponding to number of filters we use), stride (Number of pixels by which we slide the filter) and zero padding (padding images with zeros at the border). If the image is padded with zeros at the border then it is termed as wide convolution and if not, it is considered as a narrow convolution. More detailed information on convolution layer is discussed in [25].
- Nonlinear activation ReLu: After every convolution operation, before generating the feature map, additional nonlinear function such as ReLu is being used in CNN. ReLu stands for Rectified Linear Unit and is a non-linear operation. It is an element wise operation and replaces all negative pixel values in the feature ma with zero. ReLu introduces the non-linear behavior to the CNN and traditional convolution operation is linear. Other non-linear activation functions such as tanh and sigmoid can also be used instead of ReLu. More detailed information on ReLU activation and other activation functions are discussed in [26].
- Pooling Layer: Spatial pooling also termed as subsampling or down-sampling reduces the dimensionality of each feature map but retains the most important information out of the feature map. Spatial pooling can be of different types such as Max, Average, Sum etc. Max pooling has shown to work better in many applications. More detailed information on pooling layer is discussed in [27].
- Fully connected Layer: This is a traditional multi-layer perceptron that uses a softmax activation function in the output layer. The term fully connected implies that every neuron in the previous layer is connected to every neuron in the next layer. The output of the convolution and pooling layers represent the high-level features of the input image. The fully connected layer uses these features for classifying the input image into various classes based on the training dataset. More detailed information on fully connected layer is discussed in [28].

Combining the above-mentioned key parameters forms the CNN. The convolution and pooling layers act as a feature extraction mechanism out of an image while the fully connected layer act as a classifier. More detailed discussion on CNN is discussed in [29]. Figure 5 will give a detailed overview of the above-mentioned concepts in relation to our application of CNN for IDS. The detailed functionality of the implemented CNN model is discussed in the next section.

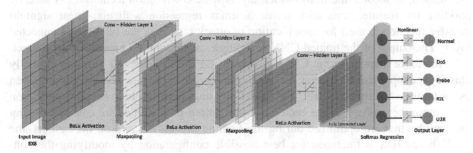

**Fig. 5.** Convolutional Neural Networks Model

## 5 Evaluation and Results

### 5.1 Implementation

Proposed architecture was implemented in MATLAB 2017b using deep learning libraries provided by MathWorks [30]. The deep learning libraries provided by MathWorks has improved a lot when compared to its previous versions and provides a lot of configuration parameters and flexibility which make the deep learning algorithms tunable to many individual applications and needs. MATLAB also provides the option of training the deep learning algorithms on CPU as well as on GPU. MATLAB also provides the real-time UDP communication which in future can be used for developing real -time deep learning based IDS [31].

From Fig. 5, we can see the MATLAB implemented CNN model. It includes the following steps:

Step 1: From pre-processing and image representation stage we generated the image dataset with each image of size 8 × 8. This is given as an input image to CNN – Hidden Layer 1.

Step 2: The CNN layers are initially initialized with random weights and filters and these are adopted during the training process.

Step 3: The network takes the input image and initiates the training process. The image goes through the forward propagation steps (convolution, ReLu and pooling operations along with forward propagation of the fully connected layers) and finds the output probabilities.

Step 4: The error value of the desired output to the generated output is calculated. And validation is performed after every 300 iterations.

Step5: Now backpropagation with gradient decent is used to update the network weights and all filter values to minimize the output error.

The above steps are continued until the validation function measures the same value for five times as the patience was set to 5. This ensure the network from over-fitting. Narrow convolution technique is used in the first convolution hidden layer. The output feature map of the first convolution hidden layer is smaller than $8 \times 8$. Due to this reason, in second and third hidden layers wide convolution techniques is used by padding the feature maps with zeros. Softmax regression with non-linear sigmoid transfer function is used for classification of attack classes at the final fully connected layer. The output of the trained CNN is multiple attacks classes present in the dataset.

The above steps train the CNN by optimizing the weights and filters to correctly classify the input trained images for attack classes. Now, the new test images are given as an input to the trained CNN. Now the CNN only perform the forward propagation and output the probability for each class (the output probabilities are calculates using the weights that are optimized during the training process). Based on the outputs, the CNN based IDS is finetuned for best possible configuration by modifying the configuration parameters such as the performance metrics are evaluated.

## 5.2 Performance Evaluation

Complete NSL-KDD and USNW-NB 15 dataset was used for evaluating the performance of the proposed model. As the ratio of attack classes vary we performed different training operations with classifying the input data into 2-Classes, 3-Classes, 4-Classes and all 5-Classes respectively for NSL-KDD and 2 Classes to 10 Classes model for UNSW-NB 15. The Fig. 5 above shows the best detection accuracies of the different attack classes and normal class by different CNN training capabilities. The best results are mentioned. This is also helpful in choosing the proper CNN for identifying the attack classes of our need based on the available dataset. From Fig. 6, we can see that the detection of attacks (R2L & U2R) in 4-Classes and 5-Classes in zero and this is obvious. From Fig. 1, we see that the percentage of R2L and U2R in the entire dataset is too low. Due to this reason, the trained CNN was unable to generalize these attack types. This is also similar in 3-classes as the percentage of Probe, U2R and R2L constitutes to less than 25% and there exists lot of subclasses in those attack types, the detection accuracies with CNN are low.

In similar manner, the performance metrics such as precision, recall, F-Measure for individual attack and normal classifications were evaluated. The below Table 1 provides the observed best performance metrics. The performance metrics are calculated based on [16].

Table 2 provides the detection accuracies of the individual attack classes present in UNSW-NB 15 dataset. The detection accuracy of the Normal packets is very accurate. The detection accuracies of attack classes are zero except generic, exploits and fuzzers and it is obvious from Fig. 2. As the ration of attacks type w.r.t other normal is very low and CNN was unable to identify the generic patterns for those attack types from the dataset provided.

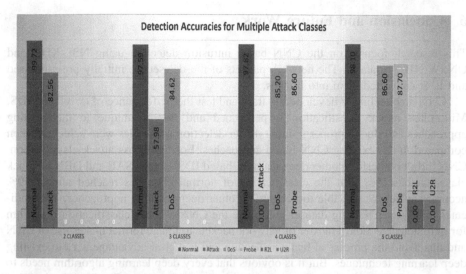

**Fig. 6.** CNN based detection accuracies for multiple attack classes NSL-KDD dataset

**Table 1.** Best performance metrics for different classes

|           | Normal | DoS   | Probe | R2L | U2R |
|-----------|--------|-------|-------|-----|-----|
| Precision | 97.82  | 84.23 | 85.46 | 0   | 0   |
| Recall    | 93.74  | 86.35 | 88.19 | 0   | 0   |
| F-Measure | 93.06  | 85.89 | 87.52 | 0   | 0   |

**Table 2.** CNN based detection accuracies for multiple attack classes UNSW-NB 15 dataset

| Attack classes | | | | | | | | | | Overall detection rate (%) |
|--------|---------|---------|--------|-----|----------------|----------|----------|-----------|-------|-----------------------------|
| Normal | Generic | Exploit | Fuzzers | DoS | Reconnaissance | Analysis | Backdoor | Shellcode | Worms | |
| 99.70% | 97.70%  | 61.80%  | 6.8%   | 0   | 0              | 0        | 0        | 0         | 0     | 94.9%                       |

Finally, we also compared the performance of our approach with other existing CNN based approaches who used NSL-KDD for training and testing. As they used the overall accuracy, we also mentioned our approach in the same manner. Following Table 3 provides the overall detection accuracies of the existing approach to our approach and the results looks promising. The performance of other deep learning techniques on NSL-KDD dataset was evaluated in [14]. From our results, CNN looks promising.

**Table 3.** Performance comparison of our approach with existing CNN based approaches

| Technique               | Test accuracy |
|-------------------------|---------------|
| CNN – ResNet 50         | 79.14%        |
| CNN – GoogLeNet         | 77.04%        |
| CNN – Proposed approach | 91.14%        |

# 6 Conclusion and Future Work

This research focuses on the CNN based intrusion detection using NSL-KDD and UNSW-NB 15 dataset. The network packets of the dataset are initially pre-processed and later converted them into images.

CNN architecture is developed to train and test the performance of developed IDS. Multi-class attack classification is performed and this is unique to the existing approaches and due to proper training, better detection accuracies were achieved when compared to the existing CNN based approaches. For multiclass attack classification, CNN didn't outperform other deep learning-based IDS such as SAE and DBN in attack classifications [16]. But the classification of normal class has reached almost 99% accuracy which was unable to achieve by other deep learning approaches. This indicates that proper training dataset will make the CNN a better classification algorithm for intrusion detection. Transfer of network packets to image format makes use of CNN and this avoid the process of feature selection and is a clear advantage w.r.t to existing deep learning techniques. But it is obvious that every deep learning algorithm needs to be evaluated for the individual case to evaluate the performance. Finally, it is clear that along with other deep learning approaches such as SAE and DBN, CNN is also a good approach in developing IDS in the ICS applications.

As a future work, a better image conversion and image representation techniques needs to be identified. In future, we will test our algorithms with this other new dataset. To counter fight with imbalanced datasets and train network efficiently for all attack types, Generative Adversarial Networks (cGAN). We also consider simulating our own dataset in the context of ICS for more precise application specific development. As MATLAB supports, real time network traffic acquisition, implementation of deep learning algorithms on the real time network traffic data will be done.

# References

1. Stallings, W.: Network security essentials : applications and standards (2000)
2. Scarfone, K., Mell, P.: Guide to intrusion detection and prevention systems (IDPS) recommendations of the National Institute of Standards and Technology. NIST Spec. Publ. **800–94**, 127 (2007)
3. Tofino Security, SCADA Security Basics: Why Industrial Networks are Different than IT Networks (2012). https://www.tofinosecurity.com/blog/scada-security-basics-why-industrial-networks-are-different-it-networks
4. Colbert, E.J.M., Kott, A. (eds.): Cyber-security of SCADA and Other Industrial Control Systems. AIS, vol. 66. Springer, Cham (2016). https://doi.org/10.1007/978-3-319-32125-7
5. M. Lincoln Laboratory, DARPA Intrusion Detection Data Sets. https://www.ll.mit.edu/ideval/data/. Accessed 07 Apr 2016
6. Sahu, S.K., Sarangi, S., Jena, S.K.: A detail analysis on intrusion detection datasets. In: Souvenir 2014 IEEE International Advance Computing Conference (IACC 2014), May, pp. 1348–1353 (2014)
7. McHugh, J.: Testing intrusion detection systems: a critique of the 1998 and 1999 DARPA intrusion detection system evaluations as performed by Lincoln Laboratory. ACM Trans. Inf. Syst. Secur. **3**(4), 262–294 (2000)

8. Revathi, D.A.M.S.: A detailed analysis on NSL-KDD dataset using various machine learning techniques for intrusion detection. Int. J. Eng. Res. Technol. **2**(12), 1848–1853 (2013)
9. Tang, T.A., Mhamdi, L., McLernon, D., Zaidi, S.A.R., Ghogho, M.: Deep learning approach for network intrusion detection in software defined networking. In: 2016 International Conference on Wireless Networks and Mobile Communications, pp. 258–263 (2016)
10. Javaid, A., Niyaz, Q., Sun, W., Alam, M.: A deep learning approach for network intrusion detection system. In: Proceedings of the 9th EAI International Conference on Bio-inspired Information and Communications Technologies (formerly BIONETICS) (2016)
11. Sheikhan, M., Jadidi, Z., Farrokhi, A.: Intrusion detection using reduced-size RNN based on feature grouping. Neural Comput. Appl. **21**(6), 1185–1190 (2012)
12. Yin, C., Zhu, Y., Fei, J., He, X.: A deep learning approach for intrusion detection using recurrent neural networks. IEEE Access **5**(c), 21954–21961 (2017)
13. Alom, Z., Bontupalli, V., Taha, T.M.: Intrusion detection using deep belief networks, pp. 339–344 (2015)
14. Potluri, S., Diedrich, C.: Deep feature extraction for multi-class intrusion detection in industrial control systems. Int. J. Comput. Theory Eng. **9**(5), 374–379 (2017)
15. Potluri, S., Diedrich, C.: Accelerated deep neural networks for enhanced Intrusion Detection System. In: IEEE International Conference on Emerging Technologies and Factory Automation, ETFA 2016 (2016)
16. Potluri, S., Henry, N.F., Diedrich, C.: Evaluation of hybrid deep learning techniques for ensuring security in networked control systems. In: 2017 22nd IEEE International Conference on Emerging Technologies and Factory Automation, pp. 1–8 (2017)
17. Shone, N., Ngoc, T.N., Phai, V.D., Shi, Q.: A deep learning approach to network intrusion detection. IEEE Trans. Emerg. Top. Comput. Intell. **2**(1), 41–50 (2018)
18. Li, Z., Qin, Z., Huang, K., Yang, X., Ye, S.: Intrusion detection using convolutional neural networks for representation learning. In: Liu, D., Xie, S., Li, Y., Zhao, D., El-Alfy, E.-S.M. (eds.) ICONIP 2017. LNCS, vol. 10638, pp. 858–866. Springer, Cham (2017). https://doi.org/10.1007/978-3-319-70139-4_87
19. Vinayakumar, R., Soman, K.P., Poornachandran, P.: Applying convolutional neural network for network intrusion detection. In: 2017 International Conference on Advanced Computing, Communications and Informatics, pp. 1222–1228 (2017)
20. Tavallaee, M., Bagheri, E., Lu, W., Ghorbani, A.A.: A detailed analysis of the KDD CUP 99 data set. In: IEEE Symposium on Computational Intelligence in Security and Defense Applications, CISDA 2009, pp. 1–6 (2009)
21. Dhanabal, L., Shantharajah, S.P.: A study on NSL-KDD dataset for intrusion detection system based on classification algorithms. Int. J. Adv. Res. Comput. Commun. Eng. **4**, 446–452 (2015)
22. Moustafa, N., Slay, J.: UNSW-NB15: a comprehensive data set for network intrusion detection systems (UNSW-NB15 network data set). In: 2015 Military Communications and Information Systems Conference, pp. 1–6 (2015)
23. Moustafa, N., Slay, J.: The evaluation of network anomaly detection systems: statistical analysis of the UNSW-NB15 data set and the comparison with the KDD99 data set. Inf. Secur. J. **25**(1–3), 18–31 (2016)
24. Moustafa, N., Slay, J.: The UNSW-NB15 data set description (2015). https://www.unsw.adfa.edu.au/unsw-canberra-cyber/cybersecurity/ADFA-NB15-Datasets/. Accessed 06 Apr 2018
25. Wu, J.: Introduction to Convolutional Neural Networks, pp. 1–28 (2016)
26. Agarap, A.F.: Deep Learning using Rectified Linear Units (ReLU), no. 1 (2018)

27. Wu, H., Gu, X.: Max-pooling dropout for regularization of convolutional neural networks. In: Arik, S., Huang, T., Lai, W.K., Liu, Q. (eds.) ICONIP 2015. LNCS, vol. 9489, pp. 46–54. Springer, Cham (2015). https://doi.org/10.1007/978-3-319-26532-2_6
28. Karn, U.: An intuitive explanation of convolutional neural networks. The Data Science Blog (2016). https://ujjwalkarn.me/2016/08/11/intuitive-explanation-convnets/. Accessed 06 May 2018
29. Bhandare, A., Bhide, M., Gokhale, P., Chandavarkar, R.: Applications of convolutional neural networks. Int. J. Comput. Sci. Inf. Technol. 7(5), 2206–2215 (2016)
30. MathWorks, Deep Learning Basics, Documentation (2018). https://www.mathworks.com/help/nnet/deep-learning-basics.html. Accessed 06 May 2018
31. MathWorks, Real-Time UDP (2018). https://www.mathworks.com/help/xpc/real-time-udp.html. Accessed 06 May 2018

# wraudit: A Tool to Transparently Monitor Web Resources' Integrity

David Salvador[✉], Jordi Cucurull[✉], and Pau Julià[✉]

Scytl Secure Electronic Voting S.A., C. Enric Granados 84, 08008 Barcelona, Spain
{david.salvador,jordi.cucurull,pau.julia}@scytl.com

**Abstract.** JavaScript has become the language of reference for programming the client-side logics of web-applications. However, there is no native full support to protect the integrity of this code from modifications conducted by the server where it is hosted. Many election applications, including internet voting solutions, are based on this language. Thus, if the server that hosts the code is compromised, a modified version of the code could be served and some election security properties affected, e.g. voter privacy, vote integrity, and so on. Furthermore, the usage of a Content Delivery Network (CDN) to mitigate Distributed Denial-of-Service (DDoS) attacks on internet voting solutions has been called into question for similar reasons. A malicious administrator of the hosting provider could have the opportunity to modify JavaScript files affecting the web application's code integrity. In order to tackle this problem, in this article we propose a solution that mitigates those risks by using a service called wraudit that transparently monitors the integrity of the published code. The service design and implementation are presented and the first insights from our experience using it are explained.

**Keywords:** Web resources · JavaScript · Code integrity
Monitoring tool · Experience

## 1 Introduction

JavaScript has become the language of reference for programming the client-side logic of web-applications. More than 90% of web sites in the internet use JavaScript as their client-side programming language [1]. JavaScript does not only make web sites more interactive, but it enables the implementation of business logic required by web applications.

All the web sites' resources, including JavaScript code, are downloaded by the browsers through HTTP connections. The integrity and privacy of those connections can be ensured with the usage of TLS [5]. However, there is no web standard to protect the users against modifications of the code performed by the hosting server.

In critical web applications, like e-voting solutions, it is key that the published resources, especially the JavaScript code, do not suffer unplanned modifications. If an attacker was able to modify some of the code, the security of

© Springer Nature Switzerland AG 2018
A. Groza and R. Prasath (Eds.): MIKE 2018, LNAI 11308, pp. 239–247, 2018.
https://doi.org/10.1007/978-3-030-05918-7_21

the web applications could be seriously compromised. For example, in e-voting solutions some election security properties could be affected, e.g. voter privacy and vote integrity. Furthermore, the use of a Content Delivery Network (CDN) solution to mitigate the Distributed Denial-of-Service (DDoS) attacks into e-voting solutions has been called into question for similar reasons [6]. A malicious administrator of the hosting provider or the CDN could have the opportunity to modify JavaScript code affecting the web application's code integrity.

In this article we introduce a tool that we have developed to monitor and guarantee the integrity of the code published in the front-end nodes; either servers managed by our company or a third-party, or by a CDN. To do so, the tool named *wraudit* downloads the web application's resources and reviews their integrity against a trusted baseline. The scans are disguised as human user's browsing to avoid bot-detection techniques that could be used to serve legit content to bots and malicious modified content to human users.

## 2　Related Work

Some security solutions are devoted to prevent the execution of manipulated code by implementing verifications on the browser. The classic solution to ensure the authenticity and integrity of code consists of signing it, using public key cryptography and enforcing its validation. For JavaScript, as opposed to other technologies such as Java Applets or mobile apps, there is no standard to sign and verify the code delivered to the browsers.

A proprietary solution [2] implemented in Mozilla browsers and, formerly, in Netscape Communicator 4.x existed, but it was discontinued. This solution encapsulated the JavaScript code and HTML files inside a signed Jar file. Unfortunately, there was no widget showing the user that the code was neither signed nor verified. Thus, a malicious non signed Jar could be used to replace the legitimate one without the voter noticing.

Recently the W3C Subresource Integrity [3] recommendation has been agreed upon, which enables the HTML code to include a hash of the referred JavaScript code. This recommendation enables the browser to validate the integrity of the code loaded from a different source, i.e. hosted in a different server than the HTML. However, this measure relies on the assumption that the HTML code itself is not manipulated. This assumption is valid when CDNs are used to serve the JavaScript code and the HTML code is served from a trusted server. In the case of e-voting systems, however, no servers are considered trusted.

From an academic point of view, there are several proposals based on signature-based whitelisting. One of the most relevant is SICILIAN [4], an approach targeted to prevent script injection attacks. The approach is based on whitelisting using code structural signatures, i.e. signatures of the code robust against syntactic changes in the scripts that do not affect their security. The main advantage of this approach is that it does not require regenerating the signatures for certain modifications of the code analyzed. The implementation of this approach requires the modification of the browsers, thus the validations are performed just when the scripts are loaded into the JavaScript parser.

Finally, other work exists that, despite not being related to security, is related to the detection of website modifications. This is the case of the Website Monitoring project of EDGI[1] that monitors and documents changes of federal websites of the USA. The purpose of this project is not to detect security attacks, but to detect website content modifications. The project has made the code publicly available.

Our proposal is based on the detection of code manipulations by performing external auditing of it. This is a similar approach to the one followed by file integrity mechanisms, such AIDE[2] or OSSEC[3]. However, these tools analyze the data directly from within the server that contains it. Our proposed tool, instead, requests the files to the HTTP server as any other user of the website would do.

## 3   Risks of Using a Content Delivery Network

The usage of Content Delivery Networks (CDNs) improves the throughput of the websites by accelerating the data access from different locations. A CDN is a network of nodes deployed in different distant physical locations that are interconnected with high speed connections and include caches to replicate the information served. Then, when users connect to a website backed with a CDN, the connection requests are served by the CDN nodes that are closest. CDNs can also be used to mitigate Distributed Denial of Service Attacks (DDoS) and to filter malicious traffic.

In order to offer all the services described, in most of the cases CDNs need to inspect, and in certain cases modify, the data transmitted through the TLS connections, i.e. the service breaks the TLS channel because it needs to be placed in between the two extremes of the connections and act as an authorized man in the middle. This requires access to the corresponding TLS server keys and certificates to inspect the data. Due to this privileged position, especially in e-voting systems [6], certain risks have to be considered:

- **Access to sensitive material.** Since the CDN has access to all the transmitted data, it can reach elements that are usually protected by the TLS connection. The HTML and JavaScript code is assumed to be public, but other elements generated during the connection such as key containers and other cryptography data are not. Despite the CDN being able to obtain the key containers, it will not be able to read their content as in most e-voting solutions those containers are password-protected. So in this case, adding a CDN does not directly renders the system as insecure, but it exposes encrypted data with a password to an additional set of nodes (the ones composing the CDN). In this case, the security of the sensitive material will rely on the strength of the password used to protect it.

---

[1] https://envirodatagov.org/website-monitoring/.
[2] http://aide.sourceforge.net/.
[3] https://www.ossec.net/.

– **Dishonest modification of the code.** As in the previous case, with a CDN having access to the data transmitted within the TLS connection, there is the risk that the HTML, JavaScript code and other resources required by the web application can be modified. In this case, there is no additional layer of security that protects the data's integrity, thus the nodes of the CDN must be trusted or a mechanism such as the W3C Subresource Integrity must be used. However, this does not protect the data if the web application's HTML resources are also served from the same CDN.

The tool that we propose in this paper will detect this last case where the code suffers a dishonest modification.

## 4   Transparently Monitoring Web Resources

Our tool named *wraudit* is a service that, based on a user-supplied baseline, performs scans on web sites looking for unexpected integrity modifications. The service features some bot-detection countermeasures in order to disguise itself as a regular human user.

If the server delivering malicious web content detects the requests made from *wraudit*, it could deliver the legit content to it while serving malicious content to the rest of the users. Many bots and crawlers can be easily detected by reviewing some of their connection's properties, like their HTTP headers [7–10] or by analyzing their navigation patterns [11,12]. The latter detection technique is based on reviewing several metadata, like the order and timing of the HTTP requests made to the server.

To avoid the possible detection, the scans are done through a headless browser which resembles the navigation behavior of a regular user: it has the same HTTP headers and it mimics the order and timing of the requests made by a user. Also, proxies can be plugged-in to disguise the scans' source origin and avoid IP detection and blacklisting. In addition, the scans are performed at different random minutes on an hourly basis.

The sites to be monitored, known as targets, can be added, modified, and deleted through an HTTP REST API. The data needed to create a new target is a list of web resources to be monitored, each of them with its associated integrity proof (SHA-256) acting as the baseline, a seed URL from where the browser will start loading the resources, an optional list of proxies to be used during the scans, and the amount of scans per hour.

A common *wraudit* flow would be as follows:

1. Baseline generation: A baseline of the new site to be monitored is created. An auxiliary tool has been developed to make this step more agile.
2. Addition of new target: The new site is added to *wraudit*. The previously created baseline and all the needed data is uploaded to the service via its API. Immediately after the site is added, a scan schedule is calculated for the current hour. That schedule will be recalculated upon every new hour.
3. Code upload: The front-end server receives the code to be published.

4. Code replication in the CDN: In the case of using a CDN, the static content is published there.
5. Periodical scanning: When the scanning service is enabled, *wraudit* will periodically scan the added targets. A headless Chromium-based browser will be used to retrieve all the web resources triggered by the navigation to the seed URL. Every downloaded web resource is stored and it will be sent back to *wraudit* once the browser finishes the navigation.
6. Comparison with baseline: For every downloaded resource, a hash of it will be calculated and compared to the one stored in *wraudit*. For every hash comparison, a log entry is written, whether it was a match or a mismatch. In the event of a resource's integrity mismatch, the detected resource content with some metadata will be stored in a special location for further forensic analysis. After comparing the integrity of the downloaded resources against the ones stored, *wraudit* will wait until the next scheduled scan.

The flow can also be seen in Fig. 1, which shows the case with a CDN. If no CDN is present, the requests are sent directly to the Front-End Server.

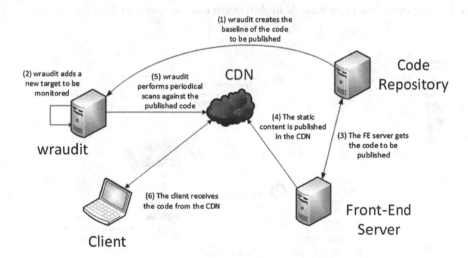

**Fig. 1.** The published content is monitored by the periodical scans that *wraudit* performs

To prevent the web servers from detecting the scans, it is crucial for *wraudit* to disguise its network presence as a regular user. If not, the malicious server or CDN node could serve a legit and non-modified version of the code to *wraudit* and defeat the purpose of the service. To avoid the detection amongst regular users the following measures have been applied:

– **Dynamic IP address**: SOCKS5 proxies are supported. One of the easiest methods to detect *wraudit* HTTP requests is by their source IP. To avoid this, one or more proxies can be plugged-in to avoid possible IP tracking. Each new scan will be performed through a randomly chosen proxy if more than one is set. Examples of proxies that could be added are: a Tor node, a commercial, public or private OpenVPN node[4], a tunnel to a private machine, and any possible combination made with a SOCKS5 connection.

– **Resources downloaded through a Browser**: *wraudit* uses a common browser, Chrome or Chromium, to load the web site and also to store the web resources. The server responding to the HTTP requests will not be able to notice if those requests were triggered by a regular user navigating the web site or by *wraudit*. The only way to detect it would be to add JavaScript code into some of the web application's resources. This added code would perform further client checks [13, 14]. However, any code addition to any web application's resources would be detected by *wraudit* as the integrity proof of the modified file would be different from the baseline.

– **Random scheduled scans**: The schedule of the scans is recalculated hourly. This means that every target will be scanned at different minutes every hour, making it more difficult to detect patterns.

A general overview of *wraudit*'s architecture can bee seen in Fig. 2.

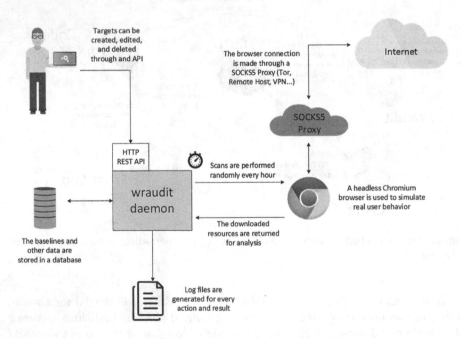

**Fig. 2.** Overview of *wraudit*'s architecture

---

[4] https://hub.docker.com/r/kizzx2/openvpn-client-socks/.

Most web applications that use the pattern single-page application (SPA[5]) can benefit from the monitoring performed by *wraudit*. SPA makes the application to load all or most of the resources on the first page load and rewrites the content without the need of loading new content, making a more responsive and fluid user experience.

Downloading all the security relevant content, mainly JavaScript and HTML, from the first page load allows *wraudit* to monitor almost the entire web application on a single action. For a sophisticated attacker, it would be easier to identify *wraudit*'s requests if several page loads were needed to monitor the web application. For example: loading the index page followed by *login.html* to cover all the relevant code.

# 5 Experiences

The *wraudit* tool has been integrated into the company's SIEM platform, which analyses the generated logs and provides an overview of the status of the service. Event alerts have been created to quickly notify the appropriate teams and act following the security incident procedure.

The tool has been used in several elections, monitoring during the whole election period the published web resources, including the JavaScript code. On these elections no CDN was used so the requests were directly sent to the front-end server. The connections from *wraudit* to the targeted web sites were made on a random basis per scan through a Tor network proxy and through the regular *wraudit*'s network connection.

During this period, the service helped the security team detect some minor customization changes made in production environments even before the standard internal communication flow informed us. These cases were flagged as false positives after validating them with the proper staff members.

No true positives were detected during the different elections periods. At the time of writing, the service has been up and running for 55 days having performed 5067 scans in a total of 7 different elections.

# 6 Conclusions

In this paper, we presented a tool to tackle the integrity concerns and risks of using JavaScript code in web applications in a monitoring-based approach. As a common user, there is no native manner to verify that the browser's downloaded code is the correct one and that it has not been modified for malicious purposes by the server.

The usage of a CDN does not solve the issue either. It will improve the availability and throughput of delivered resources, but a malicious node could deliver modified versions of the web resources and stay unnoticed.

---

[5] https://en.wikipedia.org/wiki/Single-page_application.

Our developed tool, *wraudit*, monitors the integrity of web resources based on a trusted and user-inputted baseline. To do so, it uses several bot-detection counter-measures to resemble a human user while downloading and scanning the web application's JavaScript code and any other kind of resource.

We have monitored several elections' e-voting web applications for more than 50 days. No true positive integrity mismatches were found during the 5000 scans that were performed and only a few false positives were generated by a customization task that was detected before our standard communication flow informed us. We will continue using *wraudit* as a monitoring tool during our elections to reduce the risks of JavaScript code modification whether we are using a CDN or not.

For our future work we are considering three lines: (a) development of a mobile app, (b) development of a browser plugin, and (c) addition of authenticity and integrity mechanisms to the baseline used by the different applications. The mobile app will be a smartphone version of *wraudit* targeted to a certain group of users like auditors, election officers, and system administrators or similar. The browser plugin will validate the integrity of the downloaded resources when the user is accessing the monitored website. The validation will be done using a baseline published in a third party location, making an attack on the whole system more difficult. Both applications would be using a baseline published in a third-party location. The mechanisms we consider adding to the baseline will be mostly based on using PKI and digital signatures, as well as optional immutabilization in the blockchain for extra security by using anchoring techniques, i.e. registering the hash of the baseline into the ledger [15].

# References

1. Web Technology Surveys. https://w3techs.com/technologies/details/cp-javascript/all/all. Accessed 9 July 2018
2. Signed Scripts in Mozilla. https://www-archive.mozilla.org/projects/security/components/signed-scripts.html. Accessed 9 July 2018
3. W3C Subresource Integrity. https://www.w3.org/TR/SRI/. Accessed 9 July 2018
4. Soni, P., Budianto, E., Saxena, P.: The SICILIAN defense: signature-based whitelisting of Web JavaScript. In: ACM Conference on Computer and Communications Security (2015)
5. The Transport Layer Security (TLS) Protocol Version 1.2. https://tools.ietf.org/html/rfc5246. Accessed 9 July 2018
6. Culnane, C., Eldridge, M., Essex, A., Teague, V.: Trust implications of DDoS protection in online elections. In: Krimmer, R., et al. (eds.) E-Vote-ID 2017. LNCS, vol. 10615, pp. 127–145. Springer, Cham (2017). https://doi.org/10.1007/978-3-319-68687-5_8
7. Alves, R., Belo, O., Lourenço, A.: A heuristic-regression approach to crawler pattern identification on clickstream data
8. Lourenço, A., Belo, O.: Applying clickstream data mining to real-time web crawler detection and containment using clicktips platform. In: Decker, R., Lenz, H.-J. (eds.) Advances in Data Analysis. SCDAKO, pp. 351–358. Springer, Heidelberg (2007). https://doi.org/10.1007/978-3-540-70981-7_39

9. Tan, P.-N., Kumar, V.: Discovery of web robot sessions based on their navigational patterns. Data Min. Knowl. Discov. **6**, 9–35 (2002). https://doi.org/10.1023/A:1013228602957
10. Broenink, R.: Using browser properties for fingerprinting purposes. In: 16th biennial Twente Student Conference on IT, Enschede, Holanda, p. 85, January 2012
11. Calzarossa, M.C., Massari, L.: Analysis of header usage patterns of HTTP request messages. In: 2014 IEEE International Conference on High Performance Computing and Communications, 2014 IEEE 6th International Symposium on Cyberspace Safety and Security, 2014 IEEE 11th International Conference on Embedded Software and Syst (HPCC, CSS, ICESS), pp. 847–853. IEEE, August 2014
12. Stassopoulou, A., Dikaiakos, M.D.: A probabilistic reasoning approach for discovering web crawler sessions. In: Dong, G., Lin, X., Wang, W., Yang, Y., Yu, J.X. (eds.) APWeb/WAIM -2007. LNCS, vol. 4505, pp. 265–272. Springer, Heidelberg (2007). https://doi.org/10.1007/978-3-540-72524-4_29
13. Detecting Chrome Headless. https://antoinevastel.com/bot%20detection/2017/08/05/detect-chrome-headless.html. Accessed 9 July 2018
14. Detecting Chrome headless, new techniques. https://antoinevastel.com/bot%20detection/2018/01/17/detect-chrome-headless-v2.html. Accessed 9 July 2018
15. Cucurull, J., Puiggalí, J.: Distributed immutabilization of secure logs. In: Barthe, G., Markatos, E., Samarati, P. (eds.) STM 2016. LNCS, vol. 9871, pp. 122–137. Springer, Cham (2016). https://doi.org/10.1007/978-3-319-46598-2_9

# Using Stigmergy to Incorporate the Time into Artificial Neural Networks

Federico A. Galatolo, Mario Giovanni C. A. Cimino[✉],
and Gigliola Vaglini

Department of Information Engineering, University of Pisa, 56122 Pisa, Italy
{federico.galatolo,mario.cimino,
gigliola.vaglini}@ing.unipi.it

**Abstract.** A current research trend in neurocomputing involves the design of novel artificial neural networks incorporating the concept of time into their operating model. In this paper, a novel architecture that employs stigmergy is proposed. Computational stigmergy is used to dynamically increase (or decrease) the strength of a connection, or the activation level, of an artificial neuron when stimulated (or released). This study lays down a basic framework for the derivation of a stigmergic NN with a related training algorithm. To show its potential, some pilot experiments have been reported. The XOR problem is solved by using only one single stigmergic neuron with one input and one output. A static NN, a stigmergic NN, a recurrent NN and a long short-term memory NN have been trained to solve the MNIST digits recognition benchmark.

**Keywords:** Artificial neural networks · Stigmergy · Deep learning
Supervised learning

## 1 Introduction and Background

The use of Artificial Neural Networks (ANN) in engineering is rapidly increasing in pattern recognition, data classification and prediction tasks [1, 2]. An important difference in recent generations of ANN is the fact that they try to incorporate the concept of time into their operating model. For example, in *spiking* NNs a temporal spike is used for mapping highly nonlinear dynamic models. Networks of spiking neurons are, with regard to the number of neurons, computationally more powerful than earlier ANN models [3]. Nevertheless, training such networks is difficult due to the non-differentiable nature of spike events [4]. Another relevant class of ANN which exhibits temporal dynamics is that of *recurrent* (cyclic) NNs (RNNs). Unlike feedforward (acyclic) NNs, recurrent NNs can use their internal state (memory) to process sequences of inputs, creating and processing memories of arbitrary sequences of input patterns [3]. A special class of recurrent NN is based on the *Long Short-Term Memory* (LSTM) unit, which is made of a cell, an input gate, an output gate and a forget gate. The cell remembers values over arbitrary time intervals and the three gates regulate the flow of information into and out of the cell [3]. However, the training process of recurrent NNs strongly depends on

© Springer Nature Switzerland AG 2018
A. Groza and R. Prasath (Eds.): MIKE 2018, LNAI 11308, pp. 248–258, 2018.
https://doi.org/10.1007/978-3-030-05918-7_22

the set of constraints and regularizations used in the optimization process, resulting in a not entirely unbiased task with respect to the "how" [5].

This paper focuses on a novel architecture that employs *stigmergy* to incorporate the concept of time in ANN. Stigmergy is defined as an emergent mechanism for self-coordinating actions within complex systems, in which the trace left by a unit's action on some medium stimulates the performance of a subsequent unit's action [6]. It is a fundamental mechanism in swarm intelligence and multi-agent systems, but it also models individual interactions [6]. In neuroscience, Hebb studied this phenomenon in the biological brain, as a basis for modeling synaptic plasticity, i.e., the ability of synapses to strengthen or weaken over time, in response to increases or decreases in their coordinated activity [7]. According to Hebb's theory, synaptic plasticity is one of the important neurochemical foundations of learning and memory. Specifically, the Hebb's law states that, when an axon of cell A is near enough to excite cell B and repeatedly or persistently takes part in firing it, some growth process or metabolic change takes place in one or both cells such that A's efficiency, as one of the cells firing B, is increased. This is often paraphrased as "neurons that fire together wire together" [7]. Similarly, in the phenomenon of selective forgetting that characterizes memory in the brain, neural connections that are no longer reinforced will gradually lose their strength relative to recently reinforced ones. Accordingly, computational stigmergy can be used to increase (or decrease) the strength of a connection, or the activation level, of an artificial neuron when stimulated (or unused).

To our knowledge, this is the first study that proposes and lays down a basic framework for the derivation of stigmergic NNs. In the literature, computational intelligence research using stigmergy is focused on swarm and multi-agent systems coordination, and on computational optimization [6]. Although its high potential, demonstrated by the use of stigmergy in biological systems at diverse scales, the use of stigmergy for pattern recognition and data classification is currently poorly investigated. As an example, in [8] a stigmergic architecture has been proposed to perform adaptive context-aware aggregation. In [9] a multilayer architectures of stigmergic receptive fields for pattern recognition have been experimented for human behavioral analysis. The optimization process of both systems is carried out using the Differential Evolution.

In this paper, the dynamics of stigmergy is applied to weights, bias and activation threshold of a classical neural perceptron, to derive the stigmergic perceptron (SP). To train a NN made of SPs, each stigmergic layer can be formally transformed into an equivalent static MLP, by spatial multiplication of nodes, layers and progressive removal of internal temporal steps. Once the network is totally unfolded, the resulting net is much larger, and contains a large number of weights. However, this static NN can be efficiently transformed in a computational graph. As a consequence, a given stigmergic NN can be transformed into a computational graph and trained using backpropagation.

To appreciate the impressive computational power achieved by stigmergic neurons, in this paper two experiments are shown. In the first experiment, the XOR problem is solved by using only one single stigmergic neuron with one input and one output. In the second experiment a static NN, a stigmergic NN, a recurrent NN and a LSTM NN have been trained to solve the MNIST digits recognition benchmark.

The remainder of the paper is organized as follows. Section 2 discusses the architectural design of stigmergic NNs with respect to traditional NNs. Experiments are covered in Sect. 3. Finally, Sect. 4 summarizes conclusions and future work.

## 2  Architectural Design

This section defines formally the design of a stigmergic NN. Without loss of generality it is introduced a pilot application, with suitable input and output coding. Figure 1a shows an example of static binary image, made of $4 \times 5 = 20$ pixels, in the spatial input coding. The necessary number of inputs for a static NN is $N = 20$. Figure 1b shows the same image in the temporal input coding. Considering $T = 5$ instants of time for providing the image row by row, the necessary number of inputs of a temporal NN is $N = 4$. In essence, the image is provided in terms of chunks over 5 subsequent instants of time. Once provided the last chunk, the temporal NN provides the corresponding output class. Therefore, a NN that incorporates the concept of time is able to process the image as a temporal series. In the training phase, the NN learns to adjust its internal states to follow the chunks dynamics, according to the input coding.

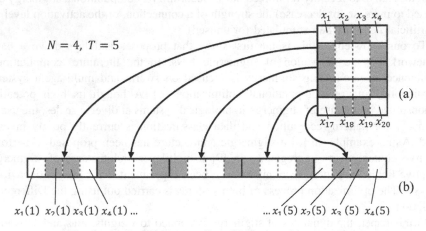

Fig. 1. (a) Spatial input coding. (b) Temporal input coding.

More formally, the conversion from spatial to temporal input coding can be represented as a spatial-to-temporal function $S2T(\cdot)$ providing a sequence of $T$ temporized chunks:

$$\langle x(1)|\ldots|x(T)\rangle = T2S(x) \tag{1}$$

where $x = [x_1, \ldots, x_{N \cdot T}]$ and $x(t) = [x_1(t), \ldots, x_N(t)]$.

Figure 2a and b show a conventional perceptron and a Stigmergic Perceptron (SP), respectively. The SP contains a smaller number of input connections, fed via temporal input coding; the weights $w_i(t)$ and the activation threshold $h(t)$ are dynamic. Note that the output value is provided only at time $T$, unless it is connected with a further SP.

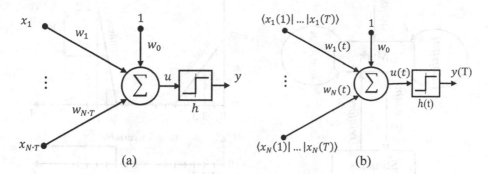

**Fig. 2.** (a) Conventional Perceptron (CP); (b) Stigmergic perceptron (SP).

More formally, let us assume a simple Heaviside step function in the activation gate without loss of generality. The conventional perceptron is modelled as follows:

$$u = w_0 + \sum_{1}^{N \cdot T} w_i \cdot x_i \tag{2}$$

$$y = H(u) = \begin{cases} 0 & if\ u < h \\ 1 & if\ u \geq h \end{cases} \tag{3}$$

whereas the SP processing is modelled as follows:

$$u(t) = w_0 + \sum_{1}^{N} w_i(t) \cdot x_i(t) \tag{4}$$

$$y(t) = H(u(t)) = \begin{cases} 0, & u(t) < h(t) \\ 1, & u(t) \geq h(t) \end{cases} \tag{5}$$

The next step is to define the stigmergy dynamics ontologically and then formally in the operating model. Figure 3a shows the stigmergy ontology [6], made by three concepts (or classes): *Time*, *Mark* and *Stimulus*. A *Stimulus* reinforces a *Mark* that, in turn, advances another *Stimulus*. The *Mark* can be reinforced up to a saturation level. Since the *Time* weakens the *Mark*, in absence of other *Stimulus* the *Mark* finishes. Figure 3b shows the dynamics of a stigmergic relationship. On the bottom, a generic variable of class *Stimulus*: a binary variable generically called $s(t)$. On the top, a generic variable of class *Mark*: a real variable generically called $m(t)$, controlled by the stimulus variable. Specifically, the mark starts from $m(0)$ and, while the stimulus value is 0, undergoes a weakening by $\partial m$ per step, up to the minimum level $\underline{m}$. While the stimulus value is 1, the mark is reinforced by $\Delta m$ per step, up to the maximum level $\overline{m}$ of saturation.

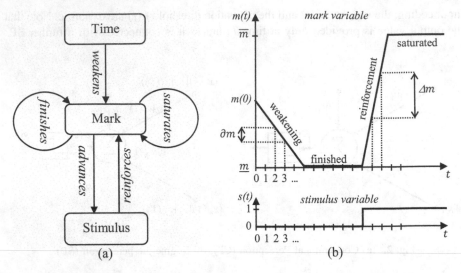

**Fig. 3.** (a) Ontology of stigmergy; (b) Dynamics of a stigmergic relationship.

More formally, the stigmergic relationship is defined as follows:

$$m(t) = \begin{cases} \max\{\underline{m}, m(t-1) - \partial m\}, & s(t, t-1, \ldots) = 0 \\ \min\{\overline{m}, m(t-1) - \partial m + \Delta m\}, & s(t, t-1, \ldots) = 1 \end{cases} \quad (6)$$

The mark dynamics can depend on current and previous values of the stimulus. According to Formula (6) the stigmergic relationships of the SP are:

$$w_i(t) = \begin{cases} \max\{\underline{w_i}, w_i(t-1) - \partial w_i\}, & x_i(t-1) = 0 \\ \min\{\overline{w_i}, w_i(t-1) - \partial w_i + \Delta w_i\}, & x_i(t-1) = 1 \end{cases} \quad (7)$$

$$h(t) = \begin{cases} \max\{\underline{h}, h(t-1) - \partial h\}, & y(t-1) = 0 \\ \min\{\overline{h}, h(t-1) - \partial h + \Delta h\}, & y(t-1) = 1 \end{cases} \quad (8)$$

In essence, the weight dynamics depends on the previous value of the input on the connection. The activation threshold depends on the previous value of the perceptron's output. The overall dynamics are parameterized via the initial mark value, the delta mark weakening, and the delta mark reinforcement. Thus, the training procedure will tune $m(0)$, $\partial m$, and $\Delta m$, i.e., $\{w_i(0)\}$, $\{\partial w_i\}$, $\{\Delta w_i\}$, $h(0)$, $\partial h$, and $\Delta h$.

Figure 4a shows a fully-connected layer of SPs. It can be demonstrated that this stigmergic NN can be represented as the standard static NN shown in Fig. 4b, called unfolded equivalent NN. Specifically, in the unfolded NN each multilayer perceptron $MLP_i$ is the static equivalent of the $SP_i$, and receives all input values from 1 to $T$. The unfolding of a stigmergic NN is based on the progressive addition of nodes, layers for progressive removal of internal temporal steps, up to a completely static NN. Once the network is totally unfolded, the resulting net is much larger, and contains a large number of weights and layers.

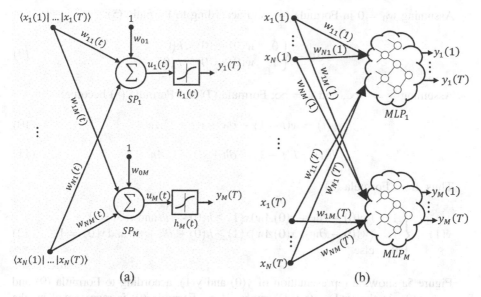

**Fig. 4.** (a) A fully-connected layer of SPs; (b) The unfolded equivalent NN.

The next step is to make the unfolded network differentiable. For this purpose, the step activation function can be approximated by a sigmoid function: $y = 1/(1 + e^{-(u-h)})$, where the midpoint $h$ corresponds to the soft threshold. Moreover, the mark variable can be modelled as a linear function with respect to the stimulus variable. Finally, the saturation/finishing constraints can be approximated by a sigmoidal clamping function applied to the mark variable.

At this step, the NN is then a static differentiable mathematical function, $y = f(x)$, which can be efficiently represented in a computation graph (CG), the descriptive language of deep learning models [10].

When training a NN, the error is a function of the parameters. A CG is a functional description of the required computation, where to compute error derivatives with respect to all the parameters, for use in gradient descent, is very efficient. A CG can be instantiated for forward or backward computation. Specifically, reverse-mode differentiation, i.e. is the backpropagation, is carried out very efficiently.

As a consequence of the equivalence between a stigmergic NN and an unfolded NN, a given stigmergic NN can be transformed into a computational graph and efficiently trained using backpropagation.

## 3 Experimental Studies

In order to appreciate the computational power of stigmergic neurons, in the first experiment the XOR problem is solved by using only one single stigmergic neuron, with one input and one output.

Assuming $w_0 = 0$ in Formula (4), and according to Formula (5):

$$y(0) = \begin{cases} 0, & w(0) \cdot x(0) < h(0) \\ 1, & w(0) \cdot x(0) \geq h(0) \end{cases} \tag{9}$$

Assuming $\underline{w} = -\infty$, and $\bar{w} = \infty$, Formula (7) and Formula (8) become:

$$w(t) = w(t-1) - \partial w + x(t-1)\Delta w \tag{10}$$

$$h(t) = h(t-1) - \partial h + y(t-1)\Delta h \tag{11}$$

Thus, from Formula (5):

$$y(1) = \begin{cases} 1, & (w(0) - \partial w + x(0)\Delta w)x(1) \geq h(0) - \partial h \text{ and } y(0) = 0 \\ 1, & (w(0) - \partial w + x(0)\Delta w)x(1) \geq h(0) - \partial h + \Delta h \text{ and } y(0) = 1 \\ 0, & \text{else} \end{cases} \tag{12}$$

Figure 5a shows a representation of y(0) and y(1), according to Formula (9) and Formula (12), in the (x(1), x(t + 1)) space. Here, Formula (9) is represented by the dashed vertical line, whereas Formula (12) is represented by the two hyperbolas. In particular, four points are highlighted, and specified in Fig. 5b, where it is apparent that the XOR problem is solved: $\overline{y(1)} = x(0) \oplus x(1)$.

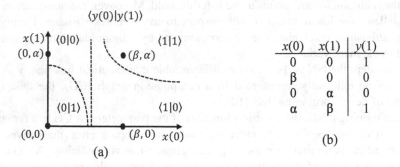

**Fig. 5.** The XOR problem with a single stigmergic neuron in the (x(1), x(t + 1)) space.

In the second experiment, a static NN, a stigmergic NN, a recurrent NN and a LSTM NN have been trained to solve the MNIST digits recognition benchmark [11]. The purpose is twofold: to measure the computational power added by stigmergy to static perceptrons, and to compare the performances of existing temporal NN. First, the static NN and the stigmergic NN have been dimensioned to achieve the best classification performance. Subsequently, the other temporal NNs have been dimensioned to have a similar number of parameters with respect to the stigmergic NN.

Figure 6 shows the architecture of the stigmergic NN. Here, the hourglass icon highlights the stigmergic relationships in the layer. Precisely, the 1$^{st}$ layer is a space-to-time coder (S2T); the 2$^{nd}$ layer is a set of fully connected perceptrons with stigmergic activation thresholds ($S_hLP$); the 3$^{rd}$ layer is a set of fully connected perceptrons with stigmergic weights and stigmergic activation thresholds $S_{wh}LP$; the 4$^{th}$ layer is a time-to-space decoder (T2S), which is the inverse transformation with respect to S2T; the 5$^{th}$ layer is a set of fully connected static perceptrons (MLP). The architecture of the static NN is made by two hidden layers of static perceptrons, and the output layer of 10 perceptrons.

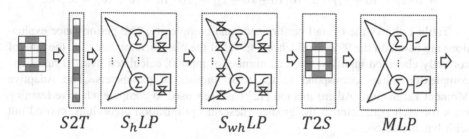

$S2T$ $S_hLP$ $S_{wh}LP$ $T2S$ $MLP$

**Fig. 6.** A deep stigmergic NN for the MNIST digits recognition benchmark.

The software has been developed with the PyTorch framework [13] and made publicly available on GitHub [14].

Precisely, an input image of the MNIST is made by $28 \times 28 = 784$ pixels, and the output is made by 10 classes corresponding to decimal digits. Overall, the data set is made of 70,000 images. At each run, the training set is generated by random extraction of 60,000 images; the remaining 10,000 images makes the testing set.

The static NN is made by 784 inputs connected to 300 perceptrons (235,200 weights and 300 biases) that, in turn, are connected to other 300 perceptrons (90,000 weights and 300 biases), that, in turn, are connected to 10 perceptrons (3000 weights and 10 biases), for a total number of parameters equals to 328,810 parameters.

The stigmergic NN is made by 28 inputs connected to 10 perceptrons with stigmergic activation (280 weights, 10 biases, 10 initial activation thresholds, 10 delta thresholds weakening, and 10 delta thresholds reinforcement) that, in turn, are connected to 10 stigmergic perceptrons with weights and stigmergic activations (100 initial weights, 100 delta weight weakening, 100 delta weight reinforcement, 10 initial activation thresholds, 10 delta thresholds weakening, 10 delta thresholds reinforcement, and 10 biases), that become 280 output after the time-to-space decoder, which, in turn, are connected to 10 static perceptrons (2800 weights and 10 biases), for a total number of parameters equals to 3,470 parameters.

The Recurrent NN is fed by 28 inputs, organized identically to the stigmergic NN inputs. Such inputs are fully connected to two parallel feed forward layers ($2 \cdot 28 \cdot 28$ weights and $2 \cdot 28$ biases); in one of these layers, each output neuron has a backward connection to the inputs of both layers ($28 \cdot 56$ weights); in the other layer, the outputs are connected to a further feed forward layer with 10 outputs (28·10 weights and 10 biases). The total number of parameters is 3,482.

The LSTM NN is fed by 28 inputs, organized identically to the stigmergic NN inputs. For each LSTM layer, the number of parameters is calculated according to the well-known formula $4 \cdot o \cdot (i + o + 1)$, where $o$ and $i$ is the number of outputs and inputs, respectively.

The topology is made by a $28 \times 10$ LSTM layer, a $10 \times 10$ LSTM layer, a $10 \times 10$ LSTM layer, and a final $10 \times 10$ Feed Forward layer. Thus, the overall number of parameters is

$$4[10(28 + 10 + 1)) + 2 \cdot 10(10 + 10 + 1)] + (10 \cdot 10 + 10 + 10) = 3,360.$$

Table 1 shows the overall performance and complexity. The performance evaluations are based on the 99% confidence interval of the classification rate (i.e., the ratio of correctly classified inputs to the total number of inputs), calculated over 10 runs. The complexity values correspond to the total number of parameters. The Adaptive Moment Estimation (Adam) method [12] has been used to compute adaptive learning rates for each parameter of the gradient descent optimization algorithms, carried out with batch method.

**Table 1.** Performance and complexity of different ANN solving the MNIST digits recognition benchmark.

| NN type | Complexity | Classification rate |
|---------|------------|---------------------|
| Static NN | 328,810 | .951 ± 0.0026 |
| LSTM NN | 3,360 | .943 ± 0.011 |
| Stigmergic NN | 3,470 | .927 ± 0.016 |
| Recurrent NN | 3,482 | .766 ± 0.033 |

It is worth nothing that the MNIST benchmark is a spatial dataset, used to favor static NN and to show the concept of space-time mapping that can be exploited with temporal NNs. As such, chunks sequences in each image are not inherently related in time. Nevertheless, the static NN employs a very large number of parameters, about two order of magnitude larger with respect to the temporal NNs.

On the other hand, Static NN, LSTM NN and Stigmergic NN have similar classification performances (differing only by 2% at the most). Comparing the classification rates of temporal NNs, which have been dimensioned to have a similar complexity, recurrent NN is largely outperformed by static NN and LSTM NN.

In consideration of the relative scientific maturity of the other comparative networks, the experimental results with the novel stigmergic NN looks very promising, and encourage further investigation activities for future work.

# 4 Conclusions

In this paper, the dynamics of computational stigmergy is applied to weights, bias and activation threshold of a classical neural perceptron, to derive the stigmergic perceptron (SP). An efficient methodology is proposed for training a multilayered NN made of SP. The methodology is based on the equivalence with static computational graphs, which can be trained using backpropagation optimization algorithms.

The effectiveness of the approach is shown via pilot experiments. Stigmergic perceptrons can be appreciated for their impressive computational power with respect to conventional perceptron. Moreover, stigmergic layers can be easily employed in deep NN architectures, and can provide performances similar to other relatively mature temporal NN, such as Recurrent NN and LSTM NN, on equal complexity.

**Acknowledgements.** This work was partially carried out in the framework of the SCIADRO project, co-funded by the Tuscany Region (Italy) under the Regional Implementation Programme for Underutilized Areas Fund (PAR FAS 2007-2013) and the Research Facilitation Fund (FAR) of the Ministry of Education, University and Research (MIUR).

This research was supported in part by the PRA 2018_81 project entitled "Wearable sensor systems: personalized analysis and data security in healthcare" funded by the University of Pisa.

# References

1. Schmidhuber, J.: Deep learning in neural networks: An overview. Neural Netw. **61**, 85–117 (2015)
2. Gu, J., Wang, Z., Kuen, J., Ma, L., Shahroudy, A., Shuai, B., Chen, T.: Recent advances in convolutional neural networks. Pattern Recognit. **77**, 354–377 (2018)
3. Pérez, J., Cabrera, J.A., Castillo, J.J., Velasco, J.M.: Bio-inspired spiking neural network for nonlinear systems control. Neural Netw. **104**, 15–25 (2018)
4. Xie, X., Qu, H., Yi, Z., Kurths, J.: Efficient training of supervised spiking neural network via accurate synaptic-efficiency adjustment method. IEEE Trans. Neural Netw. Learn. Syst. **28** (6), 1411–1424 (2017)
5. Song, H.F., Yang, G.R., Wang, X.J.: Training excitatory-inhibitory recurrent neural networks for cognitive tasks: a simple and flexible framework. PLoS Comput. Biol. **12**(2), e1004792 (2016)
6. Heylighen, F.: Stigmergy as a universal coordination mechanism I: definition and components. Cogn. Syst. Res. **38**, 4–13 (2016)
7. Greer, K.: Turing: then, now and still key. In: Yang, X.S. (ed.) Artificial Intelligence, Evolutionary Computing and Metaheuristics. SCI, vol. 427, pp. 43–62. Springer, Heidelberg (2013). https://doi.org/10.1007/978-3-642-29694-9_3
8. Cimino, M.G.C.A., Lazzeri, A., Vaglini, G.: Improving the analysis of context-aware information via marker-based stigmergy and differential evolution. In: Rutkowski, L., Korytkowski, M., Scherer, R., Tadeusiewicz, R., Zadeh, L.A., Zurada, J.M. (eds.) ICAISC 2015. LNCS (LNAI), vol. 9120, pp. 341–352. Springer, Cham (2015). https://doi.org/10.1007/978-3-319-19369-4_31

9. Alfeo, A.L., Cimino, M.G., Vaglini, G.: Measuring physical activity of older adults via smartwatch and stigmergic receptive fields. In: Proceedings of the 6th International Conference on Pattern Recognition Applications and Methods (ICPRAM), pp. 724–730. Scitepress (2017)
10. Goodfellow, I., Bengio, Y., Courville, A., Bengio, Y.: Deep Learning, vol. 1. MIT press, Cambridge (2016)
11. LeCun, Y., Cortes, C., Burges, C.J.C.: The MNIST database of handwritten digits. http:// yann.lecun.com/exdb/mnist/. Accessed 03 Sept 2018
12. Kingma, D.P., Ba, J.L.: Adam: a method for stochastic optimization. In: International Conference on Learning Representations, pp. 1–13 (2015)
13. PyTorch, Tensors and Dynamic neural networks in Python with strong GPU acceleration. https://pytorch.org. Accessed 14 Sept 2018
14. GitHub platform. https://github.com/galatolofederico/mike2018. Accessed 14 Sept 2018

# Modeling Sustainability Reporting
# with Ternary Attractor Neural Networks

Mario González[1], David Dominguez[2(✉)], Odette Pantoja[3], Carlos Guerrero[2],
and Francisco B. Rodríguez[2]

[1] SI² Lab, Universidad de las Américas, Quito, Ecuador
mario.gonzalez.rodriguez@udla.edu.ec
[2] Grupo de Neurocomputación Biológica, Dpto. de Ingeniería Informática,
Escuela Politécnica Superior, Universidad Autónoma de Madrid, 28049 Madrid, Spain
{david.dominguez,f.rodriguez}@uam.es
[3] FCA, Escuela Politécnica Nacional, Quito, Ecuador
odette.pantoja@epn.edu.ec

**Abstract.** This work models the Corporate Sustainability General Reporting Initiative (GRI) using a ternary attractor network. A dataset of 15 years evolution of the GRI reports for a world-wide set of companies was compiled from a recent work and adapted to match the pattern coding for a ternary attractor network. We compare the performance of the network with a classical binary attractor network. Two types of criteria were used for encoding the ternary network, i.e., a simple and weighted threshold, and the performance retrieval was better for the latter, highlighting the importance of the real patterns' transformation to the three-state coding. The network exceeds the retrieval performance of the binary network for the chosen correlated patterns (GRI). Finally, the ternary network was proved to be robust to retrieve the GRI patterns with initial noise.

**Keywords:** Sustainability · Ternary coding
Bi-linear and Bi-quadratic retrieval

## 1 Introduction

The classical binary coded attractor network has many known advantages as a machine learning algorithm, such as, distributed computation; robustness to noise and connection and nodes failure; association, which allows pattern completion and denoising; and dynamic learning (synaptic) and retrieval (recursive). However, the storage capacity of this system is moderate, not being adequate for pattern extensive learning [1]. Also, previous research has dealt with the pattern codification to increase the capacity retrieval, suggesting a self-control with threshold neural dynamics that attenuate the cross-talk noise improving the information performance [3]. Such adaptive threshold has been replaced by a quadratic threshold, i.e. depending on the activity of the neurons [4]. The aforementioned research has shown that a ternary coded network with bi-quadratic

© Springer Nature Switzerland AG 2018
A. Groza and R. Prasath (Eds.): MIKE 2018, LNAI 11308, pp. 259–267, 2018.
https://doi.org/10.1007/978-3-030-05918-7_23

learning improves the pattern retrieval when compared to a binary coded network [2].

Mainly, random patterns have been used to test the retrieval improvement of the model. Application of the binary coded network to real patterns can be found in [6,9–11]. In this work the use of real patterns to measure the retrieval performance of the ternary model is proposed. The selected data comes from corporate sustainability reporting patterns that have been used in [11], where it was shown that a binary coded network can deal with these type of patterns, a static and dynamical analysis of the pattern retrieval by the network was carried out. A valuable insight was obtained in terms of the temporal evolution of the Global Reporting Initiative (GRI) [12] patterns for a set of global enterprises. The aforementioned research results, for the performance of the two states network will be directly compared with the proposed ternary coded network.

In recent years, international pressure has increased sustainable practices by organizations, inducing to private and public entities to track their social and environmental activities [13]. Most of these organizations has re-oriented their strategic management to sustainable dimensions, and use GRI as a tool to report their sustainable practices. Several reporting tools exist with similar objectives, however, GRI remains as the best known and most used instrument for this purpose [7,8,15,17]. The pioneer of sustainability reporting, GRI, was designed in 1997 with the aim to offer organizations (enterprises, corporations, governmental and no-governmental institutions) a global protocol to report their positions in economical, environmental and social performance [14]. Through these standards, entities regulate and manage their corporate social responsibility (CSR) activities allowing them to follow established sets of rules [18]. About six thousands of the largest companies globally apply, manage and report GRI, with the aim of visualizing their behavior in these issues related to sustainability. G3 is the third generation of GRI which is integrated by reporting principles and performance indicators [16]. G3 framework is divide in three principal branches: strategy and profile, management approach and performance indicators. The indicators are stratified in social matters (where are involved human rights, labor, product responsibility and society), economical issues and environmental matters [13].

In this paper, a ternary Attractor Neural Network (tANN) model is proposed to predict the sustainability reporting scores (GRI) in order to improve the retrieval performance. The GRI patterns have been translated to three states and the network was able to improve the quality of the retrieval. The retrieval improvement depends on how the input data is translated to the three states. Thus, two methods of encoding were tested, a simple threshold coding value of independent items reported for each enterprise, and a weighted coding according to the relative number of items reported compared with the whole set of enterprises. The quality of the retrieval was assessed for both types of encoding. In these work we have checked for the competition between binary and bimodal codification using bi-lineal and bi-quadratic learning rules in Hopfield-Hebb type network to optimize the network performance [2–4]. The rest of the article is organized as follows. In the following Sect. 2 we describe the ternary coded bi-quadratic model. In Sect. 3 we present the preliminary results for the ternary coded network for different coding criteria. Finally, Sect. 4 concludes the paper discussing the main findings.

## 2    The Model

In this section we present the neurodynamics for the ternary attractor network. This ternary model includes the binary $\{\pm 1\}$ and the bimodal $\{0, 1\}$ representations of the neural code as special cases. We define also the performance measures of the network.

Consider a neural network consisting of $N$ neurons $\{\sigma_i | i = 1, \ldots, N\}$ which can take values from the discrete set $\sigma_i \in \{-1, 0, +1\}$. The networks aims to store a set of $P$ patterns $\{\xi^\mu | \mu = 1, \ldots, P\}$ each of which are supposed to be a collection of $\{\xi_i^\mu | i = 1, \ldots, N\}$ sites, with a probability distribution

$$p(\xi^\mu = +1) = \frac{a^\mu + b^\mu}{2}; \ p(\xi^\mu = -1) = \frac{a^\mu - b^\mu}{2}; \ p(\xi^\mu = 0) = (1 - a^\mu); \quad (1)$$

where $a^\mu$ and $b^\mu$ are the pattern activity and bias respectively, given by the averages

$$a^\mu = \langle (\xi_i^\mu)^2 \rangle; \ b^\mu = \langle \xi_i^\mu \rangle \equiv \frac{1}{N} \sum_i^N (\xi_i^\mu). \quad (2)$$

The neurons are updated according to the following dynamics,

$$\sigma_i(t+1) = g(h_i(t), \theta_i(t)); \ g(h, \theta) \equiv \text{sign}(h) \times \Theta(|h| - \theta), \quad i = 1, \ldots, N, \quad (3)$$

where $sign$ and $\Theta$ are the signum and the step functions respectively, and the lineal and threshold local fields of neuron $i$ are defined respectively by

$$h_i(t) = w \sum_j J_{ij}\sigma_j(t), \quad \theta_i(t) = (1 - w) \sum_j K_{ij}\sigma_j^2(t). \quad (4)$$

Here, $w \in [0, 1]$ is the balance. If the balance is $w = 1$, one recovers the lineal model for binary patterns, whereas if $w = 0$, there are only quadratic terms for bimodal patterns.

The bi-lineal and bi-quadratic learning weights are of the Hebb-type whose updating rules are defined respectively as

$$\Delta^\mu J_{ij} = \frac{C_{ij}}{(a^\mu)^2 N} \xi_i^\mu \xi_j^\mu, \quad \Delta^\mu K_{ij} = \frac{C_{ij}}{(\tilde{a}^\mu)^2 N} \eta_i^\mu \eta_j^\mu, \quad \mu = 1 \ldots P, \quad (5)$$

at each learned pattern $\mu$, with

$$\eta_i^\mu = (\xi_i^\mu)^2 - a^\mu, \quad \tilde{a}^\mu = a^\mu(1 - a^\mu). \quad (6)$$

The topology matrix $C = \{C_{ij}\}$ describes the connectivity structure of the neural network. In previous study [2,11] $C$ splits into local and random links, which sums up to the total number of connections per neuron: $L = L_l + L_r$. This way, the network topology is characterized by the *connectivity* ratio $\gamma = L/N$ and the *randomness* ratio $\omega = L_r/L$. As in the *small-world* model the parameter $\omega$ plays the role of a rewiring probability.

In the following, the $C$ will be the given by a fully connected network ($L = N$, $\gamma = 1$) for the ternary model, and a diluted ring of nearest neighbors with $L = 200$, $\gamma = 0.03$, $\omega = 0.0$ for the sake of comparison with the binary model in [11].

The order parameters relevant for the present model are

$$m^\mu(t) = \frac{1}{a^\mu N} \sum_i \xi_i^\mu \sigma_i(t), \quad l^\mu(t) = \frac{1}{\tilde{a}^\mu N} \sum_i \eta_i^\mu \sigma_i^2(t), \tag{7}$$

where $m^\mu$ is the usual lineal overlap, $l^\mu(t)$ is the square activity overlap. Besides these retrieval parameters one can consider also the neural activity parameter, given by $q(t) = \frac{1}{N} \sum_i \sigma_i^2(t)$, which, although is not related to the pattern information, plays a rule in the network dynamics in Eq. 3.

## 3   Results: Network Performance for GRI Dataset

### 3.1   GRI Dataset

The dataset was obtained from the GRI Reports List which gives a detailed and aggregated overview of all reports included in GRI's Sustainability Disclosure Database. A free copy of the dataset can be accessed for academic purposes [12]. A dataset comprising a total of $N = 5897$ worldwide enterprises was collected. The data contains the GRI patterns for the years 1998 to 2013, for a total of $P = 15$ patterns of size $N$. The binary representation of the pattern $\xi_i^\mu$ is given according to the items reported $I_i^\mu$ from Table 1 for each enterprise $i$ at year $\mu$. $I_i^\mu$ is defined in Eq. 8 as follows:

$$I_i^\mu = \sum GRI_{items}, \quad I_i^\mu \in \{0, 1, 2, 3, 4, 5\}. \tag{8}$$

If $I_i^\mu = 0$ then $\xi_i^\mu = 0$, and $\xi_i^\mu = 1$ otherwise, gives the binary coding. The ternary representation of the patterns is encoded according to different criteria in order to generate the three states. In each subsection is specified how the ternary patterns were encoded, and the experimental results are discussed.

### 3.2   Ternary Network with Simple Threshold Coding

The first pattern codification is defined in Eq. 9 according to the number of reported items $I_i^\mu$ using a simple threshold criteria.

$$\xi_i^\mu = \begin{cases} -1 \text{ if } I_i^\mu < 1 \\ 0 \text{ if } 1 \leq I_i^\mu < 3 \\ 1 \text{ if } I_i^\mu \geq 3. \end{cases} \tag{9}$$

**Table 1.** GRI summary coding.

| 1. Version | 2. Expertise level | 3. Situations |
|---|---|---|
| G0 | A | T, 3p: Third party |
| G1 | B | S: self-declared |
| G2 | C | U: undeclared |
| G3 | **2.1 Audited** | I: integrated |
| G3.1 | Yes or No | N: non-GRI |
| G4 | **2.2 Who is auditing?** | G: GRI-verified |
| GRI-Ref | GRI | R: referenced |
| Non-GRI | 3p: third party | IA: in accordance |
| | | CIO: content index only |

Threshold of 1 and 3 are used to define the value of $\xi_i^\mu$ according to Eq. 9.

Figure 1 depicts the network retrieval performance for the $P = 15$ years of GRI reports (patterns). The values of the linear $m$ and quadratic $l$ overlaps are depicted for different values of the balance $w$. We can appreciate the following behavior according to the value of $w$, which allows a trade-off between the linear and quadratic retrieval, expressed by the overlaps $m$ and $l$. For the extreme $w = 0$ (Fig. 1-left) we have a quadratic retrieval ($m \sim -0.8$, $l \sim 0.8$) along with the linear retrieval of the negative (inverse) of the patterns. For $w = 1$ (Fig. 1-right) only the linear retrieval is possible ($m \sim 1$, $l \sim 0$). For intermediate values, i.e. $w = 0.5$ (Fig. 1-center), it is possible to retrieve both linear and quadratic measures ($m \sim 1$, $l \sim 1$). A similar behavior can be observed for values of $0.4 < w < 0.6$, we keep $w = 0.5$ constant for comparing both types of coding in the next subsection.

In this sense the objective is to find the value of $w$ that optimizes the retrieval in terms of $m$, $l$, for the patterns intended to be stored and retrieved, which corresponds to $w = 0.5$ as shown in Fig. 1. Next, the robustness of the network in terms of initial noise in the retrieval phase is tested, as well as an alternative coding for the GRI patterns.

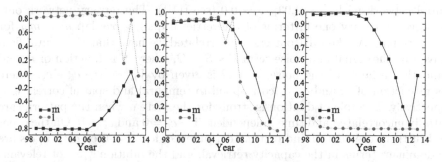

**Fig. 1.** Network retrieval overlaps $m$ and $l$ for balances of $w = 0.0$, $0.5$, and $1.0$. Simple threshold coding, noiseless case, i.e. $m^{t=0} = 1$.

### 3.3  Ternary Network Weighted Threshold Coding and Basin of Attraction

As the first years of GRI reporting are essentially blank for the majority of enterprises, due to the standard being slowly implemented in the first years, a weighted threshold is tested in order to compensate for the low level of activity of the first years. The second proposed pattern codification is the weighted threshold defined as:

$$\xi_i^\mu = \begin{cases} -1 \text{ if } I_i^\mu < B^\mu \\ \phantom{-}0 \text{ if } B^\mu \leq I_i^\mu < 2B^\mu \\ \phantom{-}1 \text{ if } I_i^\mu \geq 2B^\mu. \end{cases} \tag{10}$$

Here, $B^\mu = 2*I^\mu/3$ and the indicator level for each year, $I^\mu = \sum_i I_i^\mu/N$, counts the indicators for all the enterprises $i$, in a given year $\mu$. $I^\mu$ is equivalent to the indicators mean for each year. From this value, we calculate $B^\mu$ in order to partition each pattern $\xi_i^\mu$ as specified in Eq. 10. In this way, the coding is compensated according the level of reporting activity of each year.

Figure 2 depicts the retrieval performance of the network for $w = 0.5$ and noise of 0.1, that is the retrieval stage starts with patterns' overlap $m_{t=0} = 0.9$. Comparison of panels left and right of Fig. 2 shows the network retrieval of the weight coding outperforms that of the simple threshold coding. Thus, the weighted encoding is better for representing the structure of the GRI patterns. This issue, highlights the importance of the ternary pattern coding, and the criteria for the data transformation should be considered carefully. The initial noise allows to test the basin of attraction of the patterns' retrieval giving a measure of the network robustness to initial noise. We can appreciate that in both panels of Fig. 2 the basin of attraction is not negligible. There is no observable effect in the Fig. 2-right respect to the noiseless case in Fig. 1-center.

Both ternary codings were checked against a network with binary coding represented by $m_H$ in both panels. The (blue) dot-dashed curve represents a diluted network with $\gamma \sim 0.03$, $\omega = 0.0$ (see [11]). The ternary network outperforms the binary one in terms of the retrieval quality overlap $m > m_H$ for both encoding. As the GRI patters are correlated we have that the neural field is given by the signal and noise term $h \sim S + \Omega$, where $S$ is function of $m$ and $l$, and the variance of the noise term $\Omega$ is given by $V_\Omega \sim \alpha + c_t + c_s$, where $\alpha$ is a function of $\gamma$, and $c_t$, $c_s$ correspond to temporal and spatial correlations respectively. The role of dilution is strong for the system when the patterns are spatially uncorrelated and time independent, i.e. $c_t = 0$ and $c_s = 0$. On the other hand, if there are spatial and or time dependence, for $c_t \neq 0$ or $c_s \neq 0$, $c$'s are the dominant terms in the capacity retrieval, and the dilution $\gamma$ is not relevant. Thus, both results $m_H$ with a ring diluted network and the ternary network with $m$, $l$ can be compared in terms of retrieved patterns $P$, as in Fig. 2. One can appreciate that the ternary network with initial noise outperforms the noiseless binary retrieval.

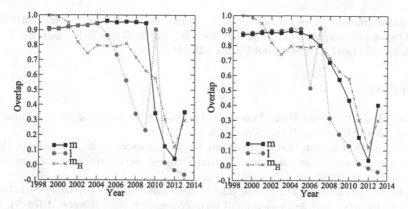

**Fig. 2.** Network retrieval overlaps $m$ and $l$ for $w = 0.5$, initial noise of 0.1, i.e. $m^{t=0} = 0.9$ and full connectivity $\gamma = 1.0$. Left: Weighted threshold coding. Right: Simple threshold coding. Binary retrieval $m_H$ for ring network $\gamma \sim 0.03$, $\omega = 0.0$. (Color figure online)

## 4    Conclusions

In this work we have presented an application of the ternary coded attractor network with bi-linear and bi-quadratic retrieval. We tested the ternary network for different encodings, with the weighted threshold outperforming the simple threshold in terms of pattern retrieval, thus the weighted threshold coding is better suited to the GRI reports encoding. These results highlight the importance of choosing carefully a preprocessing criteria in order to transform the original data into a three-state coded pattern. The network also proved to be have a non-negligible basin of attraction being robust to initial noise during the retrieval process. Also, the ternary network with noisy initial state, outperforms the binary network. We can appreciate that the transition phase to no retrieval in the quadratic retrieval parameter, coincides with the recession peak between 2007 to 2010. We conjecture that the quadratic parameter is more effective for detecting the fast fluctuation in the behavior of the GRI.

We have shown, that the ternary coded network have advantages over the binary network in terms of storage/retrieval of patterns. In this work, we have applied to GRI reporting patterns of a set of worldwide enterprises for a period of 15 years. We have improved the retrieval capacity of this patterns when compared with the binary coded network. We intend to apply the ternary network to real world data to store large amount of spatially structured and temporal correlated patterns for instance, socio-economics problems such as the Panama Papers [5], corruption, gender equality; as well as, other types of applications in Engineering such as biometrics: fingerprint, iris patterns; surveillance: automotive traffic videos; in order to assess the storage increase of the ternary network.

**Acknowledgments.** This work has been supported by Spanish grants MINECO (http://www.mineco.gob.es/) TIN2014-54580-R, TIN2017-84452-R, and by UAM-Santander CEAL-AL/2017-08, and UDLA-SIS.MG.17.02.

# References

1. Amit, D.J.: Modeling Brain Function: The World of Attractor Neural Networks. Cambridge University Press, New York (1989)
2. Bollé, D., Dominguez, D.R.C., Erichsen Jr., R., Korutcheva, E., Theumann, W.K.: Time evolution of the extremely diluted Blume-Emery-Griffiths neural network. Phys. Rev. E **68**(6), 062901 (2003)
3. Bollé, D., Dominguez, D., Amari, S.I.: Mutual information of sparsely coded associative memory with self-control and ternary neurons. Neural Netw. **13**(4–5), 455–462 (2000)
4. Carreta Dominguez, D.R., Korutcheva, E.: Three-state neural network: from mutual information to the Hamiltonian. Phys. Rev. E **62**, 2620–2628 (2000)
5. Dominguez, D., Pantoja, O., González, M.: Mapping the global offshoring network through the panama papers. In: Rocha, Á., Guarda, T. (eds.) ICITS 2018. AISC, vol. 721, pp. 407–416. Springer, Cham (2018). https://doi.org/10.1007/978-3-319-73450-7_39
6. Doria, F., Erichsen Jr., R., González, M., Rodríguez, F.B., Sánchez, Á., Dominguez, D.: Structured patterns retrieval using a metric attractor network: application to fingerprint recognition. Physica A Stat. Mech. Appl. **457**, 424–436 (2016)
7. Etzion, D., Ferraro, F.: The role of analogy in the institutionalization of sustainability reporting. Organ. Sci. **21**(5), 1092–1107 (2010)
8. Fernandez-Feijoo, B., Romero, S., Ruiz, S.: Commitment to corporate social responsibility measured through global reporting initiative reporting: factors affecting the behavior of companies. J. Cleaner Prod. **81**, 244–254 (2014)
9. González, M., Dominguez, D., Rodríguez, F.B., Sanchez, A.: Retrieval of noisy fingerprint patterns using metric attractor networks. Int. J. Neural Syst. **24**(07), 1450025 (2014)
10. González, M., Dominguez, D., Sánchez, Á.: Learning sequences of sparse correlated patterns using small-world attractor neural networks: an application to traffic videos. Neurocomputing **74**(14–15), 2361–2367 (2011)
11. González, M., del Mar Alonso-Almeida, M., Avila, C., Dominguez, D.: Modeling sustainability report scoring sequences using an attractor network. Neurocomputing **168**, 1181–1187 (2015)
12. GRI: GRI sustainability reporting standards (2018). https://www.globalreporting.org/Pages/default.aspx
13. Guthrie, J., Farneti, F.: GRI sustainability reporting by Australian public sector organizations. Public Money Manage. **28**(6), 361–366 (2008)
14. Hedberg, C.J., Von Malmborg, F.: The global reporting initiative and corporate sustainability reporting in Swedish companies. Corp. Soc. Responsib. Environ. Manag. **10**(3), 153–164 (2003)
15. Legendre, S., Coderre, F.: Determinants of GRI G3 application levels: the case of the fortune global 500. Corp. Soc. Responsib. Environ. Manag. **20**(3), 182–192 (2013)
16. Marimon, F., del Mar Alonso-Almeida, M., del Pilar Rodríguez, M., Alejandro, K.A.C.: The worldwide diffusion of the global reporting initiative: what is the point? J. Cleaner Prod. **33**, 132–144 (2012)

17. Shahi, A., Issac, B., Modapothala, J.: Intelligent corporate sustainability report scoring solution using machine learning approach to text categorization. In: 2012 IEEE Conference on Sustainable Utilization and Development in Engineering and Technology (STUDENT), pp. 227–232 (2012)
18. Vigneau, L., Humphreys, M., Moon, J.: How do firms comply with international sustainability standards? Processes and consequences of adopting the global reporting initiative. J. Bus. Ethics **131**(2), 469–486 (2015)

# Analysing a Periodical
# and Multi-dimensional Time Series

Octavian Lucian Hasna[(✉)] and Rodica Potolea[(✉)]

Technical University of Cluj-Napoca, 26-28 Baritiu Street, Cluj-Napoca, Romania
{octavian.hasna,rodica.potolea}@cs.utcluj.ro

**Abstract.** Time series analysis has become an important field of data mining in the last decade. Dynamics of real-world processes are important in domains like seismology, medicine, astrophysics, meteorology, economics and industry. In this article we develop a methodology for analysing a periodical and multi-dimensional time series so as to extract new features that improve the performance of time series classification. Our aim is to have a methodology which is independent on the measurement errors and on the level of noise. For this we analyse three methods for extracting a period, both from the perspective of methodology and performance. We experimentally compare these strategies in order to identify the minimal quantity of labelled time series required for training so as to obtain a good classification accuracy.

**Keywords:** Time series analysis · Fault diagnosis · Data mining

## 1 Introduction

Nowadays we are surrounded by a myriad of electric devices. These devices generate every second a huge amount of time series data. The purpose of time series data mining is to try to detect meaningful information from the shape of the data.

We propose a new approach to analyse periodical time series data by comparing multiple sample rates and different sizes of training instances. We have developed a process that will sample the input time series, will filter the noise and in the end will extract new features. The features are dependent on the strategy used for extracting periods from the time series data. The challenges for extracting a period are related to both the presence of measurement errors and to the noise inside the time series data. So as to eliminate these problems we will use the following strategies for extracting one period:

- the period is extracted between two consecutive intersections with the Ox axis;
- the period will have the starting position in an intersection with Ox axis and the length of the period will be fixed
- the period starting and ending position will be the same for all the dimensions of the time series

© Springer Nature Switzerland AG 2018
A. Groza and R. Prasath (Eds.): MIKE 2018, LNAI 11308, pp. 268–278, 2018.
https://doi.org/10.1007/978-3-030-05918-7_24

The rest of this paper is organised as follows. In Sect. 3 we present the concept and the properties of time series. In Sect. 4 we describe the components of our architecture and how they interact. In Sect. 5 we present result of the experiments conducted on the given use case. The final Sect. 6 contains the conclusions and the future directions of this work.

## 2  Related Work

In [13] the authors proposed an artificial neural network model for detection of faults in rotary systems by using sensor data. They state that the classical expert systems have a major weakness because it uses binary logical decisions which does not reflect the gradual nature of many real world problems. Their first model was implemented using the classical feed-forward network with back propagation. When the model will learn a new pattern it will constantly modify a previous training. The second model is based on adaptive resonance theory that refers to a class of neural networks that cluster the pattern space and produce appropriate weight vectors. This network remains open to new learning by creating a new cluster for each training set which is not similar with the previous ones. Even though the second model performs better than the first one, the problem is not related to the classification function, but to the selection of well-discriminating features as stated by the authors in [14].

Going forward with this objective the authors in [6] proposed a set of feature-based representation that tackle the insights that can be gained from time series. They group the features in global features and subsequence features. Global features quantify patterns in time series across the full time interval of measurement. Subsequence features are used for some classification problems where time series properties differs only within a specific time interval. To tackle the time series data mining problem we have to consider two aspects: the time series representations and the similarity measure. Using the whole raw data is expensive because the time series can be very long. The representations method should guarantee that the most important patterns remains and that it will not create new patterns. In literature there are a couple of comparisons between time series representations [2,5,15]. In [9] the authors grouped the time series representations in a taxonomy based on the affinity to a given time series mining task. The authors from [11] suggested that for time-series classification, 1 Nearest Neighbour (K=1) and Dynamic Time-warping are very difficult to beat.

Concerning the analysis of an electric signal for detecting faults in an electric motor there are a number of techniques that were proposed. The most common ones are: Discrete Fourier Transform (DFT) [4], Discrete Cosine Transform (DCT) [1], Discrete Wavelet Transform (DWT) [7], Park's vector approach [3] and Hilbert transform [16]. In [10] the authors presents a hybrid approach for rotor fault diagnosis. They test their single layer model with four classification algorithms: KNN, decision tree and two variants of random forests. We will use a double layer classifier to increase the robustness of the model and also we will use less data taking into account the memory constraint of an embedded device.

## 3   Terminology

A time series belongs to the family of signals and can be defined as a sequence of points at successive moments in time. Formally it can be described as follows:

$$TS = \{\langle p, t \rangle | p \in \mathbb{R}^d, t \in \mathbb{R}\} \tag{1}$$

Base on the components of the formula (1) the time series are classified in: one-dimensional (univariate) or multi-dimensional (multivariate) and discrete or continuous.

A window from a continuous time series is defined as a sequence of values that starts at $t_s$ and has a length of $\Delta t$. Formally it can be defined as:

$$TS_{s, \Delta t} = \{\langle p, t \rangle | \langle p, t \rangle \in TS, t_s \leq t < t_s + \Delta t\} \tag{2}$$

In the case of a discrete time series, the sequence contains a finite number of points $n$ starting from $t_i$ and is defined as:

$$TS_{i,n} = \{\langle p, t \rangle | \langle p, t \rangle \in TS_{discrete}, t_i \leq t < t_{i+n}\} \tag{3}$$

A continuous time series can be transformed into a discrete time series using the Nyquist-Shannon theorem. A problem can arise when the two time series are sampled at different frequencies or they have gaps (missing points). One possible solution to this problem is to use interpolation. The points that are missing from the time series that were sampled at a higher frequency are easier to be computed using interpolation compared to the missing points from the time series that were sampled at a lower frequency.

From now on we will use the term time series for a discrete and one-dimensional time series. Also we will assume that all the time series are sampled at the same frequency and so we will ignore the time parameter.

## 4   System Architecture

Our architecture (Fig. 1) contains four main modules that interact so as to classify the input time series. We constraint the input time series so as to be periodical and to have two dimensions.

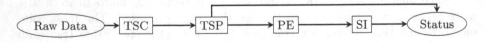

**Fig. 1.** Conceptual architecture.

## 4.1  Time Series Collector

The first module, Time Series Collector (TSC) samples the continuous multi-dimensional time series with the frequency $f_{sampling}$. According to Nyquist-Shannon theorem, the value of $f_{sampling}$ must be at least double $f_{signal}$ so as to be able to rebuild the initial signal. After the sampling, the module collects a sequence of $n$ values from the first sampled signal $TS_1$ and from the second sampled signal $TS_2$. The value of $n$ depends on the number of periods $(p)$ that we want to extract and on the number of values per one period $(|Period|)$. Because we need to align the sequences of periods in the next modules, we should extract at least one additional period. Formally the module can be described as:

$$TSC(D_{raw}) = \{(TS_1, TS_2), ...\} \tag{4}$$

with $n = |TS_1| = |TS_2|$, $|Period| = \left[\frac{f_{sampling}}{f_{signal}}\right]$, $n \geq (p+1) * |Period|$.

## 4.2  Time Series Pre-Processor

The second module, Time Series Pre-Processor (TSP) performs a filtering on the time series data. If there are values that are outside the domain of the first or second signal, the module can already predict the status. Otherwise the first and the second sequences are transformed using a moving average filter (MA). This filter is used to lower the short-term variations.

$$TSP(TS_1, TS_2) = \begin{cases} error, x \in TS_1 \wedge x \notin TS_1^{domain} \\ error, x \in TS_2 \wedge x \notin TS_2^{domain} \\ (TS_1', TS_2') \end{cases} \tag{5}$$

with $TS_1' = MA(TS_1), TS_2' = MA(TS_2)$

In this case we are using the simple moving average (SMA) filter that starts by computing the average sum of the points that are at a distance lower than a given radius $r$ from the initial point. The new values represent the transformed time series. The method can be expressed using the following formula:

$$SMA(t) = \frac{1}{2r+1} \sum_{i=t-r}^{t+r} TS(t) \tag{6}$$

## 4.3  Period Extractor

The third module, Period Extractor (PE) starts by finding all the intersections with the Ox axis for both sequences. We choose the first sequence as the one with less noise. In this case the strategy to find Ox intersection is to search for the change of value sign. For the second sequence, the more nosy of the two, this strategy doesn't work because the change of sign happens frequently. The strategy for the second sequence is to compute two sums: one before the possible intersection and one after the possible intersection. The number of elements in the sums is equal to the intersection tolerance ($\lambda$).

$$sum_x^{before} = \sum_{i=x-\lambda}^{x-1} v_i \ , \ sum_x^{after} = \sum_{i=x+1}^{x+\lambda} v_i \qquad (7)$$

with $v_i \in TS_2', \forall i = \overline{1,n}$

The next step is to choose the intersection point $x$ that will respect the following condition:

$$sum_x^{before} < 0 \wedge v_x \geq 0 \wedge sum_x^{after} > 0 \qquad (8)$$

All the positions of the intersection points are stored in $IP_1$ for the first sequence and in $IP_2$ for the second sequence.

The final step is to use the discovered intersection points for extracting the periods. The starting and the ending position for the first sequence periods can be computed in two different ways:

$$(x_{1,start}, x_{1,end}) = \begin{cases} (x_k, x_{k+1}), & \text{case 1a} \\ (x_k, x_k + |Period|), & \text{case 1b} \end{cases} \qquad (9)$$

with $x_k \in IP_1$

Because the intersection points for the first sequence are easier to compute we will have three different ways to extract the periods from the second sequence:

$$(x_{2,start}, x_{2,end})_c = \begin{cases} (x_k, x_{k+1}), & \text{case 2a} \\ (x_k, x_k + |Period|), & \text{case 2b} \\ (x_{1,start}, x_{1,end}), & \text{case 2c} \end{cases} \qquad (10)$$

with $x_k \in IP_2$

The third case has an advantage over the first two cases because it incorporates the phase difference between the two sequences (see results from Table 1). Formally the module can be described as:

$$PE(TS_1', TS_2') = \{(Period_1, Period_2, phase), ...\} \qquad (11)$$

with

$$Period_i = \{TS_i'(x) | x = \overline{x_{i,start}, x_{i,end}}\} \qquad (12)$$

$$phase = 2 * \pi * \frac{x_{2,start} - x_{1,start} + x_{2,end} - x_{1,end}}{|Period_1| + |Period_2|} \qquad (13)$$

## 4.4   Status Identifier

The last module, Status Identifier (SI) uses the extracted periods to detect the status of the device. This module is composed of two layers of classifiers. The results of the first layer of classifiers is used as features for the second layer of classifiers. The feature extractor from the first layer starts by combining $p$ consecutive periods from the two signals to form longer sequences $(S_1, S_2)$. The length of one period is $n$, so the length of a sequence is $p * n$. The values from the sequences are filtered by a moving average filter with a radius of $r$ an then normalised. The resulted sequences are sent to the classifiers from the first layer. The values of $p$, $n$ and $r$ are established in the Sect. 5 based on the results from Table 2a. Those classifiers compare the unknown sequence with a list of identified sequences by using a similarity measure. The results of this classification are sent as features to the next layer.

In the second layer, we used the sequences from the first layer and extract new features. The first feature is represented by the ratio of two signals and is calculated below:

$$ratio = \frac{rms(S_1)}{rms(S_2)} \tag{14}$$

where $rms$ represents the root mean square of the sequence and is computed as:

$$rms(S) = \sqrt{\frac{\Sigma_{i=1}^{p*n} S(i) * S(i)}{p * n}} \tag{15}$$

Another feature that we use is represented by the displacement of the signal compared to Ox axis and is computed as:

$$displacement(S) = \frac{\min(S) + \max(S)}{2} \tag{16}$$

The next features are computed based on the extreme values on each period. Firstly it extracts the sequence of minimums and maximums on each period from the sequence $S$.

$$Mins(S) = \{\min(S_{period_i})\}, \; Maxs(S) = \{\max(S_{period_i})\} \tag{17}$$

where $i = \overline{(k-1)*n+1, k*n}$ and $k = \overline{1,p}$.

Secondly, it computes the absolute differences between consecutive values in the sequences of minimums $Mins(S)$ and maximums $Maxs(S)$.

$$ad(S) = \{|S(i) - S(i+1)| | i = \overline{1,p-1}\} \tag{18}$$

Thirdly, it takes the maximum and the average values from the sequences of differences $ad(S)$ to determine the following features:$max1(S) = \max(ad(Mins(S)))$, $max2(S) = \max(ad(Maxs(S)))$, $avg1(S) = \overline{ad(Mins(S))}$ and $avg2(S) = \overline{ad(Maxs(S))}$.

For the last set of features we used the Discrete Fourier Transformation (DFT). We apply this transformation on the sequence $S$ and take the first $m$ values. These values are further transform by the formula:

$$avgDft(i) = \frac{|DFT_{i-1} - DFT_i| + |DFT_i - DFT_{i+1}|}{2} \tag{19}$$

where $i = \overline{2, m-1}$.

These previous presented features and the results of the first layer of classifiers are used by the classifier from the second layer. The result of the second layer classifier represents the result of the SI module, the identified status.

In the off-line flow this module is trained with labelled periods. Those periods were extracted from labelled time series. In the on-line flow this module classify unknown periods using the two layers classifier.

## 5    Results and Evaluation

Our use case is to detect the status of an electric device. Usually the device works correctly, but sometimes faults may occur. A fault can be drastic in which case it is labelled as an error or not so drastic in which case is a warning. From this point of view the problem of detecting the status becomes a three class classification problem: normal, warning and error. The dataset is heavily unbalanced, the normal case occurs frequently, but the warning and error cases occur rarely.

The first signal is represented by the voltage signal and the second signal is represented by the current signal. The frequency of the signals $f_{signal}$ is 50 Hz and the sampling frequency $f_{sampling}$ is 2.5 KHz and the sampling time is 4 s. The sampling frequency from [10] is 50 KHz, twenty times higher. For the following experiments we used two datasets with measurements. The data from the first dataset was measured in classic electric power properties (230 V and 50 Hz). The data from the second dataset was measured in multiple conditions (230 V, 230 V with added harmonics, 190 V and 250 V). The datasets have 4 measurements labels: normal (50% of the data) and 3 types of defects (equally distributed in the remaining 50% of the data). Both datasets have the same distributions of the measurement labels. The first dataset is used for training the classifiers and the second dataset is used for testing.

The KNN classifier works by finding the nearest labelled period that is closer to the unknown period. For this task it computes the distance between the unknown period and all the labelled periods and chooses the one that has the smallest distance. For the last feature vector there are three KNN classifiers in the first layer. If there is no majority, meaning that each classifier predict a different class, the meta-classifier from the second layer will predict the warning class.

In the first experiment we will compare different strategies for extracting the voltage and the current periods on the feature vectors: current, voltage, phase and all three combined. The features: voltage and current are represented as a sequence of numerical values and the phase is represented as one numerical value. The voltage signal has less noise compared to the current signal. The length of one period is 256 and we use 80% of the first dataset for training the model and 20% from the second dataset for testing it. The results from the Table 1 show that the best strategy for extracting the current period is **2c** and for extracting the voltage period is **1a**. This result confirm the assumption from the SubSect. 4.3. The result demonstrates the fact that is easier to extract one period from the

**Table 1.** The error rates and standard deviation for different strategies.

| Voltage case | Current case | $error_1$ | $std_1$ | $error_2$ | $std_2$ | $error_3$ | $std_3$ | $error_4$ | $std_4$ |
|---|---|---|---|---|---|---|---|---|---|
| 1a | 2a | 25.70 | 2.13 | 63.28 | 2.84 | 55.29 | 2.69 | 36.82 | 5.70 |
| 1a | 2b | 52.97 | 4.39 | 63.25 | 2.84 | 33.74 | 1.39 | 38.88 | 5.03 |
| 1a | 2c | **10.05** | **0.40** | 63.27 | 2.86 | 55.24 | 2.65 | 30.30 | 6.42 |
| 1b | 2a | 25.70 | 2.13 | 61.70 | 2.23 | 55.47 | 3.04 | 36.68 | 5.02 |
| 1b | 2b | 52.97 | 4.39 | 61.66 | 2.22 | 34.33 | 1.49 | 39.65 | 4.81 |
| 1b | 2c | 14.93 | 1.05 | 61.68 | 2.25 | 55.69 | 3.15 | 32.72 | 4.98 |

current signal using the Ox intersections from the voltage signal compared to the Ox intersection of the current signal. Because the voltage signal has higher values compared to the current signal, the noise can be removed without loosing the real data and the intersections can be found easier. Also we confirm that the best feature vector is the one that uses the current, this was expected and is in concordance with a review of fault diagnosis of electrical machines from [12].

The task of the second experiment is to select the minimum amount of data and choose the filtering techniques so as to have a small error rate. A smaller period (smaller sampling frequency) can be processed faster, but can lack important details about the time series. A longer period (higher sampling frequency) will contain more details, but it will also contain more noise so it will take more to time to be processed. For this experiment we are using the first feature vector (extracted periods with raw values from the current signal). The system was tested on a set product of period sizes ($n \in \{64, 128, 256\}$), number of periods ($p \in \{1, 2, 3, 4, 5, 6, 7, 8, 9\}$), radius lengths ($r \in \{0, 1, 2, 4, 8, 16, 32\}$) and type of normalisation (no normalisation, min-max normalisation and z-normalisation).

For the classifier we used KNN and for the similarity measure we used the Euclidean distance. We take randomly 50% (maintaining the class distribution) from the first dataset for training the classifier and for testing we take 20% from the second dataset for each iteration. We repeated this process 10 times and we reported the average error rate and the standard deviation (Tables 2a and b).

From Table 2a we observe that the smallest error rate is obtained for a sequence of 8 periods, each with 256 points and with a smoothing radius equal with 16. We can observe that if we increase the radius used for the smoothing algorithm data is lost and the error rate increases. Also min-max normalisation gave better results than z-normalisation because for our use case the amplitude and the displacement of the current signal are discriminatory features.

In the next experiment we want to decide on the set of features used for the second layer of the model. For the first layer we use a sequence of current signal with 8 periods. Each period contains 256 values and is smoothed with SMA with $r = 16$. The whole sequence is normalised with min-max normalisation. This sequence is used as feature for the KNN classifier from the first layer. Fro the similarity measurement we use the Euclidean distance. We train the KNN classifier with 1% instances from the first dataset. In the second layer we used

**Table 2.** The classification error percentage and standard deviation for:

(a) $r = 0$

(b) $Norm = MinMax$

| Norm | n | p=7 $std_7$ | p=8 $std_8$ | p=9 $std_9$ |
|---|---|---|---|---|
| Raw | 64 | 14,78 0,19 | 14,5  0 | 14,4  0 |
| Raw | 128 | 14,24 0,16 | 14,4  0 | 14,05 0,05 |
| Raw | 256 | 14,21 0,09 | 14,4  0 | 14,23 0,11 |
| MinMax | 64 | 9,25 0,61 | 8,56 0,44 | 8,52 0,53 |
| MinMax | 128 | 10,97 0,25 | 10,91 0,43 | 10,66 0,67 |
| MinMax | 256 | 9,23 1,13 | **7,98** 1,89 | 9,2 1,79 |
| ZNorm | 64 | 16,44 0,05 | 16,4  0 | 16,4  0 |
| ZNorm | 128 | 16,4  0 | 16,4  0 | 16,4  0 |
| ZNorm | 256 | 16,4  0 | 16,4  0 | 16,4  0 |

| r | p=8 $std_8$ |
|---|---|
| 0 | 7,98 1,89 |
| 1 | 3,32 0,18 |
| 2 | 3,24 0,12 |
| 4 | 3,16 0,16 |
| 8 | 3,12 0,14 |
| 16 | **3,01** 0,03 |
| 32 | 5,21 0,34 |
| 64 | 22,21 0,16 |

a decision tree classifier (C4.5 implementation from Weka library [8]) which was train with 10% from the first dataset. The first feature of the classifier from the second layer is represented by the result of the KNN classifier. The rest of the features are enumerated in the Table 3a and they are grouped in feature vectors. After experimentations we observe that DFT coefficients from index 7 to 17 are useful so they are used to compute $avgdft$.

The whole model (first layer and second layer) was evaluated with 90% of the first dataset (in-domain) and with the second dataset (cross-domain). The evaluation was repeated 10 times with a randomly chosen train set. The result of the evaluation is presented in the Table 3b. We can confirm with the result that displacement and DFT coefficients are the most important features for this use case. The feature vector 11 that has only the two features obtains an error rate of 1.84% with a standard deviation of 0.97%. The feature vector 10 that contains all the features obtain an error rate of 1.38% with a standard deviation of 1.19%. Both results are for cross-domain evaluation. Although the model that uses the feature vector 10 obtains a better result we will discard it because this

**Table 3.** Second layer results

(a) Second layer feature vectors.

| Feature | 5 6 7 8 9 10 11 |
|---|---|
| rms(V) / rms(C) | x  x x  x |
| avgdft | x  x x   x  x |
| max1(C) | x x x x  x |
| max2(C) | x x x x  x |
| avg1(C) | x x x x  x |
| avg2(C) | x x x x  x |
| displacement(C) | x  x  x |

(b) In-domain and cross-domain evaluations.

| Feature vector | $error_{in}$ | $std_{in}$ | $error_{out}$ | $std_{out}$ |
|---|---|---|---|---|
| 5 | 0,15 | 0,34 | 2,3 | 0,43 |
| 6 | 0,12 | 0,31 | 2,82 | 1,1 |
| 7 | 0,21 | 0,44 | 2,69 | 0,82 |
| 8 | 0,21 | 0,44 | 3,54 | 1,78 |
| 9 | 0,12 | 0,31 | 2,82 | 1,1 |
| 10 | 0,23 | 0,68 | **1,38** | 1,19 |
| 11 | 0,26 | 0,79 | 1,84 | 0,97 |

is probably an over-fit. We can see this at the feature vector 8 that contains almost all the feature from feature vector 10, but it obtains a much lower result (error rate = 3.54%) compared to a model with a single layer of classifiers (error rate = 3.01%). Compared to [10] our model is more stable, their model has an error rate that is between 0% and 12%.

## 6    Conclusions

This paper presents a methodology for analysing a multi-dimensional and periodic time series. We propose the use of a new strategy for extracting periods from time series. Also we incorporated a two level classifier. The first layer is composed of KNN classifiers for each of the selected features, the second layer contains a decision tree classifier that uses as feature the result of the classifiers from the first layer.

In our future work we want to change the size and the normalisation for different features of the same classifier, because not all the feature needs the same level of granularity. Also we want to test more classifier for the second layer. Finally we want to use this methodology for another class of signal analysing problems.

## References

1. Ahmed, N., Natarajan, T., Rao, K.R.: Discrete cosine transform. IEEE. Trans. Comput. **100**(1), 90–93 (1974)
2. Bagnall, A., Bostrom, A., Large, J., Lines, J.: The great time series classification bake off: An experimental evaluation of recently proposed algorithms. extended version (2016)
3. Cardoso, A.M., Cruz, S., Carvalho, J., Saraiva, E.: Rotor cage fault diagnosis in three-phase induction motors, by park's vector approach. In: IEEE Industry Applications Conference, vol. 1, pp. 642–646. IEEE (1995)
4. Faloutsos, C., Ranganathan, M., Manolopoulos, Y.: Fast subsequence matching in time-series databases, vol. 23. ACM (1994)
5. Fu, T.: A review on time series data mining. Eng. Appl. Artif. Intell. **24**(1), 164–181 (2011)
6. Fulcher, B.D.: Feature-based time-series analysis (2017)
7. Haar, A.: Zur theorie der orthogonalen funktionensysteme **69**(3), 331–371 (1910)
8. Hall, M., Frank, E., Holmes, G., Pfahringer, B., Reutemann, P., Witten, I.H.: The WEKA data mining software: an update. ACM SIGKDD Explor. Newslett. **11**(1), 10–18 (2009)
9. Hasna, O.L., Potolea, R.: Time series–a taxonomy based survey. In: Intelligent Computer Communication and Processing (ICCP), pp. 231–238. IEEE (2017)
10. Martin-Diaz, I., Morinigo-Sotelo, D., Duque-Perez, O., Osornio-Rios, R.A., Romero-Troncoso, R.J.: Hybrid algorithmic approach oriented to incipient rotor fault diagnosis on induction motors. ISA Trans. **80**, 427–438 (2018)
11. Mitsa, T.: Temporal Data Mining. Chapman and Hall/CRC, Boca Raton (2010)
12. Nandi, S., Toliyat, H., Li, X.: Condition monitoring and fault diagnosis of electrical motors-a review. IEEE Trans. Energy Convers. **20**(4), 719–729 (2005)

13. Rajakarunakaran, S., Venkumar, P., Devaraj, D., Rao, K.S.P.: Artificial neural network approach for fault detection in rotary system. Appl. Soft Comput. **8**(1), 740–748 (2008)
14. Timmer, J., Gantert, C., Deuschl, G., Honerkamp, J.: Characteristics of hand tremor time series. Biol. Cybern. **70**(1), 75–80 (1993)
15. Wang, X., Mueen, A., Ding, H., Trajcevski, G., Scheuermann, P., Keogh, E.: Experimental comparison of representation methods and distance measures for time series data. Data Min. Knowl. Disc. **26**(2), 275–309 (2013)
16. Xu, B., Sun, L., Xu, L., Xu, G.: Improvement of the hilbert method via esprit for detecting rotor fault in induction motors at low slip. IEEE Trans. Energy Convers. **28**(1), 225–233 (2013)

# Stock Price Forecasting Over Adaptive Timescale Using Supervised Learning and Receptive Fields

Mario G. C. A. Cimino[1(✉)], Federico Dalla Bona[2],
Pierfrancesco Foglia[1], Manilo Monaco[1], Cosimo A. Prete[1],
and Gigliola Vaglini[1]

[1] Department of Information Engineering, University of Pisa, 56122 Pisa, Italy
{m.cimino, p.foglia, m.monaco, a.prete,
g.vaglini}@ing.unipi.it
[2] Trading Methods, SL - 35100 San Bartolomé de Tirajana,
Las Palmas, Gran Canaria, Spain
federicodallabona@tradinglift.com

**Abstract.** Pattern recognition in financial time series is not a trivial task, due to level of noise, volatile context, lack of formal definitions and high number of pattern variants. A current research trend involves machine learning techniques and online computing. However, medium-term trading is still based on human-centric heuristics, and the integration with machine learning support remains relatively unexplored. The purpose of this study is to investigate potential and perspectives of a novel architectural topology providing modularity, scalability and personalization capabilities. The proposed architecture is based on the concept of Receptive Fields (RF), i.e., sub-modules focusing on specific patterns, that can be connected to further levels of processing to analyze the price dynamics on different granularities and different abstraction levels. Both Multilayer Perceptrons (MLP) and Support Vector Machines (SVM) have been experimented as a RF. Early experiments have been carried out over the FTSE-MIB index.

**Keywords:** Stock price forecasting · Pattern recognition
Artificial neural network · Support vector machine

## 1 Introduction and Motivation

Stock price forecasting is a challenge in financial systems. Although there is an inherent level of chaos in markets dynamics, what really matters for decision-making is upward and downwards movements. In this field, even small improvements in performance can be very profitable [1].

Typically, *long-term trading* investors use *fundamental analysis*, which involves the study of many indicators over months, concerning overall economy, industry condition, financial condition and management of companies, earnings, expenses, assets and liabilities and so on. In this field, many studies have proposed various methods for forecasting stock prices. Most of these approaches require to select

© Springer Nature Switzerland AG 2018
A. Groza and R. Prasath (Eds.): MIKE 2018, LNAI 11308, pp. 279–288, 2018.
https://doi.org/10.1007/978-3-030-05918-7_25

carefully the input variables, to establish a predictive mathematical model under professional knowledge, to adopt various statistical methods for prior analysis of indicators.

With the rapid growth of internet-based transactions, the frequency for performing operations on the stock market has increased to fractions of seconds. In the last decade, several automatic traders emerged in *short-term trading*, operating in markets without the human intervention [2, 3]. Nowadays, automatic trading is efficient for intraday operations, but starts to become inefficient on *medium-term trading*, i.e., ranging from some days to a couple of weeks, over which events may have a nonlinear impact on dynamics.

The focus of this paper is on *medium-term trading*, where financial gains are not trivial to obtain. Typically, medium-term traders use *technical analysis*, adopting stock price and, eventually, volume charts to identify patterns and trends. Current research on medium-term stock price forecasting involves artificial intelligence techniques and real time computing. A fundamental process in technical analysis is *pattern recognition*. The purpose is to identify repeating patterns in prices, and figure out the ongoing pattern in order to predict the pattern completion in the close future [4]. In contrast to a case of function approximation, the investor aims to get a maximal profit rather than a minimal standard deviation. Thus, results depend on the predicted sign of course changes, and are based on the speculation for the rise and fall of prices. Therefore, the patterns of interest represent changes of price instead of course value.

In technical analysis, many patterns have been proposed. A graphical pattern emerges from the operational decisions of buyers and sellers and summarizes the global behavior of a market in a specific time interval. Common chart patterns are *head-and-shoulders*, *double-top*, *triple-top*, *spike-top*, *1–2–3-low*, *1–2–3-high*, and so on [4]. Different people use different methods to consider the favorite patterns. There are many ways to be successful and no one strategy is the best. However, patterns are not significant without *context indicators*. Examples of context indicators are simple moving average, support, resistance, trend lines, the degree of prices volatility and momentum-based indicators. In brief, support and resistance are certain predetermined levels of the price at which the price tends to stop and reverse [5]. Under proper patterns, practitioners look to buy at support and sell at resistance. Trend lines give defined entry and exit points, which can be utilized when moving to a new context, where there is no price history. High volatility in financial time series results in a greater difficulty in forecasting [6]. Momentum-based indicators, such as Bollinger bands, tend to be used in range-bound or trendless markets [1, 7]. Thus, it is the current context which assigns a certain reliability to a given pattern. Another fundamental issue is the time frame (or horizon), to which the analysis should be carried out. The horizon is not a constant notion: it is iteratively adjusted to focus the expected patterns at different granularities, potentially ranging from days to weeks. Indeed, many patterns are inherently recursive, manifest a fractal character and can therefore be found on different time scales, and with different duration in time [8].

Given the above requirements, a novel architecture based on machine learning has been designed and realized for supporting strategies of identification of investment opportunities. Overall, the strategies focus on short-term and medium-term patterns, but taking into consideration also short-term and medium-term information furnished by indicators as a reference context. The purpose of this study is to investigate potential and perspectives of the proposed approach in terms of accuracy, but also modularity, scalability and personalization.

More technically, the architecture is organized in terms of Receptive Fields (RFs), i.e., sub-modules focusing on specific groups of patterns, that can be connected to further levels of processing [9]. This topology allows to analyze the price dynamics on different granularities and different abstraction levels [10]. Both Multilayer Perceptrons (MLP) and Support Vector Machines (SVM) have been experimented as a receptive field for detecting sub-group of patterns. Early experiments have been carried out over the FTSE-MIB index, an Italian stock market index.

The remainder of the paper is structured as follows. Section 2 discusses the architectural design. Experiments are covered in Sect. 3. Finally, Sect. 4 summarizes conclusion and future work.

## 2  Architectural Design

This section focuses on the design of an architecture supporting strategies of identification of investment opportunities. Such strategies consider the stock price oscillation in a given time window. As an example, and without losing generality, Fig. 1 shows a basic breakout strategy, using the *1–2–3 low* pattern. The strategy assumes that, under an overall rising trend, and after occurrence of waves 1, 2, and 3, the opportunity is identified when the stock price *breaks* the resistance level. To detect this opportunity, the *1–2–3 low* pattern must be recognized, as well as its context (i.e., rising trend, support and resistance levels). To recognize patterns in financial time series is not a trivial task, due to additional fluctuations (noise), the volatile context, the lack of formal definitions. Technical patterns are not exact, and can be very different over occurrences, in terms of a different amplitude and different duration, and visually the same pattern occurrences can look different despite being equivalent. Moreover, patterns do not cover every time point in the series. In addition, the classical technical patterns are often personalized by technical analysts, producing a high number of pattern variants. As a consequence, to develop and manage algorithms for automated heuristics for financial pattern detection is often neither convenient nor effective.

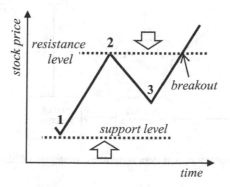

**Fig. 1.** Breakout trading strategy.

For the above reasons, during the past decades machine learning models have been developed to learn the key characteristics and to recognize technical patterns [4]. The major challenges in the field are: to recognize the input pattern reliably, to provide scalable, modular and adaptable architectures, to allow a dynamic inclusion/exclusion of personalized patterns. In particular, current research partially considers the manageability and the integrability with user's cognitive processes. For this purpose, the architectural design should explicitly address the application of the support system to human strategies. Traditionally, attention is primarily paid to interface design [13] and usability [14] or to performance evaluation. With regard to the latter aspect, the use of machine learning raises the following issues: (i) for an increasing number of patterns, there is an explosion of units needed, leading to increasing difficulties in learning; (ii) when patterns not previously considered are taken into account, the overall global learning process must be repeated. To foster scalability issues, a recent research trend considers that deep learning topology could be applied to time series forecasting, by extracting robust features that capture relevant information for each architectural layer [7]. However, this field still remains relatively unexplored, and then can produce systems that are costly, i.e., complex and engineered, and not very profitable, i.e., usable only under specific circumstances.

In this paper we propose a flexible architectural topology, where each RF can be considered as a modular "plugin" specialized for families of patterns. This approach enables a dynamic customization of patterns. Thus, to add, remove or update a family of patterns is relatively simple, since it involves mainly the training over the data of the new family. Furthermore, this modular organization allows the reusability of RFs. Figure 2 shows the overall topology, based on a collection of RFs.

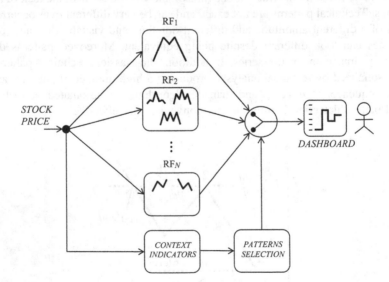

**Fig. 2.** Architectural topology of a system supporting strategies of identification of investment opportunities.

Each RF is specialized on a family of patterns, it takes as an input the stock price time series, and provides as an output the related pattern label. Some examples of family of patterns are shown in figure: *double-top* (RF1), *spike-top, head-and-shoulders, triple-top* (RF2), ..., *1–2–3 low, 1–2–3 high* (RFN), and so on. On the bottom, context indicators are calculated, to determine the significance and the reliability of the recognized patterns. The output is controlled through a pattern selector. The outcome is a temporal sequence of patterns. The pattern abstraction level sensibly reduces the complexity and the cognitive effort for the technical analyst, and can be easily represented in a dashboard.

Figure 3 represents the internal structure of a single RF. As specified, the input is made of samples of the stock price over time, $p(t)$, with sampling rate $\sigma$. To allow a scanning over a specified time scale, an adaptable windowing is carried out as a first step, selecting the values that are enclosed in the current sliding window with size $\tau$. Second, the ripple is removed, by using a triangular moving average with size $\rho$, as a smoothing function [11]. It is a weighted moving average commonly used in financial time series, providing a good balance between signal and micro noise. Third, a resampling is carried out to deliver a prefixed number of data samples $T$, independently of the time scale. Fourth, min-max normalization is made, obtaining data values between 0 and 1 aside from the price scale. Fifth, the pattern recognition system can produce none, one or more recognized patterns. In case of unknown pattern, the process restarts, adapting the time window size $\tau$, through a zoom in/out function. The process ends when setting the right time scale for that pattern, or when the minimum/maximum scale is reached.

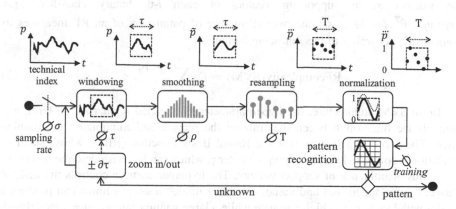

**Fig. 3.** Structure of a RF.

To speed up the execution time of the overall process, in systems where time constraints are a concern, the pipelined structure of the RFs and/or the loops can be parallelized on advanced multicore systems [15].

For the pattern recognition task, two different solutions have been studied and experimented: a Multi-Layer Perceptron (MLP), and a Support Vector Machine (SVM).

## 2.1   Multilayer Perceptron as a Receptive Field

The MLP is fed by $T$ input samples and consists of one hidden layer with size (i.e., number of neurons) $h$, and an output layer with $P$ output, where $P$ is the number of patterns that can be recognized in the family. The activation is based on a softmax function, which is commonly used in multiclass classification methods. Given the feed-forward and fully connected layers of a MLP, the overall number of parameters of a RF measures its complexity, according to the following formula:

$$\text{RFcomplexity}(\text{MLP}) = T \cdot (h+1) + h \cdot (P+1) \tag{1}$$

Given a set of labelled patterns, for a given family of patterns, the 80% of randomly extracted patterns is used as a training set, and the remaining 20% is used as a test set. The training is based on the minimization of the mean squared error with respect to the numerical output expected for each label, made through the backpropagation algorithm. The best value of the hyperparameter $h$ is determined by calculating the 99% confidence interval of the classification rate for each $h$ in a specified interval.

## 2.2   Support Vector Machine as a Receptive Field

The SVM architecture adopted is a soft-margin SVM known as C-SVM classifier. Since an SVM is designed for binary classification, the multiclass RF able to recognize a family of $P$ patterns is created decomposing the problem into a combination of the $P$ $(P-1)/2$ outputs of binary classifiers, i.e., according to a *one-vs.-one* strategy. Given the number $s_i$ of supporting vectors of each $i$-th binary classifier, $S_i = \{v_j : v_j \in \Re^T, j = 1, \ldots, s_i\}$ the overall number of parameters of an RF measures its complexity, according to the following formula:

$$\text{RFcomplexity}(\text{SVM}) = T \cdot \sum_1^{P(P-1)/2} s_i \tag{2}$$

In an SVM architecture, the hyperparameter $C$ is called regularization term, and controls the trade-off between maximizing the margin and minimizing the training error. The kernel function used is the Radial Basis Function (RBF), whose standard deviation is controlled via the hyperparameter $\gamma$, which can be considered the inverse of the radius of influence of support vectors. The hyperparameter $\gamma$ controls the tradeoff between error due to bias and variance in your model: a small gamma can produce a model with low bias and high variance while a large gamma can produce a model with higher bias and low variance. The best values of hyperparameters $C$ and $\gamma$ have been set using a grid-search with exponentially growing sequences.

## 3   Experimental Studies

The data set used for experiments comes from the stock trading prices of the FTSE-MIB index, sampled from Oct 19, 2017 to May 2, 2018, i.e., in 134 total days. Each day contains 511 observations: an observation is sampled every minute ($\sigma = 1$ sample per minute) during the opening time, i.e. from 9:00 to 17:30, i.e., 8.5 h. Overall, the data set contains 68,474 total samples. The window size $\tau$ is set within the interval [30, 120] minutes (or samples). The smoothing size is $\rho = 15$ min. The resampling size is $T = 50$ samples. Finally, the zoom in/out variation is $\partial\tau = 1$ min.

The number of instances generated from the dataset is 142 for each of the patterns *1–2–3 low* and *1–2–3 high*. A perturbation function has been applied to increase the instances up to 426 per pattern. The perturbation function adds or subtracts a small random value to each sample. After perturbation, the quality of the generated samples has been verified using a segmentation function based on the Perceptually Important Points (PIP) algorithm [12] to verify the statistics for each pattern.

Figure 4a shows an occurrence of *1–2–3 low* pattern, before and after smoothing. Figure 4b shows the signal after resampling and normalization. It is apparent that differences in micro noise, scale prices and time extension are almost completely removed. Figure 5 shows the 426 occurrences of *1–2–3 low* pattern. It is clear that the occurrences of the same pattern can look very different.

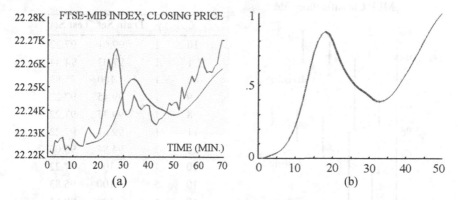

**Fig. 4.** Real sample of pattern *1–2–3 low*: (a) before and after smoothing; (b) after resampling and normalization

To compare the performances of the MLP-based and SVM-based RF, Fig. 6a shows their classification rate for different values of the respective hyperparameters. For the MLP, the best performance on the test set is achieved with 10 neurons in the hidden layer: 95.3%. For the SVM, the best performance is achieved with $C = \{9,10\}$ and $\gamma = 0.6$: 100% (training) and 98.61% (testing). It is apparent that the SVM outperforms the MLP. However, according to Formula (1) and (2), and considering the "unknown" pattern as a third class, the number of parameters is $50 \cdot 11 + 10 \cdot 4 = 590$ for the MLP, and $50 \cdot (70 + 50 + 73) = 9,650$ for the SVM. Thus, in terms of complexity, SVM is more than one order of magnitude larger than MLP.

Let us consider the effects of an increase of the number of patterns, by introducing in the same RF the following two patterns: *upward head-and-shoulders* and *downwards head-and-shoulders*. Again, a perturbation function has been applied to increase the instances up to 426 per pattern. After training, the RF is able to recognize 5 total

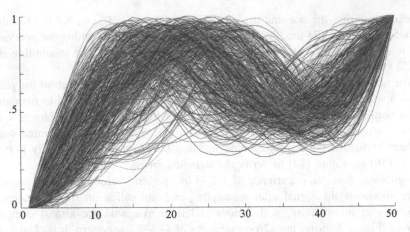

**Fig. 5.** Occurrences of *1–2–3 low* pattern available in the data set.

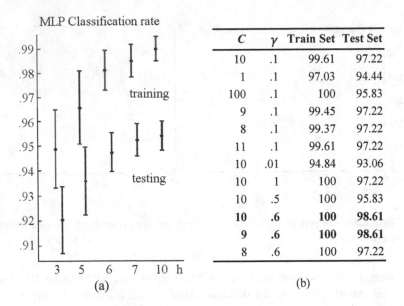

MLP Classification rate

| $C$ | $\gamma$ | Train Set | Test Set |
|---|---|---|---|
| 10 | .1 | 99.61 | 97.22 |
| 1 | .1 | 97.03 | 94.44 |
| 100 | .1 | 100 | 95.83 |
| 9 | .1 | 99.45 | 97.22 |
| 8 | .1 | 99.37 | 97.22 |
| 11 | .1 | 99.61 | 97.22 |
| 10 | .01 | 94.84 | 93.06 |
| 10 | 1 | 100 | 97.22 |
| 10 | .5 | 100 | 95.83 |
| **10** | **.6** | **100** | **98.61** |
| **9** | **.6** | **100** | **98.61** |
| 8 | .6 | 100 | 97.22 |

(a)                                (b)

**Fig. 6.** Performances of a RF with 3 patterns and for different values of hyperparameters: (a) Classification rate of MLP against $h$; (b) Classification rate of SVM against $C$ and $\gamma$.

patterns. Figure 7 shows the performances provided by the MLP-based and SVM-based RF with the related hyperparameters. Results on the test set show that SVM outperforms the MLP. However, according to Formula (1) and (2), the number of parameters is now $50 \cdot 11 + 10 \cdot 6 = 610$ for the MLP, and $50 \cdot 291 = 14,550$ for the SVM. Thus, the complexity of SVM is dramatically increased. However, the complexity of SVM is not an issue, since families of patterns are typically made by less than 5 patterns.

| RF: hyperparameters | Train Set | Test Set |
|---|---|---|
| MLP: $h = 6$ | $.973 \pm .015$ | $.938 \pm .02$ |
| MLP: $h = 10$ | $.991 \pm .003$ | $.948 \pm .02$ |
| SVM: C=12, $\gamma$=0.1 | $.998$ | $.983$ |

**Fig. 7.** Classification rate of a RF with 5 patterns, made with MLP and SVM.

## 4 Conclusions

In this paper we have designed and experimented a flexible architectural topology based on Receptive Fields, for supporting strategies of identification of financial investment opportunities based on machine learning. The approach enables a dynamic customization of patterns and foster reusability of RF. The overall system provides a pattern-based abstraction level, and sensibly reduces the complexity and the cognitive effort for the technical analyst involved in medium-term technical analysis. By improving the comfort via timely and tailored information, the system can be well integrated with the investor's decision process, thus reducing errors resulting from bias and emotion.

The paper illustrates the design of an RF considering noise, variability of amplitude, duration, shape, of equivalent pattern occurrences. MLP and SVM have been used as a RF. Experiments have shown that SVM outperforms MLP, although the SVM complexity is sensibly higher. However, such complexity is not an issue since each RF is typically devoted to few patterns.

As a future work, different machine learning techniques, which incorporate the concept of time into their operating model, will be adopted for RFs.

**Acknowledgements.** This work was carried out in the framework of the SCIADRO project, co-funded by the Tuscany Region (Italy) under the Regional Implementation Programme for Underutilized Areas Fund (PAR FAS 2007–2013) and the Research Facilitation Fund (FAR) of the Ministry of Education, University and Research (MIUR).

The authors thank Marco Gasperini for his work on the subject during his thesis.

## References

1. Zhou, X., Pan, Z., Hu, G., Tang, S., Zhao, C.: Stock market prediction on high-frequency data using generative adversarial nets. Mathematical Problems in Engineering (2018)
2. Jabbur, E., Silva, E., Castilho, D., Pereira, A., Brandão, H.: Design and evaluation of automatic agents for stock market intraday trading. In Proceedings of the 2014 IEEE/WIC/ACM International Joint Conferences on Web Intelligence (WI) and Intelligent Agent Technologies (IAT), vol. 03, pp. 396–403. IEEE Computer Society, August 2014
3. Wang, X., Bao, S., Chen, J.: High-frequency stock linkage and multi-dimensional stationary processes. Physica A: Stat. Mech. Appl. **468**, 70–83 (2017)
4. Gong, X., Si, Y.W., Fong, S., Biuk-Aghai, R.P.: Financial time series pattern matching with extended UCR Suite and Support Vector Machine. Expert Syst. Appl. **55**, 284–296 (2016)

5. Zapranis, A., Tsinaslanidis, P.E.: A novel, rule-based technical pattern identification mechanism: identifying and evaluating saucers and resistant levels in the US stock market. Expert Syst. Appl. **39**(7), 6301–6308 (2012)
6. Yi, X., Jin, X., John, L., Shouyang, W.: A multiscale modeling approach incorporating ARIMA and ANNS for financial market volatility forecasting. J. Syst. Sci. Complex. **27**, 225–236 (2014)
7. Bao, W., Yue, J., Rao, Y.: A deep learning framework for financial time series using stacked autoencoders and long-short term memory. PLoS ONE **12**(7), e0180944 (2017)
8. Volna, E., Kotyrba, M., Jarusek, R.: Multi-classifier based on Elliott wave's recognition. Comput. Math Appl. **66**(2), 213–225 (2013)
9. Cimino, M.G., Pedrycz, W., Lazzerini, B., Marcelloni, F.: Using multilayer perceptrons as receptive fields in the design of neural networks. Neurocomputing **72**(10–12), 2536–2548 (2009)
10. Alfeo, A.L., Barsocchi, P., Cimino, M.G., La Rosa, D., Palumbo, F., Vaglini, G.: Sleep behavior assessment via smartwatch and stigmergic receptive fields. Pers. Ubiquit. Comput. **22**(2), 227–243 (2018)
11. Wang, L., An, H., Xia, X., Liu, X., Sun, X., Huang, X.: Generating moving average trading rules on the oil futures market with genetic algorithms. Math. Probl. Eng. (2014)
12. Fu, T.C., Chung, F.L., Luk, R., Ng, C.M.: Stock time series pattern matching: Template-based vs. rule-based approaches. Eng. Appl. Artif. Intell. **20**(3), 347–364 (2007)
13. Dini, G., Foglia, P., Prete, C.A., Zanda, M.: Social and Q&A interfaces for app download. Inf. Process. Manage. **50**(4), 584–598 (2014)
14. Foglia, P., Prete, C.A., Zanda, M.: Relating GSR signals to traditional usability metrics: case study with an anthropomorphic web assistant. In: Instrumentation and Measurement Technology Conference Proceedings. IMTC 2008. IEEE, pp. 1814–1818. IEEE, May 2008
15. Bartolini, S., Foglia, P., Prete, C.A.: Exploring the relationship between architectures and management policies in the design of NUCA-based chip multicore systems. Future Gener. Comput. Syst. **78**, 481–501 (2018)

# Periodically Diluted BEGNN Model of Corruption Perception

Mario González[1], David Dominguez[2(✉)], Guillermo Jerez[2],
and Odette Pantoja[3]

[1] SI[2] Lab, Universidad de las Américas, Quito, Ecuador
mario.gonzalez.rodriguez@udla.edu.ec
[2] Grupo de Neurocomputación Biológica, Dpto. de Ingeniería Informática,
Escuela Politécnica Superior, Universidad Autónoma de Madrid, 28049 Madrid, Spain
david.dominguez@uam.es
[3] FCA, Escuela Politécnica Nacional, Quito, Ecuador
odette.pantoja@epn.edu.ec

**Abstract.** This study evaluates the performance provided by a Blume-Emery-Griffiths neural network (BEGNN) for two datasets of corruption indicators, namely the Corruption Perceptions Index and the Global Corruption Barometer. Bi-lineal and bi-quadratic terms are added to the Hamiltonian of the model, as well as for the order parameters to measure the network retrieval efficiency. The network is tested for different noise levels of the patterns' initial state during the retrieval phase in order to measure the robustness of the network and its basin of attraction. The network connectivity is diluted periodically and its performance is tested for different levels of dilution. The network is analyzed in terms of the pattern load, mixing the real corruption patterns with random patterns in order to assess the change from retrieval to non-retrieval phases.

**Keywords:** Three-state neural network
Corruption Perceptions Index · Global Corruption Barometer

## 1 Introduction

This article checks the effectiveness of applying a Blume-Emery-Griffiths Neural Network (BEGNN) model to detect relevant patterns in real data and to describe the behavior of sociological indicators on corruption perception data. The application of Attractor Networks to real data and engineering problems is scarce. Recent works have used a binary attractor network for fingerprint recognition [5,6], traffic video [7]. Dealing with socioeconomics problems is even more rare [10]. Ternary networks can improve the retrieval properties over the binary network, also, more information can be encoded in the three-states and recovered as bilinear and biquadratic retrieval. Thus, the complex behavior of the data in socioeconomics problems can be better captured with this model. In particular, this work tests two datasets, namely, Corruption Perceptions Index (CPI) and the Global Corruption Barometer (GCB).

© Springer Nature Switzerland AG 2018
A. Groza and R. Prasath (Eds.): MIKE 2018, LNAI 11308, pp. 289–298, 2018.
https://doi.org/10.1007/978-3-030-05918-7_26

Simulations have been carried out to quantify the BEGNN performance for different levels of noise in the input patterns parameters as well as for different levels of dilution. Artificial neural networks approach (specifically Hopfield-type networks) as a structural model is effective for categorization problems, data classification, and for faces and objects detection and identification [12,16]. In this sense, the objective of this work is to evaluate a three-state (or ternary) performance of the BEGNN [4], using as input data the Transparency International CPI and GCB datasets. To carry out this study, different aspects of the ternary network will be varied to obtain a combination of optimal parameters to make a performance analysis of the BEGNN for modeling the corruption datasets.

In recent years has been an outbreak of massive cases about corruption in the global context like the Panama Papers scandal, increasing the international concern in this area [11]. Certain institutions and institutional figures that traditionally have been a fundamental part of the state/government in many countries have suffered a serious setback in their credibility, thus deteriorating the trust that citizens placed in them [20].

Transparency International (TI) is an international non-governmental organization who denunciates the corruption and the power abuse in institutions. Since 1995, TI has been preparing and making available to the public a series of reports and indicators on this matter. Two of these indicators are analyzed in the present research, the CPI and GCB. CPI collects experts and business people opinions by their perceived levels of public sector corruption in 180 countries and territories [13,17,21], using a scale of 0 to 100, where 0 is highly corrupt and 100 is very clean. The CPI compile information from trustworthy data sources, including the assessment in areas like bribery, diversion of public funds, use of public office for private gain, nepotism in the civil service and state capture. In 2017 CPI reflected that more than two-thirds of countries scored below 50, showing high levels of corruption in public sector.

On the other hand GCB is based on citizens perceptions, experiences and attitudes towards corruption in their direct personal lives [14,15,18,19]. GCB addresses sectors like (1) political parties, (2) parliament/legislature, (3) legal system/judiciary, (4) police, (5) business/private sector, (6) tax revenue, (7) customs, (8) media, (9) medical services, (10) education system, (11) registry and permit services, (12) utilities, (13) military, (14) NGOs, and (15) religious bodies. In 2017, GCB showed that one of four people paid a bribe to access public services, as well, the most corrupt groups were identified as police and elected representatives [19].

The rest of the article is organized as follows. In the following Sect. 2 we describe the BEGNN ternary model and its performance measures. In Sect. 3 we present the main results for different model parameters and Sect. 4 concludes the paper discussing the implications of our findings.

## 2   The Model

In this section we present the BEGNN model and define the dynamics to achieve the stationary states. This BEGNN model includes the binary $\{\pm1\}$ and the bimodal $\{0,1\}$ representations of the neural code as special cases [1]. At the end we describe also the order parameters of the system.

Consider a neural network consisting of $N$ neurons $\{\sigma_i | i = 1, \ldots, N\}$ which can take values from the discrete set $\sigma_i \in \{-1, 0, +1\}$. The networks aims to store a set of $P$ patterns $\{\xi^\mu | \mu = 1, \ldots, P\}$ each of which are supposed to be a collection of random variables, $\{\xi_i^\mu | i = 1, \ldots, N\}$ with a probability distribution

$$p(\xi^\mu = +1) = \frac{a^\mu + b^\mu}{2}; \; p(\xi^\mu = -1) = \frac{a^\mu - b^\mu}{2}; \; p(\xi^\mu = 0) = (1 - a^\mu); \quad (1)$$

where $a^\mu$ and $b^\mu$ are the pattern activity and bias respectively, given by the averages

$$a^\mu = \langle (\xi_i^\mu)^2 \rangle; \; b^\mu = \langle \xi_i^\mu \rangle \equiv \frac{1}{N} \sum_i^N (\xi_i^\mu). \quad (2)$$

The energy function of the system is given by the following bi-lineal and bi-quadratic Hamiltonian,

$$H = \sum_i h_i \sigma_i + \sum_i \theta_i \sigma_i^2, \quad h_i = w \sum_j J_{ij} \sigma_j, \; \theta_i = (1 - w) \sum_j K_{ij} \sigma_j^2, \quad (3)$$

where the lineal and threshold local fields are defined respectively by $h_i, \theta_i$. If the weight $w = 1$, one recover the lineal model for binary patterns, whereas if $w = 0$, there are only quadratic terms for bimodal patterns.

The bi-lineal and bi-quadratic learning weights are of the Hebb-type defined respectively as

$$J_{ij} = \frac{C_{ij}}{(a^\mu)^2 N} \sum_\mu \xi_i^\mu \xi_j^\mu, \qquad K_{ij} = \frac{C_{ij}}{(\tilde{a}^\mu)^2 N} \sum_\mu \eta_i^\mu \eta_j^\mu, \quad (4)$$

with

$$\eta_i^\mu = (\xi_i^\mu)^2 - a^\mu, \quad \tilde{a}^\mu = a^\mu (1 - a^\mu). \quad (5)$$

In order to get the stationary states of the Hamiltonian, the neurons are updated according to the following dynamics,

$$\sigma_i(t + 1) = g(h_i(t), \theta_i(t)); \; g(h, \theta) \equiv \text{sign}(h) \times \Theta(|h| - \theta), \quad i = 1, \ldots, N, \quad (6)$$

where $sign$ and $\Theta$ are the signum and the step functions respectively [1,2].

The topology matrix $C = \{C_{ij}\}$ describes the connectivity structure of the neural network. The network topology $C$ is characterized by a periodic coupling, connecting each neuron $i$ with another neuron $j$ at every distance with $|i - j| mod D$, in a cyclical ring, randomly changing the initial $j$ for each new pattern $\mu$. Here, $D$ is the distance between connected neurons and $D \in \{1, \ldots, N\}$.

Then, the dilution of the network can be expressed as $\gamma = 1/D$. If $\gamma = 1$ one has a fully connected network. For $\gamma \to 0$, one has a extremely diluted network. A modular topology, randomly diluted instead of periodically, was studied in [8,9].

The order parameters relevant for the present model are

$$m^{\mu}(t) = \frac{1}{a^{\mu}N} \sum_i \xi_i^{\mu} \sigma_i(t), \quad l^{\mu}(t) = \frac{1}{\tilde{a}^{\mu}N} \sum_i \eta_i^{\mu} \sigma_i^2(t), \tag{7}$$

where $m^{\mu}$ is the usual lineal overlap, $l^{\mu}(t)$ is the square activity overlap. Besides these retrieval parameters one can consider also the neural activity parameter, given by $q(t) = \frac{1}{N} \sum_i \sigma_i^2(t)$, which, although is not related to the pattern information, plays a role in the network dynamics in Eq. 6. Together with $m, l$, the pattern load $\alpha = P/K$ is used to measure the performance of the network. One is interested in finding a critical value $\alpha_c$, where the equivalent number of patterns $P_c$ are recovered above a given retrieval overlap $m$.

## 3   Results: BEGNN Retrieval Performance

This section starts defining the pattern coding. Then, the performance of the network for the two selected datasets, CPI and GCB, is presented for the balance parameter $w$ in terms of bi-lineal $m$ and bi-quadratic $l$ retrieval. Finally, the analysis of BEGNN retrieval is explored for different levels of dilution $\gamma$ and noisy conditions.

### 3.1   Patterns' Coding

The original CPI dataset is encoded on a discrete scale from 0 (highly corrupt) to 100 (very clean). This value is then converted to a ternary pattern according to:

$$\xi_i^{\mu} = \begin{cases} 0 \text{ if CPI value is NaN or Empty} \\ -1 \text{ if cell value} < 60 \\ 1 \text{ Otherwise.} \end{cases} \tag{8}$$

The pattern size $N = 190$ is given then by the number of countries (once evaluated).

**Table 1.** GCB coding

| Item/sector | Year 1 | | ... | Year n | |
| --- | --- | --- | --- | --- | --- |
| | Country 1 ... | Country n | ... | Country 1 ... | Country n |
| 1 | 3.1 | 2.9 | ... | 3.4 | 3.0 |
| ⋮ | 3.3 | 2.6 | ... | 3.2 | 2.5 |
| 15 | 4.5 | 4.3 | ... | 3.6 | 4.2 |

The GCB patterns are encoded from Table 1. The original dataset GCB has 15 items/sectors (as mentioned in the Introduction 1) with a value that is continuous between 1.0 and 5.0. Each of the $N_s = 15$ items/sectors (described in the introduction), is evaluated for each of the $N_c = 125$ countries, and converted to a ternary pattern (low/medium/high corruption) according to:

$$\xi_i^\mu = \begin{cases} -1 \text{ if } 1.0 \leq GCB < 2.5 \\ 0 \text{ if } 2.5 \leq GCB < 3.5 \\ 1 \text{ if } 3.5 \leq GCB \leq 5.0 \end{cases} \tag{9}$$

The pattern $\xi_i^\mu$ have size $N = N_c \times N_s = 125 \times 15 = 1875$. Both CPI and GCB threshold/criteria for encoding, are chosen to get patterns that are unbiased, avoiding a dynamics threshold mechanism [2].

## 3.2  Bi-lineal and Bi-quadratic Retrieval

With a balance parameter $w = 0.0$, one is able to retrieve only the bi-quadratic $l$ terms for bimodal patterns in Fig. 1 left panels for CPI (top) and GCB (bottom). On the other extreme, for $w = 1.0$, only the bi-lineal $m$ terms for binary patterns is recovered. One is interested in optimizing the retrieval in terms of both bi-lineal $m$ and bi-quadratic $l$ terms. For intermediate values of the balance parameter i.c. $w = 0.5$, both $m, l$ terms are retrieved, as shown in the center panels of Fig. 1.

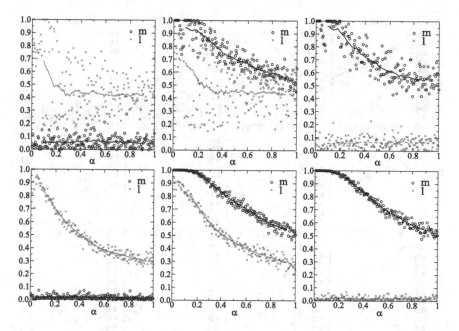

**Fig. 1.** Network retrieval overlaps $m$ and $l$ for $w = 0.0, 0.5, 1.0$ from left to right for CPI (top panels with $\gamma = 1.0$) and GCB (bottom panels with $\gamma = 0.1$).

In Fig. 1 top center and right panels, can be observed in order to compare the retrieval of a classical binary Hopfield network versus the ternary BEGNN. One can appreciate that the smoothed curve for the bi-lineal retrieval $m$ with

$w = 0.5$ drops less sharply than in the case of $w = 1.0$. That is, the ternary network improves the retrieval of the binary one. In the GCB case, Fig. 1 bottom center and right panels, the difference is less pronounced, this is due to the case that real patterns are less than in the CPI case. This is also noted in the retrieval curve being less noisy. Thus, for real patterns is more critical the improvements of the ternary network over the binary one. The value of $w = 0.5$ is kept constant in order to explore the role of the dilution and noise in the retrieval performance of the BEGNN.

### 3.3    Corruption Perceptions Index Retrieval

Figure 2 depicts the retrieval performance of the BEGNN model for the CPI dataset. Different levels of random noise are added to the initial state of the retrieval stage, $n = \{0.0, 0.2, 0.35, 0.5\}$, from left to right respectively. Different levels of dilution were also checked, $\gamma = \{1.0, 0.25, 0.08\}$ from top to bottom. The CPI database is composed of $P_{CPI} = 15$ patterns (the years from 2002 to 2016), the fully connected BEGNN ($\gamma = 1.0$) learns a total of $P = 190$ patterns, where the remaining ones are generated randomly $P_{random} = 175$, to reach a

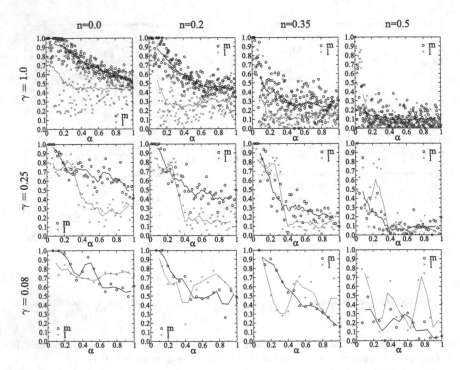

**Fig. 2.** Network retrieval overlaps $m$ and $l$ for $w = 0.5$ for CPI data. Columns with noise levels $n = \{0.0, 0.2, 0.35, 0.5\}$ from left to right respectively. Network dilution $\gamma = \{1.0, 0.25, 0.08\}$ from top to bottom respectively.

pattern load of $\alpha = 1$. On the other extreme, for a diluted connectivity $\gamma = 0.08$, the network stores only the real patterns $P_{CPI} = 15$.

One can appreciate in Fig. 2 top panels, that for the noiseless case ($n = 0.0$) the fully connected ($\gamma = 1.0$) BEGNN manages to retrieve $\alpha_c \sim 0.5$, i.e. half the patterns $P_c = 95$, with a retrieval quality over $m \geq 0.7$. The bi-quadratic parameter $l$ decays faster as the number of stored patterns increase. As the noise increase to $n = 0.2$ the number of stored patterns is around 30% $\alpha_c \sim 0.3$, given a measure of the BEGNN basin of attraction. Increasing further the noise ($n = 0.35$), only $P_c = 6$ are recovered over $m \geq 0.7$. Finally, no retrieval is possible for a noise level of $n = 0.5$. A similar qualitative behavior is observed for the periodic dilution in Fig. 2 middle panels. Figure 2 bottom-left panels, show the BEGNN model is able to store all the $P_{CPI} = 15$ real patterns with a quality $m \geq 0.5$ for the noiseless case. This panel depicts for the first 5 patterns/years (2002 to 2006), that the CPI behavior is very similar, i.e. high correlation inducing $m$ to decrease. This could be interpreted as the index is not changing that much. For the following 4 years (2007 to 2010), the retrieval behavior changes indicating changes in corruption perception, probably coinciding with the world-wide economic crisis. From 2011 to 2016, the value of $m$ decays indicating again that these years are highly correlated, indicating that the perception has not changed from the previous patterns/years. Again, increasing the noise worsens the retrieval quality of the CPI patterns.

### 3.4   Global Corruption Barometer Retrieval

Figure 3 depicts the retrieval performance of the BEGNN model for the GCB dataset. The same levels of noise used in the CPI dataset are used. Different levels of dilution were also checked, $\gamma = \{0.1, 0.016, 0.0032\}$ from top to bottom. The pattern size difference for both CPI ($N = 190$) and GCB ($N = 1875$) accounts for the different dilutions chosen. The GCB database is composed of $P_{GCB} = 6$ patterns (the years $\{2004, 2005, 2006, 2009, 2010, 2013\}$). The BEGNN with dilution $\gamma = 0.1$ learns a total of $P = 187$ patterns with the remaining patterns generated at random $P_{random} = 181$. On the minimum dilution $\gamma = 0.0032$, the BEGNN retrieves only the real $P_{GCB} = 6$ patterns without noise (bottom-left panel). Unlike the CPI case, nothing can be implied about the behavior of GCB dataset, more than that probably the perception of corruption change less in the case of citizens perception (GCB) than in the case of the expert opinions (CPI). Also, the small number of patterns could be the reason, that no behavior can be inferred. Again, the small number of real patterns accounts for smoother retrieval curves in the case of the GCB dataset. In all panels, the bi-quadratic retrieval overlap $l$ is retrieved below the bi-lineal term $m$. A more refined self-control mechanism for the dynamics should be needed [2].

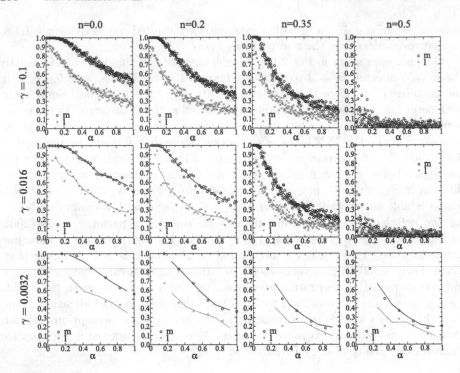

**Fig. 3.** Network retrieval overlaps $m$ and $l$ for $w = 0.5$ for GCB data. Columns with noise levels $n = \{0.0, 0.2, 0.35, 0.5\}$ from left to right respectively. Network dilution $\gamma = \{0.1, 0.016, 0.0032\}$ from top to bottom respectively.

## 4   Conclusions

In this paper, the effectiveness of the Blume-Emery-Griffiths neural network (BEGNN) was investigated. Real patterns were used mixed with random patterns in order to describe the transition of the BEGNN model from retrieval to non retrieval. Corruption Perceptions Index (CPI) and Global Corruption Barometer (GCB) datasets were chosen as real patterns. The network balance between bilineal and bi-quadratic terms was explored and an intermediate value $w = 0.5$ was proved to optimize the retrieval when compared with a binary network $w = 1.0$. This performance improvement was more notorious in the case where more real patterns were stored and retrieved by the BEGNN.

Different levels of noise and connectivity dilution were tested. The BEGNN proved to be very robust to initial noise with a non trivial basin of attraction. For the more diluted BEGNNs, only the real patterns were stored/retrieved. In the CPI case, the behavior of the index was explained by the BEGNN model, indicating a change of corruption perception around the global financial crisis (year 2010). In the case of GCB, the behavior was harder to inferred with the BEGNN retrieval behavior, although we speculate that the behavior is more steady than in the case of CPI, with citizens being more pessimistic in their perception of corruption. We intend to apply the BEGNN to a set of socio-economics problems such as sustainability reporting [10,11], the Panama Papers [3], gender equality, emigration/immigration flows.

**Acknowledgments.** This work has been supported by MINECO TIN2014-54580-R, TIN2017-84452-R, and by UAM-Santander CEAL-AL/2017-08, and UDLA-SIS.MG.17.02.

# References

1. Bollé, D., Dominguez, D.R.C., Erichsen Jr., R., Korutcheva, E., Theumann, W.K.: Time evolution of the extremely diluted Blume-Emery-Griffiths neural network. Phys. Rev. E **68**(6), 062901 (2003)
2. Bollé, D., Dominguez, D., Amari, S.I.: Mutual information of sparsely coded associative memory with self-control and ternary neurons. Neural Netw. **13**(4–5), 455–462 (2000)
3. Dominguez, D., Pantoja, O., González, M.: Mapping the global offshoring network through the panama papers. In: Rocha, Á., Guarda, T. (eds.) ICITS 2018. AISC, vol. 721, pp. 407–416. Springer, Cham (2018). https://doi.org/10.1007/978-3-319-73450-7_39
4. Dominguez, D.R.C., Korutcheva, E.: Three-state neural network: from mutual information to the Hamiltonian. Phys. Rev. E **62**(2), 2620 (2000)
5. Doria, F., Erichsen Jr., R., González, M., Rodríguez, F.B., Sánchez, Á., Dominguez, D.: Structured patterns retrieval using a metric attractor network: application to fingerprint recognition. Physica A Stat. Mech. Appl. **457**, 424–436 (2016)
6. González, M., Dominguez, D., Rodríguez, F.B., Sanchez, A.: Retrieval of noisy fingerprint patterns using metric attractor networks. Int. J. Neural Syst. **24**(07), 1450025 (2014)
7. González, M., Dominguez, D., Sánchez, Á.: Learning sequences of sparse correlated patterns using small-world attractor neural networks: an application to traffic videos. Neurocomputing **74**(14–15), 2361–2367 (2011)
8. González, M., Dominguez, D., Sánchez, Á., Rodríguez, F.B.: Capacity and retrieval of a modular set of diluted attractor networks with respect to the global number of neurons. In: Rojas, I., Joya, G., Catala, A. (eds.) IWANN 2017. LNCS, vol. 10305, pp. 497–506. Springer, Cham (2017). https://doi.org/10.1007/978-3-319-59153-7_43
9. González, M., Dominguez, D., Sánchez, Á., Rodríguez, F.B.: Increase attractor capacity using an ensembled neural network. Expert Syst. Appl. **71**, 206–215 (2017)
10. González, M., del Mar Alonso-Almeida, M., Avila, C., Dominguez, D.: Modeling sustainability report scoring sequences using an attractor network. Neurocomputing **168**, 1181–1187 (2015)
11. González, M., del Mar Alonso-Almeida, M., Dominguez, D.: Mapping global sustainability report scoring: a detailed analysis of Europe and Asia. Qual. Quant. **52**, 1–15 (2017)
12. Krizhevsky, A., Sutskever, I., Hinton, G.E.: Imagenet classification with deep convolutional neural networks. In: Advances in Neural Information Processing Systems, pp. 1097–1105 (2012)

13. Qaiser, B., Nadeem, S., Siddiqi, M.U., Siddiqui, A.F.: Relationship of social progress index (SPI) with gross domestic product (GDP PPP per capita): the moderating role of corruption perception index (CPI). Pakistan J. Eng. Technol. Sci. **7**(1), 61–76 (2018)
14. Rose-Ackerman, S., Palifka, B.J.: Corruption and Government: Causes, Consequences, and Reform. Cambridge University Press, Cambridge (2016)
15. Srivastava, S.C., Teo, T.S., Devaraj, S.: You can't bribe a computer: dealing with the societal challenge of corruption through ICT. MIS Q. **40**(2), 511–526 (2016)
16. Szegedy, C., Toshev, A., Erhan, D.: Deep neural networks for object detection. In: Advances in Neural Information Processing Systems, pp. 2553–2561 (2013)
17. TI-CPI: Transparency International Corruption Perceptions Index (2018). https://www.transparency.org/research/cpi/overview
18. TI-GCB: Transparency International Global Corruption Barometer 2004 (2018). https://www.transparency.org/whatwedo/publication/gcb_2004
19. TI-GCB: Transparency International Global Corruption Barometer 2015/16/17 (2018). https://www.transparency.org/research/gcb/gcb_2015_16
20. Villoria, M., Van Ryzin, G.G., Lavena, C.F.: Social and political consequences of administrative corruption: a study of public perceptions in Spain. Public Adm. Rev. **73**(1), 85–94 (2013)
21. Yoon, J., Klasen, S.: An application of partial least squares to the construction of the social institutions and gender index (SIGI) and the corruption perception index (CPI). Soc. Ind. Res. **138**(1), 61–88 (2018)

# Neural Machine Translation
# with Recurrent Highway Networks

Maulik Parmar[✉] and V. Susheela Devi

Indian Institute of Science, Bengaluru 560012, Karnataka, India
maulik2087@gmail.com

**Abstract.** Recurrent Neural Networks have lately gained a lot of popularity in language modelling tasks, especially in neural machine translation (NMT). Very recent NMT models are based on Encoder-Decoder, where a deep LSTM based encoder is used to project the source sentence to a fixed dimensional vector and then another deep LSTM decodes the target sentence from the vector. However there has been very little work on exploring architectures that have more than one layer in space (i.e. in each time step). This paper examines the effectiveness of the simple Recurrent Highway Networks (RHN) in NMT tasks. The model uses Recurrent Highway Neural Network in encoder and decoder, with attention. We also explore the reconstructor model to improve adequacy. We demonstrate the effectiveness of all three approaches on the IWSLT English-Vietnamese dataset. We see that RHN performs on par with LSTM based models and even better in some cases. We see that deep RHN models are easy to train compared to deep LSTM based models because of highway connections. The paper also investigates the effects of increasing recurrent depth in each time step.

**Keywords:** Recurrent highway networks · Reconstructor · Attention
Encoder-decoder

## 1 Introduction

Neural Machine Translation (NMT) is a recent approach towards machine translation [1–3,6]. In contradiction with the conventional Statistical Machine Translation (SMT) system [7] which consists of many small sub-components that are tuned separately, in neural machine translation the whole neural network is jointly trained to maximize the conditional probability of a correct translation given a source sentence, using the bilingual corpus.

The use of Neural Networks for Machine Translation leads to fluent translation. Popular neural machine translation models [1–3] use stacked LSTMs, which read through the source sentence one word at a time till it reaches the end of sequence symbol *<eos>* tag, then it starts to emit target words one by one till it generates the end of sequence *<eos>* tag.

We move in the same direction, but instead of stacking layers of LSTM, we stack layers within each time step, as illustrated in Fig. 1. Each time block is

© Springer Nature Switzerland AG 2018
A. Groza and R. Prasath (Eds.): MIKE 2018, LNAI 11308, pp. 299–308, 2018.
https://doi.org/10.1007/978-3-030-05918-7_27

recurrent highway network following the work of [4]. With this architecture we demonstrate their effect on machine translation when layers within a time step is increased one by one. Parallelly with the neural machine translation(NMT), the concept of "attention" has gained a lot of popularity in recent years [2,3]. We follow the attention model by [3] as our base model. With IWSLT English-Vietnamese dataset we found that without attention increasing the recurrent depth does not affect the BLEU [8] score much, whereas with attention it shows a significant increase in the BLEU score with increasing recurrent depth.

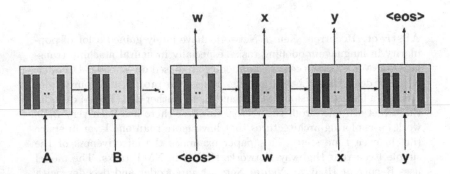

**Fig. 1.** Neural machine translation with recurrent highway architecture for translating a source sequence A B into a target sequence X Y. (Proposed Model without attention)

The problem with these vanilla attention models is that translation generated by these models often lack adequacy. There is a problem of over-translation and under-translation i.e some words are translated more than once, while some words are not translated at all. To address this problem we use reconstructor model [9] which we will discuss in Sect. 4.

## 2  Related Work

Even prior to the recent end-to-end NMT models neural networks were used for SMT based translation with some success. The concept of end-to-end learning for machine translation has been attempted in the past with limited success. From then its a long journey to the end-to-end models [1–3,6] which have outperformed the previous SMT baselines [7].

Our work being the first application of RHN in neural machine translation task, is very close to the work [1,3] and [9]. At the same time we take the motivation to apply the RHN in this area from [5]; who has shown the success of recurrent highway network (RHN) in automatic speech recognition.

## 3  Recurrent Highway Network

Recurrent state transition in RNN is described by $y^{[t]} = f(Wx^{[t]} + Ry^{[t-1]} + b)$. Similarly, a Recurrent Highway Network (RHN) layer has multiple highway layers in the recurrent state transition. RHN were first introduced in [4].

Let, $W_{H,T,C} \in R^{n \times m}$ and $R_{H_l,T_l,C_l} \in R^{n \times n}$ represent the weights matrices of the H nonlinear transform and the T and C gates at layer $l = 1, ..., L$. The biases are denoted by $b_{H_l,T_l,C_l} \in R^n$ and let $s_l$ denote a intermediate output at layer $l$ with $s_{[t_0]} = y^{[t-1]}$. Then an RHN layer with a recurrence depth of L is described by:

$$s_l^{[t]} = h_l^{[t]} * s_l^{[t]} + s_{l-1}^{[t]} * c_l^{[t]} \tag{1}$$

where

$$h_l^{[t]} = tanh(Wx^{[t]}I_{[l=1]} + R_{H_l} * s_l^{[t]} + b_{H_l}) \tag{2}$$

$$t_l^{[t]} = \sigma(Wx^{[t]}I_{[l=1]} + R_{T_l} * s_l^{[t]} + b_{T_l}) \tag{3}$$

$$c_l^{[t]} = tanh(Wx^{[t]}I_{[l=1]} + R_{C_l} * s_l^{[t]} + b_{C_l}) \tag{4}$$

and $I_{[l=1]}$ is the indicator function.

It is to be observed that a RHN layer with $L = 1$ is essentially a basic variant of an LSTM layer. The computation graph for a RHN block is illustrated in Fig. 2.

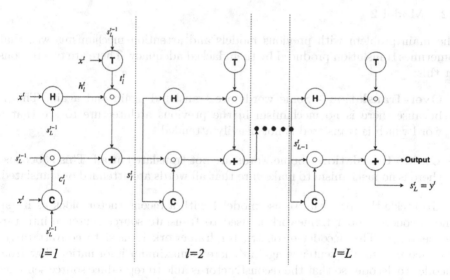

**Fig. 2.** Schematic showing computation within an RHN layer inside the recurrent loop. Vertical dashed lines delimit stacked Highway layers. Horizontal dashed lines imply the extension of the recurrence depth by stacking further layers. $H, T, C$ are the transformations described in Eqs. 2, 3 and 4, respectively [4].

# 4    Model

Many sequential processing tasks require complex nonlinear transition functions from one step to the next. However, recurrent neural networks with "deep" transition functions remain difficult to train, even when using Long Short-Term Memory (LSTM) networks as shown by [4,11]. We use existing neural machine translation models with recurrent highway networks(which extend the LSTM architecture to allow step-to-step transition depths larger than one) as their recurrent block.

## 4.1    Model 1

We propose a neural machine translation model using the recurrent highway network architecture given by [4], and we use encoder-decoder system on this architecture with attention as given by [3] as our two base models. We use RHN instead of LSTM to model conditional probability of target sentence given source.

## 4.2    Model 2

The main problem with previous models and attention mechanisms was that sometimes translation produced by them lacked adequacy. There are two reasons for this:

– **Over-Translation** - Some words are translated again and again. This is because there is no mechanism in the previous architecture to see that a word which is translated is not heavily attended.

– **Under-Translation** - Some words are not translated at all. This is because there is no mechanism to make sure that all words are attended or translated.

To tackle this problem we use model 1 with a reconstructor block as in [9]. The encoder-decoder framework is used to translate source sentence into target sentence. The decoder-reconstructor framework is used to convert target sentence into source sentence again. There is maximum information flow from encoder to decoder so that the reconstructor is able to reproduce source sentence from target sentence. By using reconstructor, model 2 tries to make sure that almost all source words are translated into target sentence so that reconstructor can reconstruct source words later. Thus, translation produced is fluent and adequate. We use RHN instead of LSTM to model conditional probability of target sentence given source and to model conditional probability of source sentence given target hidden states (in reconstructor block). The thing to be noted is that we use the reconstructor block only during training phase. During inference, we use the regular encoder-decoder framework without reconstructor block (Fig. 3). Unlike [9], we only use reconstructor in training phase and not during inference. The loss function used for training comprises of two terms, decoder loss and

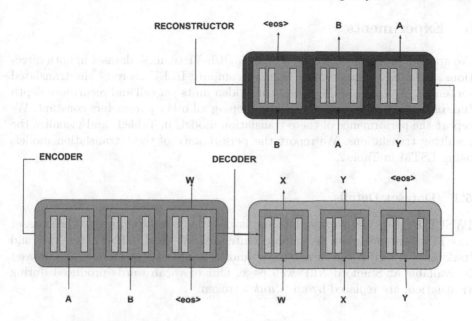

**Fig. 3.** Example of an reconstructor-based NMT system as described in [9]. Green blocks are part of reconstructor. For clarity, the embedding and projection layers are not shown in Figure. (Color figure online)

reconstructor loss. We train the neural network by minimizing two loss terms. The first term decoder loss $L_d$, is the log probability of a correct translation T given the source sentence S. So the training objective is

$$L_d = \frac{-1}{\|S\|} \sum_{(T,S)\in S} \log p(T/S) \tag{5}$$

The second term reconstructor loss $L_r$, is the log probability of a correct translation S given target hidden states H.

$$L_r = \frac{-1}{\|S\|} \sum_{(S,T)\in S} \log p(S/H) \tag{6}$$

where S is the training set. The final loss function is given by:

$$L = L_d + \beta * L_r \tag{7}$$

where $\beta$ is a hyperparameter which reflects the importance of reconstruction compared to translation task and should be tuned based on the dataset used.

# 5    Experiments

We applied our method on the IWSLT English-Vietnamese dataset in both directions. Reference sentences are used to compute BLEU score of the translated
sentences. We changed the number of hidden units per cell and recurrence depth
(no. of layer in each time step) while keeping all other parameters constant. We
report the performance of these translation models in Table 1, and visualize the
resulting translations. We report the performance of these translation models
using LSTM in Table 2.

## 5.1    Dataset Details

IWSLT English-Vietnamese data set is used for our experiment. The dataset
has $133k$ sentence pairs of training sentences. We used 'tst2012' (en—vi) and
'tst2013' (en—vi) as our development and test dataset respectively. The dataset
is available at Stanford NLP web page. Out of vocab words produced during
translation, are replaced by an '$<unk>$' token.

## 5.2    Evaluation Metrics

- Perplexity: In natural language processing, perplexity is a way of evaluating
  language models. A language model is a probability distribution over entire
  sentences or texts.

$$Perplexity = 2^{-\frac{1}{N}\sum_{n=1}^{N}\sum_{t=1}^{T} ln p_{target}} \tag{8}$$

- BLEU Score:BLEU [8], or the Bilingual Evaluation Understudy, is a score
  for comparing a candidate translation of text to one or more reference
  translations.

$$BLEU = min(1, \frac{output\_length}{reference\_length}) \sqrt[4]{(\prod_{i=1}^{4} precision_i)} \tag{9}$$

## 5.3    Training Details

- We have used SGD with a learning rate of 0.1.
- We have used a dropout of 20%.
- A batch size of 32 is used.
- Roughly all the experiments ran for 30 epochs.

**Table 1.** Test perplexity and BLEU score obtained on tst2013 test set with RHN as recurrent network. Source-English, Target-Vietnamese.

| Model | Depth | Layers | Hidden units | Test perplexity | Test BLEU |
|---|---|---|---|---|---|
| Model 1 and greedy search | 3 | 1 | 128 | 15.82 | 21.8 |
| Model 1 and greedy search | 3 | 1 | 256 | 12.56 | 23.1 |
| Model 2 with $\beta = 1$ and greedy search | 2 | 2 | 128 | 14.24 | 22.0 |
| Model 2 with $\beta = 1$ and greedy search | 2 | 2 | 256 | 14.98 | 22.6 |
| Model 2 with $\beta = 1$ and greedy search | 2 | 2 | 512 | 14.97 | 22.9 |
| Model 2 with $\beta = 0.5$ and greedy search | 2 | 2 | 128 | 14.38 | 22.8 |
| Model 2 with $\beta = 0.5$ and greedy search | 2 | 2 | 256 | 12.46 | 23.4 |
| Model 2 with $\beta = 0.5$ and greedy search | 2 | 2 | 512 | 15.46 | 22.5 |
| Model 2 with $\beta = 0.1$ and greedy search | 2 | 2 | 256 | 12.41 | 24.0 |
| Model 2 with $\beta = 0.1$ and beamsearch (bw=10) | 2 | 2 | 256 | 11.98 | 24.9 |
| Model 2 $\beta = 0.1$ and greedy search | 7 | 1 | 256 | 12.29 | 23.9 |
| Luong attention model with LSTM as in paper [10] | – | – | – | – | 23.3 |

**Table 2.** Test perplexity and BLEU score obtained on tst2013 test set with LSTM as recurrent network, $\beta = 0.1$ and 256 hidden units. Source-English, Target-Vietnamese.

| Model | Test perplexity | Test BLEU |
|---|---|---|
| Reconstructor model, with greedy search [9] | 13.31 | 22.3 |
| Reconstructor model,with beam search (bw = 10) [9] | 11.45 | 23.4 |
| Attention model, layers = 1 with greedy search | 13.52 | 22.1 |
| Attention model, layers = 2 with greedy search | 12.07 | 23.1 |

## 5.4   Sample Translations

A few example translations produced by our model 1 and model 2 along with the reference sentences are shown in Table 3. From this randomly picked sample it is visible that, NMT2 avoids problems of over translation as seen in NMT1. Now we check the translation of the randomly picked sentences for recurrence depth 3 and 4 in Table 4. From this randomly picked sample it is visible that, increasing the recurrence depth helps to capture the semantics of the language better.

**Table 3.** Translation of randomly picked sentences with Model 1 and Model 2.

| Ref | I even went through an identity crisis |
|---|---|
| NMT1 | I &apos;ve experienced a crisis crisis of my origins |
| NMT2 | I experienced the crisis of my origins |
| Ref | Where am I from? Who am I? |
| NMT1 | Where do I come from? And I m one person? |
| NMT2 | Where am I coming from? Who am I? |
| Ref | Ông là ông ca tôi |
| NMT1 | Ông là tôi |
| NMT2 | Ông là ông tôi |

**Table 4.** Translation of randomly picked sentences with 128 hidden units and recurrence depth 3 and 4 without reconstructor.

| Ref | When I was little, I thought my country was the best on the planet, and I grew up singing a song called "Nothing To Envy" |
|---|---|
| Depth-3 | When I was a little bit, I thought, "Can see this country is the best country in the world and I often sing "what I can't envy" |
| Depth-4 | When I was a little boy, I think $<unk>$ is the best country in the world and I often sing "We doesn't have to envy" |
| Ref | Since my family couldn't understand Chinese, I thought my family was going to be arrested |
| Depth-3 | Because my family didn't understand Mandarin, so I thought they would be arrested |
| Depth-4 | Because my family didn't know Chinese, so I thought they would be arrested |

## 5.5  Model Analysis

To check how good our model is learning with the change of layers i.e. recurrence depth, we plot the training perplexity of the model 1 with different number of recurrence depth.

**Table 5.** Number of parameters in reconstructor model.

| Recurrent unit | No of hidden units | Parameters (in millions) |
|---|---|---|
| LSTM with layers = 2 | 128 | 1.2 |
| RHNN with layers = 1, depth = 2 | 128 | 0.6 |
| LSTM with layers = 2 | 256 | 4.4 |
| RHNN with layers = 1, depth = 2 | 256 | 2.1 |
| RHNN with layers = 2, depth = 2 | 256 | 4.1 |
| RHNN with layers = 1, depth = 7 | 256 | 2.1 |

GLOBAL STEPS VS PERPLEXITY PLOT FOR DIFFERENT RECURRENCE DEPTH

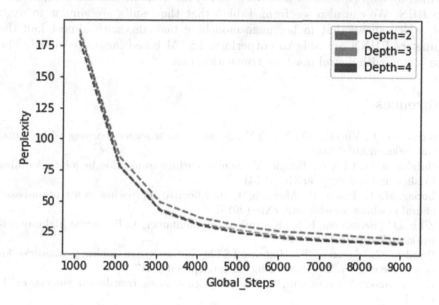

**Fig. 4.** Perplexity vs. number of tensorflow steps.

It can be seen that, there is a visible difference in the curve when we change depth from 2 to 3, and a bit less difference when we change from 3 to 4. Perplexity decreases with the increment of recurrence depth (Fig. 4). As we can see in Table 5, RHNN models have less number of parameters as compared to LSTM and are able to perform as good as LSTM models or in some cases even better.

## 6    Conclusion

We use Recurrent Highway Networks, a powerful new model designed to take advantage of increased depth in the recurrent transition while retaining the ease of training of LSTMs. Our model works reasonably well with the IWSLT English-Vietnamese dataset in terms of BLEU score. The model shows significant amount of increase in score when we increase the recurrence depth one layer at a time. The increasing trend is largely visible when we change from 2 to 3 layers, a bit less from 4 to 5 layers. It is almost negligible when we change the recurrence depth from 5 to 6. Hence, we claim in machine translation task, we get the advantage of increasing the recurrence depth, which is similar to the results as mentioned in [1]; regarding the stack depth of LSTM's. Also to further produce adequate translation, we use reconstructor model which also results in significant improvement. By using reconstructor block along with attention, we get improvement of almost 1 BLEU score compared to model without reconstruction. Also, we see that with beam search we were further able to improve translation and got improvement of around **1.5** BLEU score compared to benchmark result provided by [10]. [4] showed that deep LSTM are difficult to train compared to deep RHN. We can also see from Table 5 that the results are similar to work of [4] which shows that in language modelling task also with almost half the parameters RHNN are able to outperform LSTM based language model. The same is true with neural machine translation task.

# References

1. Sutskever, I., Vinyals, O., Le, Q.V.: Sequence to sequence learning with Neural Networks. arXiv (2014)
2. Bahdanau, D., Cho, K., Bengio, Y.: Neural machine translation by jointly learning to align and translate. arXiv (2014)
3. Luong, M.-T., Pham, H., Manning, C.D.: Effective approaches to attention-based neural machine translation. arXiv (2015)
4. Zilly, J.G., Srivastava, R.K., Koutník, J., Schmidhuber, J.: Recurrent highway networks. arXiv (2016)
5. Pundak, G., Sainath, T.: Highway-LSTM and recurrent highway networks for speech recognition. In: Proceedings of Interspeech (2017)
6. Kalchbrenner, N., Blunsom, P.: Recurrent continuous translation models. arXiv (2013)
7. Koehn, P., Och, F.J., Marcu, D.: Statistical phrase-based translation. In: NAACL (2003)
8. Papineni, K., Roukos, S., Ward, T., Zhu, W.-J.: BLEU: a method for automatic evaluation of machine translation. In: ACL (2002)
9. Tu, Z., Liu, Y., Shang, L., Liu, X., Li, H.: Neural machine translation with reconstruction. In: AAAI (2017)
10. Luong, M.-T., Manning, C.D.: Stanford neural machine translation systems for spoken language domains. arxiv (2015)
11. Pascanu, R., Gülçehre, Ç., Cho, K., Bengio, Y.: How to construct deep recurrent neural networks. CoRR abs/1312.6026 (2013)

# A Comparative Study of Methods Used in the Analysis and Prediction of Financial Data

Ioana Angela Socaci[✉] and Camelia Lemnaru

Technical University of Cluj-Napoca, Cluj-Napoca, Romania
ioana.socaci@student.utcluj.ro, Camelia.Lemnaru@cs.utcluj.ro

**Abstract.** The main goal of this paper is to present a complete pipeline solution to the problem of forecasting financial data - the closing price of two stock indices. Firstly, we explore wavelet decomposition as a powerful method for reducing noise. In the second step we analyze several approaches for feature extraction. For the final phase we consider two prediction models based on long short-term memory cells -single layer and stacked-, together with a deep feed-forward neural network architecture. Our focus is on the second and third pipeline stages, for which we compare and discuss different strategies. We are concerned with emphasizing the differences in performance for recurrent and feed-forward neural networks respectively. Also, we analyze the effect of adding a higher order feature extraction phase before prediction, and compare stacked auto-encoders to principal component analysis in this sense.

**Keywords:** Stock indices · Feature extraction · Prediction

## 1 Introduction

The aim of this study is to compare several approaches that can be used at different levels of a pipeline architecture for financial data analysis -stock index data. There are three key issues that are addressed within the pipeline: identifying and reducing noise, reducing the dimension of the input data by extracting more abstract features and predicting one step ahead the closing price value of two stock indices (Hang Seng and S&P500 [5]) given an amount of previous information.

In the following section we present several approaches proposed in the literature that try to solve similar problems – financial data forecasting. We continue with a description of our approach, which may consider wavelet decomposition for noise reduction, different strategies for high order feature extraction, and also several different prediction architectures: Long Short-Term Memory – LSTM (single layered, or stacked), together with simple feed forward neural networks. In the evaluation section we present the metrics for analyzing the performance of the proposed models, the results we obtained and conclusions regarding the best neural network architectures.

© Springer Nature Switzerland AG 2018
A. Groza and R. Prasath (Eds.): MIKE 2018, LNAI 11308, pp. 309–320, 2018.
https://doi.org/10.1007/978-3-030-05918-7_28

## 2    Related Work

Most solutions for stock index prediction employ a processing pipeline consisting of: noise elimination, high order feature extraction and a prediction stage. Several approaches can be found in literature for each stage.

### 2.1    Noise Removal

The authors of [1] propose an auto-regression statistical approach to predict financial data. Two de-noising methods are proposed for time series data pre-processing: forward-backward non-linear filter (FBF) and wavelet-based de-noising. The two filters are evaluated via the auto-regression model's fit rate and the approximate entropy method. Results show that filtering improves prediction performance. For example, the fit rate is 0.3754% using the unfiltered signal and with approximation 99% for the filtered data (with both filtering methods).

The Auto-Correlation Function (ACF) [9] computes the degree of correlation between time series observations of a variable. It can be computed for different lags and it can be used for white noise identification. For example, a lag of value 1 represents the correlation between this observation and the precedent one. The values of the function range from −1 to 1: we can have negative, positive or no correlation between observations. If for at least one lag value, a certain threshold is surpassed regardless of it being positive or negative, then we may consider that there is correlation between the observations, otherwise we deal with random data.

### 2.2    Principal Component Analysis for Feature Extraction

In [2], the authors present an Artificial Neural Network (ANN) architecture for financial forecasting, based on wavelets and Principal Component Analysis (PCA). The paper proposes three architectures. The first model (WPCA-NN) uses wavelets to de-noise Open, High, Low, Close (OHLC) prices, and applies PCA on OHL to obtain a single component. The second model (WNN) omits to apply PCA, while the last model (NN) does no pre-processing operation before the data is fed into the neural network. The paper shows that using wavelet transform in combination with PCA as pre-processing steps enhances performance of prediction model.

In [3], the authors propose a financial time series forecasting architecture that involves PCA, Affinity Propagation clustering (AP) and nested k-Nearest Neighbor regression (NkNN) – PANK model. It uses time series data consisting of relative returns obtained from the closing prices of CSI300 stock index. The evaluation metric is Hit Rate (HR) – an average over the number of correctly predicted relative returns. By considering PCA, the performance is improved: the PANK model obtains the best HR of 0.8, over 0.68 and 0.74 for kNN and AP+NkNN, respectively.

### 2.3  Auto–Encoder (AE) Based Approaches for Feature Extraction

The authors of [4] propose a deep neural network of Stacked Auto-encoders (SAEs) for obtaining high-level features from the available data. The focus of the research is on Stacked De-noising Auto-Encoders (SDAEs), for which the decoder error is minimized in the presence of corrupted input data. The architecture contains five AEs, the first being overcomplete and the next ones undercomplete. The more compact features obtained in last layer are input to a logistic regression model that predicts a rising or falling of the stock index.

Another solution is proposed in [5], where the authors present a complete pipeline for stock index prediction, based on deep learning. The methods used in each of the three main phases of the pipeline are: wavelets for de-noising (W), SAEs for deep feature extraction and Long Short-Term Memory (LSTM) based neural network for the one-step ahead prediction phase. In the last phase a simple Recurrent Neural Network (RNN) is also considered, for comparison reasons. Experiments are conducted on a series of stock indices for the following architectures: WSAEs-LSTM (main), WLSTM, LSTM and RNN. Evaluation is done in terms of predictive accuracy and profitability. Results indicate that WSAE-LSTM architecture outperforms the others. For example, Mean Average Percentage Error shows four times better results for WSAEs-LSTM (0.016) than for a simple RNN (0.075) during experiments carried on year six.

### 2.4  Non-recurrent Models for Stock Index Prediction

The authors of [6] propose a deep feed-forward neural network architecture for predicting stock indices. The authors employ windowing [6], with a window size of 10, meaning that data from the past 10 days $(n-1, ..., n-10)$ is used as input to the network, to predict the $n + t^{th}$ day's closing price. Due to the high input dimension, multi-core processing is employed using Hogwild algorithm [11], as parallelization method. This way, cores handle different data subsets. The evaluation is performed considering profitability and prediction performance metrics. The results obtained suggest that, the farther in the future the predicted day is, the higher the generalization error.

### 2.5  Long Short–Term Memory (LSTM) Based Models for Stock Index Prediction

In [7], the authors propose two LSTM based approaches for stock market prediction: an LSTM with embedded layer (ELSTM) and an LSTM with an automatic encoder (AELSTM). The concept of "stock vector", representing multiple historical stocks, is introduced too. The ELSTM model obtains the stock vector (for input dimension reduction) from an embedded layer. This vector is then fed into a three-layer LSTM network, that ends with a regression layer predicting the direction (up or down) of the stock index. AELSTM uses automatic encoder for obtaining the stock vector. In order to overcome the weight initialization issue - large values are prone to fall into a local optimum, while small values would slow down the training process -, continuous restricted Boltzman machine (CRBM) is introduced - initial weights are learned every two layers. Evaluation is done from two perspectives: Mean Squared Error (MSE) when predicting the stock index value, accuracy when ups and downs of the index are predicted. From the evaluated architectures, the authors find that LSTM based models have about 10% higher accuracy and MSE reaches minimum values. Moreover, the embedded layer approach outperforms the other.

Another solution is described in [8]. The authors compare LSTM and Support Vector Machine (SVM) performance for different stocks forecasting, by including various pre-processing techniques after normalization - PCA, Independent Component Analysis (ICA), Partial Least Squares (PLS). The LSTM architecture includes dropout layers to prevent overfitting. The SVM approach uses a radius basis function as kernel for solving the nonlinear classification problem. The prediction is represented by the next day closing price, given an amount of past information. Results indicate as best performers the models involving pre-processing techniques PCA and PLS, while LSTM is found to perform best on low volatility stocks.

## 3   Basic Pipeline

We consider three main processing stages for time series stock index prediction: noise elimination, high-order feature extraction and a prediction model. Our main purpose is to compare different approaches that can be used within the second and third pipeline stages (as seen in Fig. 1). Additionally, we want to show the role of each phase in implementing a robust solution to the considered problem – the prediction of one-step ahead closing prices for stock indices. Figure 1 shows the order of the described pipeline stages together with some intermediate steps that occur within the pipeline. We proceed with a short discussion of those additional steps.

We already described the method for identifying noise in the previous section (ACF). Another auxiliary step used within the mentioned pipeline involves scaling of data. Scaling data is important in situations in which we deal with multivariate time series, where variables belong to different ranges. If not scaled, it may alter the learning process; higher scale variables may shadow the lower scale variables, even though the later have same or even greater importance to the final prediction. So, we have to bring the data values to a common range in order to avoid such negative effects.

### 3.1   Dataset Description

We use the dataset from [5]. It contains observations of multiple stock indices, but we consider just Hang Seng and S&P500 stock indices. For Hang Seng index, daily observations are in the interval 2008-07-02 up to 2016-09-30, while for S&P index they start from 2008-07-01 up to 2016-09-30. We consider a division of the datasets with the following percentages: 70% of data is used for training, 10% is

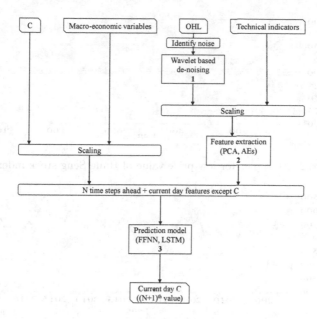

**Fig. 1.** Pipeline stages

used for validation and 20% in testing. The data contains as features the OHLC variables, a series of technical indicators and two macro-economic variables that were introduced in [5], amounting to a total of 19 features.

## 3.2 Noise Elimination

In the case of financial time series, noise elimination is considered necessary because of the presence of outliers and/or white noise, which may prevent a neural network from generalizing well. We have chosen to apply wavelet transform in order to emphasize their effectiveness in signal decomposition and noise elimination.

We mentioned before that the ACF can be used to determine whether there is white noise within the time series. Based on that, Fig. 2 shows the plot of this function on the Low Price variable of the Hang Seng stock index dataset. This way, we can conclude that the correlation between the observations decreases in time. This behavior starts to be seen from a lag of approximately 200, meaning that observations at a distance of 200 do not correlate too much with each other. Nevertheless, we may state that the Low Price variable observations are strongly correlated, as close observations actually relate.

Starting from this we show how discrete wavelet transform (DWT) can be applied on the OHL values of a stock index. Our discussion is limited to DWT because we are dealing with a set of samples, discrete values (which are part of the considered time series data). The DWT implementation that we assume in this paper is the one introduced by Mallat [13]. Figure 3 illustrates the original Low

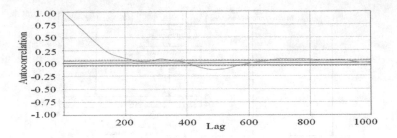

**Fig. 2.** ACF plot for low price value of Hang Seng stock index

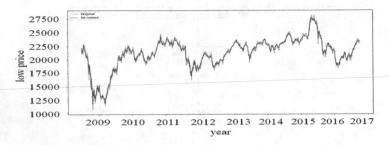

**Fig. 3.** Low price variable de-noised

Price variable, and the one reconstructed after applying the wavelet transform. We observe that only small portions of the original signal are smoothed – this way several time series components, such as trend, are more easily identified.

One of the important parameters to be considered when employing wavelets is the type of mother wavelet. For this study we have tried to use Haar and Daubechies [12]. The last one presents more vanishing moments, meaning that functions represented by the father wavelet can be more complex. In this sense, we found that Daubechies mother wavelet with 2 vanishing moments best suits our data. As we rely on a discrete sample dataset, we need to limit the number of decomposition levels, used in Mallat's algorithm, based on the N considered observations. We use the following formula for finding the number of decomposition levels:

$$round(\log_2{(N/W\ dec\_len - 1)}), \tag{1}$$

W dec_len - length of the decomposition filter associated with the mother wavelet.

Since the result of DWT consists in detail (high frequency components) and approximation (low frequency components) coefficients, and assuming that noise is accumulated in the high frequency components, some of the detail coefficients are cut off through thresholding. The method we employ to achieve this is known as universal thresholding [10]:

$$TUV = \sqrt{2\log{NL}}, \tag{2}$$

N - number of samples, L - decomposition levels.

### 3.3   High-Order Feature Extraction

In this pipeline stage we use different approaches to extract features from the raw data. One of the main reasons for introducing this processing unit is to obtain a higher level of abstraction from the available input variables. Moreover, we want to explore whether applying this step on financial data would imply a better generalization - meaning better performance on the test data - obtained by the prediction model. Previous research has shown that auto-encoder (AE) based approaches [5] are effective in obtaining an approximation of the existent features. We also consider Principal Component Analysis (PCA) as a second approach.

One of the main issues that we try to solve concerns finding an appropriate architecture for AE. We have considered several prototypes described in the literature: deep AEs (DAEs), stacked AEs (SAEs), and the simple – one hidden layer – AE. A relevant aspect to be mentioned is that the effectiveness of a particular architecture is data dependent, so we have to identify the most appropriate configuration for our particular datasets.

We continue our discussion with the key parameters that have to be modeled when training AEs. For DAEs, we need the number of encoding layers, the dimension of the code layer, and dimension of the intermediate layers (between input-code layer and between code-output layer) – from layer to layer we reduce dimension by 2 up to code layer. Those are dependent mainly on the input dimension, and type of data (in this case data belonging to different stock indices). Having too few or too many neurons within a layer degrades the training performance. Through our experiments and observations we can formulate that the code layer has to be somewhere close to half the input dimension, to have good results.

Similarly, we consider SAEs. In this case, we train separately several AEs, then stack them (the output of the code layer from one AE represents input to the next one). Lastly, we fine-tune the stack of AEs by attaching an output layer equal to the dimension of the input. Regarding the dimension of the code layer of each AE, the same substitution applies as for DAEs.

In addition to the various AE based models, we chose to explore also PCA, as one of the most prominent approaches for dimensionality reduction, by capturing the directions in which features exert most variation and building a set of components (new data features) from those. PCA can be seen as a linear AE.

### 3.4   Prediction Model

In the final pipeline stage we explore different deep learning approaches for the prediction stage of our pipeline, including recurrent and non-recurrent models.

We use several neural network architectures that involve Long Short-Term Memory (LSTM) cells, using either a single layer of LSTM cells, or a stack of LSTM (S-LSTM) layers. As with AEs, we find through experiments the best parameters for those architectures (how many layers to stack, how many memory

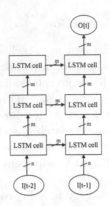

**Fig. 4.** S-LSTM, 3 layers, I[t]/O[t] - input/output representing observation at time t, n - input dimension, m - LSTM cell output dimension

cells to consider etc.). Figure 4 illustrates the architecture of a S-LSTM, with three stacked layers of two LSTM cells.

An LSTM cell can be seen as a collection of multiple simple neural networks (input, output, forget gate and cell state) for which we have to consider dimension of their output layer. We mention that an auxiliary layer (independent of the LSTM model) receives the current day features and is merged with the output layer of the LSTM. The result is input to an additional one element (neuron) layer – because our network predicts only one value (closing price).

We emphasize the power of recurrent neural networks when dealing with temporal data sequences – LSTM networks, specifically – through comparison with a Feed-Forward Neural Network (FFNN) architecture on which we apply the windowing technique [6]. This approach is used as baseline, and we expect recurrent neural networks, and specifically LSTM cells (capable of memorizing long term dependencies by keeping track of the entire context through the use of a cell state layer) to represent a powerful improvement for sequential data prediction over FFNNs with windowing.

## 4    Evaluation

The loss function that we try to optimize during the learning process is Mean Squared Logarithmic Error (MSLE). It represents a version of the Mean Squared Error (MSE) function which does not penalize large differences between the actual and predicted value when both of them are large. Nevertheless, since our data is scaled between 0 and 1 before being given to the neural networks, this metric behaves similarly with the MSE in our case. We use MSE together with the Mean Absolute Error (MAE) as metrics to evaluate the performance of our predictions.

## 4.1 Evaluation of AE Based Approaches

Table 1 illustrates the results of the best configurations of DAE, AE and SAE. For Hang Seng, these results were achieved by a DAE having a code layer of size 8 and the first intermediate layer of size 10, the AE having a code layer size of 10, and the SAE using 2 pre-trained AEs each with a code layer size of 8. For S&P500, the DAE has a code layer of size 10, the first intermediate layer dimension being 12, the AE uses a code layer of size 8, while the SAE has 2 stacked AEs, each with a code layer of size 10.

**Table 1.** Performance of AEs based approaches, given by several error metrics

| StockIndex | DAE | | | AE | | | SAE | | |
|---|---|---|---|---|---|---|---|---|---|
| | MSLE | MSE | MAE | MSLE | MSE | MAE | MSLE | MSE | MAE |
| Hang Seng | 0.00166 | 0.00365 | 0.04570 | 0.00174 | 0.00432 | 0.05106 | 0.00197 | 0.00454 | 0.05378 |
| S&P500 | 0.00141 | 0.00349 | 0.04426 | 0.00139 | 0.00338 | 0.04401 | 0.00179 | 0.00424 | 0.04817 |

Taking into account that we use 16 features as input to the AEs (we exclude closing price and the two macro-economic variables), we can emphasize the already mentioned aspect, that an appropriate code layer size is close to half the dimension of the input. If we compare the loss function results, even though they are quite similar, we obtained slightly better performance for the AE, in the case of S&P500 index, while for Hang Seng index best architecture is the DAE.

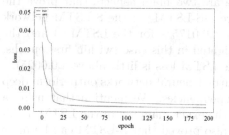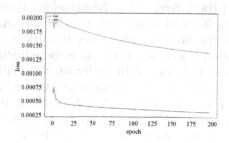

**Fig. 5.** SAE (left), AE (right) loss results for last 200 epochs (validation-yellow, train-blue) – S&P500 index (Color figure online)

Figure 5 illustrates loss function evolution of last 200 epochs on both training and validation dataset, for the AE and SAE best architectures of S&P500 index. We specify that training was carried on 400 epochs, out of which 200 epochs were considered for fine-tuning, in the case of the SAE. We can observe that the fine-tuning step of the SAE starts at an error of ≈0.05, while the AE error at the end of the 200 epoch is ≈0.02. Even though AE's error is not improved too much for the last 200 epochs, it comes with the advantage that has converged faster, so after 400 epochs AE architecture is better than SAE one.

## 4.2    Evaluation of Prediction Models

We use same loss function for training the prediction models - MSLE. In addition to the already presented metrics, we also employ Mean Absolute Percentage Error (MAPE). It is an important metric since its value is independent of the scale of the results. Its main drawback comes from the fact that it cannot be used in situations that deal with zero data values (as it was the case for the feature extraction models). The results for the LSTM, S-LSTM and FFNN best performing configurations are presented in Table 2.

**Table 2.** The performance achieved by the various prediction models, measured by different error metrics

| Stock Index | LSTM | | | | S-LSTM | | | | FFNN | | | |
|---|---|---|---|---|---|---|---|---|---|---|---|---|
| | MSLE | MSE | MAE | MAPE | MSLE | MSE | MAE | MAPE | MSLE | MSE | MAE | MAPE |
| Hang Seng | 0.0003 | 0.0008 | 0.0207 | 0.8895 | 0.0002 | 0.0006 | 0.0178 | 0.7630 | 0.0013 | 0.0035 | 0.0449 | 2.33 |
| S&P500 | 0.0024 | 0.0049 | 0.0553 | 0.9764 | 0.0020 | 0.0045 | 0.0529 | 0.9323 | 0.0030 | 0.0082 | 0.0694 | 2.56 |

For the Hang Seng index, the LSTM model uses 2 LSTM cells, each cell with an output of dimension 12, the S-LSTM model contains 3 layers each of 2 LSTM cells with same output dimension, the FFNN is composed of 3 hidden layers of dimension 12 and the window size of 7. For S&P500, the best configurations are the same, with the exception of S-LSTM, that needs only 2 layers of LSTM cells.

Convergence is reached fast by both LSTM and S-LSTM best architectures of Hang Seng index. Nevertheless, there are two main aspects that prove the efficiency of a more complex architecture – S-LSTM – : the S-LSTM network starts with a smaller error ($\approx$0.016 over $\approx$0.0175 – for the LSTM –) and the abrupt decrease of the loss is more highlighted in this case (within first epochs, S-LSTM loss is little under $\approx$0.002, while LSTM loss is little above $\approx$0.0025).

From Table 2 we can deduce that recurrent neural networks outperform deep FFNNs when we deal with temporal dependencies. We mention that using a window size equal to 2, which would be the exact mapping of the LSTM architecture produces irrelevant results. It is also proved that S-LSTM can be more efficient than single layer LSTM architectures.

## 4.3    Complete Pipeline Results

In this section we show the results of the complete pipeline. The key aspects that we are concerned about are: whether using feature extraction methods can improve the overall performance of our best prediction models and what is the best approach for feature extraction – PCA or AEs. To that end, we consider for each stock index: the best AE architecture – DAE, SAE or AE –, the best prediction model –LSTM, S-LSTM or FFNN –, assemble them together and most importantly – consider various experiments on the same architecture.

**Table 3.** Performance achieved by the complete pipeline and statistical results of the S-LSTM prediction model, for several error metrics

| Stock Index | AE+S-LSTM | | | | S-LSTM statistics | | | | PCA+S-LSTM | | | |
|---|---|---|---|---|---|---|---|---|---|---|---|---|
| | MSLE | MSE | MAE | MAPE | MSLE | MSE | MAE | MAPE | MSLE | MSE | MAE | MAPE |
| Hang Seng | 0.0004 | 0.0008 | 0.0208 | 1.04 | 0.0004 | 0.0008 | 0.0216 | 1.09 | 0.0075 | 0.013 | 0.0801 | 3.73 |
| S&P500 | 0.0014 | 0.004 | 0.051 | 1.96 | 0.0018 | 0.0044 | 0.0511 | 1.88 | 0.0011 | 0.0031 | 0.043 | 1.64 |

The results are presented in Table 3. For either of the stock indices, we can observe that the addition of feature extraction phase improves best prediction model's performance. Regarding whether PCA or AE based approaches perform better is a matter of the data we use. From our experiments it can be seen that AEs give significantly better results than PCA, for the Hang Seng index (MSLE = 0.00038 for AE approach, while MSLE = 0.00751 for PCA). A plot of the prediction (red line) and the original data (green line) is illustrated in Fig. 6. In this case, using PCA even degrades the performance of the prediction. Nevertheless, for S&P500 index the opposite situation occurs, PCA performs better, even though in this case the results are not so different from the AE based approach – which also produces an improvement of the prediction.

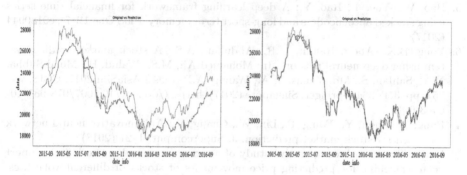

**Fig. 6.** Prediction results of PCA+S-LSTM (left) and AE+S-LSTM (right) – Hang Seng index closing price (Color figure online)

## 5    Conclusions

The objective of this paper was to provide a comparative study of different deep learning approaches that can be used at different levels within a pipeline for analyzing financial data. We show the effectiveness of wavelets in approximating time series variables and reducing noise if necessary (in our case variables did not exhibit too much randomness). Then, we present different AE based architectures for extracting features from the available data and we show that LSTM based approaches exhibit high prediction power in financial data analysis.

Summing up the results, it can be concluded that introducing the feature extraction phase improves prediction performance – by having a smaller set of features without redundancy. Also, the decision regarding the feature extraction approach is highly dependent on the type of data. In this sense, we can state that AEs generally represent a more stable approach than PCA – AEs show promising results for both types of indices, while PCA behaves differently for a different type of data.

# References

1. Leng, J.: Modelling and Analysis on Noisy Financial Time Series. Scientific Research Publishing, Wuhan (2014)
2. M'ng, J., Mehralizadeh, M.: Forecasting East Asian indices futures via a novel hybrid of wavelet-PCA denoising and artificial neural network models. PloS One **11**(6), e0156338 (2016)
3. Tang, L., Pan, H., Yao, Y.: PANK-a financial time series prediction model integrating principal component analysis, affinity propagation clustering and nested k-nearest neighbor regression. J. Interdiscip. Math. **21**(3), 717–728 (2018)
4. Li, J., Liu, G., Yeung, H., Yin, J., Chung, Y., Chen, X.: A novel stacked denoising autoencoder with swarm intelligence optimization for stock index prediction. In: 2017 International Joint Conference on Neural Networks (IJCNN), pp. 1956–1961 (2017)
5. Bao, W., Yue, J., Rao, Y.: A deep learning framework for financial time series using stacked autoencoders and long-short term memory. PloS One **12**(7), e0180944 (2017)
6. Yong, B.X., Abdul Rahim, M.R., Abdullah, A.S.: A stock market trading system using deep neural network. In: Mohamed Ali, M.S., Wahid, H., Mohd Subha, N.A., Sahlan, S., Md. Yunus, M.A., Wahap, A.R. (eds.) AsiaSim 2017. CCIS, vol. 751, pp. 356–364. Springer, Singapore (2017). https://doi.org/10.1007/978-981-10-6463-0_31
7. Pang, X., Zhou, Y., Wang, P., Lin, W., Chang, V.: An innovative neural network approach for stock market prediction. J. Supercomput. 1–21 (2018)
8. Li, Z., Tam, V.: A comparative study of a recurrent neural network and support vector machine for predicting price movements of stocks of different volatilites. In: 2017 IEEE Symposium Series on Computational Intelligence (SSCI), pp. 1–8. IEEE (2017)
9. Wei, W.: Time series analysis. In: The Oxford Handbook of Quantitative Methods in Psychology, vol. 2 (2006)
10. Cohen, R.: Signal denoising using wavelets. Project Report, Department of Electrical Engineering Technion, Israel Institute of Technology, Haifa (2012)
11. Recht, B., Re, C., Wright, S., Niu, F.: Hogwild: a lock-free approach to parallelizing stochastic gradient descent. In: Advances in Neural Information Processing Systems, pp. 693–701 (2011)
12. Misiti, M., Misiti, Y., Oppenheim, G., Poggi, J.: Wavelet Toolbox, vol. 15, p. 21. The MathWorks Inc., Natick (1996)
13. Mallat, S.: A theory for multiresolution signal decomposition: the wavelet representation. IEEE Trans. Pattern Anal. Mach. Intell. **11**, 674–693 (1989)

# Skin Lesion Images Segmentation: A Survey of the State-of-the-Art

Adegun Adekanmi Adeyinka[✉] and Serestina Viriri

School of Maths, Statistics and Computer Science,
University of KwaZulu-Natal, Durban, South Africa
218082884@stu.ukzn.ac.za, viriris@ukzn.ac.za

**Abstract.** This paper presents a detailed and robust survey of the state-of-the-art algorithms and techniques for performing skin lesion segmentation. The approach used is the comparative analysis of the existing methods for skin lesion analysis, critical review of the performance evaluation of some recently developed algorithms for skin lesion images segmentation, and the study of current evaluating metrics used for performance analysis. The study highlights merits and demerits of the algorithms examined, observing the strength and weakness of each algorithm. An inference can thus be made from the analysis about the best performing algorithms. It is observed that the advancement of technology and availability of a large and voluminous data set for training the machine learning algorithms encourage the application of machine learning techniques such as deep learning for performing skin lesion images segmentation. This work shows that most deep learning techniques outperform some existing state-of-the arts algorithm for skin lesion images segmentation.

**Keywords:** Segmentation · Skin lesion · Evaluation metrics
Deep learning

## 1 Introduction

The advancement in technology and rapid increase in the amount of computing resources such as graphical processing units (GPU) and memory sizes, and also the availability of voluminous medical imaging data set for training of machine learning algorithms has led to the rapid growth and wide acceptability of computer vision techniques for analysing medical imaging data. This has led to various researches being carried out in the development of algorithms and techniques for better diagnosis and prediction of diseases in the recent times. This work aims at performing a comparative analysis of various state-of-the-art techniques for performing segmentation of skin lesion images towards the detection of melanoma. Segmentation is a process of extracting the region of interest (ROI) of an image under analysis [1,2]. Skin lesion images which are being examined here can be described as a mole that results from the local proliferation of pigment cells also known as melanocytes and based on the colour from the skin

© Springer Nature Switzerland AG 2018
A. Groza and R. Prasath (Eds.): MIKE 2018, LNAI 11308, pp. 321–330, 2018.
https://doi.org/10.1007/978-3-030-05918-7_29

melanin, the skin lesion can be categorised into pigmented and non-pigmented while the pigmented can benign and the malignant. The benign are not harmful while the malignant are cancerous and harmful [3].

## 1.1   Image Segmentation

Segmentation is the fundamental task of the analysis of the skin lesion images for the discovery of melanoma that is the cancerous cells. This can be done through a thorough and proper examination of the lesion shapes, sizes, colours and textures. However, proper segmentation is difficult because of great varieties of the lesion shapes, sizes, colours and different types of skin textures with some lesions having irregular boundaries and in some cases there is smooth transition between the lesion and the skin. Melanoma becomes dangerous because of its ability to spread to other part of the body if not detected early.

Differentiating malignant and benign cases, as shown in Fig. 1 is a very difficult task even for experienced specialists, and the use of computing techniques and algorithms can be of a great assistance. The system always starts with pre-processing of images, that is the removing of undesired artefacts such as hair, freckles or shading effects. After the pre-processing comes the segmentation steps for the identification of the lesion boundaries [4]. The goal of segmentation is to cluster pixels in the melanoma suspicious regions of the skin lesions. This will further be subjected to analysis and prediction towards proper melanoma detection. Segmentation process involves classification of the skin lesion using their morphological structure, colour, fractal and texture properties [3].

Various techniques and operations such as thresholding, morphological analysis and texture detection have been used in the past to divide a digital image into individual objects to perform a separate analysis of each region [3].

In this study, the comparative analysis of some of these techniques and their performance using some known evaluation metrics is carried out. This work also studied the performance of various techniques used in the International Symposium on Biomedical Imaging (ISBI) challenge on "Skin Lesion Analysis towards Melanoma Detection" which was hosted by International Skin Imaging Collaboration (ISIC) 2017. The challenge was divided into three tasks namely: Segmentation of the lesion, features detection and classification of lesions as benign and malignant. The lesion segmentation process involves the automated localization of lesion areas in the form of binary masks [5]. The performance evaluation accuracies and some other evaluation metrics were taken for the techniques used. The result obtained is therefore analysed in this study.

## 2   Segmentation Algorithms and Techniques

There has been significant development in research for the development of segmentation algorithms and techniques for skin lesion analysis in the recent past. One of the most popular techniques uses a rule based on asymmetry, border

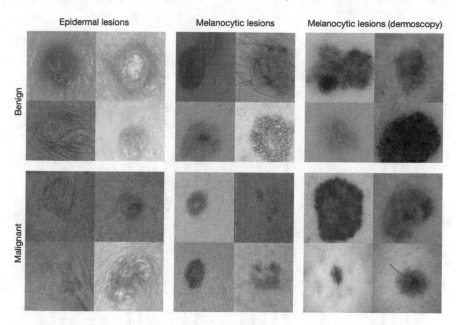

**Fig. 1.** Epidermal lesion, Melanocytic lesions and the Melanocytic lesions visualized with a dermoscope [29].

structure, variegated colour and dermatoscopical structures (ABCD). This rule has always been the basis for a diagnosis by dermatologist [6].

In the ABCD rule, asymmetry means the two sides do not match while they match for the symmetry. This can distinguish the benign from the malignant skin lesions. The border structure may also be even for benign and uneven for the malignant in most cases. The variegated color is always just one color in the case of Benign while the malignant always possess two or more colors. The general dermatoscopical structure are always very small like one-quarter inch for the benign while is always larger than that in the case of malignant. This rule has always been applied by many algorithms segmentation of skin lesions images towards the melanoma detection as it was derived from the rule commonly used by dermatologist for diagnosis of skin cancer [6].

The segmentation algorithms can be broadly classified into threshold-based, edge based or region-based methods, fused-based, Active contour-based and soft computing or Intelligence based segmentation. The comparison between these algorithms is shown in Table 1.

**Table 1.** Table showing comparison between algorithms commonly used for segmentation in the past

| Algorithm | Description | Advantages (Pros) | Disadvantages (Cons) |
|---|---|---|---|
| Edge-based segmentation | It performs the segmenting of an image based on the edges by searching for edge pixels and connecting them to form image contours. The method can be categorised into manual and automatic. Manual method uses mouse to trace lines that represent image boundaries among regions and automatic method uses edge detection filters such as Laplacian, Gaussian filter, watershed algorithm etc. [6] | Algorithms are usually less complex – Edges are important features in an image to separate regions Combination of results may often be a good idea | The results obtained can be influenced by noise levels, double edge generation, and inaccuracy in detection of borders etc. [5] |
| Region-based segmentation | Images are partitioned into regions or groups of similar pixel depending on their properties. The method employs the understanding that neighbouring pixels within the same region have same value. Each pixel is compared with its neighbours in a particular region and according to some certain condition, it is categorised [6,7] | Regions cover more pixels than edges and thus you have more information available in order to characterize your region –When detecting a region you could for instance use texture which is not easy when dealing with edges | The results can also be influenced by noise levels, double edge generation, and inaccuracy in detection |
| Threshold based segmentation | This can be described as point based or pixel based segmentation. Examples of the methods used include Otsu's thresholding, fuzzy logic8, Renyi's entropy, Adaptive thresholding etc. [6] | The advantage of the threshold method is that the calculation is simple and the operation speed is faster | The disadvantage is that it is difficult to obtain accurate results for image segmentation problems where there is no significant gray scale difference or a large overlap of the gray scale values in the image [10] |
| Intelligence based segmentation | This is the application of machine learning or soft computing techniques in segmentation process. Methods used include Co-operative Neural networks, Evolution Strategies, Fully Convolutional Residual Network, Convolutional Neural Networks etc. [5] | It has features such as adaptability, fault tolerance and optimal performance | A large amount of image data set will be required to train the algorithms |
| Fused-based segmentation | This uses the combination of two or more segmentation algorithms to produce a sophisticated segmentation for example combining thresholding with active contour [8,9] | Various thresholding methods can be combined in order to obtain the best thresholding method through threshold fusion | It has Complexity tendency and require higher computational resources |

# 3  Performance Evaluation Metrics for the State of the Arts Algorithms

This paper presents the performance evaluation of various image segmentation algorithms used on image data sets. The segmentation results are assessed by several metrics used for measuring the output quality of image segmentation algorithms. The following metrics are therefore commonly used for performance evaluation of the algorithms: Sensitivity, Specificity, Accuracy, Jaccard index, Dice coefficient and Average precision.

Four parameters are very important in getting the metrics stated above:

- True positives (TP)-when the prediction of an observation belonging to a class actually does belongs to that class in reality.
- True negatives (TN)-when the prediction of an observation not belonging to a class does not actually belong to that class in reality.
- False positives (FP)-occurs when the prediction that an observation belongs to a class when in reality it does not.
- False negatives (FN)-occurs when the prediction that an observation does not belong to a class when in reality it does.

These parameters are thus used to compute the aforementioned metrics as stated below:

- Precision: This is defined as the proportion of relevant examples that are true positives among all of the examples which were predicted to belong in a certain class. It is the proportion of predicted positives which are actual positive

$$\text{Precision} = \frac{TP}{TP + FP} \tag{1}$$

- Recall: This is defined as the proportion of examples which were predicted to belong to a class with respect to all of the examples that truly belong in the class.

$$\text{Recall} = \frac{TP}{TP + FN} \tag{2}$$

- Sensitivity: This proportion of actual positives which are predicted positive.

$$\text{Sensitivity} = \frac{TP}{TP + FN} \tag{3}$$

- Specificity: This is proportion of actual negative which are predicted negative

$$\text{Specificity} = \frac{TN}{TN + FP} \tag{4}$$

- Accuracy: This is defined as the percentage or proportion of correct predictions and it can be calculated by dividing the number of correct predictions by the number of total predictions

$$\text{Accuracy} = \frac{CorrectPredictions}{TotalPredictions} = \frac{TP + TN}{TP + TN + FP + FN} \tag{5}$$

- Jaccard index: The Jaccard index also known as Jaccard similarity index is a measure of similarity for the two sets of data and can be expressed as:

$$\text{Jaccard Index} = \frac{2 * TP}{2 * TP + FP + FN} \tag{6}$$

$$J(A, B) = \frac{|A \cap B|}{|A \cup B|} = \frac{|A \cap B|}{|A| + |B| - |A \cap B|}. \tag{7}$$

where $J(A, B)$ is Jaccard index $0 \leq J(A, B) \leq 1$.

- Jaccard distance: Jaccard similarity coefficient is used to calculate the similarity between finite sample sets, this is called the Jaccard distance:

$$d_J(A, B) = 1 - J(A, B) = \frac{|A \cup B| - |A \cap B|}{|A \cup B|}. \tag{8}$$

where $d_J(A, B)$ is the Jaccard distance $0 \leq d_J(A, B) \leq 1$.

- Dice coefficient: The Jaccard index is related to the Dice index according to:

$$\text{Dice Coefficient S} = \frac{2 * J}{(1 + J)} \tag{9}$$

$$\text{Dice Coefficient S} = \frac{2 * TP}{2 * TP + FP + FN} \tag{10}$$

It is important to note that high sensitivity and Specificity indicates high performance of a given method [3].

## 4  Performance Evaluation (Critical) Analysis of State-of-the-Arts Algorithms and Techniques Used in the ISBI Challenge for Skin Lesion Segmentation

Various algorithms have been developed and applied for segmentation of skin lesions in time past. This section captures the application of some algorithms and their performance on the segmentation of skin lesion image data sets of ISBI challenge 2017. The performance evaluation results of these algorithms is shown in Table 2.

Lin et al. [9] applied K-means clustering and ensemble of regressions for skin lesion segmentation. The results of the performance analysis of their algorithm was able to give the average score of 76.0% and 66.5% for Dice coefficient and Jaccard Index which shows that a reasonably high percentage of similarity and low level of diversity between the samples set of data used for their experiment. This algorithm does not perform well where there is high level of diversity in the sample set. The algorithm is sensitive to outliers.

Attia et al. [11] presented a proposed architecture for Recurrent Neural Networks (RNN) and Convolutional Neural Networks (CNN). Their method improves on fully convolutional neural networks (FCN and SegNet) that usually perform over-segmentation. This method tends to outperform some other state of the arts segmentation algorithms with a high sensitivity and specificity average of 95.4% and 94% showing higher rates of correct predictions but consumes high computational resources.

Wen [12] proposed a model called II-FCN that uses a lot of training methods with conditional random field technique to perform segmentation of the melanoma from dermoscopy image. Conditional random field was applied as a post processing method to fine-tune the final result. Their model can automatically segment melanoma at high jaccard index 82% and still keep learning from epoch to epoch. The conditional random field improve the jaccard index of trained data sets. The system however tries to manage overfitting.

Jahanifar et al. [13] introduced a proposed algorithm that uses supervised saliency detection method on dermoscopic images. The method was based on discriminative regional feature integration (DRFI) method. The system can easily be trained on small datasets and outperforms many systems with sensitivity and specificity of 82% and 97.8% showing higher rates of positive predictions. Increasing the number of trees increases the complexity of the system. Berseth et al. [14] proposed a U-Net architecture to provide a probability estimate for each pixel in the original image. They were able to get the average score Jaccard Index of 83% and does not really need conditional random field to improve the training images. It outperforms most of the state of the art segmentation algorithm but it requires a lot of data set to train.

Li [17] presented a framework consisting of multi-scale fully convolutional residual networks and a lesion index calculation unit (LICU). The performance analysis of their system was able to give them the average score of 78.9% and 97.5% for Sensitivity and Specificity. This shows a high rate of performance. The system requires high computation resources and very large data set for training. Dhanesh Ramachandram [16] used fully convolutional neural network for lesion segmentation trained in an end-to-end manner. It gave IOU (intersection over union) score of 64.2% for the validation set. This implies that the system can work very well with fairly dissimilar training and validation set but requires a lot of data to train and have a tendency of overfitting. Galdran et al. [18] applied the shades of gray color constancy technique to color-normalize the entire training set of images. This was used for training two deep convolutional neural networks with U-Net architecture for skin lesion segmentation and classification. This gives the average score of 81.3% and 96.8% for Sensitivity and Specificity. Chang [15] also used the U-Net architecture based neural network. The performance gives average scores of 81.2% and 95.1% for Sensitivity and Specificity but the system trains with low decreasing rate. Garcia-Arroyo et al. [20] proposed the use of Histogram thresholding combined with fuzzy classification for obtaining the segmentation mask from skin lesions. Their results of high average rate of 89.4% and 91.8% for Sensitivity and Specificity.

**Table 2.** The performance evaluation results for the various state of the arts algorithm for skin segmentation

| Techniques | Accuracy | Dice coefficient | Jaccard index | Sensitivity | Specificity |
|---|---|---|---|---|---|
| Fully convolutional-de-convolutional networks [21] | 0.934 | 0.849 | 0.765 | 0.825 | 0.975 |
| Deep convolutional networks [14] | 0.932 | 0.847 | 0.762 | 0.820 | 0.978 |
| Deep residual networks [22] | 0.934 | 0.844 | 0.760 | 0.802 | 0.985 |
| UNET deep learning [23] | 0.931 | 0.839 | 0.754 | 0.817 | 0.970 |
| Fully convolutional networks [27] | 0.930 | 0.837 | 0.752 | 0.813 | 0.976 |
| Discriminative regional feature integration (DRFI) [13] | 0.930 | 0.839 | 0.749 | 0.810 | 0.981 |
| Convolutional neural network (CNN) [18] | 0.922 | 0.824 | 0.735 | 0.813 | 0.968 |
| Deep learning network [17] | 0.922 | 0.810 | 0.718 | 0.789 | 0.975 |
| Thresholding and neural network [28] | 0.915 | 0.797 | 0.715 | 0.774 | 0.970 |
| Fully-convolutional residual networks and a lesion index calculation unit (LICU) [17] | 0.924 | 0.805 | 0.711 | 0.762 | 0.979 |
| II-FCN [12] | 0.910 | 0.795 | 0.697 | 0.790 | 0.982 |
| FCNN [24] | 0.917 | 0.774 | 0.684 | 0.784 | 0.950 |
| K-means clustering [10] | 0.900 | 0.774 | 0.679 | 0.779 | 0.962 |
| Fuzzy classification and Histogram thresholding [20] | 0.884 | 0.760 | 0.665 | 0.869 | 0.923 |
| Deep neural network [15] | 0.910 | 0.775 | 0.665 | 0.812 | 0.951 |
| Fuzzy classification and Histogram thresholding [25] | 0.899 | 0.737 | 0.644 | 0.710 | 0.977 |
| SDI algorithm Mario [19] | 0.857 | 0.697 | 0.592 | 0.692 | 0.937 |
| Hybrid deep learning [11] | 0.894 | 0.669 | 0.573 | 0.674 | 0.971 |
| CIELAB G [26] | 0.867 | 0.656 | 0.536 | 0.565 | 0.980 |
| Deep CNN [16] | 0.829 | 0.573 | 0.444 | 0.703 | 0.942 |

## 5    Conclusion

The study is a critical and analytical survey of the present state-of the-art techniques for performing segmentation of skin lesion images. Some set of algorithms were studied for their performance on skin lesion images. The evaluation techniques were also studied. Merits and demerits of these algorithms were also examined. A conclusion can be drawn from the analysis made, about the best performing algorithms. It was observed that the application of machine learning techniques such as deep learning for performing analysis of images gives a better performance in image analysis most especially in the segmentation process of skin lesions images.

## References

1. Celebi, M.E., et al.: A methodological approach to the classification of dermoscopy images. Comput. Med. Imaging Graph. **31**(6), 362–373 (2007)
2. Oliveira, R.B., Filho, M.E., Ma, Z., Papa, J.P., Pereira, A.S., Tavares, J.M.R.S.: Computational methods for the image segmentation of pigmented skin lesions: a review. Comput. Methods Programs Biomed. **131**, 127–141 (2016)

3. Okuboyejo, D.A., Olugbara, O.O.: A review of prevalent methods for automatic skin lesion diagnosis. Open Dermatol. J. **12**, 14–53 (2018)
4. Cavalcanti, P.G., Scharcanski, J.: Macroscopic pigmented skin lesion seg-mentation and its inuence on the lesion classication and diagnosis. In: Celebi, M., Schaefer, G. (eds.) Color Medical Image Analysis. Lecture Notes in Computational Vision and Biomechanics, vol. 6, pp. 15–39. Springer, Dordrecht (2013). https://doi.org/10.1007/978-94-007-5389-1_2
5. Pathan, S., Prabhu, K.G., Siddalingaswamy, P.C.: Techniques and algorithms for computer aided diagnosis of pigmented skin - a review. Biomed. Signal Process. Control **39**, 237–262 (2018)
6. Revathi, V., Chithra, A.: A review on segmentation techniques in skin lesion images. Int. Res. J. Eng. Technol. (2015). e-ISSN 2395-0056
7. Hsu, T.-Y., Fuh, C.-S.: Pedestrian Contour Detection Based on Image Segmentation, pp. 1–6 (2010)
8. Celebi, M.E., Iyatomi, H., Schaefer, G., Stoecker, W.V.: Lesion border detection in dermoscopy images. Comput. Med. Imaging Graph **33**(2), 148–153 (2010)
9. Lin, B.S., Michael, K., Kalra, S., Tizhoosh, H.R.: Skin lesion segmentation: U-Nets versus clustering. In: Proceedings of the IEEE Symposium Series on Computational Intelligence, SSCI 2017, pp. 1–7 (2018)
10. Alvarez, D., Iglesias, M.: k-Means clustering and ensemble of regressions: an algorithm for the ISIC 2017 skin lesion segmentation challenge. ArXiv preprint arXiv:1702.07333 (2017)
11. Attia, M., Hossny, M., Nahavandi, S., Yazdabadi, A.: Spatially aware melanoma segmentation using hybrid deep learning techniques. arXiv preprint arXiv:1702.07963 (2017)
12. Wen, H.: II-FCN for skin lesion analysis towards melanoma detection. In: ISIC 2017. https://arxiv.org/pdf/1702.08699.pdf. Accessed 13 Aug 2018
13. Jahanifar, M., Tajeddin, N.Z., Asl, B.M.: Supervised saliency map driven segmentation of the lesions in dermoscopic images. https://arxiv.org/ftp/arxiv/papers/1703/1703.00087.pdf. Accessed 13 Aug 2018
14. Berseth, M.: Skin lesion analysis towards melanoma detection. https://arxiv.org/ftp/arxiv/papers/1703/1703.00523.pdf. Accessed 13 Aug 2018
15. Chang, H.: Skin cancer reorganization and classification with deep neural network. https://arxiv.org/ftp/arxiv/papers/1703/1703.00534.pdf. Accessed 13 Aug 2018
16. Ramachandram, D., Devries, T.: LesionSeg: semantic segmentation of skin lesions using deep convolutional neural network. In: ISIC 2017. https://arxiv.org/pdf/1703.03372.pdf. Accessed 13 Aug 2018
17. Li, Y., Shen, L.: Skin lesion analysis towards melanoma detection using deep learning network. https://arxiv.org/ftp/arxiv/papers/1703/1703.00534.pdf. Accessed 13 Aug 2018
18. Galdran, A., Alvarez, A.: Data-driven color augmentation techniques for deep skin image analysis. https://arxiv.org/pdf/1703.03702.pdf. Accessed 13 Aug 2018
19. Guarracino, M.R., Maddalena, L.: Segmenting dermoscopic images. https://arxiv.org/pdf/1703.03186.pdf. Accessed 13 Aug 2018
20. Garcia-Arroyo, J.L., Garcia-Zapirain, B.: Segmentation of skin lesions based on fuzzy classification of pixels and histogram thresholding. https://arxiv.org/pdf/1703.03888.pdf. Accessed 13 Aug 2018
21. Yuan, Y.: Automatic skin lesion segmentation with fully convolutional-deconvolutional networks. https://arxiv.org/pdf/1703.05165.pdf. Accessed 13 Aug 2018

22. Bi, L., Kim, J., Ahn, E., Feng, D.: Automatic skin lesion analysis using large-scale dermoscopy images and deep residual networks. https://arxiv.org/ftp/arxiv/papers/1703/1703.04197.pdf. Accessed 13 Aug 2018
23. Menegola, A., Tavares, J., Fornaciali, M., Li, L.T., Avila, S., Valle, E.: RECOD Titans at ISIC challenge 2017. https://arxiv.org/pdf/1703.04819.pdf. Accessed 13 Aug 2018
24. Qi, J., Le, M., Li, C., Zhou, P.: Global and local information based deep network for skin lesion segmentation. https://arxiv.org/pdf/1703.05467.pdf. Accessed 13 Aug 2018
25. Jaisakthi, S.M., Chandrabose, A., Mirunalini, P.: Automatic skin lesion segmentation using semi-supervised learning technique. https://arxiv.org/pdf/1703.04301.pdf. Accessed 13 Aug 2018
26. Wiselin Jiji, G., Johnson Durai Raj, P.: An extensive technique to detect and analyze melanoma. https://arxiv.org/ftp/arxiv/papers/1702/1702.08717.pdf. Accessed 13 Aug 2018
27. Kawahara, J., Hamarneh, G.: Fully convolutional networks to detect clinical dermoscopic features. https://arxiv.org/pdf/1703.04559.pdf. Accessed 13 Aug 2018
28. Gutiérrez-Arriola, J.M., Gómez-Álvarez, M., Osma-Ruiz, V., Sáenz-Lechón, N., Fraile, R.: Skin lesion segmentation based on preprocessing, thresholding and neural networks. https://arxiv.org/ftp/arxiv/papers/1703/1703.04845.pdf. Accessed 13 Aug 2018
29. Andre, E., et al.: Dermatologist-level classification of skin cancer with deep neural networks. Nature 542(7639), 115 (2017)

# Skin Lesion Segmentation Using Enhanced Unified Markov Random Field

Omran Salih and Serestina Viriri[✉]

School of Maths, Statistics and Computer Science,
University of KwaZulu-Natal, Durban, South Africa
omran@aims.ac.za, viriris@ukzn.ac.za

**Abstract.** Markov Random Field (MRF) theory has a significant potential role in image segmentation field. It uses (pixels, regions, edges)-based on MRF models to detect objects, boundaries and other relevant information in an image. This paper proposes an extension of Unified Markov Random Field (UMRF) model to include edge-based features. Firstly, the proposed technique employs the likelihood function to combine the advantages of the pixel-based, region-based and edge-based MRF model, by computing the product of the pixel likelihood function, regional likelihood function and edge likelihood function. Secondly, the region-based macro texture features are extracted using the UMRF model. Then the edge-based features are extracted using the maximum gradient method to recover any significant lost information. A principled probabilistic inference is implemented to integrate various types of likelihood information and spatial constraints by iteratively updating the posterior probability of the proposed model. The segmentation process is completed when the iterations converge. The proposed enhanced UMRF technique which combines pixel-based, region-based and edge-based features achieved a higher skin lesion segmentation accuracy than MRF model which combines pixel-based and region-based only.

**Keywords:** Markov Random Field · Unified Markov Random Field
Skin lesion · Segmentation

## 1 Introduction

Image segmentation plays an important role in image processing and its applications such as medical diagnostic [3]. The role of image segmentation is to divide the image into subgroups of regions with respect to the appropriate locations. Researchers have proposed many methods to solve this problem, such as pixel-based MRF, region-base MRF [11], edge-pixel MRF [7], and pixel- and region-based MRF [4]. Although the image segmentation is still a challenges due to many factors such as, feature extraction from the image, the contextual information, the object granularity, and the contour smoothness. This paper proposes a method based on MRF theory to address these challenges in image segmentation.

© Springer Nature Switzerland AG 2018
A. Groza and R. Prasath (Eds.): MIKE 2018, LNAI 11308, pp. 331–340, 2018.
https://doi.org/10.1007/978-3-030-05918-7_30

The skin cancer foundation in the United States has been stated that the maximum frequent type of cancer is the skin cancer. Skin cancer increased over amount of time in many region in the world for instance Singapore [10], Slovakia [17], and the Netherland [14]. To date the easiest way to stop spreading of skin cancer is through detecting the skin cancer in early stage to manage to identify the abnormalities of skin cancer. In particular, to detect abnormalities of skin in early stage is very important since these abnormalities might lead to skin cancer. During the skin examination, it is very important to tell the different between non-melanoma skin cancer and melanoma skin cancer, and give the right treatment. Unfortunately, the care health systems are facing an issue to offer a potential patients of a large population with skin examination due to a few experts who deliver proper skin diagnosis and the difficulties of these location at larger center [19].

Malignant melanoma has one of the very rapidly increasing incidences on earth and has a large mortality rate. Early diagnosis is quite important because melanoma may be cured with prompt excision [8]. Dermoscopy images play a significant role in the noninvasive early detection of melanoma [2]. However, melanoma detection using human vision alone may be subjective, inaccurate and poorly reproducible even among experienced dermatologists. Obviously this is related to the challenges in interpreting images with diverse characteristics including lesions of varying sizes and shapes, lesions that will have fuzzy boundaries, different skin colors and the clear presence of hair [1]. Therefore, the automatic analysis of dermoscopy images is an invaluable aid for clinical decision making and for image based diagnosis to recognize diseases for example melanoma.

This paper presents the segmentation of the skin lesion tumors. Automatic skin cancer detection system is an ill-posed problem and depends on certain parts such as lesion segmentation, detection and localization of visual dermoscopic features and disease classification. Each of the previous parts depend on certain criteria, for example lesion segmentation needs to be grouped in a pixels such as range of intensity value, texture or gradient information. Automatic skin cancer tumor detection is not an easy task. It needs a lot of image analytical knowledge and experience but in general most of medical institution still use manual methods to detect the skin cancers tumors where expert clinician segment out the tumor manually which is time-consuming. There is room to improving the existing techniques of skin cancer detection especially with the availability of innovative computationally efficient techniques.

## 2   Method

The proposed method is a probabilistic model based on Markov Random Field (MRF) theory. It combines the benefits of several methods based on MRF into its account as depicted in Fig. 1. The proposed method put into account the advantages of three MRF methods: (i) the region-based MRF model, (ii) the pixel-based MRF model, (iii) the edge-based MRF model. The general overview of the proposed method is basically as follow. First an input image is used to extract the pixel values, the regional features, and the edge features. The initial segmentation is very important before extracting the regional feature since it could be directly affects the desire segmentation accuracy, which can be done using one of the over-segmented image algorithm (mean shift, Ncut, watersheld, turbopixel). Then the regional features formula proposed by authors in [4] is used to obtain the regional features image. The edges of a color image are extracted by the max gradient method to obtain the edge features image. Finally, the pixel values, the regional features, and the edge features are used to solve the Maximum a Posteriori (MAP) estimation to find the best estimation which leads to the desire image segmentation. Figure 1 shows the flowchart of the proposed method: First, extract the pixel features $Y^P$, the regional features $Y^R$, from the over-segmented image, and the edge features $Y^E$ extracted using the max gradient method. Then, these features together are combined using likelihood function and integrates them with spatial information of the posterior probability. The segmentation result can be given by finding the MAP estimation problem. The proposed method is described in more details as follow.

## 2.1   Problem Formulation

Let $S = \{s_i | i = 1, 2, \cdots, N \times M\}$ be an input image where $N \times M$ denotes the size of the image and $s_i$ represents each pixel in the image. $X = \{X_s | s \in S\}$ represents the label random field defined on $S$. Each random variables $X_s$ in $X$ represents the class of pixel $s$, the class set is $\Lambda = \{1, 2, \cdots, n\}$ where $n$ is the number of classes. $Y = \{y_s | s \in S\}$ represents the observed image defined on $S$. Let $x = \{x_s | s \in S\}$ an instantiation of the region label field. In the MRF method, the main goal of segmentation is to find an optimal estimation of $x$ given the observed image $Y$, formulated as the following Maximum a Posteriori (MAP) estimation problem:

$$\hat{x} = \arg\max_x P(x|Y), \tag{1}$$

where $P(x|Y)$ is the posteriori. By using Bayes' theory, the posterior $P(x|Y)$ in Eq. (1) is equivalent to

$$\hat{x} = \arg\max_x P(Y|X)P(X). \tag{2}$$

The proposed method divides the observed image $Y$ into pixel feature $Y^P = \{Y_s^P | s \in S\}$, the regional feature $Y^R = \{Y_s^R | s \in S\}$, and the edge feature $Y^R = \{Y_s^E | s \in S\}$ which means $Y = (Y^P, Y^R, Y^E)$. BY substituting $Y$ in Eq. (2), we obtain

$$\hat{x} = \arg\max_x P((Y^P, Y^R, Y^E)|X)P(X), \tag{3}$$

$$= \arg\max_x P(Y^P|X)P(Y^R|X)P(Y^E|X)P(X). \tag{4}$$

To find the estimation of Eq. (4), the distribution of $P(Y^P|X), P(Y^R|X)$, $P(Y^E, X)$, and $P(X)$ will be describe in SubSects. 2.2, 2.3 and 2.4.

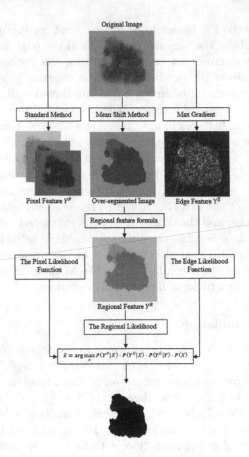

**Fig. 1.** Flowchart of the proposed method using an example.

## 2.2 Probability of the Label Random Field

The probability of the label random field $P(X)$ is used to model the label random field $X$. According to the theory of Harmercley-Clifford [13], $P(X)$ is a Gibss distribution which is given by

$$P(X = x) = \frac{1}{Z} \exp\left(-U(x)\right). \tag{5}$$

Here $Z$ is the normalisation factor defined as follows

$$Z = \sum_x U(x), \tag{6}$$

where $U(x)$ denotes the energy function, that is i.e.,

$$U(x) = \sum_{s \in S} U(x_s, x_{N_s}), \tag{7}$$

and

$$U(x_s, x_{N_s}) = \sum_{t \in N_s} V(x_s, x_t). \tag{8}$$

The $N_s$ is the set of pixel's neighbours $s$ and each $V(x_s, x_t)$ is the potential function between pixel $s$ and pixel $t, t \in N_s$. The potential function $V(x_s, x_t)$ is defined by the Multilevel Logistic (MLL) model [13] which has the following form

$$V(x_s, x_t) = \begin{cases} \beta & \text{if } x_s = x_t \\ -\beta & \text{if } x_s \neq x_t \end{cases}, \tag{9}$$

where $\beta > 0$ is the potential parameter and $t \in N_s$.

### 2.3  Conditional Probability Function

The likelihood function in our proposed method has been divided into three parts: the pixel likelihood function, the regional likelihood function, and the edge likelihood function. All these functions are described below in more details.

**The Pixel Likelihood Function.** Extract spectral value as the pixel feature to model the micro texture pattern and the detailed information using the likelihood function $P(Y_s^P|X)$. The proposed method used Gaussian distribution to determine the distribution of the likelihood function of $P(Y_s^P|X)$ which is obtained by

$$P(Y_s^P|X_s = h) = \frac{1}{(2\pi)^{D/2}\sqrt{\det(\Sigma_h^P)}} \exp\left(-\frac{(Y_s^P - \mu_h^P)^T \cdot (Y_s^P - \mu_h^P)}{2(\Sigma_h^P)}\right), \tag{10}$$

where $Y_s^P$ is the pixel feature for every pixel $s$, the Gaussian distribution parameters are $\mu_h^P, \Sigma_h^P$, and $D$ is the dimension of $Y_s^P$.

**The Regional Likelihood Function.** The proposed method used algorithm provided by [4], to extract the regional feature of an input image. It highlighted that one of over segmented should be used to obtain the initial segmentation because it is very important in the final segmentation accuracy. Several methods of over-segmented are proposed in the literature to provide a better over segmentation result, i.e., watershed [5], mean shift (MS) [6], normalisation cut (Ncut) [18], and tuberpixel [12]. In this paper, we used MS method to extract the over-segmented. The regional feature $Y_s^R$ is presented to extract the spectral value information from over-segmented image for each pixel $s$. The regional feature $Y_s^R$ is given as follows

$$Y_s^R = p_{R_s}\left[1 - \log(p_{R_s})\right] + \frac{1}{|N_{R_s}|}\sum_{T \in N_{R_s}} p_T\left[1 - \log(p_T)\right], \tag{11}$$

where $R_s$ represents the initial over-segmented region including $s$. $p_{R_s}$ denotes the area ratio of the region $R_s$ to the whole image, and $N_{R_s}$ is the set of neighbour regions of $R_s$. On solving for the likelihood function of regional feature $P(Y_s^R|X)$, the Gaussian distribution have been used to determine the distribution of the likelihood function of $P(Y_s^P|X)$, which is given by

$$P(Y_s^R|X_s = h) = \frac{\sqrt{\alpha}}{(2\pi)^{D'/2}\sqrt{\det(\Sigma_h^P)}} \exp\left(-\frac{(Y_s^P - \mu_h^P)^T \cdot (Y_s^P - \mu_h^P)}{2(\Sigma_h^P/\alpha)}\right).$$

(12)

Here $D'$ is the dimension of $Y_s^R$, $\mu_h^R$, and $\Sigma_h^R$ are the parameters of Gaussian distribution, $\det(\Sigma_h^R)$ is the determinant of $\Sigma_h^R$, $1 \leq h \leq n$, and $\alpha$ is proposed to show the interaction between the regional feature and the pixel feature.

**The Edge Likelihood Function.** Edges of a color image by the max gradient method [7] are used, to extract the edges of a color image without converting it to grayscale. This clearly shows that a significant amount of information is lost by the standard method, but it is recovered with the max gradient method [7]. The RGB color of each pixel is treated as a 3D vector, and the strength of the edge is the magnitude of the maximum gradient. This also works if the image is in any other (3-dimensional) color space. Direct formulas for the jacobian eigenvalues were used [17] to calculate the maximum eigenvalue (gradient magnitude), hence this function is vectorized and yields good results without sacrificing performance.

Assume $f : R^2 \to rgb, (x, y) \in R^2$ is a continuous color image. The color components will be denote $r(x,y), g(x,y)$ and $b(x,y)$, so that the image as a whole can be denoted by $f = (r, g, b)$ or more explicitly by $f(x,y) = (r(x,y), g(x,y), b(x,y))$. Let $J$ is the Jacobian, its elements are the partial derivatives of $r, g, b$ with respect to $x, y$. The edge strength is the greatest eigenvalue of the product of Jacobian and its transpose.

$$J' * J = \begin{pmatrix} \frac{\partial r}{\partial x} & \frac{\partial g}{\partial x} & \frac{\partial b}{\partial x} \\ \frac{\partial r}{\partial y} & \frac{\partial g}{\partial y} & \frac{\partial b}{\partial y} \end{pmatrix} \begin{pmatrix} \frac{\partial r}{\partial x} & \frac{\partial r}{\partial y} \\ \frac{\partial g}{\partial x} & \frac{\partial g}{\partial y} \\ \frac{\partial b}{\partial x} & \frac{\partial b}{\partial y} \end{pmatrix} = \begin{pmatrix} J_x & J_{xy} \\ J_{xy} & J_y \end{pmatrix}.$$

(13)

The edge color image is obtained by finding the greatest eigenvalues of Eq. (13), which is given by the following formula:

$$Y^E = (J_x + J_y) + \sqrt{|(J_x^2 - 2J_x J_y + J_y^2 + 4J_{xy}^2)|},$$

(14)

where $Y^E$ is the edge color image for a whole image. The partial derivatives is obtained by using Sobel filter. The Gaussian distribution have been used to determine the distribution of the likelihood function of $P(Y_s^E|X)$, which is given by

$$P(Y_s^E|X_s = h) = \frac{1}{(2\pi)^{D/2}\sqrt{\det(\Sigma_h^P)}} \exp\left(-\frac{(Y_s^E - \mu_h^E)^T \cdot (Y_s^E - \mu_h^E)}{2(\Sigma_h^E)}\right),$$

(15)

where $Y_s^E$ is the pixel feature for each pixel $s$, the Gaussian distribution parameters are $\mu_h^E, \Sigma_h^E$, and $D$ is the dimension of $Y_s^E$.

## 2.4 Parameters Setting

The proposed method has eighth parameters, $\mu_h^P, \Sigma_h^P, \mu_h^R, \Sigma_h^R, \mu_h^E$, and $\Sigma_h^E$, which are used in Eqs. (15) and (12). Furthermore, they are known as the mean value and the variance value for the Gaussian distribution, which can be calculated as follows

$$\mu_h^P = \frac{1}{|X^h|} \sum_{s \in X^h} Y_s^P, \qquad \Sigma_h^P = \frac{1}{|X^h|} \sum_{s \in X^h} \left(Y_s^P - \mu_h^P\right)' \left(Y_s^P - \mu_h^P\right), \qquad (16)$$

$$\mu_h^R = \frac{1}{|X^h|} \sum_{s \in X^h} Y_s^R, \qquad \Sigma_h^R = \frac{1}{|X^h|} \sum_{s \in X^h} \left(Y_s^R - \mu_h^R\right)' \left(Y_s^R - \mu_h^R\right), \qquad (17)$$

$$\mu_h^E = \frac{1}{|X^h|} \sum_{s \in X^h} Y_s^E, \qquad \Sigma_h^E = \frac{1}{|X^h|} \sum_{s \in X^h} \left(Y_s^E - \mu_h^E\right)' \left(Y_s^E - \mu_h^E\right). \qquad (18)$$

$\beta$ is the potential parameter in Eq. (9), which is used for finding $P(X)$, and $\alpha$ is used to reflect the interaction between $P(Y_s^P | X_s = h)$ and $P(Y_s^R | X_s = h)$.

## 2.5 Algorithm for the Proposed Method

Algorithm 1 shows the steps of proposed practical implementation, firstly gets an input image $Y$, and the number of the classes $n$. It gets over-segmented regions using mean shift method, then extracts the pixel, regional, and edge feature, eventually obtains the segmentation result.

---

**Algorithm 1.** The Proposed Method

---

1: **procedure** UMRF($Y$)                                     ▷ Y is an input image
2:     Extract the spectral value of $Y$ as the pixel feature $Y^P$;
3:     Use MS to obtain over-segmented regions;
4:     Extract the regional feature $Y^R$ from over-segmented using equation (11);
5:     Extract the edges features $Y^E$ using the max gradient method.
6:     Get the initial label field $X^0$ by using $k$-mean algorithm cluster the feature into $n$ classes;
7:     Start iteration. Set **itr** = 0;
8:     **while** True **do**
9:         Estimate $\mu_h^P, \Sigma_h^P, \mu_h^R, \Sigma_h^R, \mu_h^E$ and $\Sigma_h^E$ respectively, $\forall n$ classes given $X^{\text{itr}}$;
10:         Compute: $P(Y_s^P | X_s = h), P(Y_s^R | X_s = h), P(Y_s^E | X_s = h)$ and $P(X_s | X_{N_s})$;
11:         Obtain the best estimation $\hat{x} = \{\hat{x}_s | s \in S\}$ using equation (4);
12:         Set $X^{\text{itr}+1} = \hat{x}$;
13:         **if** $X^{\text{itr}+1} == X^{\text{itr}}$ **then**
14:             Stop and $X^{\text{itr}+1}$ is the best segmentation;
15:         **else if** $X^{\text{itr}+1} == X^{\text{itr}}$ **then**
16:             itr = itr + 1;
17:         repeat;
18:     **return** $X^{\text{itr}+1}$                                     ▷ $\hat{x} = \{\hat{x}_s | s \in S\}$

---

# 3    Experimental Results and Discussion

The proposed method is compared with UMRF model for the figure/ground segmentation. The UMRF model is a probabilistic model based on Markov Random Field (MRF). A UMRF model combine the benefits of the pixel-based and regional-based MRF models. Therefore, the compression between the proposed method and UMRF model will demonstrate the difference between our method and UMRF model. Furthermore, the UMRF model is one of the stat-of-art methods. Tested images and segmentation results that obtained from the proposed and UMRF model are depicted in Fig. 2. These experiments have been performed on skin cancer images from MED-NODE database [9]. Different type of images have been used to preform the experiment. As we observe in Fig. 2, the proposed method shows a better performance compared with UMRF method.

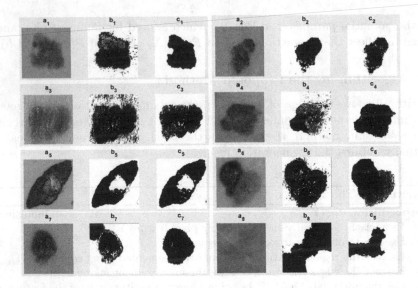

**Fig. 2.** $(a_i)$ Original images, $(b_i)$ segmented images using UMRF model, and $(c_i)$ images segmentation using the proposed method.

Quantitative evaluation of the segmentation has been done using five types of evaluation metric, to measure the effectiveness of the proposed method segmentation: (i) Jaccard Index (JI) [15], (ii) Rand Index (RI) [16], (iii) Jaccard distance (JD) [15], (iv) global consistence error (GCE), and (v) Variation of information (VoI) [6]. Table 1 shows several important insights on the performance and particularities of the proposed method. Firstly, the proposed method achieved the largest JI, which indicates that the proposed model has the strongest over all performance when compared to the UMRF model. Secondly, based on the RI, it can be observed that the proposed method has the largest performance when compared to UMRF model. Third, based on the JD, GCE, and VoI, it was observed that the proposed method is quite good. Consequently, the proposed method preforms equally on both melanoma and naevus cases.

**Table 1.** Segmentation performance metric.

| | Methods | $a_1$ | $a_2$ | $a_3$ | $a_4$ | $a_5$ | $a_6$ | $a_7$ | $a_8$ |
|---|---|---|---|---|---|---|---|---|---|
| JI | UMRF | 91.79% | 98.00% | 73.48% | 80.73% | 90.80% | 88.80% | 88.57% | 87.77% |
| | Prop | **97.73%** | **98.37%** | **89.87%** | **99.99%** | **99.90%** | **92.23%** | **97.62%** | **98.58%** |
| RI | UMRF | 0.5626 | 0.6294 | 0.5341 | 0.5170 | 0.5574 | 0.5019 | 0.6034 | 0.5007 |
| | Prop | **0.9142** | **0.8885** | **0.8692** | **0.8826** | **0.9081** | **0.7997** | **0.8023** | **0.8825** |
| JD | UMRF | 0.0821 | 0.0199 | 0.2652 | 0.1927 | 0.0920 | 0.1120 | 0.1143 | 0.1222 |
| | Prop | **0.0227** | **0.0164** | **0.1013** | **0.0006** | **0.0009** | **0.0777** | **0.0238** | **0.0142** |
| GCE | UMRF | 0.0030 | 0.0003 | 0.0003 | 0.0006 | 0.3505 | 0.0003 | 0.0003 | 0.1571 |
| | Prop | **0.0796** | **0.0977** | **0.1264** | **0.1062** | **0.0865** | **0.3363** | **0.2578** | **0.2989** |
| VoI | UMRF | 0.9080 | 0.8045 | 0.9505 | 0.9759 | 1.6167 | 0.9975 | 0.8455 | 1.3006 |
| | Prop | **0.4585** | **0.5735** | **0.7083** | **0.5550** | **0.4676** | **1.5664** | **1.4786** | **1.4542** |

# 4  Conclusion

In this paper, a proposed method for image segmentation is presented. The results are found to be highly accurate compared with UMRF model. The proposed method can be part of a system designed to assist automatic skin lesions in the field of sector health. Skin lesion experimental results using the proposed method indicate that, the proposed method potentially can provide more accurate skin lesions segmentation from images than comparable methods existing in the literature. We plan to employ the method in a full automatic skin lesion detection.

# References

1. Celebi, M.E., et al.: Automatic detection of blue-white veil and related structures in dermoscopy images. Comput. Med. Imaging Graph. **32**(8), 670–677 (2008)
2. Celebi, M.E., et al.: A methodological approach to the classification of dermoscopy images. Comput. Med. Imaging Graph. **31**(6), 362–373 (2007)
3. Celebi, M.E., Wen, Q., Iyatomi, H., Shimizu, K., Zhou, H., Schaefer, G.: A state-of-the-art survey on lesion border detection in dermoscopy images. In: Dermoscopy Image Analysis, pp. 97–129 (2015)
4. Chen, X., Zheng, C., Yao, H., Wang, B.: Image segmentation using a unified markov random field model. IET Image Process. **11**(10), 860–869 (2017)
5. Chien, S.-Y., Huang, Y.-W., Chen, L.-G.: Predictive watershed: a fast watershed algorithm for video segmentation. IEEE Trans. Circuits Syst. Video Technol. **13**(5), 453–461 (2003)
6. Comaniciu, D., Meer, P.: Mean shift: a robust approach toward feature space analysis. IEEE Trans. Pattern Anal. Mach. Intell. **24**(5), 603–619 (2002)
7. Di Zenzo, S.: A note on the gradient of a multi-image. Comput. Vis. Graph. Image Process. **33**(1), 116–125 (1986)
8. Erdei, E., Torres, S.M.: A new understanding in the epidemiology of melanoma. Expert Rev. Anticancer Ther. **10**(11), 1811–1823 (2010)
9. Giotis, I., Molders, N., Land, S., Biehl, M., Jonkman, M.F., Petkov, N.: Med-node: a computer-assisted melanoma diagnosis system using non-dermoscopic images. Expert Syst. Appl. **42**(19), 6578–6585 (2015)

10. Jemal, A., Bray, F., Center, M.M., Ferlay, J., Ward, E., Forman, D.: Global cancer statistics. CA Cancer J. Clin. **61**(2), 69–90 (2011)
11. Jie, F., Shi, Y., Li, Y., Liu,Z.: Interactive region-based MRF image segmentation. In: 2011 4th International Congress on Image and Signal Processing (CISP), vol. 3, pp. 1263–1267. IEEE (2011)
12. Levinshtein, A., Stere, A., Kutulakos, K.N., Fleet, D.J., Dickinson, S.J., Siddiqi, K.: Turbopixels: fast superpixels using geometric flows. IEEE Trans. Pattern Anal. Mach. Intell. **31**(12), 2290–2297 (2009)
13. Li, S.Z.: Markov Random Field Modeling in Image Analysis. Springer, London (2009). https://doi.org/10.1007/978-1-84800-279-1
14. Nijsten, T., Louwman, M.W., Coebergh, J.W., et al.: Skin cancer epidemic in the Netherlands. Ned. Tijdschr. Geneeskd. **153**, A768–A768 (2009)
15. Real, R., Vargas, J.M.: The probabilistic basis of jaccard's index of similarity. Syst. Biol. **45**(3), 380–385 (1996)
16. Recasens, M., Hovy, E.: Blanc: implementing the rand index for coreference evaluation. Nat. Lang. Eng. **17**(4), 485–510 (2011)
17. Rogers, H.W., Weinstock, M.A., Feldman, S.R., Coldiron, B.M.: Incidence estimate of nonmelanoma skin cancer (keratinocyte carcinomas) in the us population 2012. JAMA Dermatology **151**(10), 1081–1086 (2015)
18. Shi, J., Malik, J.: Normalized cuts and image segmentation. IEEE Trans. Pattern Anal. Mach. Intell. **22**(8), 888–905 (2000)
19. Wartman, D., Weinstock, M.: Are we overemphasizing sun avoidance in protection from melanoma? Cancer Epidemiol. Prev. Biomarkers **17**(3), 469–470 (2008)

# Texture Classification Using Deep Convolutional Neural Network with Ensemble Learning

Krishan Gupta[✉], Tushar Jain[✉], and Debarka Sengupta

Indraprastha Institute of Information Technology,
Delhi (IIIT-D), New Delhi, India
{krishang,tushar16056,debarka}@iiitd.ac.in

**Abstract.** This paper approaches the problem of texture classification from very challenging dataset, the describable texture dataset (DTD), using a combination of popular pre-trained convolutional neural networks architectures to improve the overall accuracy of the system. Different architectures include mixture of VGG, Resnet50, Inception, Xception models with different number of layers and parameters which are individually tweaked to attain maximum accuracy. The results obtained from these models are combined using different technique to obtain the best results. In order to better generalize our model we even tested for other well known datasets such as KTH-TIP-2b, FMD and CUReT. Using the ensemble techniques we were able to achieve comparable accuracy wrt to state of the art techniques.

**Keywords:** Texture classification ·
Describable Texture Dataset (DTD) · CNN

## 1 Introduction

Texture, being an inherent property of the images is frequently used in applications like image classification, image segmentation and image synthesis. In image processing literature, texture is broadly defined as the spatial variation of pixel intensities across the image. Unlike object classification, which focuses on classifying prominent object in the foreground, texture classification uses the repetition and flow of patterns within the texture. It can be further classified as tactile texture, the physical feel of the surface and visual texture which refer to visual impact due to texture on an observer. In this paper, our focus is on visual texture only and henceforth the term texture means visual texture. Visually, the texture can be described by the adjectives like banded grid, honeycombed, and woven.

The problem of object classification has been studied rigorously by the machine learning community over the last few years and many state-of-art are being reported from time to time. However, the problem of texture classification is more complex due to a large variation of objects within single texture

© Springer Nature Switzerland AG 2018
A. Groza and R. Prasath (Eds.): MIKE 2018, LNAI 11308, pp. 341–350, 2018.
https://doi.org/10.1007/978-3-030-05918-7_31

class. Various dataset have been released in order to study texture attributes
and classification. In our study we will be evaluate the performance of our architectures on describable texture dataset (DTD) [5], FMD [15], CUReT [7] and
KTH-TIP-2b dataset [3] (Fig. 1).

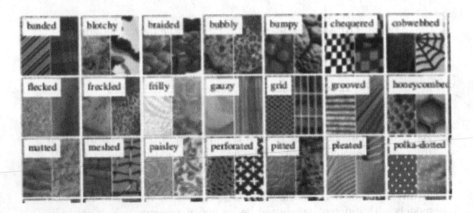

**Fig. 1.** Sample images from DTD dataset.

Ever since Krizhevsky et al. [12] produced state of the art results on Image-
Net challenge [8] Convolutional neural networks (CNNs) have provided state
of the art results in various image recognition, object detection and segmentation challenges. CNNs are built using a combination of convolutional, pooling
and fully connected layers. These layers are able to capture complex features
which are highly invariant and discriminant unlike the handcrafted features.
Pre-trained models have been extensively used in image recognition either for
feature generation or for weight initialization in CNN. They provide fast training of CNN and provide better results than a CNN model trained from scratch.
However, it is very difficult to obtain an optimal CNN architecture which can
provide the best results on every dataset.

In the last few years ensemble techniques such as stacking, bagging [2] and
boosting [9] are used in data science competitions to attain the best accuracy and
reduce the overall loss. Bagging or bootstrap aggregation reduces the variance
by training different instances of models on different subsets of data chosen randomly with replacement. Stacking improves the overall prediction by aggregating
the output from different models using a meta classifier on top using predictions
from base models as features. Boosting is a sequential method that trains multiple model on weighted data points with more weight to misclassified data points
hence decreases the overall bias of the model. All the three approaches, also
known as ensemble techniques, help in reduced manual effort of finding the optimal architecture by making use of probabilities from multiple models. As most of
the previous studies focus on using weak learners, in this paper, we are leverag-
ing the merits of ensemble techniques with pre-trained CNN models to achieve

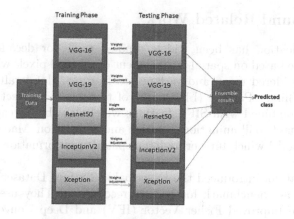

**Fig. 2.** Model architecture for approach 1

satisfactory performance on texture dataset. We are using very powerful pre-trained models VGG-16 [16], VGG-19 [10], Resnet50 [11], inception, Xception [4] model which are fine tuned on the texture dataset. The results are combined using the voting technique and the weights are assigned to each probability from each model to achieve the maximum accuracy. In our study, our model was able to use the probabilities from different model to overall attain better accuracy (Fig. 2).

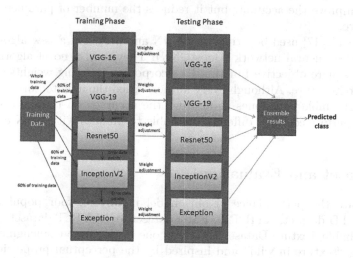

**Fig. 3.** Model architecture for approach 2

## 2   Background Related Work

Texture classification has been widely studied topic for decades. Structural approaches were based on spatial arrangement of selected pixels while statistical approaches considered mean and variance as features. Handcrafted techniques include Local Binary Pattern (LBP), Bag of textons, fisher vector, SIFT [13], Fisher vector combined with SIFT features which are able to capture features which are invariant to illumination, rotation and translation. Mao et al. [14] used bag of words model which further undergo spatial transformation to best match image region.

Cimpoi et al. [6] introduced the Describable Texture Dataset (DTD) which is state of the art benchmark for texture recognition. They used two texture descriptors: the Improved Fisher Vector (IFV) and Deep Convolutional Activation Feature (DeCAF) to extract the texture descriptors and trained SVM using them to achieve a classification accuracy of 66.7% ± 0.9. Song et al. proposed a similar technique to handle the problem of texture classification. They introduced Fisher Vector (FV-CNN), a pooling method and used it in combination with FC-CNN to define texture descriptors. SVM is trained on these texture descriptors to achieve a classification accuracy of 75.5% ± 0.8 on DTD dataset. Other methods include using CNN features and using BoW model to attain better results. Zhou et al. used pre-trained models on texture and scene dataset to achieve better results. Andrearczyk et al. [1] proposed texture CNN (T-CNN) which uses novel energy layer in which each feature map is simply pooled by calculating the average of its activated output. Though, this approach does not improve the accuracy but it reduces the number of parameters of the architecture.

Yang et al. [17] used boosting with CNN and proposed a new algorithm for boosting Deep neural network (BoostCNN). They used a novel algorithm and used least square objective function to incorporate boosting weights into deep learning architecture. Although every author varied the architecture of CNN no one used ensemble techniques to improve the accuracy on the dataset. In our study, we performed three different ensemble techniques with CNN on texture dataset.

## 3   Dataset and Evaluation

We evaluate the performance of our model mainly on four popular texture dataset: DTD dataset, KTH-T2b, FMD dataset and CUReT dataset.

Describable Texture Dataset (DTD) is one of the most challenging dataset, containing "texture in wild" and inspired by the perceptual properties of textures. Released by cimponi et al., this dataset is not generated under controlled conditions rather collected through the Internet. The dataset is divided into 47 texture categories having a total of 5640 images with 120 images in each category. CUReT (Columbia-Utrecht Reflectance and Texture) is another texture dataset consisting of 61 different textures each containing 205 images each captured under different viewing and illumination conditions in a controlled lab

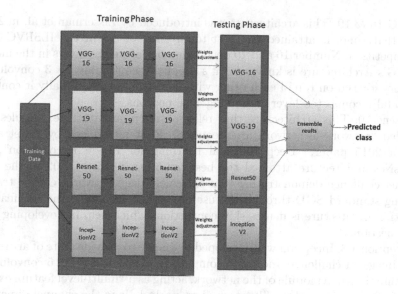

**Fig. 4.** Model architecture for approach 3

environment. Flickr Material Dataset (FMD) was constructed with the specific purpose of capturing a range of real world appearances of common materials e.g. glass, plastic. This dataset consists of 100 images each in 10 categories. Each image in this dataset was selected manually from Flickr.com to ensure a variety of illumination conditions, compositions, colors, texture and material sub-types. In our experiment images were divided into 60:10:30 for training, validation and testing for CUReT, FMD and DTD dataset. KTH-TIPS-2b dataset consist of 4752 images of 11 materials captured under controlled scale, pose and illumination. This dataset contains four samples for each category. We followed the normal approach and used one sample for training and validation and other three for testing (Fig. 4).

## 4   Evaluation Matrices

The following evaluation matrices are used for performance evaluation purpose. The first is accuracy: a measure of correct predictions by the classifier and the second is error rate: a measure of incorrect predictions by the classifier.

## 5   Methodology and Analysis

Texture CNN is an entirely CNN based approach to target texture classification. We have used popular pretrained CNN architecture namely VGG-16, VGG-19, Resnet50, InceptionV2, Xception model which have produced state of art results on ImageNet dataset. The following section discusses each model in detail.

- VGG 16 & 19: This architecture was introduced by Zisserman et al. in 2014. At that time, it attained the best top-5 error of 8.8 in the ILSRVC 2014 competition. Number 16 and 19 denote number of weight layers in the model. VGG's Architecture is known for it's simplicity containing $3 \times 3$ convolution layers stacked on top of each other with increasing depth. Finally it contains two fully connected layer containing 4096 neurons.
- Resenet50: This architecture that relies on micro-architecture modules also called "network-in-network architectures". First introduced by He et al. in their 2015 paper, "Deep Residual Learning for Image Recognition", the ResNet architecture attained the best top-5 error rate of 7.02 in the Imagenet challenge demonstrating that extremely deep networks can be trained using standard SGD through the use of residual modules. Another features of this architecture is it uses skip connections which help in developing deep connection.
- Inception V3: Inception was developed by google to provide state of art results on imagenet challenge. Inception computes $1 \times 1$, $3 \times 3$, and $5 \times 5$ convolutions within the same module of the network, acting as a "multi-level feature extractor". Output from these filters are then stacked along the channel dimension and before being fed into the next layer in the network.
- Xception was proposed by François Chollet. The original incarnation of this architecture was called GoogLeNet, but subsequent manifestations have simply been called Inception vN where N refers to the version number put out by Google. Xception is an extension of the Inception architecture which replaces the standard Inception modules with depthwise separable convolutions.

Fine tuning is the task of taking a retrained model and using it to solve a similar problem. Fine tuning is done by changing the softmax layer equal to the number of dataset classes. In our experiments, images were first resized into $200 \times 200$ before being fed into the model. Cross entropy loss was used in each model and learning rate was set at .002. These models were fine tuned and images were generated by upto 6 times using rotation, translation, scaling etc. and a softmax layer equal to the number of classes was placed on the output layer.

**Table 1.** Results using approach 1

| Dataset name | Val. Acc. | Test Acc. | Tr. Loss | Val. Loss |
|---|---|---|---|---|
| DTD | 0.64 | **0.6814** | 0.12 | 1.83 |
| CUReT | 0.98 | **0.9974** | 0.06 | .05 |
| KTH-TIPS-2b | 0.42 | **0.7084** | 0.0011 | 3.53 |
| FMD | 0.48 | **0.49** | 0.07 | 3.04 |

In our experiment we followed three different approaches. In our first approach, a variant of bagging method, we took the dataset and fed it into five

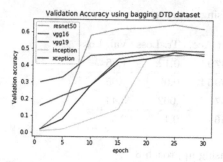 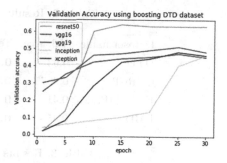

**Fig. 5.** Validation Accuracy for DTD dataset using approach 1 (left) & 2 (right). In first approach complete dataset was fed into five different models in parallel while in other approach each model was trained sequentially on the misclassified data points from previous model and 60% of original dataset as shown in Fig. 3

different pretrained models in parallel. After getting the probabilities from each model for each class, we assigned weights to different probabilities by training an SVM on training dataset and combined their results to get the final probability per class. The class with highest probability is taken as the predicted class. In second approach, a variant of boosting method, we sequentially train each model on wrongly predicted data points of a previous pretrained model and 60% of the original dataset for a model. Similar to the first one we followed the same approach to combine the results to get the final output. Validation accuracy for each of the individual models were plotted in Figs. 5, 6 and 7 for both the approaches. In the third approach, a hybrid of bagging and boosting we combined the approach 1 and 2. We used 4 pre-trained model and overfitted the dataset on each pre-trained model by training multiple instances of the model on error data points and combined the output as done in approach 1 to achieve the final results.

## 5.1    Observation

As depicted in Tables 1 and 2, Test accuracy for the final model is better than the best validation and test accuracy of the individual model for a dataset in both our approaches. As seen in Fig. 5, resnet50 model achieved the best accuracy of 62% and 63% in approach 1 & 2. Using ensemble techniques, we achieved an accuracy of 68.14% in Approach 1 and 68.95% in Approach 2 and 68.35% in Approach 3 which is better than the best accuracy of individual models. In FMD dataset, as seen in Fig. 7, individually resnet50 outperforms all other models with an accuracy of 43% in approach 1 and 48% in approach 2. Approach 2 outperforms all other models and achieved an accuracy of 56%. Our approach one performed best on CUReT dataset achieving 99.74% on test dataset which

**Table 2.** Results using approach 2

| Dataset name | Val. Acc. | Test Acc. | Tr. Loss | Val. Loss |
|---|---|---|---|---|
| DTD | 0.63 | **0.6795** | 0.12 | 1.86 |
| CUReT | 0.9875 | **0.9964** | 0.06 | .05 |
| KTH-TIPS-2b | 0.41 | **0.67** | .0021 | 3.44 |
| FMD | 0.45 | **0.56** | 0.1 | 2.5 |

**Table 3.** Results using approach 3

| Dataset name | Approach 1. Acc. | Approach 2. Acc. | Approach 3 Acc. |
|---|---|---|---|
| DTD | 0.6814 | 0.6795 | **0.6835** |
| CUReT | **0.9974** | 0.9964 | 0.9972 |
| KTH-TIPS-2b | **0.7084** | 0.67 | 0.6851 |
| FMD | 0.49 | **0.56** | 0.52 |

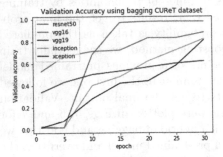 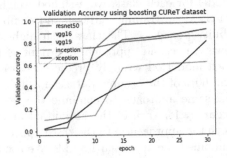

**Fig. 6.** Validation accuracy for CUReT dataset using approach 1 (left) & 2 (right)

is at par with state of the art results on this dataset [5] and better than [18]. Our approach is better than individual model can be seen as follows (Table 3):

1. For DTD, FMD and CUReT dataset Resnet50 model performed the best while for KTH dataset VGG-16 performed the best
2. As seen in Figs. 7 and 8 there is a large difference in accuracy between Resnet50 and other model in case of FMD dataset. Our final models used all the models to get the best results.
3. Approach 1 performed better than approach two in most of the cases except FMD and DTD dataset.
4. Our ensemble techniques prevented over-fitting as SVM was trained on the probabilities from all the individual model and helped in better prediction.
5. Approach 3 consistently performed at par with approach 1 & 2 for all dataset except FMD dataset.

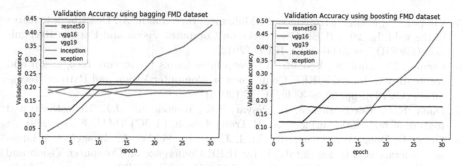

**Fig. 7.** Validation accuracy for FMD dataset using approach 1 (left) & 2 (right)

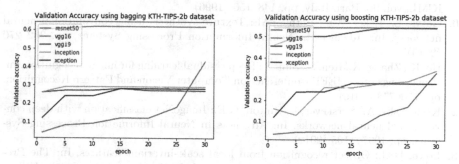

**Fig. 8.** Validation accuracy for KTH-TIP2b dataset using approach 1 (left) & 2 (right)

## 6  Conclusion

We have investigated the problem of texture and used multiple datasets to prove our results. Ensemble techniques, in general, are better than the individual model which helped in making in better decision using multiple models. These approaches can be used to achieve state of art results while reducing the overhead time on fine tuning. In order to improve our result, current state of art result CNN+fisher vectors can be used with our models to better improve the accuracy for all the datasets.

## References

1. Andrearczyk, V., Whelan, P.F.: Using filter banks in convolutional neural networks for texture classification. Pattern Recogn. Lett. **84**, 63–69 (2016)
2. Breiman, L.: Bagging predictors. Mach. Learn. **24**(2), 123–140 (1996)
3. Caputo, B., Hayman, E., Mallikarjuna, P.: Class-specific material categorisation. In: Tenth IEEE International Conference on Computer Vision, ICCV 2005, vol. 2, pp. 1597–1604. IEEE (2005)
4. Chollet, F.: Xception: deep learning with depthwise separable convolutions. arXiv preprint, 1610–02357 (2017)

5. Cimpoi, M., Maji, S., Kokkinos, I., Mohamed, S., Vedaldi, A.: Describing textures in the wild. In: 2014 IEEE Conference on Computer Vision and Pattern Recognition (CVPR), pp. 3606–3613. IEEE (2014)
6. Cimpoi, M., Maji, S., Vedaldi, A.: Deep filter banks for texture recognition and segmentation. In: 2015 IEEE Conference on Computer Vision and Pattern Recognition (CVPR), pp. 3828–3836. IEEE (2015)
7. Dana, K.J., Van Ginneken, B., Nayar, S.K., Koenderink, J.J.: Reflectance and texture of real-world surfaces. ACM Trans. Graph. (TOG) 18(1), 1–34 (1999)
8. Deng, J., Dong, W., Socher, R., Li, L.J., Li, K., Fei-Fei, L.: ImageNet: a large-scale hierarchical image database. In: IEEE Conference on Computer Vision and Pattern Recognition, CVPR 2009, pp. 248–255. IEEE (2009)
9. Freund, Y., Schapire, R.E., et al.: Experiments with a new boosting algorithm. In: ICML, vol. 96, Bari, Italy, pp. 148–156 (1996)
10. Gatys, L., Ecker, A.S., Bethge, M.: Texture synthesis using convolutional neural networks. In: Advances in Neural Information Processing Systems, pp. 262–270 (2015)
11. He, K., Zhang, X., Ren, S., Sun, J.: Deep residual learning for image recognition. In: Proceedings of the IEEE Conference on Computer Vision and Pattern Recognition, pp. 770–778 (2016)
12. Krizhevsky, A., Sutskever, I., Hinton, G.E.: ImageNet classification with deep convolutional neural networks. In: Advances in Neural Information Processing Systems, pp. 1097–1105 (2012)
13. Lowe, D.G.: Object recognition from local scale-invariant features. In: The Proceedings of the Seventh IEEE International Conference on Computer Vision, vol. 2, pp. 1150–1157. IEEE (1999)
14. Mao, J., Zhu, J., Yuille, A.L.: An active patch model for real world texture and appearance classification. In: Fleet, D., Pajdla, T., Schiele, B., Tuytelaars, T. (eds.) ECCV 2014. LNCS, vol. 8691, pp. 140–155. Springer, Cham (2014). https://doi.org/10.1007/978-3-319-10578-9_10
15. Sharan, L., Liu, C., Rosenholtz, R., Adelson, E.H.: Recognizing materials using perceptually inspired features. Int. J. Comput. Vis. 103(3), 348–371 (2013)
16. Simonyan, K., Zisserman, A.: Very deep convolutional networks for large-scale image recognition. arXiv preprint arXiv:1409.1556 (2014)
17. Song, Y., Cai, W., Li, Q., Zhang, F., Dagan Feng, D., Huang, H.: Fusing subcategory probabilities for texture classification. In: Proceedings of the IEEE Conference on Computer Vision and Pattern Recognition, pp. 4409–4417 (2015)
18. Timofte, R., Van Gool, L.J.: A training-free classification framework for textures, writers, and materials. BMVC 13, 14 (2012)

# A Novel Decision Tree Approach
# for the Handling of Time Series

Andrea Brunello[1](✉), Enrico Marzano[2], Angelo Montanari[1],
and Guido Sciavicco[3]

[1] University of Udine, Via delle Scienze 206, 33100 Udine, Italy
{andrea.brunello,angelo.montanari}@uniud.it
[2] Gap s.r.l.u., Via Antonio Pigafetta 5, 34147 Trieste, Italy
e.marzano@gapitalia.it
[3] University of Ferrara, Via Saragat 1, 44122 Ferrara, Italy
guido.sciavicco@unife.it

**Abstract.** Time series play a major role in many analysis tasks. As an example, in the stock market, they can be used to model price histories and to make predictions about future trends. Sometimes, information contained in a time series is complemented by other kinds of data, which may be encoded by static attributes, e.g., categorical or numeric ones, or by more general discrete data sequences. In this paper, we present J48SS, a novel decision tree learning algorithm capable of natively mixing static, sequential, and time series data for classification purposes. The proposed solution is based on the well-known C4.5 decision tree learner, and it relies on the concept of time series shapelets, which are generated by means of multi-objective evolutionary computation techniques and, differently from most previous approaches, are not required to be part of the training set. We evaluate the algorithm against a set of well-known UCR time series datasets, and we show that it provides better classification performances with respect to previous approaches based on decision trees, while generating highly interpretable models and effectively reducing the data preparation effort.

**Keywords:** Decision trees · Time series · Evolutionary computation

## 1 Introduction

Time series play a major role in many domains. As an example, in economy, they may be used for stock market price prediction [25], while, in medicine, they may help in forecasting the patient arrival rate in emergency centers [32]. In this work, we focus on the general problem of *time series classification*. Given a training dataset of labeled time series data, the goal is to derive a model capable of assigning a label to new, unlabeled instances. Various techniques have been used in the past for such a purpose, ranging from support vector machines [18] to neural networks [19]. However, when understanding and validating the decision

© Springer Nature Switzerland AG 2018
A. Groza and R. Prasath (Eds.): MIKE 2018, LNAI 11308, pp. 351–368, 2018.
https://doi.org/10.1007/978-3-030-05918-7_32

process is as important as the accuracy degree of the prediction itself, decision trees are still a popular choice among classification models (see, e.g., [1]).

The main contribution of this paper is a novel decision tree learner based on C4.5 [26], that we call J48SS, which is capable of exploiting static (categorical and numeric) attributes as well as sequential and time series data during the same execution cycle. Such a mixture of heterogeneous data can actually be observed in many domains. As an example, we may think of phone call classification in contact centers [5,6]: a conversation may be described by sequential data (such as the audio transcription of the call), one or more time series (for instance, the evolution of sound pressure over time), and a set of static attributes (tracking, e.g., some relevant characteristics of the speakers, or statistics synthesized from the textual transcription). Another use case is given by the medical domain, for example by the task of classifying a disease affecting a patient based on his/her sex and age (classic attributes), ECG data (time series) and a sequence of symptoms (sequential data). Clearly, the availability of a single, universal model for the classification of such heterogeneous data greatly reduces the data preparation effort, and eases the subsequent analysis phase. The proposed algorithm makes use of the concept of *shapelet*, originally introduced in [36]. A shapelet may be thought of as a time series pattern that is useful for classification purposes. In the recent years, several contributions have employed such a primitive for time series analysis [15,17,20,27,28,34], although, to the best of our knowledge, our approach is the first one that relies on multi-objective evolutionary computation for the shapelet generation process, in the context of decision tree classification. Moreover, unlike most of the previous studies, we do not require the generated shapelets to be part of the training set, and we provide an effective strategy to control their degree of complexity, which can be easily adapted to the requirements of the specific classification task.

Experimental results show that J48SS is capable of producing interpretable models, that nevertheless achieve better classification performances than previous solutions based on single decision trees, while keeping a low computation time. Moreover, preliminary insights suggest that J48SS trees might be combined in smaller and possibly more accurate ensemble models than those proposed in the past, although at the price of a loss in interpretability.

We are aware of some very recent approaches that achieve an accuracy on time series classification higher than the one of the solution we propose (see, e.g., [29]). Nevertheless, these approaches typically lack two distinctive features of J48SS, namely, the ability of natively dealing with mixed data, and the interpretability of the generated models.

## 2   Background

This section gives a short account of the main used methodologies and concepts.

## 2.1    The Decision Tree Learner J48 (C4.5)

J48 is the *Weka* [35] implementation of C4.5 [26], which, to date, is probably one of the most used machine learning algorithms for classification. This is mainly due to the fact that, over the years, it proved itself capable of providing good classification performances, while being computationally efficient with respect to both training and prediction phases, and guaranteeing the interpretability of the generated models. In short, C4.5 builds a decision tree from a set of training instances according to the traditional recursive *Top Down Induction of Decision Trees* (TDIDT) approach: starting from the root, at each node C4.5 chooses the data attribute (categorical or numeric) that most effectively splits the set of samples into subsets, according to the *Gain Ratio* criteria. The splitting process continues until the sample reaches a predefined minimum number of instances, or when no attribute proves to be useful in splitting the data. In such cases, the corresponding node becomes a leaf of the tree. After the tree construction phase, (post) *pruning* techniques are employed to reduce the size of the generated model and to improve its generalization capabilities.

## 2.2    Evolutionary Algorithms

*Evolutionary Algorithms* (EAs) are adaptive meta-heuristic search algorithms, inspired by the process of natural selection, biology, and genetics [11]. Unlike traditional random search, they rely on historical information to direct the search into the most promising regions of the search space and, in order to achieve that, they mimic the processes that in natural systems lead to adaptive evolution, through the application of operators such as *selection*, *crossover*, and *mutation*. Specifically, Our implementation is based on the well-known multi-objective evolutionary algorithm NSGA-II [9].

Multi-objective evolutionary algorithms are designed to solve a set of minimization/maximization problems for a tuple of $n$ functions $f_1(\overrightarrow{x}), \ldots, f_n(\overrightarrow{x})$, where $\overrightarrow{x}$ is a vector of parameters belonging to a given domain. A set $\mathcal{F}$ of solutions for a multi-objective problem is said to be *Pareto optimal* (or *non-dominated*) if and only if for each $x \in \mathcal{F}$, there exists no $y \in \mathcal{F}$ such that *(i)* $f_i(y)$ improves $f_i(x)$ for some $i$, with $1 \leq i \leq n$, and *(ii)* for all $j$, with $1 \leq j \leq n$ and $j \neq i$, $f_j(x)$ does not improve $f_j(y)$. The set of non-dominated solutions from $\mathcal{F}$ is called *Pareto front*. Multi-objective approaches are particularly suitable for multi-objective optimization, as they are capable of searching for multiple optimal solutions in parallel. This means that such algorithms are able to find a set of optimal solutions in the final population in a single run and, once such a set is available, the most satisfactory solution can be chosen by applying a preference criterion.

*Generalization* is the ability of a model to perform well on new cases, not belonging to the training set. On the contrary, *overfitting* is a phenomenon which occurs when a model is too closely fit to a specific and limited set of examples, and thus fails in applying its knowledge to new data. Evolutionary techniques tend to produce solutions that are as good as possible for a given set of instances, against which the fitness function is evaluated, without considering the performances on possible new cases. Thus, in the recent years, generalization in evolutionary computation has been recognized as an important open issue [14], and several efforts are being made to solve such a problem [8]. For example, to reduce overfitting and improve generalization, in [14], the authors propose to use, through the generations, a small and frequently changing random subset of the training data. Another approach is given by *bootstrapping*, i.e., the repeated re-sampling of training data with replacement, with the goal of simulating the effect of unseen data. Then, the errors of each solution with respect to the bootstrapped datasets are evaluated, speculating that the lower their variance, the higher the generalization capability of the solution [12]. Also, an independent validation set may be used to separately assess the fitness of each individual in the population, which is nevertheless still evolved with respect to the training set [13]. Other strategies are based on the concept of reducing the *functional complexity* of the solutions. This is somewhat different than reducing the *bloat* (i.e., an increase in mean program size without a corresponding improvement in fitness), as it has already been observed in the past that bloat and overfitting are not necessarily correlated [31].

## 2.3   Time Series Shapelets

Time series classification is recognized as a difficult problem in the literature. A commonly adopted solution performs a preliminary data discretization step using approaches such as *Equal Width* or *Equal Frequency* binning, or more advanced strategies like *Symbolic Aggregate Approximation* (SAX) [21]. This step allows one to build a symbolic representation of the time series, that can be then analyzed with traditional pattern mining algorithms [22]. Such an approach has been followed in many studies, e.g., in [23,24]; however, the discretization phase typically involves a loss in information, and may reduce the interpretability of the results.

Alternative approaches rely on patterns that can be generated directly from the numeric data, such as *time series shapelets*. Shapelets have been originally presented in [36] as contiguous time series subsequences which are in some sense maximally representative of a class. The overall idea is that shapelets are meant to capture local features of the time series, which should be more resistant to noise and distortions than global characteristics. Figure 1 shows an example of a shapelet, together with a time series. Since a shapelet is defined as an arbitrary-length contiguous subsequence of a training set time series, we may determine the total number of shapelets that can be obtained from a dataset. Let us consider $n$ instances, and define as $l_i$ the length of the time series of the $i$th instance. Then, the total number of shapelets that may be generated is $\sum_{i=1}^{n}(l_i!)$. Given such an enormous space, an exhaustive search for the best shapelets is unfeasible and, indeed, several contributions have concentrated on the problem of speeding up the shapelet extraction process [15,17,20,27,28,34], following, for instance, heuristic search, or random sampling of the shapelet candidates.

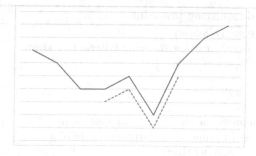

**Fig. 1.** A time series (blue solid line) and a possible shapelet (red dotted line). The two lines are intentionally shifted for the ease of comprehension. (Color figure online)

Typically, shapelets are used in the following way. Given a training dataset made by time series, $k$ shapelets are extracted through a suitable method. As a result, each of the instances is represented by $k$ predictor attributes: each one of them encodes the distance between the corresponding shapelet and the instance's time series. For its simplicity, the *Euclidean distance* is the most used distance metric: the final value corresponds to the minimum distance between the time series and the shapelet, calculated with a sliding window approach. Measures based on *Dynamic Time Warping* [30] or *Mahalanobis distance* [2] have been experimented as well.

## 3  J48SS Algorithm Description

In this section, we present J48SS, a novel decision tree learning algorithm based on J48 (Weka's implementation of C4.5, release 8 [35]) and NSGA-II multi-objective evolutionary algorithm [9]. It builds on a previous extension of J48 resulting in a decision tree capable of mixing static and sequential data during the same execution cycle [6]. The authors look forward to sharing the source code of J48SS on the web, other than asking for its addition to the *Weka* data mining suite [35] as an add-on package.

Let us now focus on the execution of J48SS. As in the classic C4.5 algorithm, the learning procedure is made of two distinct phases: a growing one, in which the tree is built, and a final pruning step, that discards the non-relevant parts of the tree, improving its generalization capability and readability.

Algorithm 1 shows the main recursive procedure used in the tree building phase. It takes in input a node (initially, the root node of the tree, in which all instances reside), and proceeds as follows. If the given node is pure (i.e., all instances have the same label) or another stopping criteria is met (e.g., based on minimum cardinality), then the node is transformed to a leaf of the tree. Otherwise, the algorithm determines the best attribute for the split. It first evaluates all static attributes (categorical and numeric), determining their *Normalized Gain* value [6], following a strategy similar to that adopted by J48/C4.5. Then, it focuses on string attributes that encode sequences: the best *closed frequent*

---

**Algorithm 1.** Node splitting procedure

---

1: **procedure** NODE_SPLIT(NODE)
2:     **if** *NODE* is "pure" or other stopping criteria met **then**
3:         make *NODE* a leaf node
4:     **else**
5:         *best_attr* ← *null*
6:         *best_ng* ← 0
7:         **for** each numeric or categorical attribute *a* **do**
8:             *a_ng* ←get normalized information gain of *a*
9:             **if** *a_ng* > *best_ng* **then**
10:                 *best_ng* ← *a_ng*
11:                 *best_attr* ← *a*
12:         **for** each sequential string attribute *s* **do**
13:             *pat, pat_ng* ←get best frequent pattern in *s*
14:             **if** *pat_ng* > *best_ng* **then**
15:                 *best_ng* ← *pat_ng*
16:                 *best_attr* ← *pat*
17:         **for** each time series string attribute *t* **do**
18:             *shap, shap_ng* ←get shapelet in *t* using NSGA-II
19:             **if** *shap_ng* > *best_ng* **then**
20:                 *best_ng* ← *shap_ng*
21:                 *best_attr* ← *shap*
22:         *children_nodes* ← split instances in *NODE* on *best_attr*
23:         **for** each *child_node* in *children_nodes* **do**
24:             call *NODE_SPLIT(child_node)*
25:             attach *child_node* to *NODE*
26:     **return** *NODE*

---

*pattern* is extracted, following the J48S strategy described in [6]. Finally, for each string attribute of the dataset that encodes a time series, it runs NSGA-II with respect to the set of instances belonging to the node (details are provided in Sects. 3.1 through 3.4). As a result, a single shapelet is returned. The shapelet is evaluated as if it was a numeric attribute, considering the Euclidean distance between each instance's time series and itself (adopting also the *subsequence distance early abandon* strategy to speed-up the computation, as suggested in [36]). In this way, its Normalized Gain value is calculated, and compared with the best found one. As a final step, the attribute with the maximum Normalized Gain is used to split the node, and the algorithm is recursively called on each of the children.

As for the input parameters specific to the new algorithm, they are listed in Table 1. Apart from *patternWeight*, which determines the degree of *complexity* of the shapelet returned to the decision tree by NSGA-II (see Sect. 3.4), they all control the evolutionary process: *crossoverP* determines the probability of breeding two individuals of the population; *mutationP* determines how often an element undergoes a random mutation (see Sect. 3.2); *popSize* determines the number of individuals in the population; *numEvals* sets the number of evaluations (and, thus, generations) that are going to be carried out during the optimization process. Note that the number of evaluations (*numEvals*) should typically be higher than the population size (*popSize*): high *popSize* values, combined with small *numEvals* values, will indeed reduce the heuristic to a blind random search. Each parameter has already a default value that has been empirically determined, though a dedicated tuning phase may be required in order to obtain the best performances, especially for *patternWeight*.

**Table 1.** Custom parameters in J48SS.

| Parameter name | Default | Description |
|---|---|---|
| CrossoverP | 0.8 | Crossover probability used in the EA |
| MutationP | 0.1 | Mutation probability used in the EA |
| NumEvals | 500 | Number of evaluations carried out by the EA |
| PatternWeight | 0.75 | Weight used for the extraction of the final shapelet |
| PopSize | 100 | Population size used by the EA |

Evolutionary algorithms have already been successfully applied to various phases of the decision tree induction process in the past [3]. The description of the implementation of an evolutionary algorithm involves the description of: *(i)* how the single solutions are represented; *(ii)* how the initial population is set up; *(iii)* which evolutionary operators (crossover, mutation) are employed; *(iv)* which fitness function is used; *(v)* in a multi-objective setting, which decision method is adopted to select a single solution from the resulting Pareto front. All these points are discussed in the following. As we shall see, unlike the majority of previous contributions, the proposed solution does not require shapelets to be part of the specific training set, but they may evolve freely through the evolutionary operators. All code pertaining to the evolutionary algorithm has been implemented in the jMetal framework [10].

## 3.1 Representation of the Solutions and Initial Population

Each shapelet in the population is represented by an ordered list of binary arrays. Each binary array in the list corresponds to a floating point value, encoded in *IEEE 754 double-precision* 64 bit format (see Fig. 2): the first, leftmost bit establishes the sign of the number, the following 11 represent the exponent, and the remaining 52 encode the fraction. As we shall see in Sect. 3.2, this kind of representation makes it extremely convenient to apply the *mutation* operator.

Given $n$ the number of elements in the population, each of the instances is initialized in the following way. A time series is randomly selected from the dataset, and then a begin and end index are randomly generated. The shapelet is then simply extracted from the portion of the time series that lies between the two indices.

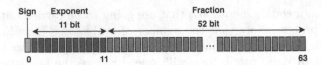

**Fig. 2.** IEEE 754 double-precision floating point format.

## 3.2 Operators

In this section, we describe the evolutionary operators that have been employed in the algorithm.

Given the nature of the problem at hand, a strategy similar to the *single-point* crossover [11] has been used. Given two parent solutions, i.e., two lists of binary arrays, two random indexes are generated, one for each parent. Such indexes define the beginning of the *tails* of the two lists, which are then swapped between the parents, generating two offspring. A graphical representation of the crossover operation, where the two indexes happen to have the same value, is shown in Fig. 3. Observe that, given the operator, the two offspring may have different lengths than those of the two parents.

As for the mutation operation, in our implementation, it is carried out by performing random flips in the binary array representation of the elements composing the shapelet. Recall that the binary arrays follow the double-precision IEEE 754 notation. Thus, the higher the index in the array, the less significant the corresponding bit. The probability of flipping the $i$th bit is thus given by $P_{mut} - P_{mut} * log_{65}(65 - i - 1))$, where $P_{mut}$ is the overall mutation probability, established by the *mutationP* parameter. Intuitively, such a formula penalizes flipping the most significant bits in the representation. The rationale behind this choice is that abrupt changes of the values of the shapelets are unwanted, since they might hinder the convergence of the algorithm to a (local) optimum. Finally, observe that randomly flipping the bits may lead to undesired results, encoded in the IEEE 754 format as *NaN* (Not a Number). To solve such infrequent cases, a further random flip is carried out in the exponent section of the binary array.

## 3.3 Fitness Function

One of the distinctive features of the proposed algorithm is the bi-objective fitness function it exploits.

The first objective is to maximize the *Information Gain* (IG) of the given shapelet, as calculated on the training instances belonging to the specific tree node. To determine the IG of a shapelet, first its minimum Euclidean distance with respect to every time series is determined, following a sliding window approach. Then, the resulting values are dealt with following the same strategy as the one used by C4.5/J48 for splitting on numeric attributes (see [26]). Note that, in principle, any other distance metric may be used in the objective, by simply defining a proper procedure.

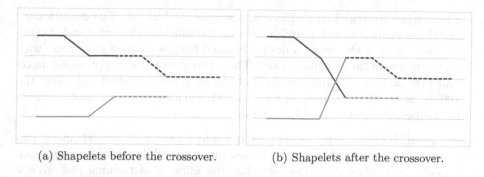

(a) Shapelets before the crossover.          (b) Shapelets after the crossover.

**Fig. 3.** Crossover operation. Dotted lines represent the tails of the shapelets, that are being swapped.

The second objective is to reduce the *functional complexity* [31] of the shapelet, in order to avoid unwanted overfitting phenomena that might occur if considering only the first objective. To do so, we rely on the well-known *Lempel-Ziv-Welch* (LZW) compression algorithm [33]: the (decimal) string representation of the shapelet is compressed through LZW, then the ratio between the lengths of the compressed and the original strings is evaluated. Note that such a ratio is typically less than 1, except for very small shapelets, in which the overhead of the LZW algorithm might make the compressed string actually larger than the original one. Finally, we set NSGA-II to minimize the ratio: the underlying idea is that "regular" shapelets should be more prone to compression than complex, overfitted ones. As a side effect, also extremely small (typically singleton) and uninformative shapelets are discouraged by the objective.

Observe again that, since a bi-objective fitness function is used, the final result is a set of Pareto-optimal solutions, with respect to the Information Gain and the compression ratio. This is an extremely important characteristic of our approach as different problems may require different functional complexities of the shapelets in order to be optimally solved. As we shall see in Sect. 3.4, a trade-off between the two objectives may be easily achieved.

It is worth mentioning that also other fitness functions have been tested, inspired by the approaches described in Sect. 2.2. Among them, the best results have been given by:

– an early-stopping strategy inspired by the separate-set evaluation discussed in [13]. The training instances are divided into two equally-sized datasets. Then, the evolutionary algorithm is trained on the first subset, with a single-objective fitness function aimed at maximizing the information gain of the solutions. The other dataset is used to separately assess a second information gain value for each of the solutions. During the algorithm computation, the best performing individual according to the separated set is kept track of, and the computation is stopped after $k$ non improving evolutionary steps. Finally, the best individual according to the separated set is returned;

– a bootstrap strategy inspired by the one presented in [12]. The evolutionary algorithm evaluates each individual along 100 different datasets (each having the same size of the original one), obtained from a random sampling (with replacement) of the original dataset. Then, two objectives are optimized: maximize the average information gain of the shapelet, as calculated along the 100 datasets, while minimizing its standard deviation, in an attempt to search for shapelets that are good in general.

Nevertheless, both of the strategies provided inferior accuracy performances than the previously discussed bi-objective fitness function. While for the first approach this might be explained by the fact that the number of training instances is greatly reduced (a problem that is exacerbated in the smallest nodes of the tree), the reason why the second one performed so poorly is still unclear, and will be investigated in further studies.

### 3.4 Decision Method

As it happens with any multi-objective optimization task, the result of the shapelet generation phase is a set of non-dominated solutions, in this case with respect to the two objectives: maximizing the information gain, while minimizing the compression ratio of the individuals. Thus, to extract a single shapelet out from the set, a decision method is needed. To this end, each solution is evaluated with respect to the following formula:

$$(1 - W) * ComprRatio_{rel} + W * (1 - InfoGain_{rel}) \tag{1}$$

where $W \in [0, 1]$ is a weight that can be customized by the user (by the *patternWeight* parameter), $ComprRatio_{rel} \in [0, 1]$ is the relative compression ratio of the shapelet, and $InfoGain_{rel} \in [0, 1]$ is the relative information gain of the shapelet, with reference to the respective highest values observed in the population. The shapelet that minimizes the value of the formula is selected as the final result of the optimization procedure, and is returned to the decision tree for the purpose of the splitting process. Intuitively, the larger the user sets $W$, the more accurate on the training set the extracted shapelet will be. On the contrary, smaller values of $W$ should result in less complex solutions being selected.

## 4 Experiments

This section describes the details of the experiments that have been carried out with J48SS. All models have been trained on a Late 2013 MacBook Pro, powered by an Intel Core i5 processor running at 2.4 GHz, and equipped with 8 GB memory.

### 4.1 Materials and Methods

All experiments are based on a selection of 16 UCR [7] datasets since, as witnessed by the recent literature, such a collection is a standard *de facto* in the

**Table 2.** The 16 UCR datasets, with the tuned values of *patternWeight* (w) and *numEvals* (evals), and the average J48SS model sizes (|J48SS|).

| Dataset | |train| | |test| | TS len | w | evals | |J48SS| |
|---|---|---|---|---|---|---|
| Adiac | 390 | 391 | 176 | 0.4 | 800 | 124.5 |
| Beef | 30 | 30 | 470 | 0.5 | 800 | 10.0 |
| ChlorineC | 467 | 3840 | 166 | 0.9 | 800 | 94.0 |
| Coffee | 28 | 28 | 286 | 0.0 | 800 | 3.0 |
| DiatomSize | 16 | 306 | 345 | 0.0 | 400 | 5.0 |
| ECGFiveD | 23 | 861 | 136 | 0.4 | 200 | 3.0 |
| FaceFour | 24 | 88 | 350 | 0.5 | 200 | 7.0 |
| GunPoint | 50 | 150 | 150 | 0.8 | 800 | 3.0 |
| ItalyPower | 67 | 1029 | 24 | 0.6 | 800 | 3.2 |
| Lighting7 | 70 | 73 | 319 | 0.9 | 800 | 15.3 |
| MedicalIm | 381 | 760 | 99 | 0.2 | 400 | 87.6 |
| MoteStrain | 20 | 1252 | 84 | 0.9 | 200 | 3.0 |
| SonyAIBO | 20 | 601 | 70 | 0.2 | 200 | 3.0 |
| Symbols | 25 | 995 | 398 | 1.0 | 800 | 11.0 |
| Trace | 100 | 100 | 275 | 0.5 | 400 | 7.0 |
| TwoLead | 23 | 1139 | 82 | 0.7 | 200 | 3.0 |

machine learning community (see, for instance, [17,20,28,29,34]). Moreover, the chosen datasets make our results comparable to the ones presented in [28]. Table 2 details the number of training and test instances, and the length of the time series in the datasets under study. Observe that, although the considered time series have fixed length, J48SS is capable of handling also time series of heterogeneous sizes.

Every dataset has been pre-processed by means of a dedicated *Python* script. As a result, each instance is described by the following set of heterogeneous attributes (other than the class label), so to exploit the capabilities of the novel algorithm: *(i)* the original time series, encoded as a string; *(ii)* the minimum, maximum, average, and variance numeric values obtained from the original time series; *(iii)* the time series *skewness* and *kurtosis* numeric values; *(iv)* the slope time series, obtained from the original one and encoded as a string; *(v)* the minimum, maximum, average, and variance numeric values obtained from the slope time series; *(vi)* the slope time series *skewness* and *kurtosis* numeric values.

Based on the selected UCR datasets, the performance of J48SS has been evaluated against the accuracy results presented in [28] (*Random Shapelet*). This work has been chosen for comparison as it is relatively recent and presents thorough details on the experimentation phase. Moreover, like in our approach, it embeds the shapelet generation phase in the decision tree inducing algorithm.

For each dataset, we built 100 single models by varying the initial seed used by the evolutionary algorithm, in order to get statistically reliable results. The two parameters that are most likely to control the degree of generalization of the models have been tuned by means of averaging the results of 100-times 10-fold cross-validation on training data: first *patternWeight*, over the range $[0.1, 0.2, \ldots, 1.0]$; then, *numEvals*, considering the values $[200, 400, 800]$. Table 2 reports the adjusted values of the two parameters for each dataset. Note that, for time constraints, we did not perform a grid-search, although such an approach would have allowed us, in principle, to find better combinations of the two values. All other parameters have been left at their default values.

Also, a series of experiments aimed at collecting statistics on the running time of the algorithm have been conducted by varying the *numEvals* parameter only, which has been tested with the values $[200, 400, 800, 1600]$ (all other parameters have been left at their default values). Again, on each selected dataset and for each value of the parameter, 100 models have been built by varying the evolutionary algorithm seed in order to get statistically meaningful results.

Although the main focus of the paper is on evaluating single, interpretable trees, it is also interesting to get at least some preliminary insights on the performances of ensembles of J48SS models. To this end, 100 ensemble models, each made of 100 trees, have been built through Weka's *Random Subspace* [16] method by varying the initial seed used by the evolutionary algorithm and keeping the tuned values for *patternWeight* and *numEvals*. The average accuracy results have been compared with those presented in [20] (*Generalized Random Shapelet Forests*) which, to the best of our knowledge, has been the only attempt so far of embedding shapelets in a forest inducing algorithm for time series classification (as an example, in [34], a shapelet extraction algorithm is used to transform the dataset *before* applying a random forest classifier). Along with the accuracy results, computation times are reported, despite the referenced paper does not present any absolute computation time. Note that the Random Subspace function has a seed that should be independently changed with respect to the one used by the evolutionary algorithm in order to get proper statistically accurate results; nevertheless, this fact has been neglected due to time constraints. The same constraints led us to test ensembles made by only 100 trees, which is a relatively small number compared, e.g., to the 500 trees that have been suggested as a suitable forest size for traditional random forests [4]. Although we acknowledge the limits of such a preliminary experimentation, the obtained results are useful to establish a baseline, and we look forward to thoroughly investigate the performances of different kinds of ensembles of J48SS models in future work.

## 4.2   Results of Single J48SS Models

Table 3 presents the results of the experimentation, along with the accuracies reported in [28] (*Random Shapelet*), which were also calculated over 100 executions of the algorithm. The *Random Shapelet* approach results are obtained by sampling different percentages of the total number of shapelets (ranging from 0.10% to 50%). The asterisk (*) symbol refers to tests that were reported not to

**Table 3.** Accuracy of the Random Shapelet approach, compared with the results obtained by J48SS. Note that, when larger sampling is used in Random Shapelet, computation times may be orders of magnitude larger than those required by J48SS.

| Dataset | Random Shapelet | | | | | | | | | | J48SS |
|---|---|---|---|---|---|---|---|---|---|---|---|
| | 0.1 | 0.2 | 0.5 | 1.0 | 2.0 | 10.0 | 20.0 | 25.0 | 33.3 | 50.0 | |
| Adiac | 45.4 | 47.7 | 49.6 | 50.6 | 51.9 | 51.6 | 51.3 | 51.7 | 50.3 | 51.8 | **60.5** |
| Beef | 40.0 | 39.3 | 36.8 | 35.5 | 33.6 | 32.4 | 31.6 | 32.0 | 31.8 | 31.2 | **55.4** |
| ChlorineC | 54.2 | 54.8 | 55.7 | 55.9 | 56.0 | 57.2 | 57.2 | 55.5 | 58.1 | * | **61.4** |
| Coffee | 69.0 | 70.3 | 73.1 | 74.1 | 76.4 | 76.9 | 78.1 | 78.3 | 78.3 | 78.3 | **100.0** |
| DiatomSize | 83.6 | **85.4** | 82.5 | 80.5 | 78.6 | 77.4 | 79.5 | 79.8 | 79.9 | 79.7 | 82.7 |
| ECGFiveD | 94.2 | 96.2 | 96.7 | 97.2 | 97.3 | **97.7** | 97.3 | 97.0 | 96.7 | 96.1 | 96.2 |
| FaceFour | 72.1 | 71.6 | 73.8 | 72.9 | 72.8 | 74.2 | 74.6 | 75.0 | 75.5 | 74.4 | **84.5** |
| GunPoint | 89.3 | 88.3 | 87.9 | 87.3 | 87.3 | 84.4 | 82.9 | 82.7 | 82.8 | 82.9 | **91.8** |
| ItalyPower | 87.1 | 87.8 | 90.0 | 90.4 | 90.8 | 92.4 | 93.0 | 93.0 | 93.1 | **93.2** | 92.7 |
| Lighting7 | 61.9 | 61.0 | 58.1 | 56.9 | 56.9 | 63.50 | 63.5 | 63.9 | 64.9 | 63.0 | **66.0** |
| MedicalIm | 58.3 | 58.5 | 58.8 | 58.9 | 58.8 | 59.2 | 59.6 | 59.8 | 59.7 | 60.6 | **65.8** |
| MoteStrain | 78.4 | 78.9 | 79.2 | 79.2 | 79.2 | 81.5 | 81.8 | **82.3** | 82.2 | 82.0 | 81.5 |
| SonyAIBO | 83.8 | 84.9 | 85.5 | 86.9 | 86.3 | 86.8 | 87.2 | 87.9 | 88.6 | **89.8** | 89.2 |
| Symbols | 78.0 | 76.1 | 76.0 | 75.2 | 76.8 | 79.5 | 80.6 | **80.8** | 80.7 | 80.6 | 77.6 |
| Trace | 94.4 | 94.5 | **95.0** | **95.0** | 94.6 | 93.4 | 93.1 | 93.1 | 93.0 | 93.0 | **95.0** |
| TwoLead | 82.2 | 85.6 | 87.4 | 89.5 | 90.2 | 91.4 | **92.1** | **92.1** | **92.1** | 92.0 | 90.6 |
| Average | 73.2 | 73.8 | 74.1 | 74.1 | 74.2 | 75.0 | 75.2 | 75.3 | 75.5 | N/A | **80.7** |

converge in a reasonable amount of time (several weeks). Regarding J48SS, we may observe that, despite the mild tuning, the algorithm is capable of achieving an overall better accuracy result than *Random Shapelet*. Even better performances may be achieved by means of a dedicated full-parameter tuning phase, using a grid-search approach, and/or extending the search range. Nevertheless, observe that, on some datasets, J48SS has shown inferior performances with respect to the largest sampling variants of the competitor. However, as reported in [28], such higher performances of *Random Shapelet* are obtained at the price of long training times: typically hundreds of seconds are required for building a single model on the smaller datasets, and thousands of seconds (or worse) are needed on the largest ones, when the larger sampling values are used. On the contrary, while J48SS training times tend to increase with the number of evaluations, they are relatively low. Specifically, Table 4 reports the average of the training times (in seconds) for the J48SS models on the 16 datasets.

With respect to the importance of weight tuning, Fig. 4 shows the average accuracy over 100 executions for the datasets *ECGFiveD* and *SonyAIBO*, over different values of *patternWeight* (all other parameters have been left at their default values). As can be seen, the two datasets behave very differently with

respect to the values of the parameter: while in *ECGFiveD* the best performances are provided by high-performing shapelets (with respect to the Information Gain), *SonyAIBO* tends to favor simple patterns. This confirms the
importance of tuning the value of *patternWeight*.

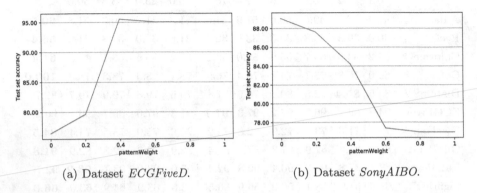

(a) Dataset *ECGFiveD*.                    (b) Dataset *SonyAIBO*.

**Fig. 4.** Average test set accuracy of J48SS, with respect to different values of *pattern-Weight*.

As for the interpretability of the generated models, Table 2 shows the average
sizes in total number of nodes of the trees built on the 16 UCR datasets. As can
be seen, decision trees are typically small, with the evident exceptions of *Adiac*,
*ChlorineC*, and *MedicalIm*. Of course, the size of the decision trees may be tuned
by customizing two parameters of J48SS that govern the *pre-* and *post-pruning*
aggressiveness (already present in J48).

## 4.3   Results of Ensembles of J48SS Models

Let us briefly report the outcomes of the experimentation with ensembles of
J48SS models. Table 5 reports the average of the accuracies and training times
of the generated models (*EJ48SS*), with respect to the accuracies reported in
[20] (*Generalized Random Shapelet Forests, gRSF*). Again, note that the EJ48SS
models are made of just 100 trees, with respect to the 500-tree forests used in
gRSF. Although the results should just be considered as a baseline for future
studies on J48SS ensembles, it is interesting to observe that in 8 out of 16 datasets
J48SS ensembles have been able to match or outperform the performance gRSF,
despite being much smaller considering the total number of trees. Moreover,
taking into account the observations done in Sect. 4.2 about the importance of
properly tuning the parameters, it seems reasonable to assume that better results
might be obtained without overly-increasing the size of the ensembles. As already
stated before, such considerations, along with the assessment of different kinds
of ensemble methods, are going to be addressed in future work.

**Table 4.** Average of J48SS training times (in seconds), given the number of evaluations of the evolutionary algorithm.

| Dataset | 200 evals | 400 evals | 800 evals | 1600 evals |
|---|---|---|---|---|
| Adiac | 14.05 | 20.81 | 37.27 | 98.88 |
| Beef | 3.73 | 5.19 | 7.7 | 14.82 |
| ChlorineC | 24.51 | 30.13 | 44.23 | 86.38 |
| Coffee | 1.1 | 1.42 | 2.01 | 3.98 |
| DiatomSize | 1.92 | 2.54 | 4.13 | 10.89 |
| ECGFiveD | 0.78 | 1.05 | 1.42 | 2.15 |
| FaceFour | 2.05 | 2.81 | 4.28 | 8.19 |
| GunPoint | 1.27 | 1.51 | 1.87 | 2.59 |
| ItalyPower | 0.76 | 0.92 | 1.3 | 2.36 |
| Lighting7 | 4.62 | 6.57 | 10.18 | 18.63 |
| MedicalIm | 8.3 | 11.01 | 17.35 | 38.39 |
| MoteStrain | 0.59 | 0.68 | 0.88 | 1.34 |
| SonyAIBO | 0.55 | 0.7 | 1.01 | 1.94 |
| Symbols | 2.71 | 3.91 | 6.33 | 14.49 |
| Trace | 2.16 | 2.93 | 4.5 | 9.48 |
| TwoLead | 0.54 | 0.71 | 0.92 | 1.54 |

**Table 5.** Accuracy and training time (in seconds) of the J48SS ensemble models (100 trees), with respect to *Generalized Random Shapelet Forests* (500 trees).

| Dataset | gRSF acc. | EJ48SS acc. | EJ48SS tr. time (s) |
|---|---|---|---|
| Adiac | 74.2 | **78.1** | 2196.8 |
| Beef | **80.0** | 67.5 | 269.1 |
| ChlorineC | 67.3 | **72.2** | 2230.9 |
| Coffee | **100.0** | **100.0** | 49.0 |
| DiatomSize | **96.4** | 86.8 | 57.6 |
| ECGFiveD | **100.0** | **100.0** | 6.2 |
| FaceFour | **100.0** | 92.8 | 36.8 |
| GunPoint | **100.0** | 98.0 | 40.2 |
| ItalyPower | 94.0 | **95.6** | 19.3 |
| Lighting7 | 69.9 | **73.1** | 410.5 |
| MedicalIm | 73.3 | **75.5** | 392.2 |
| MoteStrain | 92.1 | **92.6** | 6.5 |
| SonyAIBO | **92.5** | 90.4 | 6.4 |
| Symbols | **96.8** | 76.1 | 215.2 |
| Trace | **100.0** | 99.1 | 61.5 |
| TwoLead | **100.0** | 97.1 | 5.8 |
| Average | **89.8** | 87.2 | |

# 5    Conclusions

In this paper, a novel decision tree, called J48SS, capable of natively exploiting categoric, numeric, sequential, and time series data in the same execution cycle has been presented. The proposed solution is based on the well-known C4.5 decision tree learner and, for time series classification, it relies on the concept of time series shapelets, which are extracted from the training dataset following an evolutionary strategy. Unlike most of the previous studies, the proposed solution does not require a shapelet to belong to the training dataset. Moreover, the novel algorithm allows the user to control the degree of complexity of the shapelets, which can be easily adapted to the requirements of the specific datasets. The algorithm has been tested on a selection of 16 UCR time series datasets, and it has shown itself to be capable of providing classification performances better than those of previous approaches based on decision trees, both with respect to the test set accuracies and the training times. In addition, the generated models are interpretable, which is extremely important in domains where understanding the classification process is as important as the accuracy of the prediction. The evolutionary algorithm which we relied on for the shapelet extraction process solution has been discussed in detail, concerning its implementation, performances, and generalization capabilities. The collected results indicate that, although the solutions found by the algorithm tend to generalize well, further work on the fitness function may lead to still better results. The right choice of the parameters, such as the degree of complexity of the shapelets seems also to play a major role in determining the classification performances. Finally, some preliminary insights suggest that still higher accuracy results may be obtained by combining J48SS models into ensembles, although at the price of a loss in interpretability and longer training times. As for future work, it will be focused on testing different ensembles of J48SS trees, and on systematically applying the novel decision tree to tasks in which the mixture of static, sequential and time series attributes plays a major role, such as in call classification or in the medical field.

**Acknowledgments.** Andrea Brunello and Angelo Montanari would like to thank the PRID project *ENCASE - Efforts in the uNderstanding of Complex interActing SystEms* for the support.

# References

1. Adesuyi, A.S., Munch, Z.: Using time-series NDVI to model land cover change: a case study in the Berg River catchment area, Western Cape, South Africa. Int. J. Environ. Chem. Ecol. Geol. Geophys. Eng. **9**(5), 537–542 (2015)
2. Arathi, M., Govardhan, A.: Effect of Mahalanobis distance on time series classification using shapelets. In: Satapathy, S., Govardhan, A., Raju, K., Mandal, J. (eds.) CSI 2015. AISC, vol. 338, pp. 525–535. Springer, Cham (2015). https://doi.org/10.1007/978-3-319-13731-5_57

3. Barros, R.C., Freitas, A.A.: A survey of evolutionary algorithms for decision-tree induction. IEEE Trans. Syst. Man Cybern. Part C (Appl. Rev.) **42**(3), 291–312 (2012)
4. Boström, H.: Concurrent learning of large-scale random forests. In: SCAI. Frontiers in Artificial Intelligence and Applications, vol. 227, pp. 20–29. IOS Press (2011)
5. Brunello, A., Gallo, P., Marzano, E., Montanari, A., Vitacolonna, N.: An event-based data warehouse to support decisions in multi-channel, multi-service contact centers. J. Cases Inf. Technol. **21**(1), 33–51 (2019)
6. Brunello, A., Marzano, E., Montanari, A., Sciavicco, G.: J48S: a sequence classification approach to text analysis based on decision trees. In: Damaševičius, R., Vasiljevienė, G. (eds.) ICIST 2018. CCIS, vol. 920, pp. 240–256. Springer, Cham (2018). https://doi.org/10.1007/978-3-319-99972-2_19
7. Chen, Y., et al.: The UCR time series classification archive, July 2015
8. Dabhi, V.K., Chaudhary, S.: A survey on techniques of improving generalization ability of genetic programming solutions. arXiv preprint arXiv:1211.1119 (2012)
9. Deb, K., Pratap, A., Agarwal, S., Meyarivan, T.: A fast and elitist multiobjective genetic algorithm: NSGA-II. IEEE Trans. Evol. Comput. **6**(2), 182–197 (2002)
10. Durillo, J.J., Nebro, A.J., Alba, E.: The jMetal framework for multi-objective optimization: design and architecture. In: Proceedings of the IEEE Congress on Evolutionary Computation (CEC 2010), Barcelona, Spain, pp. 4138–4325, July 2010
11. Eiben, A.E., Smith, J.E.: Introduction to Evolutionary Computing. Springer, Heidelberg (2003). https://doi.org/10.1007/978-3-662-05094-1
12. Fitzgerald, J., Azad, R.M.A., Ryan, C.: A bootstrapping approach to reduce overfitting in genetic programming. In: Proceedings of the 15th Annual Conference Companion on Genetic and Evolutionary Computation (GECCO 2013), pp. 1113–1120. ACM (2013)
13. Gagné, C., Schoenauer, M., Parizeau, M., Tomassini, M.: Genetic programming, validation sets, and parsimony pressure. In: Collet, P., Tomassini, M., Ebner, M., Gustafson, S., Ekárt, A. (eds.) EuroGP 2006. LNCS, vol. 3905, pp. 109–120. Springer, Heidelberg (2006). https://doi.org/10.1007/11729976_10
14. Gonçalves, I., Silva, S.: Balancing learning and overfitting in genetic programming with interleaved sampling of training data. In: Krawiec, K., Moraglio, A., Hu, T., Etaner-Uyar, A.Ş., Hu, B. (eds.) EuroGP 2013. LNCS, vol. 7831, pp. 73–84. Springer, Heidelberg (2013). https://doi.org/10.1007/978-3-642-37207-0_7
15. Grabocka, J., Wistuba, M., Schmidt-Thieme, L.: Scalable discovery of time-series shapelets. arXiv preprint arXiv:1503.03238 (2015)
16. Ho, T.K.: The random subspace method for constructing decision forests. IEEE Trans. Pattern Anal. Mach. Intell. **20**(8), 832–844 (1998)
17. Hou, L., Kwok, J.T., Zurada, J.M.: Efficient learning of timeseries shapelets. In: Proceedings of the 30th AAAI Conference on Artificial Intelligence (AAAI 2016) (2016)
18. Kampouraki, A., Manis, G., Nikou, C.: Heartbeat time series classification with support vector machines. IEEE Trans. Inf. Technol. Biomed. **13**(4), 512–518 (2009)
19. Karim, F., Majumdar, S., Darabi, H., Chen, S.: LSTM fully convolutional networks for time series classification, **6**, 1662–1669 (2018). arXiv preprint arXiv:1709.05206
20. Karlsson, I., Papapetrou, P., Boström, H.: Generalized random shapelet forests. Data Min. Knowl. Discov. **30**(5), 1053–1085 (2016)
21. Lin, J., Keogh, E., Lonardi, S., Chiu, B.: A symbolic representation of time series, with implications for streaming algorithms. In: Proceedings of the 8th ACM SIGMOD Workshop on Research Issues in Data Mining and Knowledge Discovery (SIGMOD 2003), pp. 2–11. ACM (2003)

22. Mabroukeh, N.R., Ezeife, C.I.: A taxonomy of sequential pattern mining algorithms. ACM Comput. Surv. **43**(1), 1–41 (2010)
23. Mörchen, F., Ultsch, A.: Optimizing time series discretization for knowledge discovery. In: Proceedings of the 11th ACM SIGKDD International Conference on Knowledge Discovery in Data Mining (KDD 2005), pp. 660–665. ACM (2005)
24. Moskovitch, R., Shahar, Y.: Classification-driven temporal discretization of multivariate time series. Data Min. Knowl. Discov. **29**(4), 871–913 (2015)
25. Nerlove, M., Grether, D.M., Carvalho, J.L.: Analysis of Economic Time Series: A Synthesis. Academic Press, New York (2014)
26. Quinlan, J.R.: C4.5: Programs for Machine Learning. Morgan Kaufmann, San Francisco (1993)
27. Rakthanmanon, T., Keogh, E.: Fast shapelets: a scalable algorithm for discovering time series shapelets. In: Proceedings of the 2013 SIAM International Conference on Data Mining (SIAM 2013), pp. 668–676 (2013)
28. Renard, X., Rifqi, M., Erray, W., Detyniecki, M.: Random-shapelet: an algorithm for fast shapelet discovery. In: Proceedings of the 2015 IEEE International Conference on Data Science and Advanced Analytics (DSAA 2015), pp. 1–10. IEEE (2015)
29. Schäfer, P., Leser, U.: Fast and accurate time series classification with WEASEL. In: Proceedings of the 2017 ACM on Conference on Information and Knowledge Management (CIKM 2017), pp. 637–646. ACM (2017)
30. Shah, M., Grabocka, J., Schilling, N., Wistuba, M., Schmidt-Thieme, L.: Learning DTW-shapelets for time-series classification. In: Proceedings of the 3rd IKDD Conference on Data Science (CODS 2016), p. 3. ACM (2016)
31. Vanneschi, L., Castelli, M., Silva, S.: Measuring bloat, overfitting and functional complexity in genetic programming. In: Proceedings of the 12th Annual Conference on Genetic and Evolutionary Computation (GECCO 2010), pp. 877–884. ACM (2010)
32. Wei, L.Y., et al.: A hybrid time series model based on AR-EMD and volatility for medical data forecasting: a case study in the emergency department. Int. J. Manag., Econ. Soc. Sci. (IJMESS) **6**(Spec. Issue), 166–184 (2017)
33. Welch, T.A.: A technique for high-performance data compression. Computer **17**(6), 8–19 (1984)
34. Wistuba, M., Grabocka, J., Schmidt-Thieme, L.: Ultra-fast shapelets for time series classification. arXiv preprint arXiv:1503.05018 (2015)
35. Witten, I.H., Frank, E., Hall, M.A., Pal, C.J.: Data Mining: Practical Machine Learning Tools and Techniques. Morgan Kaufmann (2016). https://www.cs.waikato.ac.nz/ml/weka/book.html
36. Ye, L., Keogh, E.: Time series shapelets: a new primitive for data mining. In: Proceedings of the 15th ACM SIGKDD International Conference on Knowledge Discovery and Data Mining (KDD 2009), pp. 947–956. ACM (2009)

# A Proposal to Estimate the Variable Importance Measures in Predictive Models Using Results from a Wrapper

Hugo Dorado[1,2(✉)], Carlos Cobos[1], Jose Torres-Jimenez[3],
Daniel Jimenez[2], and Martha Mendoza[1]

[1] Information Technology Research Group (GTI), Universidad del Cauca,
Sector Tulcán Office 422 FIET, Popayán, Colombia
h.a.dorado@cgiar.org, {ccobos,
mmendoza}@unicauca.edu.co
[2] International Center for Tropical Agriculture (CIAT),
Km 17 Recta Cali-Palmira, Apartado Aéreo 6713, 763537 Cali, Colombia
{h.a.dorado,d.jimenez}@cgiar.org
[3] Center for Research and Advanced Studies of the National Polytechnic
Institute, Ciudad Victoria, Tamaulipas, Mexico
jtj@cinvestav.mx

**Abstract.** The methods for variable importance measures and feature selection in the task of classification/regression in data mining and Big Data enable the removal of noise caused by irrelevant or redundant variables, the reduction of computational cost in the construction of models and facilitate the understanding of these models. This paper presents a proposal to measure the importance of the input variables in a classification/regression problem, taking as input the solutions evaluated by a wrapper and the performance information (quality of classification expressed for example in accuracy, precision, recall, F measure, among others) associated with each of these solutions. The proposed method quantifies the effect on the classification/regression performance produced by the presence or absence of each input variable in the subsets evaluated by the wrapper. This measure has the advantage of being specific for each classifier, which makes it possible to differentiate the effects each input variable can generate depending on the model built. The proposed method was evaluated using the results of three wrappers - one based on genetic algorithms (GA), another on particle swarm optimization (PSO), and a new proposal based on covering arrays (CA) - and compared with two filters and the variable importance in Random Forest. The experiments were performed on three classifiers (Naive Bayes, Random Forest and Multi-Layer Perception) and seven data sets from the UCI repository. The comparisons were made using Friedman's Aligned Ranks test and the results indicate that the proposed measure stands out for maintaining in the first input variables a higher quality in the classification, approximating better to the variables found by the feature selection methods.

**Keywords:** Classification · Variable importance · Filters · Wrappers
Genetic algorithms · Particle swarm optimization · Covering arrays

© Springer Nature Switzerland AG 2018
A. Groza and R. Prasath (Eds.): MIKE 2018, LNAI 11308, pp. 369–383, 2018.
https://doi.org/10.1007/978-3-030-05918-7_33

# 1   Introduction

The variables importance is a measure of numerical quantification that is given to each input variable in a classification-regression model and represents an indicator of relevance or contribution to the prediction of the response variable [1, 2]. With this measure it is possible to establish a ranking of the input variables, from the most important to the least important. This result has been used in different investigations to understand the results of a model beyond the simple prediction, to the detailed study of the quality of the model against the presence or absence of certain input variables.

Feature selection, meanwhile, is pre-processing method in classification-regression models, and seeks to identify an optimal subset of input variables to predict a response variable, in such a way that the process seeks to remove input variables that are irrelevant or redundant [3]. With this reduction, the performance of the algorithm that is being built can be improved and its interpretation facilitated through the construction of less complex and more informative models. Among the types of feature selection, wrappers are a computationally expensive task, because in the exploration of subsets of variables, the classifier is evaluated several times, and from each evaluated solution a performance measure is obtained, such as accuracy, precision, or others [4, 5].

While the objective of a wrapper is to find the best subset of variables in which the performance measure of the algorithm is optimum, so far, no studies have been reported that have used the subsets of variables that have been evaluated by the wrapper to estimate the variable importance measures. In this investigation it was therefore decided to use this information to calculate a measure of variable importance measures so that, using an added value in the interpretation of feature selection, the researcher not only obtains a subset of variables (feature selection) but also an estimate of the partial influence each of these has on the classification.

In this paper we present a proposal to estimate the variable importance measures of a model using the solutions that a wrapper evaluates during the search process. To do this the results of three wrappers were tested. The variable importance measures from the wrappers were compared with the results of the Random Forest Variable Importance measure (RFVI) (permutation-based) and the Information Gain (IG) and Gain Ratio (GR) filters, obtaining promising results.

The rest of the document is organized as follows: Sect. 2 presents concepts related to the importance of variables and wrappers. It then presents a summary of the three wrappers used in the experimentation. Section 3 presents the proposal to establish the measure of importance of variables with the data delivered by the wrappers. Section 4 shows the results of the experimentation, and the analysis and comparison of the proposed algorithm against others of the state of the art. Finally, Sect. 5 presents the conclusions, together with future work the research group hopes to carry out in the short term.

## 2  Related Work

Variables importance measures can be understood from different definitions according to the method being implemented to estimate it. Common definitions include: (i) an indicator that quantifies the change in the value of the response of the model with respect to the change in the permutation of an input variable or a set of them, (ii) an indicator that estimates the contribution of the uncertainty of an input variable, or set of them, to the uncertainty of the response variable of a model, and (iii) an indicator that quantifies the strength of the dependence between the response variable of a model with respect to one or a set of input variables [1, 6, 7].

### 2.1  Feature Selection via Wrappers

The main characteristic of feature selection via wrappers is that it uses the classification-regression algorithm within the evaluation process on each subset of variables - hence making the process computationally intensive. The search for the best subset of variables is an NP problem that becomes computationally prohibitive as the number of input variables grows. Defining a search strategy is a pre-requisite, which directs the algorithm to evaluate the most promising solutions [8]. An evaluation criterion is also necessary. This defines the performance of the algorithm that is obtained from a subset of variables. Several variations have been adapted for the implementation of wrappers. The main feature that differentiates them is the search strategy used to define the subsets of variables that need to be evaluated [9]. Below we define some of the strategies used for wrappers: genetic algorithms, particle swarm optimization, and a new algorithm based-on covering arrays proposed by the authors.

**Genetic Algorithms** (GA) are methods based on evolution, whose approach is inspired by the process of change that species have as a result of continuous evolution over time, emphasizing the fact that recent species adapted better to changes generated in the environment compared to those that disappeared [10, 11]. In a GA for feature selection, solutions are presented expressed in sequences of binary numbers, 0 indicating the absence of a variable and 1 its presence; each candidate solution represents a subset of variables and is called a chromosome. During each iteration to the population of solutions, a set of operations of selection, crossing, mutation and replacement are applied with the purpose of improving the quality of the solutions in terms of the aptitude (fitness) function. The GAs applied to different search tasks, including feature selection, do not guarantee finding the global optimum of the problem, but in most cases they allow finding a local optimum that is appropriate in relation to the time constraints in the execution of the algorithm [12]. The operators used for the tests in this paper were: roulette wheel selection, HUX crossover, one-bit mutation and replace the worst. The values assigned to the parameters involved in the operators were taken from [13], where they make a comparison of evolutionary algorithms for feature selection.

**Particle Swarm Optimization** (PSO) is an algorithm that works very well in various continuous, discrete and binary problems. In the binary PSO that was implemented for the process of feature selection, the particles (solutions) have the same characteristics of the chromosomes in the GA with respect to the binary sequence that represents the presence and absence of variables (known in PSO as the position of the particle) and their fitness value, but also has two important components, the best position visited by the particle in its search process and the velocity of the particle. The change of the position and the velocity of each particle in each iteration is influenced by the information it contains in its current position and the best position found by it, information of the position of nearby or related particles (informants) and the position of the best particle in the swarm [14]. The implementation of binary PSO applied in the tests presented below was made following the proposal of [15] and the configuration of parameters assigned as in the genetic algorithms was based on [13].

**Covering Arrays** (CA) are mathematical objects in which several factors, parameters or variables of interest are evaluated, and each factor contains a certain number of possibilities or values. Their application includes several fields, especially in software and hardware testing, the aim being to provide quality products without incurring inflated costs. CAs may be expressed using the notation CA (N, t, k, v), which represents a two-dimensional array (matrix) of size N × k, where N refers to the number of tests (rows), k the number of factors, parameters, or variables (columns), v the alphabet indicating the possible number of values that each factor can take (for example, an array whose values are 0 and 1 is said to have an alphabet of 2, or is binary) and t is the strength or degree of interaction between parameters. The special feature of CAs is that any set of columns that are extracted from the array contains all the possible combinations of $v^t$ tuples in at least one of the rows [16].

In the adaptation made of the CAs for feature selection, the value of k equals the number of input variables of the dataset, v is equal to 2 for binary CAs and each row of the CA guides the search, representing a candidate solution with a structure equivalent to that of a chromosome in GA or position of a particle in PSO. In the paper, CA is proposed as an attractive method to estimate the variable importance measures, due to its properties that allow it to reach the greatest coverage (tests of interactions between variables) with the least possible effort (efficiently), that is, with the lowest number of evaluations of the fitness objective (EFOs). In addition, this algorithm can be easily parallelized.

An example of subsets of variables formed by a CA of strength 2 (t = 2) and 4 factors or variables (k = 4) is shown on Fig. 1. The first row was removed because in this subset no variables were selected. This figure also shows a W matrix that represents the CA cleaned (the rows that have only zeros have been removed), and ready to use. The result of the performance metric (e.g. accuracy) for each row of W using the selected classifier or regression algorithm is presented in vector $\alpha$.

$$\begin{bmatrix} 0 & 0 & 0 & 0 \\ 0 & 1 & 1 & 1 \\ 1 & 0 & 1 & 1 \\ 1 & 1 & 0 & 1 \\ 1 & 1 & 1 & 0 \end{bmatrix} => Subsets => \begin{bmatrix} x_2, x_3, x_4 \\ x_1, x_3, x_4 \\ x_1, x_2, x_4 \\ x_1, x_2, x_3 \end{bmatrix}; W = \begin{bmatrix} 0 & 1 & 1 & 1 \\ 1 & 0 & 1 & 1 \\ 1 & 1 & 0 & 1 \\ 1 & 1 & 1 & 0 \end{bmatrix}; \alpha = \begin{bmatrix} \alpha_1 \\ \alpha_2 \\ \alpha_3 \\ \alpha_4 \end{bmatrix}$$

**Fig. 1.** Extraction of a subset of variables using CA (N = 5, t = 2, k = 4, v = 2)

Regardless of which feature selection algorithm is used (GA, PSO or CA wrappers), a binary matrix W is defined with the description of the variables of the dataset that were included or not in each gene, particle or test, together with the vector $\alpha$ indicating the quality of each test in relation to the performance metric selected for the classifier. Both W and $\alpha$ are the entries of the proposed algorithm to define the variable importance measures. In the case of PSO and GA, all the generated solutions are taken, not only the final population, which means that the algorithm executes n EFOs, this being the number of rows in W and $\alpha$. In the case of CA, this value corresponds to the number N of rows of the CA, or to N-1 if there is a row full of zeros, where no variable is selected (as in the example of Fig. 1).

## 3   Algorithm Proposal

The algorithm for variable importance measures detects the presence of each input variable within the subsets of variables used by the wrapper and saves from each of them the accumulated quality or performance (e.g. accuracy), when it was present and when it was absent. The algorithm also counts the number of times in which each variable was present in the solutions. At the end, the accumulated qualities and counts are used to calculate for each of the input variables the difference of the quality average when the input variable was present with respect to the quality average when the input variable was absent. With this we obtain a measure of relevance that indicates the balance in the performance that the presence of each input variable produced in the classifier. This formulation lets unimportant or irrelevant input variables approach to zero where their presence in the classifier has no effect on performance, negative importance where their presence reduces performance and positive values for the input variables that are important; the larger the value, the more important the variable. This result is an easy ranking to interpret by the user. Figure 2 presents the algorithm for defining variable importance measures starting from the solutions evaluated by a wrapper, which has an order of complexity $O\ (n \times p)$ of basic operations that do not involve the execution of a classifier or regression algorithm.

## 4   Results and Discussion

The experimentation was conducted using seven data sets taken from the real world and recognized as test sets in several studies: Glass, Ionosphere, Sonar, Vehicle, WDBC, Wine, and Zoo. The details and description of these datasets can be found in the UCI Repository [17]. To build the CA-based wrapper, a covering of strength 4 and alphabet 2 (binary) was used, given that with this strength the number of test cases (rows or N value) has been enough in terms of effectiveness in other fields such as black box software testing, area where CAs have been widely used. GA configuration was performed with an initial population of 20 individuals and a mutation probability of 0.01. In PSO it was used with an initial population of 20 particles, a maximum velocity of 6 and a minimum of –6 and acceleration constants of 2. These configurations were chosen according to the tests carried out in [13]. The number of EFOs was

| Inputs: | Matrix W with p columns and n rows // where p is the number of input variables of the dataset and n is the amount of EFOs executed by the wrapper |
| | Vector $\alpha$ with n rows // for each row in W this vector stores the performance/quality metric (accuracy, F-measure, precision or other) of the classification |
| Output: | vector V with p columns // for each column an importance value is defined |

| 1. | **begin** |
| 2. | V1 = empty vector with length equal to p |
| 3. | V2 = empty vector with length equal to p |
| 4. | C1 = empty vector with length equal to p |
| 5. | **for** r = 1 **to** n **do** |
| 6. | **for** i =1 **to** p **do** |
| 7. | **if** W [r, i] == 1 **then** |
| 8. | C1 [i] = C1 [i] + 1 |
| 9. | V1 [i] = V1 [i] + $\alpha_i$ |
| 10. | **else** |
| 11. | V2 [i] = V2 [i] + $\alpha_i$ |
| 12. | **end if** |
| 13. | **end for** |
| 14. | **end for** |
| 15. | **for** i = 1 **to** p **do** |
| 16. | V [i] = (V2 [i] / C1 [i]) – (V1 [i] / (n - C1 [i])) |
| 17. | **end for** |
| 18. | **return** V |
| 19. | **End** |

**Fig. 2.** Pseudocode of algorithm proposed for defining variables importance measures

meanwhile adjusted according to the total number of tests implemented by the CA, to make the results of the three wrappers comparable.

Regarding the selected classifiers, three were chosen with different approaches. Each can be seen in Table 1 with its main configuration parameter. Within each solution that evaluates the wrapper, when constructing the classification model with the specific subsets of variables, an optimization was made to its respective parameter based on a greedy search. This search divides the parameter space into 6 values, then evaluates the classifier using cross validation with 10 folders and 5 repetitions, to finally select the value of the parameter whose classification power is maximum. This strategy of feature selection and optimization was taken from [18].

For GA and PSO, 30 experiments were performed with different seeds in the initialization to define the average behavior of the results delivered by these algorithms. The final results of all the data sets are shown later in Tables 2 and 3, but to achieve a better understanding of the results obtained, a detailed review of the results of the Zoo data set is initially made.

In Fig. 3, the results of GA and PSO are represented by a boxplot. This is due to the 30 experiments that were executed. On the other hand, only one measure is obtained for

**Table 1.** Classifiers and their corresponding parameters

| Acronym | Classifier | Parameter |
|---------|-----------|-----------|
| NB | Naïve Bayes | Factor for Laplace correction |
| MLP | Multi-layer perceptron | Number of units in the hidden layer |
| RF | Random Forest | Number of variables randomly sampled as candidates at each split |

**Table 2.** Comparison of the accuracy from the best subset (BS) of variables found, and the obtained with an equivalent number of variables in the importance variable for GA, CA, PSO, RF, GR and IG. FART applied to all accuracies excluding BS. Best results per row in bold

| Model | Dataset | BA | GA | CA | PSO | RFVI | GR | IG |
|-------|---------|-----|-----|-----|-----|------|-----|-----|
| NB | Glass | 0.698 | **0.678** | **0.678** | **0.678** | 0.621 | 0.523 | 0.598 |
| | Ionosphere | 0.951 | 0.932 | 0.923 | 0.923 | **0.937** | 0.923 | 0.920 |
| | Sonar | 0.872 | 0.789 | 0.774 | **0.794** | 0.745 | 0.741 | 0.741 |
| | Vehicle | 0.664 | 0.645 | **0.651** | 0.629 | 0.644 | 0.617 | 0.630 |
| | WDBC | 0.978 | 0.967 | **0.967** | 0.956 | 0.961 | 0.942 | 0.942 |
| | Wine | 0.994 | **0.989** | 0.984 | 0.984 | 0.972 | 0.967 | 0.972 |
| | Zoo | 0.922 | **0.842** | 0.832 | 0.801 | 0.832 | 0.782 | 0.782 |
| | Rank mean | | **1.710** | 2.210 | 3.290 | 3.210 | 5.640 | 4.930 |
| | FART | T = 21.62, df = 5, p-value < 0.01 | | | | | | |
| | Pos hoc | | a | ab | ab | abc | d | Cd |
| MLP | Glass | 0.716 | 0.672 | 0.664 | **0.678** | **0.678** | 0.673 | 0.673 |
| | Ionosphere | 0.947 | 0.918 | 0.912 | 0.918 | **0.920** | 0.912 | 0.912 |
| | Sonar | 0.892 | 0.837 | 0.837 | **0.847** | 0.842 | 0.798 | 0.798 |
| | Vehicle | 0.830 | 0.807 | **0.819** | 0.804 | 0.809 | 0.774 | 0.792 |
| | WDBC | 0.985 | 0.967 | **0.970** | 0.967 | 0.970 | 0.967 | 0.963 |
| | Wine | 0.995 | 0.995 | 0.978 | **0.978** | 0.973 | 0.995 | 0.972 |
| | Zoo | 0.984 | **0.960** | 0.912 | 0.950 | 0.911 | 0.930 | 0.911 |
| | Rank mean | | 2.930 | 3.570 | **2.430** | 2.640 | 4.290 | 5.140 |
| | FART | T = 10.85, df = 5, p-value = 0.054 | | | | | | |
| | Pos hoc | | – | – | – | – | – | – |
| RF | Glass | 0.821 | **0.781** | 0.776 | 0.776 | **0.781** | **0.781** | **0.781** |
| | Ionosphere | 0.960 | 0.940 | **0.949** | 0.940 | 0.946 | 0.923 | 0.943 |
| | Sonar | 0.929 | 0.866 | **0.899** | 0.870 | 0.866 | 0.818 | 0.818 |
| | Vehicle | 0.780 | 0.773 | **0.780** | 0.776 | 0.765 | 0.741 | 0.749 |
| | WDBC | 0.982 | **0.972** | 0.965 | **0.972** | **0.972** | 0.953 | 0.954 |
| | Wine | 0.993 | 0.978 | 0.978 | **0.984** | **0.984** | 0.978 | **0.984** |
| | Zoo | 0.994 | 0.981 | **0.970** | 0.950 | **0.970** | 0.911 | 0.931 |
| | Rank mean | | 3.000 | 2.860 | 3.210 | **2.640** | 5.290 | 4.000 |
| | FART | T = 14.98, df = 5, p-value = 0.01 | | | | | | |
| | Pos Hoc | | a | ab | ab | a | c | bc |

**Table 3.** Comparison of matched percentage from the features in the best subset (BS) and the features from GA, CA, PSO, RF, GR and IG when they are evaluated in the same number of features from BS, for seven datasets and three classifiers. Best results per row in bold.

| Model | Dataset | GA | CA | PSO | RFVI | GR | IG |
|---|---|---|---|---|---|---|---|
| NB | Glass | **80** | **80** | **80** | 40 | 60 | 40 |
| | Ionosphere | 60.0 | 53.3 | 53.3 | 60.0 | 53.3 | **66.7** |
| | Sonar | 39.1 | **65.2** | 47.8 | 47.8 | 39.1 | 39.1 |
| | Vehicle | 44.4 | **77.8** | 44.4 | 55.6 | 44.4 | 44.4 |
| | WDBC | 58.3 | **75.0** | 58.3 | 33.3 | 33.3 | 33.3 |
| | Wine | 88.9 | **88.9** | 77.8 | 44.4 | 55.6 | 55.6 |
| | Zoo | 33.3 | **66.7** | **66.7** | 50.0 | 50.0 | 50.0 |
| | Rank mean | 3.43 | **1.86** | 3 | 3.93 | 4.57 | 4.21 |
| | FART | T = 14.79, df = 5, p-value = 0.011 | | | | | |
| | Post hoc | ab | a | ab | b | b | b |
| MLP | Glass | **83.3** | 66.7 | 83.3 | 50.0 | 66.7 | 66.7 |
| | Ionosphere | 62.5 | **68.8** | **68.8** | 56.3 | 43.8 | 62.5 |
| | Sonar | 52.0 | 48.0 | **56.0** | 40.0 | 28.0 | 28.0 |
| | Vehicle | 86.7 | **93.3** | 80.0 | 86.7 | 86.7 | 86.7 |
| | WDBC | **50.0** | 30.0 | 40.0 | 40.0 | 30.0 | 20.0 |
| | Wine | 77.8 | **88.9** | 66.7 | 55.6 | 66.7 | 66.7 |
| | Zoo | **66.7** | **66.7** | **66.7** | 33.3 | 33.3 | 50.0 |
| | Rank mean | **2.21** | 2.43 | 2.64 | 4.64 | 4.71 | 4.36 |
| | FART | T = 17.02, df = 5, p-value < 0.01 | | | | | |
| | Post hoc | a | a | ab | c | c | bc |
| RF | Glass | **87.5** | **87.5** | **87.5** | **87.5** | **87.5** | **87.5** |
| | Ionosphere | **63.6** | 45.5 | 45.5 | 63.6 | 36.4 | **63.6** |
| | Sonar | 57.1 | **75.0** | 57.1 | 60.7 | 32.1 | 32.1 |
| | Vehicle | **80.0** | **80.0** | 60.0 | 50.0 | 50.0 | 50.0 |
| | WDBC | 38.5 | 53.9 | **69.2** | 46.2 | 46.2 | 46.2 |
| | Wine | 62.5 | **75.0** | 62.5 | 37.5 | 50.0 | 50.0 |
| | Zoo | 57.1 | **71.4** | 42.9 | 42.9 | 42.9 | 42.9 |
| | Rank mean | 3 | **2.07** | 3.21 | 3.86 | 4.71 | 4.14 |
| | FART | T = 11.20, df = 5, p-value = 0.048 | | | | | |
| | Post hoc | ab | a | abc | abc | c | bc |

CA. This is because a random process is not used in CA and for this reason there is only a single value of relevance (30 experiments are not required). At this point, the importance provided by each wrapper allows a better understanding of the relationships that occur between the set of input variables and the response variable, because the input variables that most affect the performance of the classification can be prioritized, and it is even possible to highlight some input variables.

Regarding the order of relevance, in Fig. 3 regardless of the wrapper and the classifier, the X13 variable always occupies one of the first few places, suggesting that

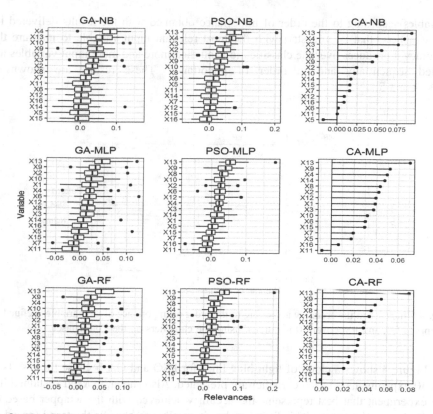

**Fig. 3.** Variable importance measures estimated for wrappers GA, PSO and CA on classifiers NB, MLP and RF on the Zoo dataset

it is, if not the most important, one of the most relevant input variables. The X9 variable meanwhile seems to have important weight in the MLP and RF algorithms but not so relevant in NB. In addition, X4 loses importance in MLP and in the others it always remains in the top 3 positions of importance. Finally, several input variables, such as X11, X15, X16, do not reach the top positions, which implies they are redundant or irrelevant.

The differences in the results of Fig. 3 were expected because some classifiers are better at detecting the interactions, associations or scale effects between the input variables, and for this reason the variable importance measures can vary from one classifier to another. But it is also clear that depending on the exploration and exploitation activities carried out by the wrapper, the results change over the same classifier. One question arises here of which of the three wrappers provides better information to define the variable importance measures. The answer to this question is presented later.

To carry out a comparison of the effect the order of the input variables has on the variable importance measures versus the performance measure evaluated in the model (in this case accuracy), the accuracy of the classifiers constructed by subsets of input variables according to the order of importance obtained with the results delivered by the wrappers, that is, you start with the most relevant input variable to measure the accuracy it produces over the classification and then more and more input variables are added sequentially and in order of importance. These results are shown in Figs. 4 and 5.

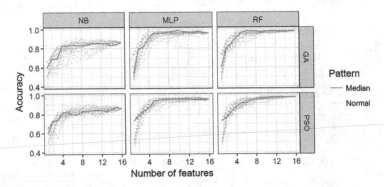

**Fig. 4.** Increase in the accuracy according to the order of importance of the variables defined by wrappers GA and PSO over 30 iterations, using the classifiers on the Zoo dataset

Figure 4 shows a cloud of light blue lines for PSO and GA because the results of the 30 experiments on each classifier are presented. Also shown in a red sustained line the experiment that best represents the accuracy achieved with the wrapper based on the median of the values. This figure makes it possible to observe the trend (based on the median) and the degree of dispersion of the results obtained, highlighting a high value of dispersion in GA when the NB classifier is used. In this figure all the curves are increasing with a logarithmic trend, i.e. after a certain number of input variables there is no significant increase in the accuracy of the classifier, which suggests that it is not necessary to add all the input variables to obtain a good quality classification.

In Fig. 5 it can be seen that the point of intersection of the horizontal line of the best known quality (Best accuracy) with the vertical line of the number of input variables found in the best known solution for the dataset (Best subset of features) is where algorithms tend to reach the best solutions (best quality) and then stabilize that value. The IG curve seems to fall and rise, due to the sudden inclusion of input variables that can negatively affect the accuracy, which may be a consequence of the fact that this measure does not consider the multivariate effect between the input variables. It is also observed that IG and GR tend to be below the other measures of importance of variables, which can be explained by the fact that these measures do not include information from the classifier. Additionally, the RFVI is the method that most closely matches the results obtained with the proposed method of variable importance measures, which works on the results of the wrappers.

From Table 2 onward shows the results that include the other data sets with which the experiments were done to evaluate the variable importance measures. Two indicators are used to evaluate the performance of the variable importance measures, which

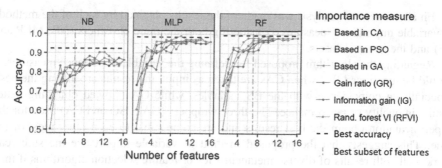

**Fig. 5.** Increase in the performance measure (accuracy) according to the order of variable importance measures estimated by the wrappers on the classifiers

are constructed using as reference the best subset (BS) of input variables composed of a total of $k$ variables known by the authors. The first indicator is the cumulative accuracy of the subset of $k$ input variables that top each of the lists of the variable importance measures. The second is established by the percentage of input variables that coincide between the first $k$ in the variable importance measures and those found in the BS.

In Tables 2 and 3, the level of significance selected for the statistical tests was 0.05, in both tables the comparisons were made using the Friedman's Aligned Ranks test (FART), which is suggested for multiple comparisons in artificial intelligence and machine learning by [19, 20]. Given the case of finding significant differences, the post hoc test recommended for FART in [19] was used. The results are represented by the letters a, b, c and d. In this notation, in case there are no significant differences in the comparison of two methods, then both will have at least one letter in common. In the case of significant difference there will be no letter in common. Also, for easy comparison the average range of each approach obtained by FART is shown. The values go from 1 to 6, where the values close to 1 represent high levels of accuracy in Table 2, and high levels of coincidence between variables with the BS in Table 3.

In Table 2 it can be seen that in terms of accuracy, the significant differences in the results obtained using the most important variables reported by the evaluated algorithms were presented in the NB and RF classifiers, while with MLP the ranking is not significant, given that the p value does not exceed the level of significance established (0.05). Therefore, in this classifier any of the results of the algorithms can be comparable in terms of accuracy. The results based on Friedman's rank show that through all the classifiers, both GR and IG are in the last places because they frequently collect the lowest values of accuracy.

Table 3 shows the percentage of coincidence of the first input variables selected by each algorithm and classifier in relation to the best-known solution (BS of the previous table). There it is observed that for the three classifiers there are significant differences between the methods of variable importance measures (p-values less than 0.05). Later, according to Friedman's rank and to the post hoc analyzes, CA which is classified within the group of letter a, twice occupies first place and takes second place once, always outperforming GR and IG that belong to the groups by d. GA was found to be comparable with GA and PSO since no significant differences are evident.

Finally, a general analysis was made of the results obtained by each of the methods of variable importance measures, considering both the three classifiers (NB, MLP and RF) and the seven datasets.

Regarding the algorithm proposed for defining the variable importance measures, it should be mentioned that when CAs are taken as input, the results are among the best, especially in coincidence with the BS variables, while GA allowed obtaining better results in quality or performance. The three wrappers (GA, PSO and CA) used for the experimentation obtain the best results and are comparable to each other most of the time. This suggests that the proposed method of variable importance measures can work well with results of diverse metaheuristics or feature selection algorithms if they deliver the appropriate inputs.

Table 4 shows that between GA, CA and PSO there is no significant difference in terms of accuracy, but these three methods outperform RFVI, GR and IG with 95% confidence. In addition, it is observed that GA obtains the best position (lowest value in the Rank column). On the other hand, CA obtained first place in the ranking for the percentage of coincidence with BS in the input variables selected as the most important, and in this indicator, the differences are not significant between GA, CA, PSO and RFVI. This group of feature selectors however outperform GR and IG with 95% confidence.

**Table 4.** Summary of FART and its post hoc over the totality of the results. Best values of Rank in bold.

| | Accuracy | | | | | | | % Match of variables with the BS | | | | | | |
|---|---|---|---|---|---|---|---|---|---|---|---|---|---|---|
| | RM[a] | Model index[b] | | | | | | RM[a] | Model index[b] | | | | | |
| | | 1 | 2 | 3 | 4 | 5 | 6 | | 1 | 2 | 3 | 4 | 5 | 6 |
| GA (1) | **2.6** | – | | | ● | ● | ● | 2.9 | – | | | | ● | ● |
| CA (2) | 2.9 | | – | | ● | ● | ● | **2.1** | | – | | | ● | ● |
| PSO (3) | 3.0 | | | – | ● | ● | ● | 3.0 | | | – | | ● | ● |
| RF-VI (4) | 2.8 | ○ | ○ | ○ | – | | | 4.1 | | | | – | ● | ● |
| GR (5) | 5.1 | ○ | ○ | ○ | | – | | 4.7 | | | | | – | |
| IG (6) | 4.7 | ○ | ○ | ○ | | | – | 4.2 | | | | | | – |

(a) **RM**: Friedman ranking average.
(b) **Model index**: The number reference used in the first column for each model.

Variable importance measures estimated from GA, CA and PSO stands out with respect to the other measures of variable importance measures, explained by the fact that the proposed method is based on the effect that the presence of each input variable has on different combinations evaluated within the wrapper. In addition, because wrappers involve in their calculation a measure of performance or quality (accuracy in this case) on the different subsets, there are greater guarantees that the first input variables will be the ones that most influence and contribute in the classification.

The filters on the other hand obtain the lowest results, which can be explained in that they do not take into account information from the classifier [3] and that analysis, which is faster, only takes into account the information provided by each input variable individually, this without involving the effect of simultaneously including other variables.

Regarding the RFVI method, it was observed that it is a measure that presents results quite close to those proposed in this paper, especially in including variables that coincide with those of BS. RFVI uses out of bagging (OOB) and permutations in the input variables to define the variable importance measures [21] within the Random Forest algorithm, specializing its use only on this classifier, which is a disadvantage.

Regarding the algorithm proposed for defining the variable importance measures, it should be mentioned that when CAs are taken as input, the results are among the best, especially in coincidence with the BS variables, while GA allowed obtaining better results in quality or performance. The three wrappers (GA, PSO and CA) used for the experimentation obtain the best results and are comparable to each other most of the time. This suggests that the proposed method of variable importance measures can work well with results of diverse metaheuristics or feature selection algorithms if they deliver the appropriate inputs.

## 5 Conclusions and Future Work

This paper proposes a method to estimate the variable importance measures based on the data collected from the performance of the solutions evaluated by a wrapper. This method measures the performance of the classifier in the presence or absence of each of the input variables. This proposed measure provides an added value to the computational effort of the wrapper and its cost is insignificant compared to the same effort made by the wrapper. In addition, it contributes to the interpretation of the classifier or regression model, by establishing a ranking to define an order of the most influential input variables and allows the possibility of generating variable importance measures proper to each classification algorithm. This proposal applies to different types of wrappers such as GA and PSO, even for new search strategies, such as the one proposed in this paper based on the use of covering arrays.

The new proposal of variable importance measures based on wrappers showed to be superior to information gain and gain ratio filters and most of the times to the variable importance measures in random forest. It achieves this by: (i) maintaining a subset of input variables with greater accuracy in the first few positions and (ii) maintaining a match between the most relevant input variables and the best solution found in feature selection. Meanwhile, although in the general test between the variable importance measures obtained from the three search strategies based on GA, PSO and CA the results did not show significant differences, the proposal based on CA has the advantage of being more easily parallelized, which would make it possible to build faster solutions. Moreover, implementation of the wrapper to obtain variable importance measures can be a tedious task when you have high dimensional datasets. Although it could guarantee good results, the process can take long execution times especially in obtaining the wrapper result.

As future work, it is proposed to evaluate the effect that this proposed measure of importance of variables has on correlated, discrete and nominal input variables. Additionally, it is intended to perform tests on other classifiers and include other measures of importance of variables in the comparison. The tests were performed with accuracy, but other performance measures can be used such as precision, recall, F-measure or Kappa index.

# References

1. Cui, L., Lu, Z., Wang, P., Wang, W.: The ordering importance measure of random variable and its estimation. Math. Comput. Simul. **105**, 132–143 (2014)
2. Li, L., Lu, Z.: Importance analysis for models with correlated variables and its sparse grid solution. Reliab. Eng. Syst. Saf. **119**, 207–217 (2013)
3. Chandrashekar, G., Sahin, F.: A survey on feature selection methods. Comput. Electr. Eng. **40**, 16–28 (2014)
4. Aggarwal, C.C.: Feature selection for classification: a review. In: Tang, J., Alelyani, S., Liu, H. (eds.) Data Classification: Algorithms and Applications, 1st edn., pp. 37-64. Chapman & Hall/CRC (2014)
5. Kohavi, R., John, G.H.: Wrappers for feature subset selection. Artif. Intell. **97**, 273–324 (1997)
6. Wei, P., Lu, Z., Song, J.: Variable importance analysis: a comprehensive review. Reliab. Eng. Syst. Saf. **142**, 399–432 (2015)
7. Altmann, A., Toloşi, L., Sander, O., Lengauer, T.: Permutation importance: a corrected feature importance measure. Bioinformatics **26**, 1340–1347 (2010)
8. Kotsiantis, S.B.: Feature selection for machine learning classification problems : a recent overview. (2011)
9. Jovi, A., Brki, K., Bogunovi, N.: A review of feature selection methods with applications, pp. 25–29 (2015)
10. Abd-Alsabour, N.: A review on evolutionary feature selection. In: Proceedings - UKSim-AMSS 8th European Modelling Symposium on Computer Modelling and Simulation, EMS 2014, pp. 20–26 (2014)
11. Khan, G.M.: Evolutionary computation. In: Evolution of Artificial Neural Development, pp. 29–37. Springer, Boston (2018). https://doi.org/10.1007/978-1-4899-7687-1
12. Sastry, K., Goldberg, D.E., Kendall, G.: Genetic algorithms. In: Search Methodologies, pp. 93–117. Springer, Boston (2014). https://doi.org/10.1007/0-387-28356-0_4
13. Wan, Y., Wang, M., Ye, Z., Lai, X.: A feature selection method based on modified binary coded ant colony optimization algorithm. Appl. Soft Comput. **49**, 248–258 (2016)
14. Xue, B., Zhang, M., Browne, W.N.: Particle swarm optimization for feature selection in classification: a multi-objective approach. IEEE Trans. Cybern. **43**, 1656–1671 (2013)
15. Kennedy, J., Eberhart, R.C.: A discrete binary version of the particle swarm algorithm. IEEE Int. Conf. Syst. Man, Cybern. Comput. Cybern. Simul. **5**, 4104–4108 (1997)
16. Tzanakis, G., Moura, L., Panario, D., Stevens, B.: Constructing new covering arrays from LFSR sequences over finite fields. Discrete Math. **339**, 1158–1171 (2016)
17. Dheeru, D., Karra Taniskidou, E.: UCI Machine Learning Repository. http://archive.ics.uci.edu/ml
18. Lin, S.-W., Lee, Z.-J., Chen, S.-C., Tseng, T.-Y.: Parameter determination of support vector machine and feature selection using simulated annealing approach. Appl. Soft Comput. **8**, 1505–1512 (2008)

19. García, S., Fernández, A., Luengo, J., Herrera, F.: Advanced nonparametric tests for multiple comparisons in the design of experiments in computational intelligence and data mining: experimental analysis of power. Inf. Sci. (Ny) **180**, 2044–2064 (2010)
20. Zarshenas, A., Suzuki, K.: Binary coordinate ascent: an efficient optimization technique for feature subset selection for machine learning. Knowl.-Based Syst. **110**, 191–201 (2016)
21. Strobl, C., Boulesteix, A.-L., Zeileis, A., Hothorn, T.: Bias in random forest variable importance measures: illustrations, sources and a solution. BMC Bioinform. **8**, 25 (2007)

# Author Index

Printed in the United States
By Bookmasters